Lecture Notes in Artificial Intelligence 1441

Subseries of Lecture Notes in Computer Science
Edited by J. G. Carbonell and J. Siekmann

Lecture Notes in Computer Science

Edited by G. Goos, J. Hartmanis and J. van Leeuwen

Springer
Berlin
Heidelberg
New York
Barcelona
Budapest
Hong Kong
London
Milan
Paris
Singapore
Tokyo

Wayne Wobcke Maurice Pagnucco
Chenqi Zhang (Eds.)

Agents and Multi-Agent Systems

Formalisms, Methodologies, and Applications

Based on the AI'97 Workshops on
Commonsense Reasoning, Intelligent Agents,
and Distributed Artificial Intelligence
Perth, Australia, December 1, 1997

Springer

Series Editors
Jaime G. Carbonell, Carnegie Mellon University, Pittsburgh, PA, USA
Jörg Siekmann, University of Saarland, Saarbrücken, Germany

Volume Editors

Wayne Wobcke
BT Laboratories, Intelligent Systems Research Group
Martlesham Heath, Ipswich, Suffolk IP5 3RE, UK
E-mail: wobckew@info.bt.co.uk

Maurice Pagnucco
Macquarie University
School of Mathematics, Physics, Computing and Electronics
Sydney NSW 2109, Australia
E-mail: morri@mpce.mq.edu.au

Chengqi Zhang
The University of New England
School of Mathematical and Computer Science
Armidale NSW 2351, Australia
E-mail: chengqi@cs.une.edu.au

Cataloging-in-Publication Data applied for

Die Deutsche Bibliothek - CIP-Einheitsaufnahme

Agents and multi-agent systems : formalisms, methodologies and applications ;
based on the AI '97, Workshops on Commonsense Reasoning, Intelligent Agents,
and Distributed Artificial Intelligence, Perth, Australia, November 30 -
December 1, 1997. Maurice Pagnucco ... (ed.). - Berlin ; Heidelberg ; New York
; Barcelona ; Budapest ; Hong Kong ; London ; Milan ; Paris ; Singapore ;
Tokyo : Springer, 1998
 (Lecture notes in computer science ; Vol. 1441 : Lectures notes in artificial
 intelligence)
 ISBN 3-540-64769-4

CR Subject Classification (1991): I.2.11, I.2, C.2.4

ISBN 3-540-64769-4 Springer-Verlag Berlin Heidelberg New York

© Springer-Verlag Berlin Heidelberg 1998
Printed in Germany

Typesetting: Camera ready by author
SPIN 10638025   06/3142 – 5 4 3 2 1 0   Printed on acid-free paper

Preface

This volume contains selected papers from three workshops held in conjunction with the Tenth Australian Joint Conference on Artificial Intelligence (AI'97), held in Perth, Australia, in December 1997: the Second Australian Workshop on Commonsense Reasoning, the Second Workshop on Theoretical and Practical Foundations of Intelligent Agents, and the Third Australian Workshop on Distributed Artificial Intelligence.

From the outset, the organizers of the three workshops planned a series of coordinated sessions which would enable participants to move freely between workshops. The idea was first to cater for the varying interests of the attendants, but, more importantly, to foster interaction amongst the three research communities which, we felt, were becoming more and more disparate in research topics and methodologies.

To this end, we are grateful for the participation of two invited speakers: Hector Levesque from the University of Toronto, who addressed a joint session of all three workshops, and James Delgrande from Simon Fraser University, who addressed a joint session of the Commonsense Reasoning and Intelligent Agents workshops. Levesque's work is particularly appropriate because it represents an effort to apply techniques from commonsense reasoning to the design of practical agent-based systems. Both speakers provided valuable feedback to the presenters of papers in the workshops, and participated in a lively, if somewhat controversial, panel discussion (as panel discussions ought to be!) on the strengths and weaknesses of the research paradigms within the Commonsense Reasoning and Intelligent Agents communities.

The papers selected for publication were revised (in some cases quite substantially) following comments from referees and workshop participants before inclusion in this volume. In addition to an invited contribution from Hector Levesque (with Steven Shapiro and Yves Lespérance), we have solicited a number of papers from researchers whose work covers the combined areas of interest of the three workshops. Randy Goebel from the University of Alberta has worked extensively on the implementation of logical reasoning systems, and is well known for the Theorist system. His paper (with Li-Yan Yuan and Jia-Huai You) is on providing a possible model semantics for disjunctive logic programs. Michael Wooldridge from Queen Mary and Westfield College, University of London, has contributed a paper (with Afsaneh Haddadi) that presents a formal model of multi-agent cooperation which does not require the agents to agree on a complete joint plan before execution can commence. We especially thank these authors for helping to identify research issues at the intersection of the topic areas of the three workshops, and for thus contributing to the coherence of the collection of papers in this volume.

In keeping with the spirit of the joint workshops, the papers in this volume are organized by topic rather than by workshop. There are 17 papers grouped around five topics: formal models of agency, reasoning agents, communication and coordination, social interaction and practical issues for DAI systems. The papers on formal models of agency concern logical issues in the design of agents and multi-agent systems, while those on reasoning agents concern logical approaches to commonsense reasoning. The papers on communication and coordination all report work on multi-agent systems using an explicit "high level" model of agents and communication, whereas those on social interaction use simpler "low level" agent models and formalize the (sometimes emergent) properties of multi-agent systems using game theory or decision theory. The final section consists of papers focussing on practical issues in the design and implementation of Distributed Artificial Intelligence applications.

Formal Models of Agency

This section contains papers addressing logical issues in the design of intelligent agents.

Shapiro, Lespérance and Levesque's invited paper presents an extension of the situation calculus to enable representation of both the knowledge of multiple agents and the evolution of situations (and knowledge) through time. The formalism is then used to specify communicative actions (including the speech acts of *request* and *inform*), and these, in turn, are used to specify a meeting scheduling program written in ConGolog, the authors' concurrent logic programming language for developing agent applications. Thus the paper demonstrates that commonsense reasoning formalisms are sufficiently powerful for specifying a nontrivial multi-agent system.

Wooldridge and Haddadi's invited paper concerns cooperation in multi-agent systems. Specifically, they present a formal model of cooperation which does not require that the agents agree in advance to a complete joint plan: rather, cooperation arises out of the individual decisions made by each agent at each time point as execution proceeds. By giving each agent the right of veto over the other agents' proposed actions so that conflicts are avoided, a group of agents can collectively progress towards a common goal.

Wobcke discusses the logic of ability and the related question of what defines an agent. Broadly speaking, the paper is an attempt to reconcile two different intuitions about agents' abilities to perform simple actions: on the one hand, an ability must be reliable, i.e., able to be exercised at the command of the agent, while, on the other hand, agents are not infallible, and their ability to perform an action is dependent on the context in which the action is executed. The ability to perform an action is treated as the condition that the action (reliably) succeeds in the "normal" course of events, and the paper presents a logical formalization of normality and ability based on situation semantics.

Lomuscio and Ryan develop the connections between modal logic as developed by logicians (especially Kripke) and the application of models of knowledge to the study of distributed algorithms. In particular, the paper gives a precise translation between Kripke models for logics with multiple modalities (one knowledge modality for each agent) and the "interpreted systems" of Fagin, Halpern, Moses and Vardi, and provides a condition under which the two types of system are isomorphic. The paper thus bridges the gap (in a precise and formal manner) between these two areas of research.

Reasoning Agents

This section contains papers broadly concerned with issues in logical approaches to commonsense reasoning.

Yuan, You and Goebel identify three kinds of logic programming semantics—sceptical, stable and partial-stable—and distinguish two interpretations of default negation: "consistency based" as in Reiter's default logic, and "minimal-model based" as in McCarthy's circumscription. The main result of the paper is to furnish a possible model semantics for disjunctive logic programs, introducing the notion of a partial-stable model. Variants of this model coincide with each of the six semantic categories identified.

Nakamatsu and Suzuki present a translation from one class of nonmonotonic ATMS (with out-assumptions used to express nonmonotonic justifications) to the class of annotated logic programs with strong negation (ALPSN). They show a direct correspondence between nonmonotonic ATMS extensions and ALPSN stable models under this translation, and provide an algorithm for implementing the ALPSN model.

Gibbon and Aisbett argue for a reasoning system in which new information is solicited from the user when there is insufficient or inconsistent information, and propose a reasoning architecture which is based on integrating a number of standard inference techniques. Of particular interest is the definition of relative importance (relevance) of information to a query, which enables the system to ask the user questions pertinent to the evaluation of the query.

Communication and Coordination

The papers in this section all draw on explicit models of agency and agent communication to study issues of coordination in multi-agent systems. Two papers (Moulin, Norman and Jennings) discuss issues in communication and negotiation, while another two papers (Ossowski and García-Serrano, C. Zhang and Li) are concerned with coordinated activity arising from multi-agent plans. The papers by Moulin and Ossowski and García-Serrano also present an interesting contrast: both emphasize the role that social relationships play in achieving coordinated activity, but the first paper formalizes this using predefined social roles, while the second uses dependency relationships arising from the structure of multi-agent plans.

Moulin discusses the influence of different social relationships between agents in defining the manner in which they interact. He proposes a modified speech act formalism in which the speaker and hearer fulfil assigned social roles that indicate the power relationship between them. The hearer's interpretation of a speech act, and hence the appropriate response, depends on this role.

Norman and Jennings present a model of negotiation, considered as a process through which agents reach agreement. The main idea is that each phase of a negotiation involves an agent granting a right to one or more other agents. The other agents may then (legitimately) act on the permission granted to exercise the right, e.g., by accepting a proposal of the first agent, or by offering a counter-proposal. Granting a right therefore involves an agent in making conditional commitments: commitments to acting appropriately whenever another agent exercises a right. Using a specific language of allowed "moves" in a negotiation, a number of protocols are formalized using the notion of rights.

Ossowski and García-Serrano are concerned with characterizing the "social dependencies" that arise between agents that have possibly conflicting plans. The problem of conflict resolution facing such agents is formalized as a decision problem, and utility theory is used to determine which compromise plans the agents can use to achieve "globally rational" coordinated behaviour. This paper and a related paper by Bui, Venkatesh and Kieronska, also appearing in this volume (see below), address the important question of how utility theory can be generalized to a multi-agent setting.

C. Zhang and Li present an improvement to Katz and Rosenschein's algorithm for the verification of multi-agent plans. In this work, a plan is represented as a directed acyclic graph whose nodes stand for actions and whose arcs stand for constraints on the order in which actions in the plan can be executed. Each graph, then, generates a set of possible execution orders. The problem of plan verification is to determine whether a particular plan achieves its goal, given only a STRIPS-like description of each action. The algorithm must take into account (in an efficient way) the possible conflicts arising from different execution orders. The algorithm presented here is superior in both time and space complexity to the original algorithm of Katz and Rosenschein.

Social Interaction

The papers in this section are all concerned with the properties of systems of relatively simple agents which may, however, interact in complex ways. This interaction is modelled using the approach of game theory. The authors all adopt an experimental methodology in evaluating their work.

Bui, Venkatesh and Kieronska present a framework in which coordination and learning of teams of decision-theoretic agents can be formalized. The paper is thus related to the work of Ossowski and García-Serrano reported in this volume (see above), although the present paper uses the definition of plan as strategy (from decision theory) rather than the notion of plan as sequence of actions (from Artificial Intelligence). The present paper also focusses on the important problem that agents face in estimating the utility of a team strategy in order to apply the technique, and the authors present experimental results based on a meeting scheduling scenario showing how this function may be learnt as the agents interact with one another over a period of time.

Carlsson and Johansson also discuss conflict resolution using a game theoretic framework. They present an experimental comparison of different strategies applied in an iterated setting to three games that have (formally) similar payoff matrices: the Prisoner's dilemma, a chicken game and a hawk-and-dove game. The authors investigate the evolutionary stability of the strategies; a strategy is evolutionary stable if (roughly) once all members of a population adopt the strategy, any mutations of the strategy are inferior and hence the strategy remains dominant in the population.

Yoshida, Inuzuka, Naing, Seki and Itoh also consider game theoretic models in a multi-agent setting, extending the model to one in which teams of agents compete with each other. Each member of a team adopts the same strategy, and contributes to the overall success of the team as measured by repeated iterations of the game between two randomly selected team members. This allows teams of agents with differing strategies to be compared.

Practical Issues for DAI Systems

The final section in this volume contains papers concerned broadly with issues in developing Distributed Artificial Intelligence systems.

C. Zhang and Luo present a translation from the EMYCIN model of uncertainty based on certainty factors, to Bayesian networks based on probability theory. This would enable existing systems using the EMYCIN model to be combined with systems using Bayesian networks. Thus both this paper and the paper by M. Zhang (see below) address issues of combining solutions in distributed expert systems.

D.M. Zhang, Alem and Yacef present a multi-agent framework for the design of instruction systems which can be used in conjunction with simulators to enable users to acquire skills in dynamic domains. The framework allows for separate agents responsible for simulating the domain, monitoring the user's progress to learn a model of the user, selecting new goals for instruction, and generating new learning scenarios, amongst other functions. They present an application of the model to developing a system for training air traffic controllers.

M. Zhang presents a case-based strategy for combining different solutions to problems in a distributed expert system. A heuristic for comparison of solutions is described and then evaluated experimentally on a sample data set.

Acknowledgements

The editors would like to thank the other organizers of the three workshops: Abhaya Nayak (Commonsense Reasoning), Lawrence Cavedon and Anand Rao (Intelligent Agents), and Dickson Lukose (Distributed Artificial Intelligence), for their efforts in arranging and coordinating the workshops. We would also like to thank the programme committee members and additional reviewers for each of the workshops, the organizers of the conference, and Griffith University (especially Abdul Sattar), the University of New South Wales (especially Norman Foo) and the University of Newcastle (especially Mary-Anne Williams) for funding the visits to Australia of the invited speakers. Finally, we would once again like to thank the invited speakers and all the workshop presenters and participants for contributing to the success of the three workshops.

Programme Committee (Commonsense Reasoning)

Grigoris Antoniou	Griffith University, Australia
Joseph Davis	University of Wollongong, Australia
Peter Eklund	University of Adelaide, Australia
Krishna Rao Madala	Griffith University, Australia
Pavlos Peppas	Macquarie University, Australia
Anand Rao	Australian Artificial Intelligence Institute, Australia
Mary-Anne Williams	University of Newcastle, Australia

Workshop Organizers

Abhaya Nayak	University of New South Wales, Australia
Maurice Pagnucco	University of New South Wales, Australia

Programme Committee (Intelligent Agents)

Hector Levesque	University of Toronto, Canada
Jörg Müller	Zuno Limited, UK
Hideyuki Nakashima	Electrotechnical Laboratory, Japan
Abdul Sattar	Griffith University, Australia
Munindar Singh	North Carolina State University, USA
Liz Sonenberg	University of Melbourne, Australia
Michael Wooldridge	Queen Mary and Westfield College, UK

Workshop Organizers

Lawrence Cavedon	Royal Melbourne Institute of Technology, Australia
Anand Rao	Australian Artificial Intelligence Institute, Australia
Wayne Wobcke	University of Sydney, Australia

Programme Committee (Distributed Artificial Intelligence)

Keith Decker	University of Delaware, USA
Yves Demazeau	IMAG-Leibniz Grenoble, France
Rose Dieng	INRIA Sophia Antipolis, France
Mark d'Inverno	University of Westminster, UK
Norbert Glaser	INRIA Sophia Antipolis, France
Victor Lesser	University of Massachusetts, USA
Michael Luck	University of Warwick, UK
Bernard Moulin	Laval University, Canada
Timothy Norman	Queen Mary and Westfield College, UK
Douglas Norrie	University of Calgary, Canada
Jeffrey Rosenschein	Hebrew University of Jerusalem, Israel
Toshiharu Sugawara	NTT Basic Research Laboratory, Japan
Minjie Zhang	Edith Cowan University, Australia

Workshop Organizers

Dickson Lukose	University of New England, Australia
Chengqi Zhang	University of New England, Australia

Contents

Formal Models of Agency

Reasoning Agents

Communication and Coordination

Specifying Communicative Multi-Agent Systems[*]

Steven Shapiro[1], Yves Lespérance[2], and Hector J. Levesque[1]

[1] Department of Computer Science
University of Toronto
Toronto, ON, Canada M5S 3G4
e-mail: {steven,hector}@ai.toronto.edu
[2] Department of Computer Science
Glendon College, York University
Toronto, ON, Canada M4N 3M6
e-mail: lesperan@yorku.ca

Abstract. In this paper, we describe a framework for specifying communicative multi-agent systems, using a theory of action based on the situation calculus to describe the effects of actions on the world and on the mental states of agents; and the concurrent, logic programming language ConGolog to specify the actions performed by each agent. Since ConGolog has a well-defined semantics, the specifications can be used to reason about the behavior of individual agents and the system as a whole. We extend the work presented in [7] to allow the specifications to mention agents' goals explicitly. The framework presented here allows the behavior of different agents to be specified at different levels of abstraction, using a rich set of programming language constructs. As an example, we specify a meeting scheduler multi-agent system.

1 Introduction

Many agent theorists (some examples are [1, 14, 19]) follow a similar methodology. They present a framework for representing the mental states of agents and the physical states of the world and axiomatize the relationships between the various components (beliefs, goals, intentions, etc.) of the agents' mental states. They then prove success theorems which state that agents will achieve their intentions under certain conditions (e.g., the agents are committed to their intentions, they possess the ability to achieve them, etc.). While this methodology can lead to some interesting theories, the facts that one can conclude from them are quite weak. One may be able to surmise that the agent will eventually achieve its intentions, but not when or by what means. It is not at all clear that these theories can be used to represent and reason about the actual behavior of agents in a detailed way, especially in the context of *complex* multi-agent systems with communicating agents.

On the other hand, there are formalisms for representing and reasoning about concurrent processes, e.g., [2, 5]. However, the representations of these formalisms are at a

---

[*] This research received financial support from the Information Technology Research Centre (Ontario, Canada), the Institute for Robotics and Intelligent Systems (Canada), and the Natural Sciences and Engineering Research Council (Canada). We thank Wayne Wobcke for helpful comments on an earlier version of this paper.

low level. They typically do not allow the specification of agents in terms of their mental states, nor do they explicitly represent actions in terms of their effects on the world.

In this paper, we explore a middle ground. We use the situation calculus [10] with Reiter's solution to the frame problem [15]—enhanced with predicates to describe agents' knowledge [18] and goals—to formally, perspicuously, and systematically describe the effects of actions on the world and the mental states of agents. We add INFORM and REQUESTUNLESS actions as primitive situation calculus actions to model inter-agent communication. We then use the notation of the concurrent, logic programming language ConGolog [4] to specify the behavior of agents. Since ConGolog has a well-defined semantics, the specifications can be used to reason about the behavior of individual agents and the system as a whole. Since ConGolog is based on the situation calculus, it is easy to add the capacity to specify the behavior of agents in terms of their mental states. In addition, ConGolog offers a wide variety of programming-language constructs (e.g., nondeterministic choice of actions, nondeterministic iteration, waiting for arbitrary first-order formulae to hold, concurrent execution with different priorities, and interrupts), which make it easy to specify a wide range of complex behaviors.

This paper extends the work presented in [7]. In that paper, the agents' mental states consisted only of knowledge. We have added the capacity to specify agents' goals. This addition allows us to dispense with the explicit representation of message queues for agents introduced in [7], yielding a cleaner account of communicative actions. We reformulate the meeting scheduler application described in [7] in this enhanced framework.

In the next section, we describe the situation calculus. In Sect. 3, we make time explicit in the situation calculus, and in Sect. 4, we add knowledge and goals to the situation calculus. In Sect. 5, we present ConGolog, and in Sect. 6, the meeting scheduler application is described. Finally, we conclude and discuss future work.

2 Situation Calculus

2.1 Theory of Action

Our action theory is based on an extended version of the situation calculus [15], a predicate calculus dialect for representing dynamically changing worlds. In this formalism, the world is taken to be in a certain situation. That situation can only change as a result of an agent performing action. The term $do(a, s)$ represents the situation that results from the agent of action a executing a in situation s. For example, the formula $ON(A, B, do(PUTON(agt, A, B), s))$ could mean that A is on B in the situation resulting from agt putting A on B in s. Predicates and function symbols whose value may change from situation to situation (and whose last argument is a situation) are called *fluents*. There is also a special constant, S_0, used to denote the actual[1] initial situation.

An action is specified by first stating the conditions under which it can be performed by means of a *precondition axiom*. For example,[2]

$$Poss(PICKUP(agt, x), s) \Leftrightarrow \forall z \neg HOLDING(agt, z, s) \land NEXTTO(agt, x, s)$$

---

[1] There can be alternative initial situations, see Sect. 4.

[2] We adopt the convention that unbound variables in a formula are universally quantified in the widest scope.

means that it is possible for *agt* to pick up an object x in situation s iff *agt* is not holding anything and it is standing next to x in s.

We adopt Reiter's solution to the frame problem [15],[3] which shows how one can transform axioms defining the effects of actions on fluents into a set of *successor state axioms*, one for each fluent, that imply the effect axioms as well as all the frame axioms. Successor state axioms have the following form, for each fluent, R:

$$Poss(a, s) \Rightarrow$$
$$[R(x, do(a, s)) \Leftrightarrow \gamma_R^+(x, a, s) \vee (R(x, s) \wedge \neg\gamma_R^-(x, a, s))],$$

where $\gamma_R^+(x, a, s)$ ($\gamma_R^-(x, a, s)$, respectively) denotes a formula which defines the conditions under which R changes truth value to becomes true (false, respectively) after a is performed in s. γ_R^+ and γ_R^- will usually contain conditions of the form: $a = t$, where t is term and a is the unbound action variable, since more than one action can change the truth value of a fluent (see for example the successor state axiom for ATMEETING in Sect. 6). This necessitates unique names axioms for actions, so that different action terms denote different actions. We assume that we have the following axioms: for distinct action types A and A',

$$A(x) \neq A'(y),$$

and

$$A(x_1, \ldots, x_n) = A(y_1, \ldots, y_n) \Rightarrow x_1 = y_1 \wedge \ldots \wedge x_n = y_n.$$

2.2 Foundational Axioms

We need some domain-independent axioms to characterize the set of situations and to define an ordering over situations [16]. To characterize the set of situations, we start with a set of initial situations (including S_0) with no predecessors, i.e., we have the following axioms:

$$\text{INIT}(S_0),$$
$$\text{INIT}(s) \Leftrightarrow \neg\exists a, s'(s = do(a, s')).$$

We then define the set of situations to be the least set containing the initial situations and closed under the application of *do* to an action and a situation. We do not present this second-order axiom, but a suitable one is given in [6]. We also need a unique names axiom for situations:

$$do(a_1, s_1) = do(a_2, s_2) \Rightarrow a_1 = a_2 \wedge s_2 = s_2.$$

It will be useful to define an ordering on situations. $s < s'$ means that there is a possible sequence of actions that can be performed starting in situation s and which results in situation s'. We define $<$ using two axioms adapted from [16]:

$$\text{INIT}(s) \Rightarrow \forall s'(\neg s' < s),$$
$$s < do(a, s') \Leftrightarrow Poss(a, s') \wedge s \leq s',$$

where $s \leq s' \overset{\text{def}}{=} s < s' \vee s = s'$.

---

[3] For treatments of the ramification and qualification problems compatible with our approach see [9, 11].

2.3 Formulae as Terms

We will need to have terms that represent formulae for two reasons. Firstly, we have actions (INFORM, REQUESTUNLESS) which take formulae as arguments. Secondly, we quantify over ConGolog programs when defining their semantics (although we do not give the semantics here). As we will see in Sect. 5, programs can contain first-order formulae, thus quantifying over programs can involve quantifying over formulae as well.

In [3], an encoding of formulae as first-order terms, called pseudo-formulae, is given, which we adopt and slightly extend to handle path formulae (see Sect. 3) and quantification over situations and paths. The encoding involves defining constants (pseudo-variables) denoting variables, and functions that correspond to situation calculus predicates and functions, and logical operators, as well as defining substitution for pseudo-variables, etc. Pseudo-formulae are related to actual formulae using the predicate HOLDS. We omit the details of the encoding and simply assume that we have the necessary axioms. However, to simplify the notation, we use actual formulae as arguments of actions and in programs. The reader should keep in mind that these formulae should really be pseudo-formulae.

3 Time

In our example application, we will need to model time: what has happened, what will happen, the actual time at a situation, and periods of time. In the situation calculus, the *do* function structures the situations as a tree (or a forest when there are several possible initial situations, as is the case here). Each situation has a linear past and a branching future. The past of a situation is well defined. It is simply the (unique) sequence of situations from the initial situation (the root of the tree) to the current situation. **Previously**(a, ϕ, s) is true if the action a has occurred in the past of s and ϕ holds after the occurrence of a:

$$\textbf{Previously}(a, \phi, s) \stackrel{\text{def}}{=} \exists s' (do(a, s') \leq s \land \phi[do(a, s')]),$$
$$\textbf{Previously}(a, s) \stackrel{\text{def}}{=} \textbf{Previously}(a, \text{True}, s).$$

To model the future of a situation, we need a way to select one future among the many possible futures. We do this using *action selection functions* (ASFs), which are functions from situations to actions. Given a starting situation, an ASF defines an infinite path of situations. For each situation in the path, the ASF selects the action that is to be performed next to yield the next situation in the path. We define the predicate **OnPath** to mean that situation s' is in the situation sequence defined by ASF σ and situation s:

$$\textbf{OnPath}(\sigma, s, s') \stackrel{\text{def}}{=} s \leq s' \land \forall a, s^* (s < do(a, s^*) \leq s' \Rightarrow \sigma(s^*) = a).$$

We can use **OnPath** to define predicates that talk about the future. For example, we could define **Eventually**(ψ, σ, s) to mean that eventually ψ will hold along the path defined by σ starting at s:[4]

$$\textbf{Eventually}(\psi, \sigma, s) \stackrel{\text{def}}{=} \exists s^* (\textbf{OnPath}(\sigma, s, s^*) \land \psi[\sigma, s^*]).$$

---

[4] We use ψ to denote a formula whose fluents may contain two placeholders sit and asf instead of a situation argument and an ASF argument (respectively), e.g., **Next**$(a, \text{asf}, \text{sit})$, which means

We also introduce a functional fluent TIME(s) which maps a situation into the current time at a situation. We assume that all actions in the domain increment TIME by DURATION(a), the amount of time it takes to perform the action a.

Since meetings take place over periods of time, we also model periods of time. A *period* is a pair of times. The first and second elements of the pair are denoted by START(*period*) and END(*period*), respectively. We use the predicate **During**(*period*, ϕ, σ, s) to stipulate that ϕ^5 holds throughout *period* on the path defined by σ and s:

$$\textbf{During}(period, \phi, \sigma, s) \stackrel{\text{def}}{=}$$
$$\exists s', s''(\textbf{OnPath}(\sigma, root(s), s') \wedge \textbf{OnPath}(\sigma, root(s), s'') \wedge$$
$$\text{TIME}(s') \leq \text{START}(period) < \text{TIME}(do(\sigma(s'), s')) \wedge$$
$$\text{TIME}(s'') < \text{END}(period) \leq \text{TIME}(do(\sigma(s''), s'')) \wedge$$
$$\forall s^*(s' \leq s^* \leq do(\sigma(s''), s'') \Rightarrow \phi[s^*])),$$

where *root*(s) is the initial situation, s_i, such that $s_i \leq s$. Since actions are of extended duration, the endpoints of a time period might fall between two adjacent situations on the path. Therefore, the definition stipulates that ϕ holds starting at the latest situation on the path (s') whose time is earlier than or equal to the start of the period until the earliest situation on the path ($do(\sigma(s''), s'')$) whose time is later than or equal to the end of period. Note that in this definition and elsewhere, we overload the $<$ and $\leq$ operators, using them to relate times as well as situations. For other approaches to adding time to the situation calculus, see [13, 17].

4 Mental Attitudes

4.1 Knowledge

Moore [12] showed how agents' knowledge could be modelled in the situation calculus by adapting the possible worlds model of knowledge to the situation calculus. We adopt his approach, using the notation of [18]. $K(agt, s', s)$ will be used to denote that in situation s, agt thinks that it could be in situation s'. We call s' a *K-alternative situation* for agt in s. **Know**(agt, ϕ, s) is then defined to be $\forall s'(K(agt, s', s) \Rightarrow \phi[s'])$, and **KWhether**($agt, \phi, s$) is defined as **Know**(agt, ϕ, s) $\vee$ **Know**($agt, \neg\phi, s$).

Scherl and Levesque [18] show how to obtain a successor state axiom for K that completely specifies how knowledge is affected by actions. In their framework, the knowledge-producing actions were performed by the agent itself, i.e., sensing actions. In this paper, we model communicative actions, which are actions that affect the mental state of an agent other than the one performing the action. However, Scherl and

---

that a is the next action to be performed. The placeholders get replaced by an ASF and a situation by an outer construct, in this case **Eventually**. $\psi[\sigma, s]$ is the formula that results from replacing asf with σ and sit with s. Where the intended meaning is clear, we suppress the placeholders, e.g., **Next**(a).

[5] We use ϕ to denote a formula that may contain the placeholder sit, but not asf. Again, we suppress the placeholder where possible. $\phi[s]$ is the formula that results from substituting s for sit in ϕ.

Levesque's successor state axiom for K is easily adapted to handle communicative actions. Here is the axiom we would use for a domain where the only knowledge-producing action is INFORM:[6]

$$Poss(a, s) \Rightarrow$$
$$[K(agt, s'', do(a, s)) \Leftrightarrow$$
$$\exists s'(K(agt, s', s) \land s'' = do(a, s') \land Poss(a, s') \land$$
$$\forall informer, \phi(a = \text{INFORM}(informer, agt, \phi) \Rightarrow \phi[s']))]$$

First note that for any action other than an INFORM action directed towards agt, the specification ensures that the only change in knowledge that occurs in moving from s to $do(a, s)$ is that it is known (by all agents) that the action a has been successfully performed. This is true because the K-alternative situations to $do(a, s)$ are the situations that result from doing a in a K-alternative situation to s where a is possible. Note that unlike [7], we assume that all actions are public, i.e., every agent is aware of the actions performed by all other agents. For the action INFORM($informer, agt, \phi$), the idea is that in moving from s to $do(\text{INFORM}(informer, agt, \phi), s)$, agt not only knows that the action has been performed (as above), but it also knows that ϕ. In this case, the K-alternative situations to $do(a, s)$ for agt are the situations that result from performing a in a K-alternative situation to s where a is possible, except the ones where ϕ is false.

Scherl and Levesque [18] showed that one could place constraints on the K-relation in the initial situation[7], and the constraints would continue to hold after any (possible) sequence of actions because the successor state axiom for K preserves these constraints. Since we are modelling knowledge (i.e., true beliefs), we constrain K to be reflexive.

4.2 Goals

We extend the framework described in [7] by modelling the goals of agents. The behavior of agents will be specified, in part, in terms of their own goals and what they know about the goals of other agents. Following Cohen and Levesque [1], we characterize the goals of an agent by specifying the paths in which all its goals (both maintenance goals and achievement goals) are achieved. Our approach differs slightly from Cohen and Levesque's in that our accessibility relation, $H(agt, \sigma, s', s)$, is used to state that in situation s, the path defined by σ and s' is consistent with what agt wants. We think of these paths as defining what the agent wants independently of what the agent knows. Cohen and Levesque restricted the G-accessible worlds (their version of H) to be a subset of the B-accessible worlds (their version of K). The end result is the same, however, as we define the goals of the agent to be the formulae true in the H-accessible paths that start in a K-accessible situation:

$$\textbf{Goal}(agt, \psi, s) \stackrel{\text{def}}{=} \forall \sigma, s'(K(agt, s', s) \land H(agt, \sigma, s', s) \Rightarrow \psi[\sigma, s'])$$

---

[6] In our example system, we have no need for sensing actions, but they could easily be added if necessary.

[7] In particular, they show that K can be constrained to be reflexive, symmetric, transitive, and/or Euclidean.

In the meeting scheduler application, the personal agents will need to be able to revise their goals. Unfortunately, we do not have a general method to handle goal revision. Instead, we assume that requests are made using a conditional request action, which we call REQUESTUNLESS. When *requester* performs the REQUESTUNLESS (*requester*, *agt*, ψ, ϕ) action, it is requesting that *agt* adopt the goal that ψ, unless ϕ obtains. We call ψ the *conditional goal* of the request and ϕ the *condition* of the request. The idea is that once the request is made (and *agt* is willing to serve it), *agt* acquires the disjunctive goal that $\psi \vee \phi$. If *agt* comes to know that ϕ does not hold, then it will have the definite goal that ψ (because agents' goals are a superset of what they know). If instead *agt* comes to know that ϕ, then it can consider the conditional goal to have been cancelled since the disjunctive goal is already satisfied. Thus, after making a REQUESTUNLESS, *requester* can cancel the request by informing *agt* that ϕ holds. In the meeting scheduler application, an agent will not adopt $\neg\psi$ as a goal after receiving a request that ψ unless ϕ, therefore the agent will not adopt ϕ as a goal.

There is a potential problem if an agent gets a request for ψ_1 unless ϕ_1, followed by a request for ψ_2 unless ϕ_2 before it knows whether ϕ_1 holds, and where the first conditional goal ψ_1 is incompatible with the new conditional goal ψ_2. If the agent adopts both goals and then finds out that both $\neg\phi_1$ and $\neg\phi_2$, then its goals will be inconsistent. To avoid this problem, we prevent agents from accepting a request involving a conditional goal that may conflict with an existing conditional goal, such as when the agent does not know that the condition associated with the existing conditional goal holds. We use the predicate POSSIBLECONFLICT to express that there was a previous request that might conflict with a request for ψ:

POSSIBLECONFLICT$(agt, \psi, s) \stackrel{\text{def}}{=}$
$\quad \exists requester, \psi'', \phi' (\textbf{Previously}(\text{REQUESTUNLESS}(requester, agt, \psi', \phi'), s) \wedge$
$\qquad\qquad \textbf{Goal}(agt, \psi' \vee \phi', s) \wedge \textbf{Goal}(agt, \psi' \Rightarrow \neg\psi, s) \wedge$
$\qquad\qquad \neg\textbf{Know}(agt, \phi', s))$

The successor state axiom for H has the same form as the one for K:

$Poss(a, s) \Rightarrow$
$\quad [H(agt, \sigma, s'', do(a, s)) \Leftrightarrow$
$\quad \exists s' (H(agt, \sigma, s', s) \wedge s'' = do(\sigma(s'), s') \wedge$
$\qquad \forall requester, \psi, \phi(a = \text{REQUESTUNLESS}(requester, agt, \psi, \phi) \wedge$
$\qquad\qquad \text{SERVES}(agt, requester, \psi) \wedge$
$\qquad\qquad \neg\text{POSSIBLECONFLICT}(agt, \psi, s) \Rightarrow (\psi \vee \phi)[\sigma, s']))]$

If the action, a, is not a REQUESTUNLESS action directed towards *agt*, then the paths (represented by σ, s'') accessible at $do(a, s)$ are the same as the ones that were accessible at s (represented by σ, s'), but the current situation (s'') is advanced by one action along the path ($do(\sigma(s'), s')$). If a is a REQUESTUNLESS action directed towards *agt*, *agt* is willing to serve the request, and there is no possible conflict with a previous request, then only those paths that also satisfy $\psi \vee \phi$ are accessible in $do(a, s)$. The SERVES predicate is used to characterize which requesters and requests the agent is willing to serve. For simplicity, SERVES is not a fluent and we omit the axioms that define it. H is constrained to be initially non-empty, i.e., the agent's wishes are initially consistent.

5 ConGolog

We have just presented a framework in which one can systematically and perspicuously describe the effects of actions on the world and on the mental states of multiple, communicating agents. In order to describe a multi-agent system, we must also specify what actions the agents perform.

We specify the behavior of agents with the notation of the logic programming language ConGolog [4], the concurrent version of Golog [8]. While versions of both Golog and ConGolog have been implemented, we are mainly interested here in the potential for using ConGolog as a specification language. A ConGolog program[8] is composed of a sequence of procedure declarations, followed by a complex action. Complex actions are composed of various constructs:

a,	primitive action
ϕ?,	wait for a condition
$\delta_1; \delta_2$,	sequence
$\delta_1 \mid \delta_2$,	nondeterministic choice between actions
δ^*,	nondeterministic iteration
if ϕ **then** δ_1 **else** δ_2,	conditional
for $x \in \Sigma$ **do** δ,	for loop
while ϕ **do** δ,	while loop
$\delta_1 \parallel \delta_2$,	concurrency with equal priority
$\delta_1 \rangle\!\rangle \delta_2$,	concurrency with δ_1 at a higher priority
$\langle\, x : \phi \to \delta \,\rangle$,	interrupt
$\beta(p)$,	procedure call.

a denotes a situation calculus action, as described above. The ConGolog specification can be for a single agent or multiple agents, depending on whether the primitive actions contain an argument for the agent of the action. ϕ denotes a situation calculus formula with the situation argument of its fluents suppressed. δ, δ_1, and δ_2 stand for complex actions, Σ is a set, x is a set of variables, β is a procedure name, and p denotes the actual parameters to the procedure. These constructs are mostly self-explanatory. Intuitively, the interrupts work as follows. Whenever $\exists x.\phi$ becomes true then δ is executed with the bindings of x that satisfied ϕ.

Procedures are defined with the following syntax: **proc** $\beta(y)\ \delta$, where β is the procedure name, y denotes the formal parameters to the procedure, and δ is a complex action. The semantics of ConGolog programs are defined using the Do predicate (see [4] for details). Informally, $Do(\rho, s, s')$ holds if situation s' is a legal terminating situation of program ρ starting in situation s.

6 Specification of a Meeting Scheduler Multi-Agent System

In our example system, we have meeting organizer agents, which are trying to schedule meetings with personal agents, which manage the schedules of their (human) owners. To

---

[8] We retain the term 'program' even though it is not our intention to execute the programs directly.

simplify the system, we assume that the personal agents have the authority to schedule meetings on behalf of their owners without consulting them. They simply inform their owners of a pending meeting fifteen minutes before it starts.

A significant feature of our approach is that different agents can be modelled at different levels of detail. The program for the personal agents mentions both their knowledge and their goals, whereas the program of the meeting organizer agents only mentions what they know. In other contexts, we might find it useful to model some agents without referring to their mental state at all.

In order to specify our multi-agent system, we must first axiomatize the actions and fluents of our domain. The actions are INFORM and REQUESTUNLESS which were previously described, and

- GOTOMEETING(*user, chair*): (the human) *user* goes to a meeting chaired by (the human) *chair*,
- LEAVEMEETING(*user, chair*): *user* leaves the meeting chaired by *chair*, and
- TICK: the time increases by one minute.

The fluents are K, H, and TIME, which were previously described, and

- ATMEETING(*user, chair, s*): *user* is at a meeting chaired by *chair* in *s*.

In addition, we have two non-fluent functions: PAG(*user*), whose value is the personal agent of *user*, and DURATION(*a*), which maps an action to its duration. For simplicity, we omit the axioms that specify these functions.

Here are the axioms that specify the actions and fluents (other than the successor state axioms for K and H which were stated previously):

Precondition axioms:

$Poss(\text{INFORM}(\textit{informer, agt}, \phi), s) \Leftrightarrow \textbf{Know}(\textit{informer}, \phi, s)$
$Poss(\text{REQUESTUNLESS}(\textit{requester, agt}, \psi, \phi), s) \Leftrightarrow \textbf{Goal}(\textit{requester}, \psi \vee \phi, s)$
$Poss(\text{GOTOMEETING}(\textit{user, chair}), s) \Leftrightarrow$
$\quad \neg \exists \textit{chair}'(\text{ATMEETING}(\textit{user, chair}', s))$
$Poss(\text{LEAVEMEETING}(\textit{user, chair}), s) \Leftrightarrow \text{ATMEETING}(\textit{user, chair}, s)$
$Poss(\text{TICK}, s)$

Successor state axioms:

$Poss(a, s) \Rightarrow$
$\quad [\text{ATMEETING}(\textit{user, chair}, do(a, s)) \Leftrightarrow$
$\quad\quad a = \text{GOTOMEETING}(\textit{user, chair}) \vee$
$\quad\quad (\text{ATMEETING}(\textit{user, chair}, s) \wedge a \neq \text{LEAVEMEETING}(\textit{user, chair}))]$
$Poss(a, s) \Rightarrow$
$\quad [\text{TIME}(do(a, s)) = t \Leftrightarrow \text{TIME}(s) = t' \wedge t = t' + \text{DURATION}(a)]$

Depending on the properties to be proven about the system, it will often be necessary to stipulate some conditions about the initial state of the system. This is accomplished by adding axioms that specify what holds in the initial situation, S_0, for example:

proc ORGANIZEMEETING(*oa*, *chair*, *Participants*, *period*)
  for $p \in$ *Participants* **do**
    REQUESTUNLESS(*oa*, PAG(*p*), **During**(*period*, ATMEETING(*p*, *chair*)),
                      SOMEONEDECLINED(*chair*, *chair*, *Participants*)));
  KWhether(*oa*, SOMEONEDECLINED(*period*, *chair*, *Participants*))?;
  for $p \in$ *Participants* **do**
    INFORMWHETHER(*oa*, PAG(*p*), SOMEONEDECLINED(*period*, *chair*, *Participants*));
  INFORMWHETHER(*oa*, *chair*, SOMEONEDECLINED(*period*, *chair*, *Participants*));
endProc,
where:
SOMEONEDECLINED(*period*, *chair*, *Participants*, *s*) $\stackrel{\text{def}}{=}$
  $\exists p \in$ *Participants*(DECLINEDREQUEST(PAG(*p*),
                  During(*period*, ATMEETING(*p*, *chair*)), *s*)),
and where:
DECLINEDREQUEST(*agt*, ψ, *s*) $\stackrel{\text{def}}{=}$
  $\exists requester$, ϕ(**Previously**(REQUESTUNLESS(*requester*, *agt*, ψ, ϕ), ¬**Goal**(*agt*, $\psi \vee \phi$), *s*))

proc INFORMWHETHER(*agt*, *agt'*, ϕ)
  Know(*agt*, ϕ)?; INFORM(*agt*, *agt'*, ϕ) |
  Know(*agt*, ¬ϕ)?; INFORM(*agt*, *agt'*, ¬ϕ) |
  ¬**KWhether**(*agt*, ϕ)?; INFORM(*agt*, *agt'*, ¬**KWhether**(*agt*, ϕ))
endProc

Fig. 1. Procedure run by the meeting organizer agents.

Initial state axioms:

$$\textbf{Know}(agt, \text{TIME} = 9{:}00 \wedge \neg \text{ATMEETING}(user, chair), S_0)$$
$$\text{PAG}(user') = agt \Rightarrow$$
$$\neg \textbf{Goal}(agt, \textbf{During}(period, \text{ATMEETING}(user, chair)), S_0)$$

We are now ready to use ConGolog to define the behavior of the agents. We start with
the meeting organizer agents. The procedure that defines the behavior of these agents is
given in Fig. 1. Their task is to organize a meeting for a given period and set of participants on behalf of the chair of the meeting. They do this by asking the personal agent
of each participant to have their owner meet during the given period unless someone
declines the meeting. Someone declines the meeting if following a conditional request
to a participant's personal agent—such that the conditional goal of the request is that
the participant be at the meeting—the agent has not adopted the corresponding goal,
i.e., the disjunction of the conditional goal and the condition of the request. The participants' agents will then reply whether they have declined the meeting. In our example,
a personal agent declines the meeting if it has a possible scheduling conflict. The meeting organizer waits until it knows whether one of the participants' agents declined the
meeting. This will happen when either someone has declined the meeting or everyone

proc MANAGESCHEDULE(*pa, user*)
  ⟨*period, chair* :
    Goal(*pa*, **During**(*period*, ATMEETING(*user, chair*))) ∧
    Know[*pa*, ¬**Previously**(INFORM(*pa, user*,
                Goal(*pa*, **During**(*period*, ATMEETING(*user, chair*))))) ∧
             START(*period*) − :15 ≤ TIME ≤ START(*period*)] →
             INFORM(*pa, user*,
                    Goal(*pa*, **During**(*period*, ATMEETING(*user, chair*)))) ⟩
  ⟩⟩
  ⟨*oa, period, Participants, chair* :
    Know[*pa*, **Previously**(REQUESTUNLESS(*oa, pa*,
               During(*period*, ATMEETING(*user, chair*)),
               SOMEONEDECLINED(*period, chair, Participants*))) ∧
         ¬**Previously**(INFORMWHETHER(*pa, oa*,
            DECLINEDREQUEST(*pa*,
               During(*period*, ATMEETING(*user, chair*)))))] →
                INFORMWHETHER(*pa, oa*,
                    DECLINEDREQUEST(*pa*, **During**(*period*,
                         ATMEETING(*user, chair*)))) ⟩
  endProc

Fig. 2. Procedure run by the personal agents.

has agreed to it. Once the organizer knows the answer, it informs all the participants' agents and the chair whether someone has declined.

The procedure that specifies the behavior of the personal agents is given in Fig. 2. Its arguments are the personal agent and the user, i.e., the owner of the personal agent. The procedure is defined with two interrupts, the first running at higher priority than the second. The first interrupt fires when the agent has the goal that the user be at a meeting that starts in less than fifteen minutes, and the agent knows that it has not previously informed the user to go to the meeting. The action taken by the agent is to inform the user that it wants the user to go the meeting.

The second interrupt handles meeting requests; it fires when the agent knows that an organizer agent has requested a meeting, and it knows that it has not yet replied to the request. The action taken is to inform the organizer whether it declines the meeting request.

A complete meeting scheduler system is defined by composing instances of the two agent procedures in parallel, thereby modelling the behavior of several agents acting independently.[9] We also need to compose the nondeterministic iteration of the tick action in parallel (at a lower priority) with the calls to the agent procedures to allow time to pass when the agents are not acting. For example, let the program ρ consist of the three

---

[9] The model is only approximate, since the *Do* relation defines interleaved executions of parallel actions, whereas one would expect that in practice different agents will be running on different processors allowing them to act simultaneously.

procedure definitions given in Figs. 1 and 2, followed by:

$$[\text{MANAGESCHEDULE}(\text{PA}_1, \text{USER}_1) \parallel$$
$$\text{MANAGESCHEDULE}(\text{PA}_2, \text{USER}_2) \parallel$$
$$\text{MANAGESCHEDULE}(\text{PA}_3, \text{USER}_3) \parallel$$
$$\text{ORGANIZEMEETING}(\text{OA}_1, \text{USER}_1, \{\text{USER}_1, \text{USER}_3\}, 12{:}00{-}2{:}00) \parallel$$
$$\text{ORGANIZEMEETING}(\text{OA}_2, \text{USER}_2, \{\text{USER}_2, \text{USER}_3\}, 1{:}30{-}2{:}45)]$$
$$\rangle\!\rangle \text{ TICK}^*$$

A sequence of actions a that satisfies:

$$\textit{Axioms} \models Do(\rho, S_0, do(a, S_0)),$$

where *Axioms* are the axioms mentioned above and suitable initial state axioms, will represent a possible evolution of the system.

In this example, the meeting organizers will both try to obtain USER$_3$'s agreement for meetings that overlap; there will thus be two types of execution sequences, depending on who obtains this agreement.

7 Discussion and Future Work

We have stressed that we are using ConGolog programs as specifications of agent behavior that can be used to prove properties of multi-agent systems rather than as implementations of agents. However, since ConGolog is a programming language, we could simulate the behavior of a system by running its program. A ConGolog interpreter has been implemented. Unfortunately, the interpreter does not handle queries about goals or knowledge. However, if the interpreter had access to a first-order logic theorem prover (since our definitions of **Know** and **Goal** are first-order), the program defined in Sect. 6 could be run (though not very efficiently).

If we did run the program, we would have a simulation of the multi-agent system. What we really want, however, is a method of transforming the program into a set of programs, one for each agent, that could be executed on different processors to yield a true multi-agent system that implements the original specification. Since the program is composed of separate procedures for each agent, this should not be too hard to accomplish. However, once again, we would have to find a way of dealing with queries about the mental states of agents, or find a transformation that could produce single-agent programs that do not refer to mental states. It would be interesting to identify a large class of multi-agent ConGolog programs that could be decomposed into single-agent ConGolog programs, and show that properties that were proven about the multi-agent program ought still to hold for a system composed of the agents running the single-agent programs on separate processors.

The multi-agent meeting scheduler application described above is very simplistic. We would like to expand it by modelling more complex communicative interactions between the agents, and between the agents and their owners. In order to accomplish this, we would have to develop a more sophisticated theory of communicative interaction than the one presented in Sect. 4. Also, we want to develop a method for handling goal (and belief) revision in our framework.

References

1. Philip R. Cohen and Hector J. Levesque. Intention is choice with commitment. *Artificial Intelligence*, 42:213–261, 1990.
2. Michael Fisher. Towards a semantics for Concurrent METATEM. In Michael Fisher and Richard Owens, editors, *Executable Modal and Temporal Logics*. Springer-Verlag: Heidelberg, Germany, 1995.
3. Giuseppe De Giacomo. Concurrency (notes). Unpublished manuscript, 1996.
4. Giuseppe De Giacomo, Yves Lespérance, and Hector J. Levesque. Reasoning about concurrent execution, prioritized interrupts, and exogenous actions in the situation calculus. In *Proceedings of the Fifteenth International Joint Conference on Artificial Intelligence (IJCAI-97)*, pages 1221–1226, Yokohama, Japan, 1997.
5. C.A.R. Hoare. *Communicating Sequential Processes*. Prentice Hall Int., 1985.
6. Gerhard Lakemeyer and Hector J. Levesque. AOL: a logic of acting, sensing, knowing, and only knowing. In *Proceedings of Knowledge Representation and Reasoning (KR&R-98)*, 1998. To appear.
7. Yves Lespérance, Hector J. Levesque, Fangzhen Lin, Daniel Marcu, Raymond Reiter, and Richard B. Scherl. Foundations of a logical approach to agent programming. In Michael Wooldridge, Jörg P. Müller, and Milind Tambe, editors, *Intelligent Agents II: Agent Theories, Architectures, and Languages (LNAI Volume 1037)*, pages 331–346. Springer-Verlag: Heidelberg, Germany, 1996.
8. Hector J. Levesque, Raymond Reiter, Yves Lespérance, Fangzhen Lin, and Richard B. Scherl. GOLOG: A logic programming language for dynamic domains. *Journal of Logic Programming*, 31:59–84, 1997.
9. Fangzhen Lin and Raymond Reiter. State constraints revisited. *Journal of Logic and Computation*, 4(5):655–678, 1994.
10. John McCarthy and Patrick J. Hayes. Some philosophical problems from the standpoint of artificial intelligence. In Bernard Meltzer and Donald Michie, editors, *Machine Intelligence 4*. Edinburgh University Press, 1969.
11. Sheila A. McIlraith. *Towards a Formal Account of Diagnostic Problem Solving*. PhD thesis, Department of Computer Science, University of Toronto, Toronto, ON, 1997.
12. Robert C. Moore. A formal theory of knowledge and action. In Jerry R. Hobbs and Robert C. Moore, editors, *Formal Theories of the Common Sense World*, pages 319–358. Ablex Publishing, Norwood, NJ, 1985.
13. Javier Pinto and Raymond Reiter. Adding a time line to the situation calculus. In *The Second Symposium on Logical Formalizations of Commonsense Reasoning*, pages 172–177, Nagoya, Japan, 1993.
14. Anand S. Rao and Michael P. Georgeff. Modeling rational agents within a BDI-architecture. In Richard Fikes and Eric Sandewall, editors, *Proceedings of Knowledge Representation and Reasoning (KR&R-91)*, pages 473–484. Morgan Kaufmann Publishers: San Mateo, CA, April 1991.
15. Raymond Reiter. The frame problem in the situation calculus: A simple solution (sometimes) and a completeness result for goal regression. In Vladimir Lifschitz, editor, *Artificial Intelligence and Mathematical Theory of Computation: Papers in Honor of John McCarthy*, pages 359–380. Academic Press, San Diego, CA, 1991.
16. Raymond Reiter. Proving properties of states in the situation calculus. *Artificial Intelligence*, pages 337–351, December 1993.
17. Raymond Reiter. Natural actions, concurrency and continuous time in the situation calculus. In *Proceedings of Knowledge Representation and Reasoning (KR&R-96)*, pages 2–13, 1996.

18. Richard B. Scherl and Hector J. Levesque. The frame problem and knowledge-producing actions. In *Proceedings of the Eleventh National Conference on Artificial Intelligence*, pages 689–695, Washington, DC, July 1993. AAAI Press/The MIT Press.
19. Munindar P. Singh. *Multiagent Systems: A Theoretical Framework for Intentions, Know-How, and Communications (LNAI Volume 799)*. Springer-Verlag: Heidelberg, Germany, 1994.

Making It Up As They Go Along: A Theory of Reactive Cooperation

Michael Wooldridge[†]   and   Afsaneh Haddadi[‡]

[†] Department of Electronic Engineering, Queen Mary & Westfield College
University of London, London E1 4NS, United Kingdom
M.J.Wooldridge@qmw.ac.uk

[‡] Daimler-Benz AG, Forschung und Technik, Alt-Moabit 96a,
10559 Berlin, Germany
afsaneh@DBresearch-berlin.de

Abstract. In this article, we present a formal theory of *on-the-fly cooperation*. This is a new model of joint action, which allows for the possibility that a group of cooperating agents will, in general, have neither the information nor the time available to compute an entire joint plan before beginning to work. It proposes that cooperating agents need therefore only reason about what to do *next*; what represents a *believable next action*. Thus, agents literally *make it up as they go along*: a plan only unfolds as cooperation continues. A detailed rationale is presented for the new model, and the components of the model are discussed at length. The article includes a summary of the logic used to formalise the new model, and some remarks on refinements and future research issues.

1 Introduction

A common assumption in early AI planning research was that in order to achieve a goal φ, an agent should first compute an entire plan π for φ, and then execute π [11]. Within the AI planning community, this strategy has long been recognised to be a severe oversimplification [15]. In the real world, the assumptions that underpin plan execution are continually made false, either through the interference of other agents, or else by actions simply failing to have their intended effects. Recognition of this led to work on planning systems that could integrate planning, execution, and, if required, re-planning, in order to achieve their goals [23].

In multi-agent systems research, however, the recognition of this fact has had little impact on theoretical models of cooperative action. For example, in one of the best-known theories of cooperation, [17], it is assumed that a group of agents have an entire, pre-computed joint plan, which they will carry on executing until certain conditions arise — at which point cooperation ends. While the theory *does* recognise that plans can fail, it nevertheless makes some strong assumptions, which, as the AI planning experience shows, must be called into doubt. In brief, the purpose of this paper is to present a new theory of cooperative action, which does not make such limiting assumptions. In this model, which we call *on-the-fly cooperation*, it is not required that agents have an entire, pre-computed joint plan in order to begin work. Nor is it assumed that once a plan fails, cooperation will end. Rather, it is assumed that in order for cooperation to continue, agents need only know *what to do next* — what makes a believable next move. Hence agents may *make it up as they go along*, and a global plan might only emerge as cooperation progresses. This is not necessarily a good strategy in all situations, but for some dynamic domains, it has been shown to have certain advantages [13].

The remainder of this paper is structured as follows. First, in the following subsection, we present a more detailed rationale for our work. In section 2, we give an overview of the logic we use to express our new theory, and in section 3, we present the new model itself. Finally, some concluding remarks are presented in section 4.

1.1 Background

Perhaps the best-known theory of cooperative action is that due to Levesque-Cohen [17]. The aim of this model is to give an account of the mental states of agents that are engaged in cooperative, team activities[1]. The theory implicitly requires that a group of agents involved in such an activity have a pre-computed joint plan, which they intend to execute until some agent becomes aware either that the goal of the plan is achieved, or else that the plan has failed, and the goal is unachievable. If such a situation arises, then the agent who recognised it is required to make the group mutually aware of the new circumstances. Building on this work, others have attempted more refined theories of cooperation. For example, in earlier work, we extended the theory to account for the whole process of cooperation, from recognition of the potential of cooperation by some agent, through to the collective development of a plan by the group, which they jointly intend to execute [28].

These theories explain many aspects of collective action. However, they also fail to account for several important features of real-world cooperation. Perhaps most importantly, they pre-suppose the development of an entire plan of collective action. We argue that this assumption is often unrealistic. A group of agents committed to cooperation with respect to some goal do not, in general, have sufficient *resources* to develop a complete joint plan. By resources, we mean both informational and computational. With respect to information, Moore [19] observed that agents often need to *find out* how to achieve a goal: they do not always have enough information to develop a complete plan in advance. Consider telephoning a friend. You may have several perfectly good plans for this, which involve either using the phone on your desk, stopping off at a pay-phone on the way home, and so on, but they all require that you know the number before you dial. You might therefore only be able to develop *part* of the plan in advance. The same is true in the multi-agent case. Consider a group of agents writing a joint paper for an important conference. They may not know *all* the required information as they begin — it may not even be possible to obtain some important information until quite late on. For example, the formatting instructions and submission details for the conference may not be available far enough in advance to actually write the paper if this information must be obtained before cooperation can begin. In any case, such information is not usually significant until close to the submission deadline. In this example, not only is it not *necessary* for the agents to have an entire, pre-computed plan, it is not *possible* for them to do so. But this does not stop them writing the paper.

---

[1] More precisely, the aim is to define the notion of *joint intention*.

With respect to computational resources, developing a joint plan is at least as complex as single-agent planning, which, as Chapman proved, is *hard* [3]. Even if the agents have sufficient pre-compiled plan fragments to achieve the goal, it will often be unrealistic to try to put these fragments together to make a complete plan before execution commences. Consider an (admittedly extreme) example: building a skyscraper. No one ever has a *complete* plan for erecting such a building, and in fact, low-level details are worked out as construction progresses.

In this paper, we present a new model of cooperative action which does not presuppose an entire pre-computed plan. (Though as a special case, this possibility is allowed for.) Rather, the model proposes that agents are only ever *required* to consider *what to do next*. A global plan *may* be available as cooperation starts — in which case the agents use it. But a plan might only emerge in *retrospect*, as the agents go along. More precisely, the model proposes that a group of agents attempting to achieve φ will continually execute a cycle of trying to find an action π that will take them *closer* to φ, (in the sense of "reducing the distance to φ, as is meant in, for example, means-ends analysis [1]) and then executing π. They do this until either they believe that φ is achieved, or that it is unachievable. While this is not always the *best* cooperation strategy, experimental results indicate that it is well-suited to dynamic domains [13].

2 The Logical Framework

The logic $\mathcal{L}$ that we use to represent our theory of on-the-fly cooperation is a many-sorted first-order version of the expressive branching time logic CTL* [9] with functions and equality, enriched by the addition of modal connectives for representing the *beliefs*, *desires*, and *intentions* of a group of *agents*, as well as the *plans* they have available to them, and the *execution* of these plans. The logic is quite complex, and a complete formal presentation is no possible in the space available. However, such a presentation is available in [25]; in this section, we simply give a summary.

The most obvious thing to say about $\mathcal{L}$ is that it contains the usual connectives and quantifiers of sorted first-order logic: we take as primitive the connectives ¬ (not) and ∨ (or), and the universal quantifier ∀ (for all), and define the remaining classical connectives and existential quantifier in terms of these. As $\mathcal{L}$ is based on CTL*, a distinction is made between *state formulae* and *path formulae*. The idea is that $\mathcal{L}$ is interpreted over a tree-like branching time structure. Formulae that express a property of nodes in this structure are known as *state formulae*, whereas formulae that express a property of paths through the structure are known as *path formulae*. State formulae can be ordinary first-order formulae, but various other additional modal connectives are also provided for making state formulae. Thus (Bel i φ) is intended to express the fact that the agent denoted by i believes φ (where φ is some state formula). The semantics of belief are given in terms of an accessibility relation over possible worlds, in much the standard modal logic tradition [4], with the properties required of belief accessibility relations ensuring that the logic of belief corresponds to the normal modal system KD45 (weak S5). The state formulae (Goal i φ) and (Int i φ) mean that agent i has a desire or intention of φ, respectively: the logics of desire and intention correspond to the normal modal system KD.

$\mathcal{L}$ contains various connectives for representing the *plans* possessed by agents. Plans have two components: a *plan descriptor* and a *plan body*. The plan descriptor characterises the pre- and post-conditions of the plan: the pre-condition represents the conditions under which a plan may be executed, and the post-condition represents the effects of the plan. A plan body is the 'program' part of a plan, which specifies a course of action. Each agent has associated with it a plan library, representing its 'procedural know-how': information it has available to it about how to achieve its intentions. The state formula (Has i π) is used to represent the fact that in the current state, agent i is in possession of the plan denoted by π. Being in possession of a plan simply means that the plan is in that agent's plan library. Restrictions on the logical model mean that an agent cannot execute a plan unless the plan is in its plan library. Note that π is a *term* of the language, not a formula. We have functional and variable terms that can stand for plans, and the ability to quantify over them is in fact crucial when we come to present our model.

The state formulae (Pre π) and (Post π) represent the fact that the pre- and postconditions of the plan π respectively are satisfied in the current world-state. The formula (Body π β) is used to represent the fact that β is the body of the plan denoted by π. We also have a connective (Holds c), which means that the *condition* denoted by c is satisfied in the current world state: the use of this connective, and the rationale behind it, is described in [25].

Turning to path formulae, (Exec β) means that the plan body denoted by β is executed on the current path. We will sometimes abuse notation by writing (Exec π) to mean that body of plan π has been executed on the current path. State formulae may be related to path formulae by using the CTL* *path quantifier* A. This operator means 'on all paths'. It has a dual, existential operator E, meaning 'on some path'. Thus Aφ means that the path formula φ is satisfied on all histories originating from the current world state, and Eφ means that the path formula φ is satisfied on at least one history that originates from the current world state. Path formulae may be built up from state formulae (or other path formulae) by using two *temporal connectives*: the U connectives means 'until', and so a formula $\varphi U\psi$ (where φ and ψ are state formulae) means 'φ is satisfied until ψ is satisfied'. The $\bigcirc$ connective means 'next', and so $\bigcirc\varphi$ means that the state formula φ will be satisfied in the next state.

2.1 Derived Connectives

In addition to the basic connectives discussed above, it is useful to introduce some *derived* constructs. These derived connectives do not add to the expressive power of the language, but are intended to make formulae more concise and readable. First, we assume that the remaining connectives of classical logic, (i.e., $\wedge$ — 'and', $\Rightarrow$ — 'if... then...', and $\Leftrightarrow$ — 'if, and only if') have been defined as normal, in terms of $\neg$ and $\vee$. Similarly, we assume that the existential quantifier, $\exists$, has been defined as the dual of $\forall$. Next, we introduce the *existential path quantifier*, E, which is defined as the dual of the universal path quantifier A. Thus a formula Eφ is interpreted as 'on some path, φ', or 'optionally, φ':

$$E\varphi \stackrel{\text{def}}{=} \neg A\neg\varphi.$$

It is also convenient to introduce further temporal connectives. The unary connective $\Diamond$ means 'sometimes'. Thus the path formula $\Diamond\varphi$ will be satisfied on some path if φ is satisfied at some point along the path. The unary $\Box$ connective means 'now, and always'. Thus $\Box\varphi$ will be satisfied on some path if φ is satisfied at all points along the path. We also have a weak version of the U connective: $\varphi W\psi$ is read 'φ *unless* ψ'.

$$\Diamond\varphi \stackrel{\text{def}}{=} \text{true}\,U\varphi \qquad \Box\varphi \stackrel{\text{def}}{=} \neg\Diamond\neg\varphi \qquad \varphi W\psi \stackrel{\text{def}}{=} (\varphi U\psi) \vee \Box\varphi.$$

Thus $\varphi W\psi$ means that either: (i) φ is satisfied until ψ is satisfied, or else (ii) φ is always satisfied. It is *weak* because it does not require that ψ be eventually satisfied.

Rather than introduce a further primitive modal connective for knowledge, we define it as true belief.

$$(\text{Know } i \; \varphi) \stackrel{\text{def}}{=} \varphi \wedge (\text{Bel } i \; \varphi)$$

It is often convenient to make use of *mutual* mental states, although such states are idealisations, not realisable in any system that admits the possibility of communication failure [10, pp176–183]. The mutual belief of φ in a group of agents g is written $(\text{M-Bel } g \; \varphi)$; the mutual goal of φ in g is written $(\text{M-Goal } g \; \varphi)$, and the mutual knowledge of φ is written $(\text{M-Know } g \; \varphi)$. We define mutual mental states as the *maximal fixed points* of the following formulae (cf. [10, pp402–411]):

$$(\text{M-Bel } g \; \varphi) \stackrel{\text{def}}{=} \forall i \cdot (i \in g) \Rightarrow (\text{Bel } i \; \varphi \wedge (\text{M-Bel } g \; \varphi))$$
$$(\text{M-Goal } g \; \varphi) \stackrel{\text{def}}{=} \forall i \cdot (i \in g) \Rightarrow (\text{M-Bel } g \; (\text{Goal } i \; \varphi))$$
$$(\text{M-Know } g \; \varphi) \stackrel{\text{def}}{=} \varphi \wedge \forall i \cdot (i \in g) \Rightarrow (\text{M-Bel } i \; (\text{M-Know } g \; \varphi))$$

Talking about Groups: The language L provides us with the ability to use simple (typed) set theory to relate the properties of agents and groups of agents. The operators $\subseteq$ and $\subset$ relate groups together, and have the obvious set-theoretic interpretation; $(\text{Singleton } g \; i)$ means g is a singleton group with i as the only member; $(\text{Singleton } g)$ simply means g is a singleton.

$$(g \subseteq g') \stackrel{\text{def}}{=} \forall i \cdot (i \in g) \Rightarrow (i \in g') \qquad (\text{Singleton } g \; i) \stackrel{\text{def}}{=} \forall j \cdot (j \in g) \Rightarrow (j = i)$$
$$(g \subset g') \stackrel{\text{def}}{=} (g \subseteq g') \wedge \neg(g = g') \qquad (\text{Singleton } g) \stackrel{\text{def}}{=} \exists i \cdot (\text{Singleton } g \; i)$$

$(\text{Agt } \beta \; i)$ means that i is the only agent required to perform plan body β.

$$(\text{Agt } \beta \; i) \stackrel{\text{def}}{=} \forall g \cdot (\text{Agts } \beta \; g) \Rightarrow (\text{Singleton } g \; i)$$

Talking about Plans: Next, we introduce some operators that will allow us to conveniently represent the structure and properties of plans. First, we introduce two constructs, $(\text{Pre } \pi \; \varphi)$ and $(\text{Post } \pi \; \varphi)$, that allow us to represent the pre- and post-conditions of plans as formulae of L. Thus $(\text{Pre } \pi \; \varphi)$ means that φ corresponds to the pre-condition of π — that φ is satisfied in just those situations where the pre-condition of π is satisfied:

$$(\text{Pre } \pi \; \varphi) \stackrel{\text{def}}{=} A\,\Box((\text{Pre } \pi) \Leftrightarrow \varphi).$$

Similarly, (Post π φ) means that φ is satisfied in just those situations in which the post-condition of π is satisfied:

$$(\text{Post } \pi \ \varphi) \stackrel{\text{def}}{=} A\square((\text{Post } \pi) \Leftrightarrow \varphi).$$

We write (Plan π φ ψ β) to express the fact that plan π has pre-condition φ, post-condition ψ, and body β:

$$(\text{Plan } \pi \ \varphi \ \psi \ \beta) \stackrel{\text{def}}{=} (\text{Pre } \pi \ \varphi) \wedge (\text{Post } \pi \ \psi) \wedge (\text{Body } \pi \ \beta).$$

It is often useful to be able to talk about the *structure* of plans bodies. We allow such plan bodies to be composed from atomic actions using sequential composition, parallel composition, test, non-deterministic choice, and iteration. We introduce some logical functions, which operate on terms denoting plan bodies, and return other plan bodies corresponding to each of these operations. We introduce one function for each of the plan constructors:

seq for ;   *par* for $\parallel$ *test* for ?   *or* for $\mid$ *iter* for $*$.

These functions are required to satisfy certain properties. For example, for all plan bodies β, β', we require that $seq(\beta, \beta')$ returns the plan body obtained by conjoining the plan bodies denoted by β and β' with the sequential composition constructor. These functions allow us to construct plan bodies within our language. However, complex plan bodies written out in full using these functions become hard to read. To make such expressions more readable, we introduce a *quoting convention*. The idea is best illustrated by example. We write

$\ulcorner\beta;\beta'\urcorner$ to abbreviate $seq(\beta, \beta')$
$\ulcorner\beta;(\beta' \parallel \beta'')\urcorner$ to abbreviate $seq(\beta, par(\beta', \beta''))$
$\ulcorner\beta;(\beta' \parallel \beta'')*\urcorner$ to abbreviate $seq(\beta, iter(par(\beta', \beta'')))$

and so on. In the interests of consistency, we shall generally use quotes even where they are not strictly required. By means of a rather involved technical construction, we can apply tests to state formula in plan bodies. So, for example, if φ is a state formula, then φ? is an acceptable plan body, which will be executed on a path just in case the formula φ is satisfied on the first state of that path. (Readers interested in how we avoid breaking the type rules of our language in using this construction are urged to consult [25].)

The readability of plan body expressions may be further improved by the introduction of derived constructs corresponding to the high-level statement-types one would expect to find in a standard imperative language such as PASCAL. First, the *if... then...* construct:

$$\ulcorner\text{if } \varphi \text{ then } \beta \text{ else } \beta' \text{ end-if}\urcorner \stackrel{\text{def}}{=} \ulcorner(\varphi?;\beta) \mid (\neg\varphi;\beta')\urcorner.$$

While and *repeat* loops are similarly easy to define:

$$\ulcorner\text{while } \varphi \text{ do } \beta \text{ end-while}\urcorner \stackrel{\text{def}}{=} \ulcorner(\varphi?;\beta)*;\neg\varphi?\urcorner$$
$$\ulcorner\text{repeat } \beta \text{ until } \varphi\urcorner \stackrel{\text{def}}{=} \ulcorner\beta;\text{while } \neg\varphi \text{ do } \beta \text{ end-while}\urcorner.$$

The case structure has a similar use to such statements in languages like PASCAL (cf. the switch statement in C).

$$\begin{array}{l} \lceil \text{case} \\ \quad \varphi_1 : \pi_1 \\ \quad \cdots \\ \quad \varphi_n : \pi_n \\ \quad \text{else} : \pi_{n+1} \\ \text{end-case} \rceil \quad \overset{\text{def}}{=} \lceil (\varphi_1?; \pi_1) | \cdots | (\varphi_n?; \pi_n) | ((\neg\varphi_1 \wedge \cdots \wedge \neg\varphi_n)?; \pi_{n+1}) \rceil \end{array}$$

Thus exactly one of the actions π_1 to π_{n+1} is executed. The else clause is a default action, which is executed if none of the other conditions evaluates to true. Note that the conditions $\varphi_1, \ldots, \varphi_n$ are assumed to be mutually exclusive.

Finally, we define an await construct:

$$\lceil \text{await } \varphi \rceil \overset{\text{def}}{=} \lceil \text{repeat true? until } \varphi \rceil.$$

Thus await φ will be executed on a path p if there is some point on p at which φ is true.

3 On-the-Fly Cooperation

In this section, which represents the main contribution of this article, we present our model of on-the-fly cooperation. We begin, in the remainder of this sub-section, with an overview.

Informally, the structure of the model is very easy to understand. Suppose that a group of agents g are cooperating in order to achieve φ (for the sake of argument, we shall assume throughout this article that φ represents a world state). Then the model proposes that g repeatedly perform a cycle of finding a plan π that will in some sense advance them towards φ, and then executing π. They carry on doing this until either they succeed in bringing about φ, or else they become aware that they are no longer able to achieve φ. Of course, figuring out a course of action that will move you towards your goal is far from being trivial: much of AI, (and in particular, the whole of the AI planning paradigm), is directed at precisely this problem. In our model, finding out what to do involves a simple cooperative search of every agent's plan library, in an attempt to find a plan that will reduce the 'distance' to the goal. Agents in our model do no first-principles planning at all. However, we do not assume that agents will *blindly* execute any plan that will reduce the distance to the goal: agents are *autonomous*, with their own desires and intentions, and may *object* to a particular plan. (They may also have strong preferences in *favour* of a particular plan, though we shall not concern ourselves with this possibility here.) The search for a plan must take account of such objections. This leads us to the informal summary of our model in Figure 1, where a group of agents g are attempting to bring about φ.

The remainder of this section is structured as follows. First, in the following section, we informally lay out the assumptions that underpin our model; in section 3.2, we formally define some of the key concepts used in the model, and in section 3.3, we formally define the communication primitives (performatives) that agents can use. Finally, in section 3.4, we present the model itself.

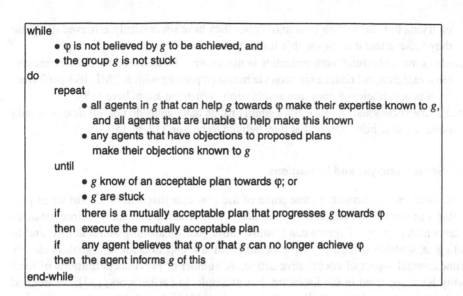

```
while
    • φ is not believed by g to be achieved, and
    • the group g is not stuck
do
    repeat
            • all agents in g that can help g towards φ make their expertise known to g,
              and all agents that are unable to help make this known
            • any agents that have objections to proposed plans
              make their objections known to g
    until
            • g know of an acceptable plan towards φ; or
            • g are stuck
    if     there is a mutually acceptable plan that progresses g towards φ
    then   execute the mutually acceptable plan
    if     any agent believes that φ or that g can no longer achieve φ
    then   the agent informs g of this
end-while
```

Fig. 1. On-the-Fly Cooperation: An Overview

3.1 Assumptions

It is important to realise that the model we present in this paper is a *first approximation* to a theory of on-the-fly cooperation. *Real* cooperation, of the type that most of us take part in every day of our lives, is, of course, a much more subtle and complex process than our model might indicate. This complexity is likely to prevent complete attempts at formalisation for the foreseeable future. So, rather than attempting to present a complete formalisation, we have selected a simple, stylized, but, we argue, plausible subset of the phenomenon, which we make tractable by the use of some limiting assumptions. Obviously, it is important that these assumptions should strike a balance between being too strong and being too weak. Too strong, and the model becomes trivial; too weak, and it becomes too complex. We believe that the following assumptions are reasonable for a first approximation.

Agents are autonomous: As Castelfranchi shows, [2], autonomy is a slippery subject. For our purposes, we simply take autonomy to mean that agents will not blindly commit to courses of action that conflict with their own intentions. (Agents are therefore not benevolent, since it is not assumed that they share all their intentions [21, p91].)

Agents are helpful: Autonomy does not imply meanness: we assume that agents are happy to perform actions on behalf of a group, provided that the performance of such actions does not conflict with their autonomy.

Agents are accommodating: This is really an aspect of helpfulness: agents will take on board the objections that other agents might have to a plan.

Agents are fanatical: We mean this in the sense of [5]. A group of agents will carry on trying to achieve their goal until either they have successfully achieved it, or else they believe that it is impossible for them to do so.

Agents communicate: Communication is not universally assumed in multi-agent systems research, but communication via message passing with KQML-like performatives is nevertheless a common assumption, which we adopt here [18].

Agents are veracious: By which we simply mean that agents do not tell lies: they only communicate information that they believe to be true [12, pp159–165].

3.2 Some Concepts and Definitions

In this section, we formally define some of the concepts that will be useful when presenting our model. We begin with *joint ability*, by which we mean the circumstances under which a group of agents can achieve some goal. Reasoning about ability, and in particular, whether it is in principle possible for a group to achieve a goal, is clearly a fundamental aspect of cooperative action. A number of previous definitions of joint ability have appeared in the literature. For example, in earlier work, [27], we defined ability in the sense of 'potential': what an agent could *potentially* bring about. This definition did not refer to the *know-how* of a group at all. The formalisation was based on earlier work by Werner, [24], who defined a notion of joint ability for φ as the group having a 'winning strategy' for φ, in the game-theoretic sense. However, such definitions do not capture the everyday sense of ability, as they ignore what a group of agents need to know in order to *realise* their potential. For example, we might have the *potential* to become millionaires within the next year, by performing some sequence of actions. But this information is, sadly, useless without knowing *which* actions to perform. So, we define a notion of joint ability in line with the definition of single agent ability developed by Moore [19]. Crudely, his definition of ability runs as follows: an agent *i* can achieve φ if *i* knows the *identity* of some action α that it can perform, such that it knew that after it did α, either φ would be achieved, or else *i* would be able to achieve φ. The point is that this definition allows for the possibility of *i finding out* how to do φ. Thus the agent need not have an entire, pre-computed plan.

In order to formalise this concept, we first define what it means for a group to be *sufficient* to carry out a plan. The idea is that group *g* will be *sufficient* to do plan π, (notation: (Suff *g* π)), iff the agents required to do π are a subset of *g*.

$$(\text{Suff } g \ \pi) \stackrel{\text{def}}{=} \forall \beta \cdot \forall g' \cdot (\text{Body } \pi \ \beta) \wedge (\text{Agts } \beta \ g') \Rightarrow (g' \subseteq g).$$

We then adapt the single-agent definition in the following way. A group *g* can *jointly achieve* φ, (notation: (J-Can *g* φ)), iff there exists some plan π, such that it is mutually known in *g* that π is possessed by some member of *g* (whose identity is known), that *g* are sufficient to do π, and either:

1. it is mutually known in *g* that φ is a post-condition of π; or else
2. it is mutually known in *g* that the post-condition of π is that *g* can jointly achieve φ.

Ability is thus defined as the *least fixed point* of the following formula:

$$(\text{J-Can } g \; \varphi) \stackrel{\text{def}}{=} \exists i \cdot \exists \pi \cdot (\text{M-Know } g \; (i \in g) \wedge (\text{Has } i \; \pi) \wedge (\text{Suff } g \; \pi)) \wedge$$
$$((\text{M-Know } g \; (\text{Post } \pi \; \varphi)) \vee (\text{M-Know } g \; (\text{Post } \pi \; (\text{J-Can } g \; \varphi)))).$$

Note that the variables i and π are quantified *outside* the scope of the M-Know connectives. This implies that the *identities* of i and π are known to g. Thus if the group do *not* know the identities of the agent and plan, but they know there there is *some* agent and *some* plan, this is not sufficient for joint ability. In the terminology of quantified modal logic, these variables are said to be quantified *de re* [14, pp183–188].

Next, an agent i is said to *object* to plan π, (notation: (Objects $i \; \pi$)), iff i intends that π is not executed.

$$(\text{Objects } i \; \pi) \stackrel{\text{def}}{=} \forall \beta \cdot (\text{Body } \pi \; \beta) \Rightarrow (\text{Int } i \; A\neg(\text{Exec } \beta)).$$

A plan will be mutually acceptable to a group if the group is mutually aware that no member of the group objects to it.

$$(\text{Acceptable } \pi \; g) \stackrel{\text{def}}{=} (\text{M-Bel } g \; \forall i \cdot (i \in g) \Rightarrow \neg(\text{Objects } i \; \pi)).$$

Note that it is not possible for an agent within a group to object to a plan, and yet for that plan to be mutually acceptable to the group. Next, we consider the notion of a plan progressing a group towards a goal. Intuitively, we say that a plan does this if either it achieves the goal, or else the plan makes it possible for the group to achieve the goal (cf. the definition of J-Can, above). The former case (where the plan directly achieves the goal) is, in a sense, more desirable than the latter. We formalise this as follows:

$$(\text{Progresses } \pi \; g \; \varphi) \stackrel{\text{def}}{=} (\text{Suff } g \; \pi) \wedge ((\text{Post } \pi \; \varphi) \vee (\text{Post } \pi \; (\text{J-Can } g \; \varphi))).$$

(Note that although the two cases in this definition correspond to those in J-Can, above, it is not possible to define J-Can in terms of Progresses, or Progresses in terms of J-Can.) Next, we define what it means for an agent to be able to *help* the group with its goal. The idea is that agent i can help group g with respect to φ, (notation: (CanHelp $i \; g \; \varphi$)), iff i has a plan π such that:

1. π progresses g towards φ;
2. i does not object to π; and
3. i does not believe that π is unacceptable to g.

$$(\text{CanHelp } i \; g \; \varphi) \stackrel{\text{def}}{=} \exists \pi \cdot (\text{Has } i \; \pi) \wedge (\text{Progresses } \pi \; g \; \varphi) \wedge$$
$$\neg(\text{Objects } i \; \pi) \wedge \neg(\text{Bel } i \; \neg(\text{Acceptable } \pi \; g)).$$

Note that i is quantified *de re*, implying that g know the identity of i. Finally, it is useful to identify certain facts as being *communicable*. The idea is that φ will be communicable to g if φ is true, but φ is not (yet) mutually believed to be true in g.

$$(\text{Comm } \varphi \; g) \stackrel{\text{def}}{=} \varphi \wedge \neg(\text{M-Bel } g \; \varphi).$$

Finally, a group will be *stuck* with respect to a goal φ if they are aware of no plan that progresses them towards φ.

$$(\text{Stuck } g \; \varphi) \stackrel{\text{def}}{=} \forall i \cdot (i \in g) \Rightarrow (\text{M-Bel } g \; \neg(\text{CanHelp } i \; g \; \varphi))$$

3.3 Performatives

The cooperative search for a mutually acceptable plan proceeds via the exchange of messages, in which agents make the group aware of both plans they have that might be useful for the group, and any objections they have with respect to plans. The exchange of messages continues until it becomes clear either that there is a mutually acceptable plan that advances the group, (i.e., the group CanProgress), or else that no such plan is available to the group (i.e., the group are Stuck).

Ultimately, the search for a mutually acceptable plan is a simple form of negotiation [22]. In human negotiation, the participants have preferences, goals, and intentions that they may ultimately compromise on, or they may threaten, lie, bluff, appeal, plead, promise, and so on, in an attempt to bring about their desires. Negotiation becomes a game of give-and-take. Rather than attempting to represent this rather complex process, we simply observe assume that agents have certain inviolable intentions; negotiation is an attempt to find a plan that is acceptable to all with respect to their intentions.

In essence, our simple model of negotiation involves agents proposing various plans, and then informing one-another of their preferences with respect to these plans. Proposing and informing are done by agents executing communicative actions: performatives. These performatives are modelled within the logic as functional terms that denote actions. The two performatives are:

$propose(i, g, \pi, \varphi)$ i proposes that g might do π to achieve φ

$inform(i, g, \varphi)$ i informs g that φ

We do not intend that proposing indicates any *preference* on the part of the proposer with respect to the proposed plan: it is simply a way for an agent to communicate to a group one way of achieving a goal. However, we do assume that:

– agents only propose plans that they have no objection to; and
– agents only propose plans that they are in possession of.

This leads us to the following semantics for *propose*:

$$\forall \pi' \cdot (\text{Body } \pi' \ulcorner propose(i, g, \pi, \varphi) \urcorner) \Rightarrow (\text{Pre } \pi' \ p) \wedge (\text{Post } \pi' \ (\text{M-Bel } g \ p)) \qquad (1)$$

where

$$p \stackrel{\text{def}}{=} \neg(\text{Objects } i \ \pi) \wedge (\text{Has } i \ \pi) \wedge (\text{Suff } g \ \pi) \wedge (\text{Post } \pi \ \varphi).$$

(There are actually some further assumptions hidden within this definition, such as, for example, the fact that communication is guaranteed, and that messages will be delivered instantaneously.) The semantics of the *inform* performative are also quite simple:

$$\forall \pi \cdot (\text{Body } \pi \ulcorner inform(i, g, \varphi) \urcorner) \Rightarrow (\text{Pre } \pi \ (\text{Bel } i \ \varphi)) \wedge (\text{Post } \pi \ (\text{M-Bel } g \ \varphi)) \qquad (2)$$

Note that in both (1) and (2), the pre-condition represents the sincerity condition associated with the performative, capturing the veracity assumption that we mentioned earlier. Also, note that we are not attempting to define a semantics of speech acts [6]: our aim is simply to define some message types that agents can use when cooperating.

```
while ¬(Bel i φ) ∧ (Bel i (J-Can g φ)) do
  /* phase 1: finding an acceptable plan */
  repeat
    /* phase 1.1: propose any plans that help */
    if (CanHelp i g φ) then
        ∃π·(Comm ((Has i π φ) ∧ ¬(Objects i π)) g) ⇒ (Exec ⌈propose(i,g,π,φ)⌉)?
    else
      ⌈inform(i,g,¬(CanHelp i g φ))⌉
    end-if
    /* phase 1.2: wait until everyone has announced */
    await ∀j·(j ∈ g) ⇒ (Bel i (CanHelp j g φ)) ∨ (Bel i ¬(CanHelp j g φ))
    /* phase 1.3: veto any unacceptable plans */
    while ∃π·(Progresses π g φ) ∧ (Comm (Objects i π) g) do
        ∃π·(Progresses π g φ) ∧ (Comm (Objects i π) g) ⇒ (Exec ⌈inform(i,g,(Objects i π))⌉)?
    end-while
  until (Bel i (Stuck g φ) ∨ (CanProgress g φ))
  /* phase 2: execute acceptable plan */
  if ∃π·(Bel i (Acceptable π g) ∧ (Progresses π g φ) ∧ (Agt π i) then
      ∃π·(Bel i (Acceptable π g) ∧ (Progresses π g φ) ∧ (Agt π i) ⇒ (Exec ⌈π⌉)?
  end-if
  /* phase 3: post results */
  case
    (Bel i φ)              : inform(i,g,φ)
    (Bel i ¬(J-Can g φ))   : inform(i,g,¬(J-Can g φ))
    else                   : true?  /* i.e., NOP */
  end-case
end-while
```

Fig. 2. A Model of Reactive Cooperation

3.4 Finally, the Model

We now come to the model itself. This model is formalised as a single-agent plan: each agent individually executes the plan in order to generate the overall behaviour summarised in 1. The model is presented in Figure 2; the agent assumed to be executing the plan is i.

The outer loop represents the fanatical commitment that agents have with respect to φ: they will carry on attempting to bring about φ while they believe they have not yet achieved it (the first conjunct), and that they can still achieve it (the second conjunct). We do not claim that one would want these conditions for *every* type of on-the-fly cooperative action: different problem domains call for different types of commitment [20]. Within the main loop are three main phases:

- finding an acceptable plan that "progresses" the group towards the goal (phase 1);
- executing such an acceptable plan (phase 2);
- updating the group with respect to the current status of group action (phase 3).

Phase 1: Finding a mutually acceptable plan. This first phase represents the key problem in on-the-fly cooperation: finding a plan that will progress the agents towards the goal, such that this plan is acceptable to all. The process of finding a plan involves agents repeatedly proposing plans that they believe will move them closer to the goal, and then vetoing any proposed plans that they object to, until eventually either the agents have considered all possible plans and found none to be acceptable (they are Stuck), or else they have found a plan that is acceptable to all (they CanProgress). This phase thus involves repeatedly executing the following steps:

- proposing any plan that may help, or else informing the group of the inability to help (phase 1.1);
- waiting until everyone else has done likewise (phase 1.2);
- vetoing any plans that are unacceptable (phase 1.3).

In stage 1.1, if an agent can help towards a goal, (i.e., it has a plan that progresses the group towards the goal, and it does not believe this plan is unacceptable to the group), then it proposes the plan to the group. Otherwise it informs the group that it is unable to help, i.e., it has no plans that progress the group towards the goal that would be acceptable to the group. Note that stage 1.3 (vetoing unacceptable plans, below), will ensure that an agent does not propose a plan that has been vetoed by some other agent. Thus an agent will eventually either propose all acceptable plans in its plan library, or else will announce that it cannot help.

Stage 1.2, (the await loop) represents a simple synchronization condition: an agent will simply wait until every other agent has informed it of the fact that it can or cannot help.

In stage 1.3, the agent repeatedly informs the group of any plans that it objects to. It will carry on doing this until either the group has found a plan that is mutually acceptable, or else the group is aware that no such plan is available.

Phase 2: Executing Acceptable Plans. If the group succeeds in finding a mutually acceptable plan that progresses them towards their goal, then the next thing they should do is execute it. From the point of view of an individual agent, this means simply executing a plan that it is the agent of, such that the agent is the only one required to carry out the plan, the plan is acceptable to all, and the plan progresses the group to the goal.

Phase 3: Posting Results. For this part of the process, we simply require that agents who either believe that the goal has been achieved, or else believe that the goal is unachievable, make the group mutually aware of this fact. If an agent neither believes that the goal is achieved, or that the goal is unachievable, then it does nothing.

4 Conclusions

We conclude with some general remarks on the formalisation. First, we note that the *layered* approach, pioneered by Cohen and Levesque [5], which we have adopted in this paper, allows us to present the formal model with comparative ease. Another obvious point to make is that presenting an agent's plan directly as a "procedure" by using a dynamic logic-style program logic, and combining this with a BDI logic, allows a number of complex ideas to be succinctly represented.

However, there are a number of points at which the formalisation is weak, and, it could be argued, inadequate. In particular, the fact that our simple plan language does not have assignment statements makes it hard to express a number of concepts, requiring a rather ugly technical kludge to be used instead. (An example is the if statement in phase 2 of Figure 2.) An obvious enhancement to the underlying formalism would be the inclusion of such statements into a richer plan language.

With respect to the specifics of the formalism, there are at least two points at which more work needs to be done. First, the notion of "progression", (i.e., the notion of agents moving towards the goal), is not satisfactorily defined. It may be that a utility-theoretic definition is more appropriate: a plan progresses the team towards the goal if the expected cost of achieving the goal after executing the plan is less than the cost of achieving it before. Similarly, we have not attempted to formalise any notion of *preference* with respect to the plans that are executed. A more realistic model would include such notions. The formalisation of *negotiation* could also be refined. Some preliminary attempts to give logical specifications of negotiation appear in [16]. Incorporating such models into our model may prove useful.

With respect to other areas for future work, it may prove helpful to attempt to marry our work on formal models of social action with the various models of cooperation and coordination that have been developed by practitioners of agent systems. For example, building on the work of Durfee on partial global planning [8], Decker has investigated five general techniques for coordinating dynamic multi-agent systems [7]. It would be interesting to investigate the extent to which such techniques could be represented using our modal/dynamic logic approach. Finally, the relationship between our theory of on-the-fly cooperation and implementations of cooperative protocols could also bear further examination.

Acknowledgments: This work was carried out while the first author was a visiting researcher at Daimler-Benz research institute in Berlin. Thanks to Kurt Sundermeyer, who made the visit possible, and everyone at DB for being so friendly.

References

1. J. F. Allen, J. Hendler, and A. Tate, editors. *Readings in Planning*. Morgan Kaufmann Publishers: San Mateo, CA, 1990.
2. C. Castelfranchi. Guarantees for autonomy in cognitive agent architecture. In M. Wooldridge and N. R. Jennings, editors, *Intelligent Agents: Theories, Architectures, and Languages (LNAI Volume 890)*, pages 56–70. Springer-Verlag: Berlin, Germany, January 1995.
3. D. Chapman. Planning for conjunctive goals. *Artificial Intelligence*, 32:333–378, 1987.
4. B. Chellas. *Modal Logic: An Introduction*. Cambridge University Press: Cambridge, England, 1980.

5. P. R. Cohen and H. J. Levesque. Intention is choice with commitment. *Artificial Intelligence*, 42:213–261, 1990.
6. P. R. Cohen and H. J. Levesque. Rational interaction as the basis for communication. In P. R. Cohen, J. Morgan, and M. E. Pollack, editors, *Intentions in Communication*, pages 221–256. The MIT Press: Cambridge, MA, 1990.
7. K. Decker and V. Lesser. Designing a family of coordination algorithms. In *Proceedings of the First International Conference on Multi-Agent Systems (ICMAS-95)*, pages 73–80, San Francisco, CA, June 1995.
8. E. H. Durfee. *Coordination of Distributed Problem Solvers*. Kluwer Academic Publishers: Boston, MA, 1988.
9. E. A. Emerson and J. Y. Halpern. 'Sometimes' and 'not never' revisited: on branching time versus linear time temporal logic. *Journal of the ACM*, 33(1):151–178, 1986.
10. R. Fagin, J. Y. Halpern, Y. Moses, and M. Y. Vardi. *Reasoning About Knowledge*. The MIT Press: Cambridge, MA, 1995.
11. R. E. Fikes and N. Nilsson. STRIPS: A new approach to the application of theorem proving to problem solving. *Artificial Intelligence*, 5(2):189–208, 1971.
12. J. R. Galliers. *A Theoretical Framework for Computer Models of Cooperative Dialogue, Acknowledging Multi-Agent Conflict*. PhD thesis, Open University, UK, 1988.
13. M. P. Georgeff and F. F. Ingrand. Decision-making in an embedded reasoning system. In *Proceedings of the Eleventh International Joint Conference on Artificial Intelligence (IJCAI-89)*, pages 972–978, Detroit, MI, 1989.
14. G. E. Hughes and M. J. Cresswell. *Introduction to Modal Logic*. Methuen and Co., Ltd., 1968.
15. L. P. Kaelbling. An architecture for intelligent reactive systems. In M. P. Georgeff and A. L. Lansky, editors, *Reasoning About Actions & Plans — Proceedings of the 1986 Workshop*, pages 395–410. Morgan Kaufmann Publishers: San Mateo, CA, 1986.
16. S. Kraus, M. Nirke, and K. Sycara. Reaching agreements through argumentation: A logical model. In *Proceedings of the Twelfth International Workshop on Distributed Artificial Intelligence (IWDAI-93)*, pages 233–247, Hidden Valley, PA, May 1993.
17. H. J. Levesque, P. R. Cohen, and J. H. T. Nunes. On acting together. In *Proceedings of the Eighth National Conference on Artificial Intelligence (AAAI-90)*, pages 94–99, Boston, MA, 1990.
18. J. Mayfield, Y. Labrou, and T. Finin. Evaluating KQML as an agent communication language. In M. Wooldridge, J. P. Müller, and M. Tambe, editors, *Intelligent Agents II (LNAI Volume 1037)*, pages 347–360. Springer-Verlag: Berlin, Germany, 1996.
19. R. C. Moore. A formal theory of knowledge and action. In J. F. Allen, J. Hendler, and A. Tate, editors, *Readings in Planning*, pages 480–519. Morgan Kaufmann Publishers: San Mateo, CA, 1990.
20. A. S. Rao and M. P. Georgeff. Modeling rational agents within a BDI-architecture. In R. Fikes and E. Sandewall, editors, *Proceedings of Knowledge Representation and Reasoning (KR&R-91)*, pages 473–484. Morgan Kaufmann Publishers: San Mateo, CA, April 1991.
21. J. S. Rosenschein and M. R. Genesereth. Deals among rational agents. In *Proceedings of the Ninth International Joint Conference on Artificial Intelligence (IJCAI-85)*, pages 91–99, Los Angeles, CA, 1985.
22. J. S. Rosenschein and G. Zlotkin. *Rules of Encounter: Designing Conventions for Automated Negotiation among Computers*. The MIT Press: Cambridge, MA, 1994.
23. S. Vere and T. Bickmore. A basic agent. *Computational Intelligence*, 6:41–60, 1990.
24. E. Werner. What can agents do together: A semantics of co-operative ability. In *Proceedings of the Ninth European Conference on Artificial Intelligence (ECAI-90)*, pages 694–701, Stockholm, Sweden, 1990.

25. M. Wooldridge. Practical reasoning with procedural knowledge: A logic of BDI agents with know-how. In D. M. Gabbay and H.-J. Ohlbach, editors, *Practical Reasoning — Proceedings of the International Conference on Formal and Applied Practical Reasoning, FAPR-96 (LNAI Volume 1085)*, pages 663–678. Springer-Verlag: Berlin, Germany, June 1996.
26. M. Wooldridge, S. Bussmann, and M. Klosterberg. Production sequencing as negotiation. In *Proceedings of the First International Conference on the Practical Application of Intelligent Agents and Multi-Agent Technology (PAAM-96)*, pages 709–726, London, UK, April 1996.
27. M. Wooldridge and M. Fisher. A first-order branching time logic of multi-agent systems. In *Proceedings of the Tenth European Conference on Artificial Intelligence (ECAI-92)*, pages 234–238, Vienna, Austria, 1992.
28. M. Wooldridge and N. R. Jennings. Formalizing the cooperative problem solving process. In *Proceedings of the Thirteenth International Workshop on Distributed Artificial Intelligence (IWDAI-94)*, pages 403–417, Lake Quinalt, WA, July 1994.

Agency and the Logic of Ability

Wayne Wobcke
Basser Department of Computer Science
University of Sydney, Sydney NSW 2006, Australia

Abstract

Theories of ability based on the dynamic logic of programs often presuppose that the agent has complete control over its actions to the extent that execution of the action never fails. Similarly, logical theories of 'seeing to it that', Belnap and Perloff (1988) and 'bringing it about', Segerberg (1989), model the result of an action without regard to the original intention of the agent, so these logics are not of direct use to formalizing the reasoning of a planning agent which must make a judgement about the likelihood of its action succeeding. In this paper, we propose an analysis of simple ability, i.e. considering only atomic actions, which is compatible with both the present and future directed sense of intention, whilst admitting the possibility of action failure. The basic idea is that an agent has the ability to do an action *A* to achieve some goal *G* if it *normally* brings about *G* when attempting to do so by doing *A*. We shall assume a primitive notion of 'attempting' or, as Bratman (1987) calls it, endeavouring, to perform an action to achieve some goal. Thus goal-directed behaviour is central to defining ability. In the latter part of the paper, we argue that this concept is also central to defining agency. We propose that agency is best understood as self-controlled goal-directed activity, where the notion of an action being under the control of an agent is intimately tied to the agent's ability to perform that action successfully under normal conditions.

1. Introduction

There are two conflicting intuitions about abilities. On the one hand, an agent only has the ability to perform an action if it can repeatedly, and reliably, do so, Kenny (1975). After all, we wouldn't say someone had the ability to hit the bull's eye on the dart board if he had done so only once. On the other hand, taking an example from Elgesem (1993), the world record long jumper *has* only jumped the world record distance once; we wouldn't want to say he did so as a kind of fluke, i.e. without exercising his ability to jump the distance. There is a related, but different, conflict in the logic of action. This conflict stems from the fact that intention is Janus-faced, to use Bratman's (1987) term: intention is both forward looking (in its role in plan formation), and present directed (in its application to intentional action). Under the forward looking point of view, intentions can only do the job required of them if the agent's ability to fulfil them is repeatable and reliable. Under the present directed view, an agent's action can be intentional even if it was not part of the agent's original intention.

There are related tensions in approaches to formalizing actions and intentions. For example, Brown (1988) takes Kenny's notion of ability as a starting point, and similar intuitions underlie the approach to formalizing ability in Artificial Intelligence based on the dynamic logic of computer programs, e.g. Singh (1994), van der Hoek, van Linder and Meyer (1994). However, humans and agent-based AI systems differ in one very significant respect from ordinary computer programs: the possibility of action failure. In the case of humans, Austin (1961) emphasized the point that having an ability and an opportunity does not always guarantee success. In the case of computer programs, whereas the kinds of failure that result in say, a program failing to execute an assignment statement, are not worth considering to have any bearing on the 'ability' of the program to calculate its output, in AI systems, this kind of failure is perhaps all too frequent. On the other hand, in approaches to formalizing locutions such as 'seeing to it that', Belnap and Perloff (1988), and 'bringing it about', Segerberg (1989), the future directed aspect of intention and action is ignored. It is as if, after the agent has executed its action, a third party comes along and describes what the agent has actually done, totally ignoring what the agent originally set out to do. The agent might have intended to fill the vase with water; what it actually brought about was that the vase was broken and water was on the floor. Thus the logic of 'bringing it about' is not directly applicable to formalizing ability or the relation of intention to action.

In this paper, we propose an analysis of simple ability, i.e. considering only atomic actions, which is compatible with both the present and future directed sense of intention, whilst admitting the possibility of action failure. The basic idea is that an agent has the ability to do an action A to achieve some goal G if it *normally* brings about G when attempting to do so by doing A. We shall assume a primitive notion of 'attempting' or, as Bratman (1987) calls it, endeavouring, to perform an action to achieve some goal. Thus goals, attempts to achieve goals, and goal-directed behaviour are central in the definition of ability. In the latter part of the paper, we argue that these concepts are also central to defining agency. This topic has received considerable attention recently, with a plethora of proposed definitions of computational autonomous agents failing to result in an agreed standard usage. We propose that agency is best understood as self-controlled goal-directed activity, where the notion of an action being under the control of an agent is intimately tied to the agent's ability to perform that action successfully under normal conditions.

A feature of the proposed theory is that abilities are *situated*. This term is used more in the sense of Barwise and Perry's (1983) situation semantics than the more loose AI sense of an agent's being connected to its environment via sensors and effectors. More precisely, we will argue that an agent's abilities are relative to the situation of the agent in exactly the same way that information flow is relative to the situation of the agent, Dretske (1981). That is, the current situation determines the background conditions with respect to which the agent's abilities are assessed. In particular, what counts as the 'normal' conditions under which an agent can achieve its goals is also situated, i.e. determined by context. This, we think, goes some way towards resolving the seeming ambiguity associated with attributions of ability. We often attribute ability without opportunity, e.g. to use an example discussed by Austin, one might say someone has the ability to read *Emma* even though there is no copy of the book available (assuming only that a certain reading maturity has been reached); equally, one might say that the ability is lacking when the opportunity is also lacking. We take the conflict with these cases to be an artifact of what one might *say* in different situations as a result of making different assumptions about those situations. Furthermore, there seems to be a pragmatic rule in force in everyday speech: assume as little as necessary about the background situation when attributing abilities, or more positively, assume that the most favourable circumstances for the agent obtain when ascribing it abilities.

A simple example will help illustrate the situated nature of abilities, as well as the tension between present and future directed senses of intention. Consider the often discussed ability of a golfer to successfully putt a golf ball into the hole. This has elements in common with both throwing a bull's eye (it is an action often attempted) and jumping the world record long jump (a particularly difficult putt may only ever be made once). First, it seems clear that the ability to putt a golf ball into the hole is not an all-or-nothing capacity. Rather, putting ability is a matter of degree: practice makes perfect. What we mean by the statement that abilities are situated is that the ability of a golfer to putt the ball in the hole is relative to the particular situation, which includes any number of relevant background factors. Depending on those factors, the ability is more or less reliable, the action more or less reproducible. Consider a golfer of considerable ability such as Greg Norman. If the distance of the ball from the hole is less than 1 metre, he can be relied on to make the putt almost always. If the distance is 2 metres, perhaps not so, but then if the green is flat rather than bumpy, perhaps he can be relied on to make the putt. Alternatively, if he is only 1 metre away from the pin but off the green, perhaps he can not be relied on to make the putt. As is usual in situation semantics analyses of information flow, the background conditions underlying an ability may never be able to be determined precisely. Similarly, we take it that the precise conditions underlying the world champion long jumper's ability to jump that distance may never again arise, but if they were to do so, he would normally jump the distance.

Elgesem (1993) emphasizes that ability to perform an action is closely related to the notion of control, in that the action's performance must be under the control of the agent. Kenny (1975) takes this to mean in that the successful action must be repeatable at will. We do not take such a (strong) view of ability: we do not require the action and its outcome to be *completely* under the agent's control. With the golf putting example, no agent can guarantee to make the putt no matter what the circumstances. Sometimes the agent just misses; it is not infallible, Austin (1961). What we require instead is that the action normally succeed when it is attempted by the agent. In addition, we accept the point that the action is only under the control of the agent to the extent that the agent can influence the outcome of the attempt. In turn, we treat this as the (weak) condition that the goal of the action would not normally come about except for the action of the agent. For example, no agent has the ability to make the sun rise because this is an event that will happen anyway. Finally, we require that the action be within the control of the agent in the sense that it is within the agent's power not to do the action. Thus the action results from a 'choice' of the agent. This may not be a conscious choice: e.g. we want to say that some simple organisms have the ability to avoid light, etc. We treat this as the property that the agent could (possibly) not have done the action. This condition precludes too simple devices from having abilities, e.g. while a device such as a thermostat does control the temperature in one sense, it cannot but do so, and in this sense it is really us who control the temperature through the instrument of the thermostat.

Returning now to the future directedness of action, it is clear that any agent which is playing golf and deciding whether to attempt a putt will need to know about its abilities. Furthermore, an agent would only be rational in intending to putt the ball if it believed that this was within its capabilities. As Bratman (1987) has pointed out, it is quite a different matter whether the agent holes the putt intentionally. Intentions play a role in reasoning and the future action of the agent; an action is intentional if it is the result of the agent's (successfully executed) chosen intentional action. The difference is that intentional actions, but not intentions, are 'belief-extendable', Bratman (1987, p. 135). What this means is that if an agent intentionally does A and believes that by doing A it will thereby do B, then the agent intentionally does B. However, Bratman claims that the agent could have intended to do A but not to do B. In the putting scenario, suppose the ball is hit and, as a result, ends up in the hole. In this case, whether or not the agent intended to hole the putt, if he acted with the intention of making the putt, his making the putt is done intentionally.

One additional point that has been mentioned so far only in passing is the connection between ability and opportunity. An agent does not have the ability to perform a particular action in a particular situation unless it has the opportunity to do so, although sometimes we might say it has the capability or the capacity to perform the action if the opportunity is absent. Opportunity is also related to the issue of control, not in that the outcome of the action is controllable, but in that the attempt of performing the action is within the agent's control. In this sense, no matter what the agent's capacity for putting golf balls, if there are no golf courses, it does not have the ability to putt any golf ball into any hole. Opportunity seems more a matter of the preconditions for performing the action (rather than the outcome of the action) being under the agent's control.

To summarize, the account of simple ability that we propose is that an agent has the ability to perform an action A in order to achieve/bring it about that G in some background situation if (i) the agent normally succeeds in achieving G when attempting A in the situation, (ii) the outcome of the action A is influenced by the agent's attempt to do A in the situation, i.e. G does not normally happen regardless of the agent's actions, (iii) the agent has the choice not to attempt A in the situation, i.e. without this, the agent does not really have power over its action, and (iv) the agent has the opportunity to perform A in the situation. Central to formalizing this notion is a logic of 'normality'.

2. A Logic of Normality

In this section, we present a modal logic of normality, i.e. a formalization of the intuition that with respect to some background situation, some extensions of the situation are normal while others are abnormal. The approach draws on the intuitions of Delgrande (1987), Boutilier (1990) and, particularly in the technical details, Asher and Morreau (1991), who present conditional logics of 'normality' intended to formalize nonmonotonic inference. In the present paper, a more simple approach is taken: extensions of a situation are either normal or abnormal; there is no grading of normality. In addition, the basis of the axiomatization is a conditional connective similar to the strict implication operator, although it will obviously differ because of the use of situations rather than propositions. Furthermore, by reinterpreting the definition of information flow from Dretske (1981), the logic of normality will turn out to be identical to the logic of information flow. Our starting point is then the logical modelling of situations and information flow.

2.1. Modelling Situations and Information Flow

Our modelling of situations comes from Devlin (1991) and Barwise and Perry (1983). A situation is just a set of infons which are themselves issues with an assigned polarity. An issue is just some basic property of an object or relation between objects which can either hold (positive polarity) or not hold (negative polarity) at some situation. We work only with conjunction, disjunction and negation of infons, and follow Devlin in borrowing from data semantics, Veltman (1981), to define a supports and rejects relation between situations and infons (further discussion of partial logic can be found in Blamey (1986)). We impose a restriction on the logical language that ensures that all infons are persistent, i.e. guaranteeing that if an infon holds at a situation, it holds at all extensions of that situation (Langholm (1988) gives a more general study of persistence). We begin with the basic definitions, assuming a given collection of issues.

Definition. A *basic infon* is an issue together with a polarity (positive or negative).

Definition. The *simple infons* are defined as follows. A basic infon is a simple infon, and if A and B are simple infons then so are $\sim A$, $A \wedge B$ and $A \vee B$.

Definition. The *persistent infons* are defined as follows. A simple infon is a persistent infon, and if A and B are persistent infons then so are $\sim\sim A$, $A \wedge B$, $A \vee B$ and $A \Rightarrow B$.

Definition. The *infons* are defined as follows. A simple infon is an infon, and if A and B are infons and C and D are persistent infons, then $\sim A$, $A \wedge B$, $A \vee B$ and $C \Rightarrow D$ are infons.

Definition. The *dual* A^* of a basic infon A is the issue of A with opposite polarity. The dual operation can be extended to all infons by defining $(A \wedge B)^*$ as $A^* \vee B^*$, $(A \vee B)^*$ as $A^* \wedge B^*$, and $(\sim A)^*$ as A (this is justified by Lemma 2.1 below).

Definition. A *situation* is a set of basic infons.

Definition. A situation is *coherent* if it does not contain any basic infon and its dual.

Definition. A situation τ *extends* σ, written $\sigma \leq \tau$, iff $\sigma \subseteq \tau$. The set of extensions of a situation σ is denoted σ^+, i.e. $\sigma^+ = \{\tau: \sigma \leq \tau\}$.

Definition. A coherent situation σ *supports (rejects)* a simple infon A, written $\sigma \models A$ ($\sigma \dashv A$), under the following conditions.

$$
\begin{array}{ll}
\sigma \models A & \text{if } A \in \sigma \text{ for a basic infon } A \\
\sigma \models \sim A & \text{if } \sigma \dashv A \\
\sigma \models A \wedge B & \text{if } \sigma \models A \text{ and } \sigma \models B \\
\sigma \models A \vee B & \text{if } \sigma \models A \text{ or } \sigma \models B \\[4pt]
\sigma \dashv A & \text{if } A^* \in \sigma \text{ for a basic infon } A \\
\sigma \dashv \sim A & \text{if } \sigma \models A \\
\sigma \dashv A \wedge B & \text{if } \sigma \dashv A \text{ or } \sigma \dashv B \\
\sigma \dashv A \vee B & \text{if } \sigma \dashv A \text{ and } \sigma \dashv B
\end{array}
$$

Lemma 2.1. A coherent situation supports an infon A iff it rejects A^*.

The above definitions are standard in situation semantics and are closely related to those of Devlin (1991). However, they are not enough to define an interesting logic: if a theorem corresponds to the simple infons which are supported by every situation then there are no theorems at all! Any such formula A fails to be not supported by the situation which is the empty set of basic infons. A logic of situations can be defined by incorporating a conditional connective corresponding to information flow: the formula $A \Rightarrow B$ stands for 'A carries the information B'. Such a formula holds in a situation σ if B is supported by all relevant alternative situations to σ that support A, Dretske (1981). To model this idea, we associate with each situation σ a collection of alternative situations σ^*: thus σ supports $A \Rightarrow B$ if every situation in σ^* that supports A also supports B, Wobcke (1989). In the present paper, the alternative situations of a situation are identified with the normal extensions of the situation.

Definition. An *information flow model* is a set Σ of coherent situations together with a function $*$ assigning to each coherent situation $\sigma \in \Sigma$ a nonempty set of coherent situations σ^* such that (i) $\sigma^* \subseteq \sigma^+$, (ii) $\sigma \in \sigma^*$, (iii) $\sigma^* = \cup\{\tau^*: \tau \in \sigma^*\}$, and (iv) whenever $\sigma \leq \tau$, $\tau^* = \sigma^* \cap \tau^+$.

Definition. A coherent situation σ *supports (rejects)* a conditional infon under the following conditions. The truth conditions given above are now understood to apply to all infons.

$$
\begin{array}{ll}
\sigma \models A \Rightarrow B & \text{if for all situations } \tau \in \sigma^* \text{ with } \tau \models A, \tau \models B \\
\sigma \dashv A \Rightarrow B & \text{if for some situation } \tau \in \sigma^* \text{ with } \tau \models A, \tau \dashv B
\end{array}
$$

Definition. An infon A is *semantically persistent* if for any situation σ, if $\sigma \models A$ then $\tau \models A$ whenever $\sigma \leq \tau$.

Lemma 2.2. A persistent infon is semantically persistent.

Proof. By induction on formulae. The interesting case is that of the conditional connective. Suppose $\sigma \vDash A \Rightarrow B$ and $\sigma \leq \tau$. Then since $\tau^* = \sigma^* \cap \tau^+$, any situation in τ^* is contained in σ^*, hence if such a situation supports A, it also supports B. □

The following scheme defines the axioms of the 'infon calculus' IC, where we use $A \Leftrightarrow B$ as an abbreviation for $(A \Rightarrow B) \wedge (B \Rightarrow A)$ and $A \to B$ as an abbreviation for $\sim A \vee B$. Note that we only allow instantiations of A, B and C that result in infon formulae.

(I1) $A \Rightarrow (A \vee B), B \Rightarrow (A \vee B)$

(I2) $(A \wedge B) \Rightarrow A, (A \wedge B) \Rightarrow B$

(I3) $A \Rightarrow (B \Rightarrow (A \wedge B))$

(I4) $A \Leftrightarrow \sim\sim A$

(I5) $(A \wedge (B \vee C)) \Rightarrow ((A \wedge B) \vee (A \wedge C))$

(I6) $((A \vee B) \wedge (A \vee C)) \Rightarrow (A \vee (B \wedge C))$

(I7) $\sim(A \wedge B) \Leftrightarrow (\sim A \vee \sim B)$

(I8) $\sim(A \vee B) \Leftrightarrow (\sim A \wedge \sim B)$

(I9) $(A \wedge (A \to B)) \Rightarrow B$

(I10) $(A \Rightarrow B) \to (A \Rightarrow B)$

(I11) $((A \Rightarrow B) \wedge (A \Rightarrow C)) \Rightarrow (A \Rightarrow (B \wedge C))$

(I12) $((A \Rightarrow C) \wedge (B \Rightarrow C)) \Rightarrow ((A \vee B) \Rightarrow C)$

(I13) $((A \Rightarrow B) \wedge (B \Rightarrow C)) \Rightarrow (A \Rightarrow C)$

(I14) $(A \Rightarrow (B \Rightarrow C)) \Leftrightarrow ((A \wedge B) \Rightarrow C)$

(RI1) From A and $A \Rightarrow B$ infer B

(RI2) If $\vdash B$ then infer $A \Rightarrow B$

The axiom schemas (I1)–(I8) and rule (RI1) capture the basic logical properties of infons. Axiom schema (I9) relates to the coherence property of situations, (I14) refers to the special conditions on the * function, and the remaining axiom schemas and rules come from modal logics of strict implication. Soundness and completeness of IC can be proven.

Definition. A set of infons Γ is *closed* if $A \in \Gamma$ whenever $\Gamma \vdash A$.

Definition. A set of infons Γ is *prime* if whenever Γ contains $A \vee B$, Γ contains A or B.

Lemma 2.3. The set of infons supported by a coherent situation is prime and closed.

Proof. By definition, $\sigma \vDash A \vee B$ iff $\sigma \vDash A$ or $\sigma \vDash B$, so the set of infons supported by any situation is prime. Closure is proven by induction on proofs in IC. More precisely, let Γ be the set of formulae supported by σ and suppose $\Gamma \vdash A$. The induction shows that $\sigma \vDash A$, hence A is contained in Γ. □

Theorem 2.4. For every prime closed consistent set of infons Γ, there is an information flow model containing a coherent situation which supports all and only the infons in Γ.

Proof. We define a mapping $[\,.\,]$ from sets of infons to situations. For any prime closed consistent set of infons Γ, define $[\Gamma]$ to be the set of basic infons contained in Γ: fixing a particular such set Γ, the information flow model consists of the set Σ of all extensions of $[\Gamma]$. For any situation σ contained in Σ, define σ^* to be the set of all $[\Gamma^*]$ where Γ^* is a prime closed consistent set of infons containing Γ_A, defined as $\{B: A \Rightarrow B \in \Gamma\}$, for some A. We must check that the four conditions on the * function are satisfied. Condition (i), $\sigma^* \subseteq \sigma^+$, follows from the fact that $B \Rightarrow (A \Rightarrow B)$ is a theorem of IC, so that whenever $B \in \Gamma$, $B \in \Gamma_A$ for any A. Condition (ii), $\sigma \in \sigma^*$, follows from the fact that $\Gamma_A = \Gamma$ when A is an IC theorem. Condition (iii) is $\sigma^* = \cup\{\tau^*: \tau \in \sigma^*\}$. Since $\sigma \in \sigma^*$, the inclusion $\sigma^* \subseteq \cup\{\tau^*: \tau \in \sigma^*\}$ is trivial. The opposite inclusion follows from (I14). More precisely, any situation in τ^* is derived from a set $\{C: B \Rightarrow C \in \Gamma_A\}$ for some formula A. Any such set is identical to the set $\{C: (A \wedge B) \Rightarrow C \in \Gamma\}$, so the corresponding situation is contained in σ^*. This observation also establishes condition (iv). Finally, we prove by structural induction that for all infons A, $\sigma \vDash A$ iff Γ contains A. The only interesting case is the conditional connective. If $A \Rightarrow B \in \Gamma$ then $\sigma \vDash A \Rightarrow B$ by construction, here using the fact that $A \Rightarrow B$ is persistent. Conversely, if $A \Rightarrow B \notin \Gamma$ then $B \notin \Gamma_A$ and so by construction, some situation in Σ supports A but not B. $\square$

Corollary 2.5. IC is sound and complete with respect to the class of information flow models.

Proof. Soundness is easy to check, noting that it relies heavily on the persistence property. Completeness follows from Theorem 2.4, using the fact that any consistent set is contained in a prime closed consistent set. $\square$

Finally, we can define a modal operator N representing normality by setting $NA \equiv (true \Rightarrow A)$ for an arbitrary persistent IC theorem *true* (it is easy to see that this is well defined). It then follows that the logic of normality contains theorems analogous to KTD4, where these are defined as follows. Note that this is not the same as the usual modal logic of this name because of the absence of PC and the use of strict rather than material implication. In particular, note that (D) does not follow from (T) because of the absence of contraposition.

(K) $N(A \Rightarrow B) \Rightarrow (NA \Rightarrow NB)$

(T) $NA \Rightarrow A$

(D) $NA \Rightarrow {\sim}N{\sim}A$

(4) $NA \Rightarrow NNA$

(N) If $\vdash A$ then infer NA

2.2. Modelling Actions and Results

In this section, we extend the logic of situations with a simple formulation of action. The approach we adopt is based on the work of Moore (1985), in which actions are modelled as state transitions, and is thus similar to other AI work based on game theory, e.g. Werner (1991), and dynamic logic, e.g. Singh (1994), van der Hoek, van Linder and Meyer (1994). This approach has also been adopted by Belnap and Perloff (1988) to formalize 'seeing to it that' and Segerberg (1989) to formalizing 'bringing it about'.

In Segerberg's system, for every proposition A, there is an 'action' δA standing for 'bringing it about that A', or more simply, 'doing A'. However, as noted above, this takes no account of the future directed aspect of intention as needed by a planning agent. What the agent brings about can only be determined *after* the agent has acted. Thus an agent's bringing about A has nothing to do with the agent's ability: the agent may intend to bring about A, but actually bring about ${\sim}A$. What is needed is a modelling that respects the difference between what at agent tries to do and what it actually does. We adopt an approach inspired by Segerberg's logic, and define an 'action' εA, standing for 'endeavouring to A'. Following Bratman (1987), we take it that there are objective facts about what an agent endeavours, i.e. that endeavouring to perform A reflects some psychological state of the agent. In the model, there will be a state transition from σ to τ labelled εA when τ is the actual result of the agent's endeavouring to perform A in σ. We shall also assume an 'action' ${\sim}\varepsilon A$, which is assigned to a transition when A is *not* attempted on that transition. Also following Segerberg, we use dynamic logic notation to represent action outcomes, i.e. $[\varepsilon A]B$ holds in a state σ if B holds in all possible states resulting from an attempt to perform A. Of course, the agent does not always succeed in bringing about A when endeavouring to A, so in contrast to Segerberg's logic, $[\varepsilon A]A$ is not a valid formula. We will place the following constraints on endeavourings: (i) an attempt to do A counts as an attempt to do B whenever A implies B, (ii) an attempt to do A and B (together) counts as an attempt to do $A \wedge B$.

Definition. An *atomic action formula* is a formula of the form εA where A is a simple infon.

Definition. The *action formulae* are defined as follows. An atomic action formula is an action formula, and if A and B are action formulae then so are $\sim A, A \wedge B$ and $A \vee B$.

Definition. An *dynamic formula* is a formula of the form $\Diamond A$ or $[A]B$ where A is an action formula and B is an infon.

Definition. A *labelled state transition model* is is a set Σ of coherent situations together with a transition function t assigning to coherent situation $\sigma \in \Sigma$ a set of labelled transitions $<\tau, \lambda>$ where $\tau \in \Sigma$ and λ is a set of action formulae, such that for all simple infons A and B (i) whenever $\text{IC} \vdash A \Rightarrow B, \varepsilon A \in \lambda$ implies $\varepsilon B \in \lambda$, (ii) λ contains $\varepsilon(A \wedge B)$ whenever it contains εA and εB, and (iii) λ contains $\sim\varepsilon A$ iff it does not contain εA.

Definition. The *result* of attempting an action A in σ, $r(\sigma, A)$, is defined as $\{\tau: <\tau, \lambda> \in t(\sigma), \lambda \text{ contains a label } A\}$.

Definition. A coherent situation σ *supports (rejects)* a dynamic formula under the following conditions.

$$\sigma \models \Diamond A \quad \text{if some } \lambda \text{ such that } <\tau, \lambda> \in t(\sigma) \text{ contains a label } A$$
$$\sigma \models [A]B \quad \text{if for all situations } \tau \in r(\sigma, A), \tau \models B$$
$$\sigma \dashv \Diamond A \quad \text{if no } \lambda \text{ such that } <\tau, \lambda> \in t(\sigma) \text{ contains a label } A$$
$$\sigma \dashv [A]B \quad \text{if for some situation } \tau \in r(\sigma, A), \tau \dashv B$$

Note that as in Singh (1994), the model allows multiple states resulting from the attempt to perform an action, which models the nondeterminism of actions. The fact that there may be transitions out of a particular state labelled with different actions captures the choice available to the agent at that state. That is, it is understood that there is a transition out of a state σ labelled εA if A is one action the agent can endeavour to perform in σ, and that such a transition leads to a result state τ if τ is a possible result of that endeavouring.

The following scheme defines the axioms of a simple 'action calculus' SAC, which also includes the IC axioms and rules obtained by counting dynamic formulae as additional infons. For ease of expression, it is assumed that the schemas apply only to legal formulae.

(A1) $\Diamond(\varepsilon A \wedge \varepsilon B) \Rightarrow \Diamond\varepsilon(A \wedge B)$
(A2) $\Diamond\sim\varepsilon(A \wedge B) \Rightarrow (\Diamond\sim\varepsilon A \vee \Diamond\sim\varepsilon B)$
(A3) $[A](B \Rightarrow C) \Rightarrow ([A]B \Rightarrow [A]C)$
(A4) $[\varepsilon A]C \wedge [\varepsilon B]C \Rightarrow [\varepsilon(A \wedge B)]C$
(RA1) If $\text{IC} \vdash A \Rightarrow B$ then infer $\Diamond\varepsilon A \Rightarrow \Diamond\varepsilon B$
(RA2) If $\text{IC} \vdash B$ then infer $[A]B$
(RA3) If $\text{IC} \vdash A \Rightarrow B$ then infer $[\varepsilon A]C \Rightarrow [\varepsilon B]C$
(RA4) If $\text{IC} \vdash A \Rightarrow B$ then infer $[\sim\varepsilon B]C \Rightarrow [\sim\varepsilon A]C$

Theorem 2.6. The logic SAC is sound and complete with respect to the class of labelled state transition models.

Proof. (Sketch) Given a maximal consistent set Γ of SAC sentences, define a labelled state transition model as follows. First, let an initial state σ be the situation constructed from Γ using Theorem 2.4. Then, for each action formula A such that $\varepsilon A \in \Gamma$, define a transition from σ labelled with εA and all formulae εB where B is a logical consequence of A. The result states are defined as the set of situations corresponding to the set of formulae $\{B: [A]B \in \Gamma\}$. $\square$

3. A Logic of Ability

We are finally in a position to express the properties of ability using the logic of infons IC and the action logic SAC. Above we have motivated a four part definition of ability: an agent has the ability to perform A to achieve goal G in a situation if (i) the agent normally succeeds in achieving G when attempting A in the situation (the success condition), (ii) the outcome of the action A is influenced by the agent's attempt to do A in the situation (the control condition), (iii) the agent has the choice not to attempt A in the situation (the choice condition), and (iv) the agent has the opportunity to perform A in the situation (the opportunity condition).

For convenience, let us define five modal operators Success$A$, Control$A$, Choice$A$, Opportunity$A$ and Ability$A$, corresponding to the above conditions.

Definition. Success$A$ $\equiv$ N([εA]A); Control$A$ $\equiv$ ~N([~εA]A); Choice$A$ $\equiv$ $\Diamond$~εA; Opportunity$A$ $\equiv$ $\Diamond \varepsilon A$; Ability$A$ $\equiv$ Success$A$ $\wedge$ Control$A$ $\wedge$ Choice$A$ $\wedge$ Opportunity$A$.

It is clear that the following properties hold.

Success$A$ $\wedge$ Success$B$ $\Rightarrow$ Success$(A \wedge B)$

Control$A$ $\wedge$ Control$B$ $\Rightarrow$ Control$(A \wedge B)$

Choice$A$ $\wedge$ Choice$B$ $\Rightarrow$ Choice$(A \wedge B)$

Choice$(A \vee B)$ $\Rightarrow$ Choice$A$ $\wedge$ Choice$B$

Opportunity$(A \wedge B)$ $\Rightarrow$ Opportunity$A$ $\wedge$ Opportunity$B$

Opportunity$A$ $\Rightarrow$ Opportunity$(A \vee B)$

The logic of ability turns out to be extremely weak. In fact, we have little more than the following principles.

Opportunity$(A \wedge B)$ $\wedge$ Ability$A$ $\wedge$ Ability$B$ $\Rightarrow$ Ability$(A \wedge B)$

If IC $\vdash A \Leftrightarrow B$ then infer Ability$A$ $\Leftrightarrow$ Ability$B$

Intuitively, the first formula is invalid without the opportunity condition because even though the agent can achieve A and B separately, it may not be able to achieve them together because this may simply not be possible.

Brown (1988) presents a logic of ability based on a nesting of two modal operators, a possibility operator and a necessity operator, Ability$A$ $\equiv$ $\Diamond\Box A$. The following are the only properties concerning only ability that are listed as valid in Brown (1988).

Ability$A$ $\Rightarrow$ Ability$(B \vee$ ~$B)$

Ability$(A \wedge B)$ $\Rightarrow$ Ability$A$ $\wedge$ Ability$B$

Ability$A$ $\vee$ Ability$B$ $\Rightarrow$ Ability$(A \vee B)$

They are all invalid on our interpretation of ability. The first thesis is an artifact of the possible worlds semantics, and fails on our modelling simply because not every situation satisfies $B \vee$ ~B, see also Elgesem (1993). The second and third theses fail for the same reason, i.e. because our logic does not have any theorems of the form Ability$A$ where A is a theorem. Such formulae A are not taken to be under the control of the agent, i.e. Control$A$ will be false (it cannot but be possible that A obtains). Concerning the second thesis, if A is a theorem, the agent can have the ability to perform $A \wedge B$ by having the ability to perform B, but it will not have the ability to perform A. For the third thesis, again if A is a theorem, the ability to perform B does not imply the ability to perform $A \vee B$ because then $A \vee B$ is a theorem and so beyond the agent's control.

It is also often accepted that the logic of ability should reject the following theses.

(T) $A \Rightarrow$ Ability$A$

(C$\Diamond$) Ability$(A \vee B)$ $\Rightarrow$ Ability$A$ $\vee$ Ability$B$

These are invalid in our system, and for much the same reason as they are invalid in Brown's logic. First, the usual reading of (T) is that if the agent does A then it has the ability to do A. This ignores the problem that A might have been a fluke, thus the performance of A is not repeatable. It confuses the present and future directed senses of action. Second, (C◊) is invalid because of nondeterminism, i.e. an agent may be able to guarantee an outcome of $A \lor B$ while not being able to guarantee A and B separately, e.g. when tossing a coin, an agent can guarantee *heads* $\lor$ *tails* but not each individual outcome.

4. What is an Agent?

A recent volume resulting from the Third International Workshop on Agent Architectures, Theories and Languages contained a series of papers on defining the term 'agent' as used in Artificial Intelligence. The fact that there is a need for such a collection of papers suggests that something is amiss with the use of the terminology. The article by Franklin and Graesser (1997) provides a survey of definitions employed by researchers, together with a taxonomy of agent systems; see also Bradshaw (1997). Most definitions require an agent to be 'situated' in an environment from which it receives perceptual input and which it affects by acting autonomously. In addition, the work of Maes (1994) emphasizes the idea that an agent's actions must realize its goals or accomplish the tasks for which it is designed. This helps only to the extent we can further define 'acting autonomously to achieve goals'. Here, many researchers, explicitly or otherwise, adopt Dennett's (1987) intentional stance, wherein the issue becomes not so much which objects are agents, but which can be so *described* according to the predictive convenience afforded to some observer.

A good place to start with terminological disputes is the dictionary: a typical dictionary distinguishes at least the following main senses of agency: (i) the actor of some event or one who has the power to act, i.e. the intentional agent of some event, (ii) one who represents and acts on behalf of another, e.g. a travel agent or company representative, and (iii) the instrumental cause of some event, e.g. the chemical agent of a reaction. Sense (i), the 'actor' sense, is the standard one in the philosophical literature on free will and the one most commonly cited by AI researchers, although the issue is muddied somewhat by adoption of the intentional stance (do agents really have goals, or are goals ascribed to them?). However, it is possible that there is equivocation between sense (i) and sense (ii), the 'assistant' sense, especially in the area of so-called 'software agents', Nwana and Azarmi (1997): certainly if one wants one's software to be 'helpful' and if it is up to the observer what counts as an agent, why not call a payroll system an agent? Sense (iii), which at first glance looks irrelevant to the discussion, is on further examination also a serious possibility: one can view a computer program as a mere instrument to achieve one's own goals, especially if one denies that computers are capable of acting either autonomously or on anyone's behalf. However, since the intended sense seems to be the 'actor' sense, I shall henceforth concentrate on this sense.

If agency requires action, what does it mean to act? Action is distinguished from mere random behaviour in that action is goal directed whereas not all behaviour need be. The clearest cases of action involve deliberation, choice, intention, and subsequent execution of an intention, but not all agents have intentions. A definition that rules out Brooks's insect-like robots, or for that matter, real insects, would be too narrow. These agents engage in goal-directed activity whilst not being aware of their goals. But on the other hand, a definition that includes any object engaged in goal-directed activity seems too broad: it must be a goal of the agent itself towards which the action is directed. This is why the intentional stance advocated by Dennett (1987) is not sufficient for characterizing action and agency. It allows, for example, 'agents' such as a boulder rolling down a hill with the 'goal' of reaching the bottom, or a light switch with the 'goal' of turning on the light whenever it is pressed. We take Dennett's point that it might be useful to treat such objects as agents for predictive purposes, but disagree that agency is best defined this way.

So first, an agent's action is goal-directed. Dretske (1988) includes an extensive discussion of desires and goal-directed behaviour, which we follow here. Essentially, desires are conditions which the agent receives some reward for attaining, and behaviour is goal-directed if it occurs because it tends to produce the desired goal. It is important to note that a goal need not be explicitly represented by an organism for it to have that goal. But neither are goals assigned by an observer. Rather, goals and goal-directed behaviour (for organisms) are the outcomes of natural selection; more precisely, an organism has the goals it has and behaviours have the goal-directedness they have by being part of the 'design' of the agent as produced by evolution, Millikan (1984). This ties in well with Maes' view of software agents as computational systems designed to achieve goals, where in this case, the goals are built in to the system by the programmer, not assigned by an observer.

Second, what distinguishes genuine examples of agency from rocks and light switches is that in the cases of agency, the action is under the control of the agent. The notion of control is central to agency, as emphasized by Elgesem (1993), who gives an analysis of control based on the approach favoured by engineers, mathematicians in the field of 'control theory', biologists and cyberneticists. The idea is that an agent's activity towards a particular goal is under the agent's control if small perturbations in the environment that deflect the agent away from its goal result in compensatory modifications to the behaviour of the agent so that its activity is redirected towards the goal. This is a very weak sense of control which covers cases of non-agency such as the systems controlling the power supply or the stability of a nuclear reactor. Again, while such systems do control aspects of the environment, they can not be said themselves to have the goal of doing so; this is our goal. Moreover, even if such systems are designed to have built in goals, they will not be in control of the actions leading to the satisfaction of those goals. This is because in every situation in which the system has a goal G, under normal circumstances there is no alternative except for the system to perform the action leading to G (under abnormal circumstances such as a breakdown of the machinery, the action may not be performed). Thus to model the control of an agent over its actions, a more complex notion of self-control is required.

We have proposed that self-control involves at least three necessary conditions. First, an action is under the control of an agent only if it is within the agent's ability: it is here that the connection between agency and ability arises. According to our proposal, an agent can only act in a goal-directed manner if when acting to fulfil its goals, it normally achieves its goals. As we have noted above, this does not mean that the agent has complete control nor infallibility: the agent may only be able to achieve its goals if the conditions are favourable, and even then, it may fail in its execution. Second, we propose that a goal-directed action is only within the control of the agent if it is somehow brought about by the agent's activities, and not by external factors irrespective of those activities. Dretske (1988) analyses this as requiring that events internal to the agent must be a primary cause of the resulting behaviour; however, he notes that defining which causes are 'primary' is problematic. Hence we adopted the weaker condition that but for the agent's activities, the result of the the agent's action would normally have been different. Third, we propose that an action is only under the control of the agent if it is within the agent's power not to have performed the action. This is the connection to the 'free will' sense of control.

Of the three conditions, the third requires more explanation. We follow the standard philosophical literature in taking this to mean that the agent 'could have done otherwise', but what does 'could' mean here? Dennett (1984) contains an extensive discussion on the notion of free will, contrasting it with determinism. Determinism is taken to be the claim that had circumstances been identical, the agent would have done the same thing. However, he argues that an agent has free will to the extent that it might have done otherwise had circumstances been slightly different. This perspective is supposed to be more useful to a planning agents, and so ties in with Bratman's (1987) 'two faces' of intention. However, Dennett is left claiming that the nature of the modality 'could' is partly epistemic: i.e. the agent's own knowledge partly determines what circumstances are sufficiently similar to some actual case. This places him at odds with the philosophical tradition, wherein the modality is agent independent. I think the notion of situatedness can help here: we are supposing that an agent has abilities with respect to some situation describing the background conditions obtaining when an action is attempted. Hence we can take 'the agent could have done otherwise' to hold in a situation iff there is a possible transition out of the situation not labelled with the attempt to perform the action. The modelling of actions is understood to reflect the true possibilities for the agent's actions in a situation, and is thus supposed to be disconnected from the agent's knowledge of what it might do in those situations.

In summary, we propose that an agent is an entity capable of self-controlled goal-directed activity. The goals of the agent must be inherent to the agent, rather than being assigned according to a pragmatic 'stance' of an observer. A goal-directed action is under an agent's control if (i) the goal normally comes about as the result of the agent's attempt to perform the action, (ii) the goal does not normally come about except as the result of the agent's action, and (iii) the agent could have not performed the action. This notion of self-control is our way of analysing the concept of autonomy proposed in many definitions of agent systems. The definition is a fairly broad one. It includes most animals, but not plants (whose actions are not under their control). It does not include power plant control systems (which control the environment but do not have their own goals, or if they do, they have no choice over their actions). It includes insects and insect-like robots, assuming these have built in goals such as staying upright. The definition includes some computer programs but not others. The deciding factors here include (i) whether the program is designed to include goals in its internal state, and (ii) whether the system has control over the achievement of those goals, i.e. (a) the system's actions normally lead to the goal being achieved, and (b) the system might (in the relevant sense) not have done the action that led to the goal's satisfaction. This will make many systems based on a BDI-architecture, e.g. Rao and Georgeff (1991), genuine agents, while purely algorithmic processes such as payroll systems and deterministic devices such as electronic calculators will turn out not to be agents.

5. Related Work

In this section, we briefly consider some issues raised by work on formalizing action and ability in the AI literature. In particular, we shall discuss the work of Moore (1985), which focuses on the relationship between knowledge and action, and that of Cohen and Levesque (1990), which includes a formalization of attempts for use in speech act theory. As an initial remark, we note that both papers are formalizing ability for a more restricted class of agents than our definition is intended to cover, i.e. planning agents having knowledge of actions (Moore) and communicating agents having beliefs, desires and intentions (Cohen and Levesque). We intend that the above discussion of ability apply to such agents, yet there may be additional conditions on when such an agent has the ability to perform a complex action.

A major theme of Moore's work is that a planning agent needs to have knowledge of its abilities if it is able to plan reliably. In addition, some of the preconditions for executing an action (and presumably for having the ability to perform that action) are knowledge preconditions. The standard example is that in order to call someone on the telephone, it is necessary to know that person's telephone number. Our discussion is silent on what, exactly, it means to know someone's telephone number: all our definition requires is that in order for an agent to have the ability to call someone, the agent must be capable of reliably executing the action in appropriate contexts. Moore (1985) proposes a particular formalization of action and ability. Essentially, he uses a first order formalism with the added suggestion that knowing an object (such as a telephone number) amounts to knowing a rigid designator for that object. A rigid designator for an object, following Kripke (1972), is an expression that denotes that object in all possible worlds. Morgenstern (1986) points out one problem with this idea: knowing a rigid designator for an object involved in an action is not sufficient for having the ability to execute that action. She notes, for example, that dialling 911 requires one sequence of movements for a rotary telephone, but a quite different sequence for a push-button telephone, so that as all the rotary telephones are gradually replaced by push-button telephones, one's ability to dial 911 disappears. Moreover, it also seems that knowing a rigid designator for the objects in an action is not necessary for having the ability to perform the action. Consider the emergency number again. Children are taught how to dial this number by showing them which sequence of movements to make, long before they know anything about numbers. Far from being a special case, even for reasoning agents it seems that a rigid designator for an object in the action is typically not needed: what counts is the ability to translate the description of an object into action at execution time. For example, I may remember my bank account access code by forming a word out of the letters that are associated with the number keys on the keypad. This description of my number is clearly non-rigid, yet it works every time in the actual world. The point is that although reasoning agents sometimes may require particular kinds of representations of the objects employed in their actions, there is nothing special that this implies about their abilities: the ability of a planning agent to perform a (primitive) action is similar in character to the ability of a non-planning agent to perform an action. The difference between reasoning agents and simpler agents is rather that sometimes the ability of a planning agent to perform a complex action is grounded in its abilities to perform that action's component subactions, and it is this relationship that is formalized by theories of ability based on dynamic logic.

The work of Cohen and Levesque (1990) concerns formalizing the theory of speech acts developed by Searle (1969). One aspect of Searle's theory is the use of essential conditions on actions in order for them to count as speech acts of particular sorts. For some illocutionary acts, the essential condition is that the action be an attempt to achieve some goal of the speaker. Hence Cohen and Levesque's formalization of speech acts includes a definition of attempts. In their theory, an attempt has three aspects: an event the agent performs (e), an intended effect of the event (q), and a goal the agent desires to achieve (p). Their example is the attempt to produce a winning shot in a basketball game. The event e is a certain sequence of bodily movements; the intention q is that the ball go towards the hoop; the goal p is that the ball should end up in the basket. The definition, in summary form, is that an agent attempts to achieve p by doing e with the intention q iff (i) it believes $\sim p$, (ii) its goal is that e should happen and then p should be true, (iii) it should intend that q hold after e occurs, and (iv) it then does e. The question is whether the definition provides a reductive analysis of Bratman's notion of endeavouring in terms of the beliefs, desires and intentions of the agent, and the events that occur. While this certainly appears to be the case from the definition, it seems to me that rather than explaining the notion of endeavouring via attempting, the definition actually presupposes the notion of endeavouring, i.e. goal-directed action. This is because what is missing from the definition is the idea that the event e is performed by the agent *with the intention to achieve q*. All the formal definition requires is that the agent intend to do e, after which q will hold; nothing says that e actually results in q holding (of course if e is not such an event, the agent is being irrational, but that is a different story). Far from being a minor quibble, this is at the heart of the matter. For on Bratman's or Dretske's account, an agent's action is goal-directed only if it is performed in order to achieve the goal. Thus we can make two points. First, Cohen and Levesque's formal definition is not an adequate characterization of attempts. Second, the definition does not reduce goal-directed behaviour to an agent's beliefs, desires and intentions and the events it produces. But this is as it should be: it is important for Dretske (1988) that simple organisms, i.e. those not having beliefs or intentions, be capable of goal-directed behaviour, and this is the property we have argued is central to defining agency.

6. Conclusion

In this paper, we proposed a logical formalization of normality and used this to state properties of ability and opportunity. The logic of normality is based on information flow in situation semantics, and is formalized using a modal logic of strict entailment. The analysis of ability is based on a notion of self-controlled goal-directed activity. We proposed that an agent be defined as an entity capable of such activity. Control is the key concept, and there are at least three aspects to control. First, an agent has control over an action if it normally succeeds in performing the action when it is attempted. Second, the agent can only control actions that will not eventuate regardless of its attempts. Third, the agent only controls actions which it has the choice not to perform.

Acknowledgements

This work was supported by the Australian Research Council. Thanks also to the reviewers of the workshop paper for helpful suggestions leading to the section on related work, and to Dag Elgesem for sending me a copy of his unpublished Ph.D. thesis.

References

Asher, N. & Morreau, M. (1991) 'Commonsense Entailment: A Modal Theory of Nonmonotonic Reasoning.' *Proceedings of the Twelfth International Joint Conference on Artificial Intelligence*, 387-392.

Austin, J.L. (1961) *Philosophical Papers*. Clarendon Press, Oxford.

Barwise, J. & Perry, J. (1983) *Situations and Attitudes*. MIT Press, Cambridge, MA.

Belnap, N.D. & Perloff, M. (1988) 'Seeing To It That: A Canonical Form for Agentives.' *Theoria*, 54, 175-199.

Blamey, S. (1986) 'Partial Logic.' in Gabbay, D.M. & Guenthner, F. (Eds) *Handbook of Philosophical Logic. Volume 3*. Reidel, Dordrecht.

Boutilier, C. (1990) 'Conditional Logics of Normality as Modal Systems.' *Proceedings of the Eighth National Conference on Artificial Intelligence (AAAI-90)*, 594-599.

Bradshaw, J.M. (1997) 'An Introduction to Software Agents.' in Bradshaw, J.M. (Ed.) *Software Agents*. AAAI Press, Menlo Park, CA.

Bratman, M.E. (1987) *Intention, Plans and Practical Reason*. Harvard University Press, Cambridge, MA.

Brown, M.A. (1988) 'On the Logic of Ability.' *Journal of Philosophical Logic*, **17**, 1-26.

Cohen, P.R. & Levesque, H.J. (1990) 'Rational Interaction as the Basis for Communication.' in Cohen, P.J., Morgan, J.L. & Pollack, M.E. (Eds) *Intentions in Communication*. MIT Press, Cambridge, MA.

Delgrande, J.P. (1987) 'A First-Order Conditional Logic for Prototypical Properties.' *Artificial Intelligence*, **33**, 105-130.

Dennett, D.C. (1984) *Elbow Room*. MIT Press, Cambridge, MA.

Dennett, D.C. (1987) *The Intentional Stance*. MIT Press, Cambridge, MA.

Devlin, K. (1991) *Logic and Information*. Cambridge University Press, Cambridge.

Dretske, F.I. (1981) *Knowledge and the Flow of Information*. MIT Press, Cambridge, MA.

Dretske, F.I. (1988) *Explaining Behavior*. MIT Press, Cambridge, MA.

Elgesem, D. (1993) 'Action Theory and Modal Logic.' Ph.D. Thesis, Institute for Philosophy, University of Oslo.

Franklin, S. & Graesser, A. (1997) 'Is It an Agent, or Just a Program?: A Taxonomy for Autonomous Agents.' in Müller, J., Wooldridge, M. & Jennings N. (Eds) *Intelligent Agents III*. Springer-Verlag, Berlin.

Kenny, A. (1975) *Will, Freedom and Power*. Blackwell, Oxford.

Kripke, S.A. (1972) *Naming and Necessity*. Blackwell, Oxford.

Langholm, T. (1988) *Partiality, Truth and Persistence*. Center for the Study of Language and Information, Stanford, CA.

Maes, P. (1994) 'Modeling Adaptive Autonomous Agents.' *Artificial Life Journal*, **1**, 135-162.

Millikan, R.G. (1984) *Language, Thought, and Other Biological Categories*. MIT Press, Cambridge, MA.

Moore, R.C. (1985) 'A Formal Theory of Knowledge and Action.' in Hobbs, J.R. & Moore, R.C. (Eds) *Formal Theories of the Commonsense World*. Ablex, Norwood, NJ.

Morgenstern, L. (1986) 'A First Order Theory of Planning, Knowledge, and Action.' in Halpern, J.Y. (Ed.) *Theoretical Aspects of Reasoning About Knowledge: Proceedings of the 1986 Conference*. Morgan Kaufmann, Los Altos, CA.

Nwana, H.S. & Azarmi, N. (Eds) (1997) *Software Agents and Soft Computing*. Springer-Verlag, Berlin.

Rao, A.S. & Georgeff, M.P. (1991) 'Modeling Rational Agents within a BDI-Architecture.' *Proceedings of the Second International Conference on Principles of Knowledge Representation and Reasoning*, 473-484.

Searle, J.R. (1969) *Speech Acts*. Cambridge University Press, Cambridge.

Segerberg, K. (1989) 'Bringing It About.' *Journal of Philosophical Logic*, **18**, 327-347.

Singh, M.P. (1994) *Multiagent Systems*. Springer-Verlag, Berlin.

van der Hoek, W., van Linder, B. & Meyer, J.-J. Ch. (1994) 'A Logic of Capabilities.' *Proceedings of the Third International Symposium on the Logical Foundations of Computer Science*, 366-378.

Veltman, F. (1981) 'Data Semantics.' in Groenendijk, J.A.G., Janssen, T.M.V. & Stokhof, M.B.J. (Eds) *Formal Methods in the Study of Language. Part 2*. Mathematisch Centrum, Amsterdam.

Werner, E. (1991) 'A Unified View of Information, Intention and Ability.' in Demazeau, Y. & Müller, J.-P. (Eds) *Decentralized Artificial Intelligence. Volume 2*. Elsevier North-Holland, Amsterdam.

Wobcke, W.R. (1989) 'A Schema-Based Approach to Understanding Subjunctive Conditionals.' *Proceedings of the Eleventh International Joint Conference on Artificial Intelligence*, 1461-1466.

On the Relation Between Interpreted Systems and Kripke Models

Alessio Lomuscio and Mark Ryan

School of Computer Science
University of Birmingham
Birmingham B15 2TT, UK
Email {A.R.Lomuscio, M.D.Ryan}@cs.bham.ac.uk
Phone +44 121 414{3734,7361}
Fax +44 121 4144281

Abstract. We compare *Kripke models* and hypercube systems, a simplified notion of *Interpreted Systems*, as semantic structures for reasoning about knowledge. Our method is to define a map from the class of hypercube systems to the class of Kripke frames, another in the opposite direction, and study their properties and compositions. We show that it is possible to characterise semantically the frames that are images of the hypercube systems.

1 Introduction

The need for specifications of complex systems in Artificial Intelligence (AI), as in mainstream computer science, has brought forward the use of logic as formal tool for reasoning and proving properties about systems. In this respect, Multi-Agent Systems (MAS) constitute no exception and in the last thirty years many logics for modelling MAS have been proposed.

The design of a knowledge based agent is a central issue in agent theory, as knowledge is a key property of any intelligent system. Arguably the most successful approach is the modal logic $S5_n$, which was first proposed in Philosophical Logic by Hintikka ([Hin62]) and later used in Distributed Computing Theory by Halpern and Moses ([HF85]) and others.

The logic $S5_n$ models a community of *ideal* knowledge agents. Ideal knowledge agents have, among others, the properties of veridical knowledge (everything they know is true), positive introspection (they know what they know) and negative introspection (they know what they do not know). The modal logic $S5_n$ (see for example [HC96] and [Gol87]) can be axiomatised by taking all the propositional tautologies; the schemas of axioms

$K_i(\phi \Rightarrow \psi) \Rightarrow K_i\phi \Rightarrow K_i\psi$	Distribution of knowledge over implication
$K_i\phi \Rightarrow \phi$	Veridical knowledge
$K_i\phi \Rightarrow K_iK_i\phi$	Positive introspection
$\neg K_i\phi \Rightarrow K_i\neg K_i\phi$	Negative introspection

where $i \in A$ represents an agent in the set of agents $A = \{1, \ldots, n\}$; and the inference rules Modus Ponens and Necessitation.

The logic $S5_n$ has also been extended to deal with properties that arise when we investigate the state of knowledge of the group. Subtle concepts like common knowledge and distributed knowledge have been very well investigated ([FHMV95]). The logic $S5_n$ is a successful tool for the agent theorist also because, even in its extensions to common knowledge and distributed knowledge, it has important meta-properties like completeness and decidability (see for example [MvdH95]).

Two apparently different semantic treatments are available in symbolic AI to interpret the language of modal logic: *interpreted systems* and *Kripke models*.

Interpreted systems were first proposed by Fagin, Halpern, Moses and Vardi [HF85] to model distributed systems. The growing interest in complex MAS and in their specifications has brought forward the concept of interpreted system as useful formal tool to model key characteristics of the agents, such as the evolution of their knowledge, communication, etc. This work has culminated in the publication of [FHMV95] in which the authors use the notion of interpreted system to explore systematically fundamental classes of MAS (such as synchronous, asynchronous, with perfect recall ability, etc.) by the use of interpreted systems.

Kripke models [Kri59] were first proposed in Philosophical Logic and later used in Logic for AI as semantic structures for logics for belief, logics for knowledge, temporal logics, logics for actions, etc, all of which are modal logics. Over the last thirty years, many formal techniques have been developed for the study of modal logics grounded on Kripke semantics, such as completeness proofs via canonical models, decidability via the finite model property [HC96], and more recently, techniques for combining logics [KW91, Gab96].

The two approaches have different advantages and disadvantages. On the one hand, interpreted systems are more intuitive to model real MAS, on the other hand Kripke models come with a heritage of fundamental techniques (see for example [Gol87, HC96] that can allow the user to prove properties about his or her specification.

Given the common purpose of the two approaches, some questions arise naturally. Is one of the approaches more specialised than the other? What is the difference between the two generated logics? Is it possible to use the powerful techniques developed for Kripke models to MAS defined in terms of the more intuitive systems? Is it possible to identify in terms of frames key MAS usually defined in terms of interpreted systems? The rest of the paper answers only partially to some of these questions, but tries to bring us a step further in our understanding of the two notions.

In the article we isolate and study a special class of interpreted systems that we call hypercube systems or simply hypercubes, which are defined by taking not an arbitrary subset (as interpreted systems are defined) but the *full* Cartesian product of the local states for the agents. We show that hypercube systems are semantically equivalent to a special class of frames defined on equivalence relations commonly used to interpret an epistemic language.

Hypercube systems are a special case of interpreted systems but we hope that the methods we introduce to analyse them can be extended to analyse interpreted systems in the general settings.

The paper is organised as follows: In Section 2 we remind the reader of some basic mathematical notions that we will use throughout the paper. In Section 3 we define interpreted systems, Kripke models, and hypercube systems. In section 4 we define maps between hypercubes and Kripke models. In Section 5 we analyse the composition of these maps and we present results that relate the two semantics. In Section 6 we draw our conclusions and we suggest further work. Proofs of all theorems and lemmas are given in the Appendix.

2 Mathematical Preliminaries

We assume a modal propositional language, defined in the usual way from a set of propositional variables by the use of classical connectives, the operators K_i and D_B. The index i varies over a set $A = \{1, \ldots, n\}$, representing the agents of the system and B varies over subsets of A. The modal operator K_i represents the knowledge of the agent i, while D_B represents the distributed knowledge among the group B (the reader is referred to [FHMV95] for an introduction to this terminology). We use the standard definitions for satisfaction for formulas on states, and validity for formulas on frames, on models, on class of frames, and on class of models - see [HC96] for details. If W is a set, id_W is the identity relation on W. If $\sim$ is an equivalence relation on W and $w \in W$, then $W/\sim$ is the set of equivalence classes, and $[w]_\sim$ is the equivalence class containing w.

3 Hypercube Systems

We briefly remind the key definitions of Kripke frames and interpreted systems; then we define hypercube systems.

3.1 Kripke models

Kripke models are the fundamental semantic structures used in modal logic to reason about possibilities, necessities, knowledge, obligation, etc. In the case of epistemic logic the usual approach is to take Kripke models grounded on equivalence relations so that they constitute a complete semantics for the logic $S5_n$ described above. We report here the key definition.

Definition 1 (Equivalence frames). An *equivalence frame* $F = (W, \sim_1, \ldots, \sim_n)$ is a tuple where W is a non-empty set and for every i in A, $\sim_i$ is an equivalence relation over $W \times W$. Elements of W are called worlds and are denoted as: $w_1, w_2, \ldots$ $\mathcal{F}$ denotes the class of frames.

Intuitively points of W represent epistemic alternatives, i.e. possible configurations. Relations represent epistemic possibility between points; for example with

$w \sim_i w'$ we capture the fact that "w' is possible according to i's knowledge in the state w".

An equivalence Kripke model $M = (F, \pi)$ is a pair, where F is an equivalence frame and π is an interpretation for the atoms of the language.

For ease of reference, we state here the notion of validity on a class of frames.

Definition 2 (Validity on Kripke frames). A formula ϕ is valid on a class $\mathcal{F}$ of Kripke frames if for any frame $F \in \mathcal{F}$ for any valuation π, $(F, \pi) \models \phi$.

3.2 Interpreted systems

Interpreted systems can be defined as follows ([FHMV95]). Consider n sets of local states, one for every agent of the MAS, and a set of states for the environment.

Definition 3 (Global states of interpreted systems). *A set of global states for an interpreted system is a subset S of the Cartesian product $L_e \times L_1 \times \cdots \times L_n$, where $L_e, L_1, \ldots, L_n$ are non-empty sets. The set L_i represents the local states possible for agent i and L_e represents the possible states of the environment.*

A global state represents the configuration of all the agents and of the environment at a particular instant of time. The idea behind considering a subset is that some of the tuples that originate from the Cartesian product might not be possible because of explicit constraints present in the MAS. By considering functions (runs) $r : N \to S$ from the natural numbers to the set of global states, it is possible to represent the temporal evolution of the system. An interpreted system $IS = (R, \pi)$ is a set of functions $R = \{r : N \to S\}$ on the global states with a valuation π for the atoms of the language. Since here we carry out an analysis of the static properties of knowledge, we will not consider runs explicitly and we will consider interpreted systems to be pairs $IS = (S, \pi)$.

Interpreted systems can represent the knowledge of the MAS by considering two global states to be indistinguishable for an agent if its local state is the same in the two global states. Thus, a set of global states S denotes the Kripke frame $F = (W, \sim_1, \ldots, \sim_n)$, if $W = S$, $(l_1, \ldots, l_n) \sim_i (l'_1, \ldots, l'_n)$, if $l_i = l'_i, i \in A$.

3.3 Hypercube systems

Given n sets of local states for the agents of the MAS, the interpreted systems we analyse in this paper and that we call hypercube systems or hypercubes, result by considering the admissible state space of the MAS to be described by the full Cartesian product of its sets of local states. This means that every global state is in principle possible, i.e. there are no mutually exclusive configurations between such local states. Various scenarios comply with this specification, such as distributed systems that have just crashed, and more generally in MAS in which no information is available about their configuration[1]. In these cases the state space of the system is the whole full Cartesian product of the sets of locals states for the agents.

With hypercubes we are imposing a further simplification on the notion presented in Definition 3: in the tuples representing the configuration of the system we do not consider a slot for the environment. The presence of the environment in the notion of Fagin et al. is motivated in order to keep track of the changes in the system and in general to represent everything that cannot be captured by the local states of the single agents (most importantly messages in transit, etc.). By neglecting the dimension of the environment or, which comes to be the same thing, by treating it as a constant, we are projecting the notion of Fagin et al. of a time-dependent interpreted system to the product of its local states. Since we are focusing on a static case, in a way we can see this restriction as fixing the environment at the time in analysis, and investigate the possible configurations of the states of the agents. We formally define hypercube systems.

Definition 4 (Global states of hypercube systems). A *hypercube system*, or *hypercube*, is a Cartesian product $H = L_1 \times \cdots \times L_n$, where $L_1, \ldots, L_n$ are nonempty sets. The set L_i represents the local states possible for agent i. Elements of a local state L will be indicated with $l_1, l_2, \ldots$ The class of hypercube systems is denoted by $\mathcal{H}$.

Aim of the paper is to relate hypercube systems to Kripke models. More specifically we would like to identify the class of Kripke models that satisfy exactly the same formulas satisfied by the hypercubes. Given the notion of validity of formulas on interpreted systems and Kripke models, it is appropriate to compare the two underlying semantic structures: Kripke frames and global states of hypercube systems. This is what we do in the next two Sections, where, for brevity, we will use the terms "hypercube systems" and "hypercubes" also to refer to sets of global states of hypercube systems as in Definition 4.

4 Mapping Between Hypercubes and Frames

Although hypercubes are intuitively a special class of Kripke frames, it is clear that they are not simply a subset. In order to clarify the relationship, we have to use the construction given implicitly in [FHMV95] for obtaining a frame from a system. Our framework will be the following (proofs are reported in the Appendix):

- We define the class of hypercubes $\mathcal{H}$, and the class of Kripke frames $\mathcal{F}$.
- We define two maps, $\mathcal{H} \xrightarrow{f} \mathcal{F}$ (based on [FHMV95]) and $\mathcal{F} \xrightarrow{g} \mathcal{H}$.
- We analyse the compositions of the maps f and g.

---

[1] It has also been suggested by Ron van der Meyden that there may be a connection between the full Cartesian product and the states of knowledge in certain classes of broadcast systems.

– We isolate the images of $\mathcal{H}$ in $\mathcal{F}$.

Hypercubes and frames are always defined over a set A of n agents, which we assume as given.

Every hypercube generates a frame ([FHMV95]):

Definition 5 (Hypercubes to frames). $f : \mathcal{H} \to \mathcal{F}$ is the function that maps the system H onto a Kripke frame in the following way:
If $H = L_1 \times \cdots \times L_n$, $f(H) = (L_1 \times \cdots \times L_n, \sim_1, \ldots, \sim_n)$, where $\sim_i$ is defined as: $(l_1, \ldots, l_n) \sim_i (l'_1, \ldots, l'_n)$ if and only if $l_i = l'_i$.

Lemma 6. *If H is a hypercube system, and $f(H) = (W, \sim_1, \ldots, \sim_n)$ is the frame defined from it by Definition 5, then*

1. $\bigcap_{i \in A} \sim_i = id_W$;
2. *For any $w_1, \ldots, w_n$ in W there exists a $\overline{w}$ such that $\overline{w} \sim_i w_i$, $i = 1, \ldots, n$.*

The proof of this (and other) results is given in the Appendix.

This shows that Kripke frames that we build from the hypercubes by means of the standard technique ([FHMV95]) constitute a subset of all the possible reflexive, symmetric and transitive Kripke frames. To relate the two semantic classes, we have to analyse the properties of Lemma 6.

The first one expresses the fact that in the images of the hypercubes there cannot be two states related by all the equivalence relations. This is a peculiarity of the construction f given in [FHMV95].

The second property reflects the fact that hypercubes are defined on full Cartesian products. The property expresses the circumstance that for every pair of points in the n dimensions space of the images of the hypercubes, there are $n!$ ways to connect them in two steps. In particular, we can change $n-1$ coordinates in n possible ways and change the last one in the last step.

Given these differences between the class of hypercubes and equivalence frames, it is likely that the two semantic structures satisfy different formulas. In fact we have the following.

Condition 1 of Lemma 6 imposes the following Lemma.

Lemma 7. *Consider a frame $F = (W, \sim_1, \ldots, \sim_n)$.*
$\bigcap_{i \in A} \sim_i = id_W$ *if and only if $F \models \phi \Leftrightarrow D_A \phi$.*

Corollary 8. *If H is a hypercube system, $f(H) \models \phi \Leftrightarrow D_A \phi$.*

This means that on hypercubes the notion of truth of a formula collapses to the one of distributed knowledge of the formula.

Condition 2 of Lemma 6 forces the frames generated from hypercubes to satisfy the following formula.

Lemma 9. *If H is a hypercube system, $f(H) \models \neg K_i \neg K_j \phi \Rightarrow K_j \neg K_i \neg \phi$, where $i \neq j$.*

The formula in Lemma 9 is an axiom that relates private knowledge between two arbitrary agents of the model.

It is easy to check that Formulas in Lemmas 7 and 9 are not generally valid on the class $\mathcal{F}$ of frames. In Figure 1 M_1 does not validate the Formula in Lemma 7 and M_2 does not validate the Formula in Lemma 9. In fact w_0 in M_1 does not satisfy $p \Leftrightarrow D_A p$, where $D_A p$ is as usual computed by taking the equivalence relation defined by the intersection of the equivalence relations $\sim_1, \sim_2$. In M_2, w_0 does not satisfy $\neg K_1 \neg K_2 p \Rightarrow K_2 \neg K_1 \neg p$.

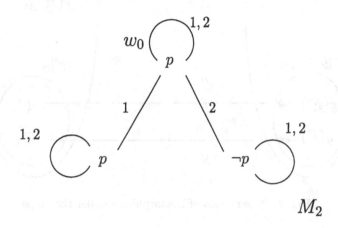

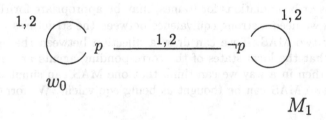

Fig. 1. Equivalence models not satisfying Formulas in Lemma 7 and Lemma 9

It is also possible to generate a system from a frame:

Definition 10 (Frames to hypercubes). $g : \mathcal{F} \to \mathcal{H}$ is the function that maps a frame $F = (W, \sim_1, \ldots, \sim_n)$ onto the hypercubes $g(F) = W/\sim_1 \times \cdots \times W/\sim_n$.

We now have defined maps between the two semantic structures. Our aim is to use them to identify the class of equivalence frames that are semantically equivalent, i.e. that satisfy the same formulas, to the hypercubes. In order to do

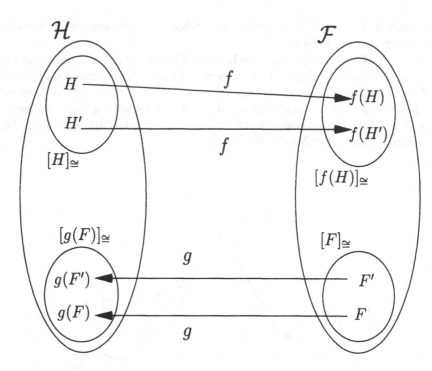

Fig. 2. Preservation of isomorphisms under the maps

so, we introduce a notion of isomorphism on $\mathcal{F}$ and $\mathcal{H}$. Many notions (such as p-morphisms or bisimulations for frames) may be appropriate for this task, but for our aims we need a strong equivalence between the structures.

Consider two MAS. If we can draw a bijection between the agents of the MAS such that the local states of the corresponding agents are themselves in a bijection, then in a way we can think that one MAS can simulate the other, and so the two MAS can be thought as being equivalent. We formalise this as follows:

Definition 11 (Isomorphism of hypercubes). Two hypercubes $H = L_1 \times \cdots \times L_n$, $H' = L'_1 \times \cdots \times L'_n$ are isomorphic ($H \cong_{\mathcal{H}} H'$) if $|L_i| = |L'_i|$ for $i = 1, \ldots, n$.

To reason about equivalent frames we take the standard notion of isomorphism.

Definition 12 (Isomorphism of frames). Two frames $F = (W, \sim_1, \ldots, \sim_n)$, $F' = (W', \sim'_1, \ldots, \sim'_n)$ are isomorphic ($F \cong_{\mathcal{F}} F'$) if and only if:

- There exists a bijection $b : W \to W'$,
- For all $s, t \in W$, and all $i \in A$, $s \sim_i t$ if and only if $b(s) \sim'_i b(t)$.

We can prove that the maps we defined preserve isomorphisms:

Lemma 13. *If $H \cong_{\mathcal{H}} H'$, then $f(H) \cong_{\mathcal{F}} f(H')$.*

Lemma 14. *If $F \cong_{\mathcal{F}} F'$, then $g(F) \cong_{\mathcal{H}} g(F')$.*

Figure 2 shows the preservation of isomorphisms under f and g between frames and hypercubes as proved Lemmas 13 and 14. Since we want to import and export results from one structure into the other, this is the result we need.

5 Characterisation of the Class of Hypercube Systems

We now investigate the extent to which the composition of f with g (or g with f) results in a hypercube (frame) which is isomorphic to the one we started with. We do this for two reasons. First we want to check whether by going back and forth between the two class of structures we are going to lose information, i.e. the structure we obtain satisfies different formulas from the original one. Secondly, this will help us prove a result on the correspondence of the hypercubes into a subclass of frames. We operate as follows.

Given a hypercube $H = L_1 \times \cdots \times L_n$, consider the image under f of H, $f(H)$. Let $H' = (L_1 \times \cdots \times L_n)/\sim_1 \times \cdots \times (L_1 \times \cdots \times L_n)/\sim_n$ be the image under g of $f(H)$. We want to investigate the relationship between H and H'.

Theorem 15. *For any system H in $\mathcal{H}$, $H \cong_{\mathcal{H}} g \circ f(H))$.*

In other words, if we start from a system H, build the corresponding Kripke frame $f(H)$, it is still possible to extract all the information from the frame by applying the function g that produces another system H', which is in a bijection with the original H.

We now investigate the other side of the relation. Consider a frame F and its image under g, $g(F)$. If we take the image under f of $g(F)$, that frame will satisfy the property stated by Lemma 6 and therefore will not in general be isomorphic to F. As we made clear in the previous Section, property one of Lemma 6 corresponds to the validity of a formula on such frames. Therefore, $f(g(F))$ is not only non-isomorphic to F, but it is not even even a p-morphic image of F.

What we can prove is the following:

Lemma 16. *If F is a frame such that there exists a system H, with $F \cong_{\mathcal{F}} f(H)$, then $F \cong_{\mathcal{F}} f \circ g(F)$.*

If we consider a frame $F = (W, \sim_1, \ldots, \sim_n)$ such that $\bigcap_{i \in A} \sim_i = id_W$, $f \circ g(F)$ will not in general be isomorphic to F. As an example, consider:

$$F = (\{w_1, w_2\}, \{(w_1, w_1), (w_2, w_2)\}, \{(w_1, w_1), (w_2, w_2)\}).$$

We need to restrict our attention to *both* the properties inherited from the mapping from hypercubes. Results of Lemmas 15 and 16 are shown in Figure 3.

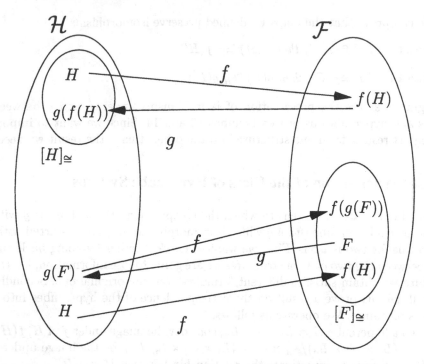

Fig. 3. Compositions of maps between frames and hypercubes as in Theorem 15 and Lemma 16

Theorem 17. If $F = (W, \sim_1, \ldots, \sim_n)$ is a frame such that:

- $\bigcap_i \sim_i = id_W$,
- $\forall w_1, \ldots, w_n, \exists \overline{w}$ such that $\overline{w} \sim_i w_i$, $i = 1, \ldots, n$;

then $F \cong_{\mathcal{F}} f \circ g(F)$.

Theorem 17 and Lemma 6 allows us to characterise the frames that are images of some system:

Theorem 18. Let $F = (W, \sim_1, \ldots, \sim_n)$ be a frame. The following are equivalent:

1. $\bigcap_i \sim_i = id_W$ and $\forall w_1, \ldots, w_n, \exists \overline{w}$ such that $\overline{w} \sim_i w_i$, $i = 1, \ldots, n$;
2. there exists an H, such that $F \cong_{\mathcal{F}} f(H)$.

Theorem 18 characterises the frames that we obtain by applying the map f to the class of hypercubes. Every member of this class of frames is isomorphic to a system and a frame not included in this class is not.

We can now identify a class of frames which is semantically equivalent to hypercube systems. To do this, we remind that satisfaction on a system H is defined by considering the image under f of H. In this context we need the notion of validity on a system:

Definition 19. A formula ϕ is valid on a system H, $(H \models \phi)$, if $f(H) \models \phi$.

Validity of ϕ on the frame $f(H)$ in Definition 19 was defined in Definition 2.

We can no prove that:

Theorem 20. *Let $\mathcal{G}$ be the class of equivalence frames that satisfy property 1 and 2 of Lemma 6, then $\forall \phi (\mathcal{H} \models \phi$ if and only if $\mathcal{G} \models \phi)$.*

Proof: From right to left. If $\mathcal{G} \models \phi$, then, since $f(\mathcal{H}) \subseteq \mathcal{G}$, $f(\mathcal{H}) \models \phi$. So, by Definition 19 $\mathcal{H} \models \phi$.

From left to right. Assume $\mathcal{H} \models \phi$, i.e. $f(\mathcal{H}) \models \phi$, we want to show that for any $F \in \mathcal{G}$, $F \models \phi$. By Lemma 17 and Theorem 18, $F \cong_{\mathcal{F}} f(g(F))$. But then $F \models \phi$ if and only if $f(g(F)) \models \phi$. But $g(F) \in \mathcal{H}$, and so $f(g(F)) \models \phi$, and so $F \models \phi$.   □

Theorems 18 and 20 completely characterise the hypercubes we focus in this note in terms of Kripke frames.

6 Conclusions and Further Work

Interpreted systems are a useful formalism for representing MAS knowledge. In this note we have analysed their relation with Kripke models in a simplified setting by looking at the case of hypercube systems.

We have defined mappings between hypercube systems and Kripke frames and we have completely characterised the Kripke structures which are semantically equivalent to hypercubes.

The methodology we presented here to map hypercubes into Kripke models suggests that further research could be undertaken to attempt to have a general methodology for translating interesting classes of interpreted systems into classes of Kripke models. This would help in the process of axiomatising key MAS defined in terms of interpreted systems as the analysis could be carried out in the class of Kripke models.

Should such a general methodology for inter-translating the two classes be achieved, this may also help in the attempt to apply combining logics techniques for modal logics (for example [KW91]) to the case of complex MAS defined in terms of systems. The idea is that complex MAS specifications would benefit from an approach focused on the identification of classes of interactions between basic and well-understood modal logics with respect to the transfer of important properties such as completeness (see [LR97a] for details).

Hypercubes seem to capture an interesting property concerning the relation between private knowledge of the agents of the group. Given the semantic equivalence expressed by Theorem 20 it is possible to axiomatise hypercubes by analysing the corresponding Kripke frames. This was presented in [LR97b] where a sound and complete axiomatisation for equivalence frames that satisfy properties 1 and 2 of Lemma 6 is shown.

Acknowledgements The authors gratefully acknowledge partial funding from the following sources: British Telecom; AISB; the Nuffield Foundation; and the European Union (ESPRIT Working Group FIREworks). We wish to thank Joe Halpern, J.-J. Meyer, and Mathias Kegelmann for useful discussions on some of the issues addressed in this article.

References

[FHMV95] Ronald Fagin, Joseph Y. Halpern, Yoram Moses, and Moshe Y. Vardi. *Reasoning about Knowledge*. MIT Press, Cambridge, 1995.

[Gab96] D. M. Gabbay. Fibred semantics and the weaving of logics. Part 1. Modal and intuitionistic logics. *Journal of Symbolic Logic*, 61(4):1057–1120, December 1996.

[Gol87] R. Goldblatt. *Logics of Time and Computation, Second Edition, Revised and Expanded*, volume 7 of *CSLI Lecture Notes*. CSLI, Stanford, 1992 (first edition 1987). Distributed by University of Chicago Press.

[HC96] G. E. Hughes and M. J. Cresswell. *A new introduction to modal logic*. Routledge, New York, 1996.

[HF85] J. Y. Halpern and R. Fagin. A formal model of knowledge, action, and communication in distributed systems: Preliminary report. In *Proceedings of the Fourth ACM Symposium on Principles of Distributed Computing*, pages 224–236, 1985.

[Hin62] Jakko Hintikka. *Knowledge and Belief, an introduction to the logic of the two notions*. Cornell University Press, Ithaca (NY) and London, 1962.

[Kri59] S. A. Kripke. Semantic analysis of modal logic (abstract). *Journal of Symbolic Logic*, 24:323–324, 1959.

[KW91] Marcus Kracht and Frank Wolter. Properties of independently axiomatizable bimodal logics. *The Journal of Symbolic Logic*, 56(4), 1991.

[LR97a] A. Lomuscio and M. Ryan. Combining logics for multi-agent system (abstract). In A. Cesta and P.-Y. Schobbens, editors, *Proceedings of the 4th ModelAge Workshop on Formal Models of Agents*, January 1997.

[LR97b] A. Lomuscio and M. Ryan. Ideal agents sharing (some!) information. Manuscript, 1997.

[MvdH95] J.-J. Ch. Meyer and W. van der Hoek. *Epistemic Logic for AI and Computer Science*, volume 41. Cambdridge University Press, 1995.

A   Proofs of Theorems

Lemma 6 *If H is a system, and $f(H) = (W, \sim_1, \dots, \sim_n)$ is the frame defined from it by Definition 5, then*

1. $\bigcap_{i \in A} \sim_i = id_W$;
2. *For any $w_1, \dots, w_n$ in W there exists a $\overline{w}$ such that $\overline{w} \sim_i w_i$, $i = 1, \dots, n$.*

Proof: For 1, Consider any two elements $w = (l_1, \dots, l_n), w' = (l'_1, \dots, l'_n)$ in W such that $w(\bigcap_{i \in A} \sim_i)w'$. Then for all i in A, $(l_1, \dots, l_n) \sim_i (l'_1, \dots, l'_n)$. Therefore by definition, for all i in A, $l_i = l'_i$, that is $w = w'$.

For 2, consider any $w_1 = (l_1, \dots, l_n), \dots, w_n = (m_1, \dots, m_n)$. Now let $\overline{w} = (l_1, \dots, m_n)$. By definition 5, the element $\overline{w}$ is in W and for each i, $\overline{w} \sim_i w_i$. □

Lemma 7 *Consider a frame* $F = (W, \sim_1, \ldots, \sim_n)$. $\bigcap_{i \in A} \sim_i = id_W$ *if and only if* $F \models \phi \Leftrightarrow D_A \phi$.

Proof. Left to right. Let M be a model based on F such that $M \models_w \phi$. Since $\bigcap_{i \in A} \sim_i = id_W$, then $M \models_w D_A \phi$. Analogously, suppose $M \models_w D_A \phi$. Since $w(\bigcap_{i \in A} \sim_i) w'$ implies $w = w'$, then $M \models_w \phi$.

Right to left. Suppose $F \models \phi \Leftrightarrow D_A \phi$ and for all i $w_1 \sim_i w_2$. Take a valuation π such that $\pi(p) = \{w_1\}$. Since $F, \pi \models_{w_1} p \Leftrightarrow D_A p$ and $F, \pi \models_{w_1} p$, we have $F, \pi \models_{w_1} D_A p$ and so $F, \pi \models_{w_2} p$. But since $\pi(p) = \{w_1\}$, it must be that $w_1 = w_2$. $\square$

Lemma 9 *If H is a system,* $f(H) \models \neg K_i \neg K_j \phi \Rightarrow K_j \neg K_i \neg \phi$, *where* $i \neq j$.

Proof: For a contradiction suppose that $f(H) \not\models \neg K_i \neg K_j \phi \Rightarrow K_j \neg K_i \neg \phi$. Then there exists a point w and a valuation π such that $(F, \pi) \models_w \neg K_i \neg K_j \phi \wedge \neg K_j \neg K_i \neg \phi$. Therefore there must exist two points w_1 and w_2 such that $w \sim_i w_1$ and $w \sim_j w_2$ and $(F, \pi) \models_{w_1} K_j \phi$ and $(F, \pi) \models_{w_2} K_i \neg \phi$. But by property 2. of Lemma 6 there exists a point $\overline{w}$ such that $\overline{w} \sim_j w_1$ and $\overline{w} \sim_i w_2$. Since $(F, \pi) \models_{w_1} K_j \phi$ and the relations symmetric, we have $(F, \pi) \models_{\overline{w}} \phi$, but this contradicts $(F, \pi) \models_{w_2} K_i \neg \phi$ that requires $\overline{w}$ to satisfy $\neg \phi$. $\square$

Lemma 13 *If $H \cong_{\mathcal{H}} H'$, then $f(H) \cong_{\mathcal{F}} f(H')$.*

Proof: Let $H = L_1 \times \cdots \times L_n$, and $H' = L_1' \times \cdots \times L_n'$. Since $H \cong_{\mathcal{H}} H'$ there is a family of bijections $b_i : L_i \to L_i'$. Consider $b = b_1 \times \cdots \times b_n$. The function b is a bijection, and therefore the universes of the frames $f(H)$ and $f(H')$ are in a bijection.

Consider now $s = (l_1, \ldots, l_i, \ldots, l_n), s' = (l_1', \ldots, l_i', \ldots, l_n')$ such that $s, s' \in H$, and $s \sim_i s'$ on $f(H)$. Consider $b(s) = (b_1(l_1), \ldots, b_i(l_i), \ldots, b_n(l_n))$ and $b(s') = (b_1(l_1'), \ldots, b_i(l_i'), \ldots, b_n(l_n'))$. Since, by definition, $l_i = l_i'$, then $b_i(l_i) = b_i(l_i')$ and therefore $b(s) \sim_i' b(s')$.

Let now be $b(s) \sim_i' b(s')$. Then, by definition $b_i(l_i) = b_i(l_i')$ and then $l_i = l_i'$, that implies $s \sim_i s'$. $\square$

Lemma 14 *If $F \cong_{\mathcal{F}} F'$, then $g(F) \cong_{\mathcal{H}} g(F')$.*

Proof: Consider two isomorphic frames $F = (W, \sim_1, \ldots, \sim_n), F' = (W', \sim_1', \ldots, \sim_n')$ such that $b : W \to W'$ is a bijection. We want to prove that there is a family of bijections c_i between the components of $g(F) = W/\sim_1 \times \cdots \times W/\sim_n$ and $g(F') = W'/\sim_1' \times \cdots \times W'/\sim_n'$. Let $c_i : W/\sim_i \to W'/\sim_i'$ such that $c_i([w]_{\sim_i}) = [b(w)]_{\sim_i'}$.

The function c_i is well defined. In fact, let $[w]_{\sim_i} = [w']_{\sim_i}$, with $w, w' \in W$. Then $c_i([w]_{\sim_i}) = [b(w)]_{\sim_i'} = [b(w')]_{\sim_i'} = c_i([w']_{\sim_i})$.

The function c_i is injective. $c_i([w]_{\sim_i}) = c_i([w']_{\sim_i})$, then $[b(w)]_{\sim_i'} = [b(w')]_{\sim_i'}$, that is $b(w) \sim_i b(w')$, $w \sim_i w'$ and then $[w]_{\sim_i} = [w]_{\sim_i'}$.

The function c_i is surjective. Consider $[w']_{\sim_i'}$, such that $w' \in W'$ and let $w \in W$ be such that $b(w) = w'$. Then $c_i([w]_{\sim_i}) = [w']_{\sim_i'}$. $\square$

Theorem 15 *For any system H in $\mathcal{H}$, $H \cong_{\mathcal{H}} g \circ f(H)$.*

Proof: We prove that the function $b_i : L_i \to (L_1 \times \cdots \times L_n)/\sim_i$, defined as $b_i(l_i) = [(l_1, \ldots, l_i, \ldots, l_n)]_{\sim_i}$, where $l_j, i \neq j$, is any element in L_j, is a bijection.

The function b_i is well defined. In fact, let $l_i = l_i'$. So $b_i(l_i) = [(l_1, \ldots, l_i, \ldots, l_n)]_{\sim_i}$ and $b_i(l_i') = [(l_1', \ldots, l_i', \ldots, l_n')]_{\sim_i}$. But $(l_1, \ldots, l_i, \ldots, l_n) \sim_i (l_1', \ldots, l_i', \ldots, l_n')$ and therefore $b_i(l_i) = b_i(l_i')$.

The function b_i is an injection: let $b_i(l_i) = b_i(l_i')$, so $[(l_1, \ldots, l_i, \ldots, l_n)]_{\sim_i} = [(l_1', \ldots, l_i', \ldots, l_n')]_{\sim_i}$, that implies $l_i = l_i'$.

The function b_i is a surjection. In fact, consider any $[(l_1, \ldots, l_i, \ldots, l_n)]_{\sim_i} \in (L_1 \times \cdots \times L_n)/\sim_i$. $b_i(l_i) = [(l_1', \ldots, l_i, \ldots, l_n')]_{\sim_i} = [(l_1, \ldots, l_i, \ldots, l_n)]_{\sim_i}$. $\quad\square$

Theorem 17 *If* $F = (W, \sim_1, \ldots, \sim_n)$ *is a frame such that:*

- $\bigcap_i \sim_i = id_W$,
- $\forall w_1, \ldots, w_n, \exists \overline{w}$ *such that* $\overline{w} \sim_i w_i$, $i = 1, \ldots, n$;

then $F \cong_{\mathcal{F}} f \circ g(F)$.

Proof: Consider the frame $f \circ g(F) = (W/\sim_1 \times \cdots \times W/\sim_n, \sim_1', \ldots, \sim_n')$ built according to Definition 10 and Definition 5. Let now h be a mapping $h : W \to W/\sim_1 \times \cdots \times W/\sim_n$, defined by $h(w) = ([w]_{\sim_1}, \ldots, [w]_{\sim_n})$. We prove that h is a bijection.

Injective: suppose $h(w_1) = h(w_2)$, so $([w_1]_{\sim_1}, \ldots, [w_1]_{\sim_n}) = ([w_2]_{\sim_1}, \ldots, [w_2]_{\sim_n})$. Therefore, for all i, $[w_1] \sim_i [w_2]$, but since $\bigcap_i \sim_i = id_W$, it must be $w_1 = w_2$.

Surjective: consider any element $([w_1]_{\sim_1}, \ldots, [w_n]_{\sim_n})$ in $W/\sim_1 \times \cdots \times W/\sim_n$. By Hypothesis on F, there exists a world $\overline{w}$ in W, such that $[\overline{w}]_{\sim_i} = [w_i]_{\sim_i}$, for each $i = 1, \ldots, n$. Therefore $([w_1]_{\sim_1}, \ldots, [w_n]_{\sim_n}) = ([\overline{w}]_{\sim_1}, \ldots, [\overline{w}]_{\sim_n}) = h(\overline{w})$.

Now we prove that $w_1 \sim_i w_2$ in F if and only if $h(w_1) \sim_i' h(w_2)$ in $f \circ g(F)$. Suppose $w_1 \sim_i w_2$, that is $[w_1]_{\sim_i} = [w_2]_{\sim_i}$; by definition of $\sim_i$, this is equivalent to $([w_1]_{\sim_1}, \ldots, [w_1]_{\sim_n}) \sim_i' ([w_2]_{\sim_1}, \ldots, [w_2]_{\sim_n})$.

This proves that F and $f \circ g(F)$ are isomorphic. $\quad\square$

Theorem 18 *Let* $F = (W, \sim_1, \ldots, \sim_n)$ *be a frame. The following are equivalent:*

1. $\bigcap_i \sim_i = id_W$ *and* $\forall w_1, \ldots, w_n, \exists \overline{w}$ *such that* $\overline{w} \sim_i w_i$, $i = 1, \ldots, n$;
2. *there exists an* H, *such that* $F \cong_{\mathcal{F}} f(H)$

Proof: 1 implies 2: Under these conditions by Theorem 17, $F \cong_{\mathcal{F}} f \circ g(F)$. That is: $H = g(F)$.

2 implies 1: By Lemma 6 the frame $f(H)$ has the properties expressed by proposition 1. But F is isomorphic to $f(H)$ and therefore it has those properties as well. $\quad\square$

Disjunctive Logic Programming and Possible Model Semantics

Li-Yan Yuan, Jia-Huai You, and Randy Goebel

Department of Computer Science
University of Alberta
Edmonton, Canada T6G 2H1
{yuan, you, goebel}@cs.ualberta.ca

Abstract. We use Kripke structures of autoepistemic logic to classify various semantics for disjunctive logic programs with default negation. We have observed that nonmonotonic reasoning can be characterized by Kripke structures whose beliefs are justified. We also observed that two different types of negative introspection in autoepistemic reasoning present two different interpretations of default negation: consistency-based and minimal-model-based; we further observed that all logic program semantics fall into three semantical points of view: the skeptical, stable, and partial-stable. Based on these observations, we classify disjunctive logic program semantics into six different categories, and discuss the relationships among various semantics.

1 Introduction

Recently the study of theoretical foundations of disjunctive logic programs with default negation has attracted considerable attention [3, 15, 17]. This is mainly because the additional expressive power of disjunctive logic programs significantly simplifies the problem of modeling disjunctive statements of various nonmonotonic formalisms in the framework of logic programming, and consequently facilitates the use of logic programming as an inference engine for nonmonotonic reasoning.

One of the major challenges is how to define a suitable semantics for various applications. A semantics of logic programs is usually specified by how default negation is justified. Different ways of justification lead to different semantics. Many promising semantics for disjunctive programs have been proposed, such as the answer set semantics [9], the static semantics [15], and the well-founded and stable circumscriptive semantics [21] but searching for suitable semantics for disjunctive programs has proved to be far more difficult than for normal programs (logic programs without disjunction) whose semantics is now fairly well understood.

Three major semantical points of view have been established for logic programs: the skeptical, stable, and partial-stable.

Roughly speaking, a *skeptical semantics* justifies a default negation **not**α if and only if α cannot possibly be derived under any circumstance. A *stable* *semantics* is based on the idea of *perfect introspection*, in that **not**α is justified if and only if α is not true in the semantics (usually in terms of a stable model or stable extension). Obviously, a stable semantics disallows any *undefined atoms*. (α is undefined if neither α nor **not**α is true in the semantics.)

A stable semantics characterizes an ideal credulous semantics for logic programs but a stable semantics of many less-than-ideal programs may not be consistent, which motivates the introduction of the third semantical point of view: the *partial-stable semantics*. A partial-stable semantics can be viewed as a relaxed stable semantics that allows a minimum number of undefined atoms.

The standard semantics in the three semantical categories for normal programs are the well-founded semantics [6], the stable semantics [8], and the regular semantics [18], respectively.

Not surprisingly, many semantics for disjunctive programs have been proposed in each of these three semantical categories. For example, the static semantics, the well-founded circumscriptive semantics, the disjunctive well-founded semantics [2], and the skeptical well-founded semantics [22] are representatives of the skeptical semantical category; the answer set semantics and the stable extension semantics [13] (based on the autoepistemic translation of logic programs) are representatives of the stable semantical category. For the partial-stable semantical category, there are the partial-stable model semantics [14], the regular model semantics [18], and the maximal stable model semantics [5]. These three partial-stable semantics, as well as many others, defined weaker stable semantics for disjunctive programs but experienced various difficulties [5]. A notable new entry in the field is the the partial-stable assumption semantics [17]. The partial-stable assumption semantics extends the answer set semantics into the partial-stable semantical category in the same way as the regular semantics extends the stable semantics for normal programs.

In addition to three semantical points of view, it has also been realized that the interpretations for default negation can be divided into two camps: those in default logic and autoepistemic logic, which are *consistency-based*, and those in circumscription and the like, which are *minimal-model-based* [12]. In the former case, default assumptions are made on the basis of certain hypotheses being consistent with a current theory; in the latter case, default assumptions are made on the basis of their being true in all minimal models of a current theory.

Our general goal here is to use Kripke structures of autoepistemic logic as a tool to classify disjunctive program semantics. Logics of knowledge and belief provide a theoretical foundation for logic programming semantics while Kripke structures capture model semantics of the logic. However, logic programming semantics have rarely been characterized in terms of Kripke structures, which is quite unusual. The main reason, we believe, is that the Kripke structure, as with any other model theoretical tools, is an ideal tool for capturing monotonic semantics of logic of knowledge and belief but it has inherent difficulty in characterizing *negative introspection*, which forms the basis for default reasoning. Intuitively, negative introspection in autoepistemic reasoning is an inference process by which a rational agent concludes **not**α by somehow failing to infer α on the basis of its available knowledge [7].

We have observed that, in order to characterize negative introspection, all beliefs held in a Kripke structure must be justified, and consequently we define the *partial-stable model* of an autoepistemic theory as a Kripke structure whose beliefs are justified with respect to the theory. We then define six different semantical categories in terms of different partial-stable models, according to three semantical points of view and two interpretations of default negation. We show that all the six semantics have been proposed earlier in some frameworks, and that all promising semantics either coincide with, or are essentially the same as, one of these six semantics.

Our study provides a basis for much needed insights into the theoretical foundations of logic programming with default negation.

The rest of the paper is organized as follows: Sections 2 and 3 briefly review logic program semantics and possible model semantics of autoepistemic logic respectively. Sections 4 and 5 define three partial-stable model semantics of autoepistemic logic based on belief justification as well as three different semantical points of view. The six different semantics of disjunctive logic programs are redefined in Section 6. Semantical analysis and comparisons are in Section 7.

2 Logic Programs with Default Negation

We consider instantiated programs in a finite language containing the binary connectivities $\vee, \wedge, \leftarrow$, and a unary connective **not**. A logic program is a set of clauses of the form

$$A_1 \vee \cdots \vee A_q \leftarrow B_1, \ldots, B_m, \mathbf{not}C_1, \ldots, \mathbf{not}C_n,$$

where A_i, B_j, C_k are atoms, $\mathbf{not}C_k$ are *default negations*, also called *assumed negations*, and $q \geq 1$. Π is considered a *normal* program if $q = 1$; and a *positive* program if $n = 0$. We use $\Pi \vdash \alpha$ to denote the fact that α can be derived from Π in the sense of classical consequence.

Assume Π is a program. A *negation set* N is defined as a set of default negations that appear in Π, which represents a possible interpretation (values) of default negations contained in Π. The GL-translation Π^N is defined as a program obtained from Π by first deleting all $\mathbf{not}c_j s$ if $\mathbf{not}c_j \in N$ and then deleting all clauses with $\mathbf{not}c_k$ in the body if $\mathbf{not}c_k \notin N$.

The main challenge is how to define a suitable semantics for logic programs. Since a negation set specifies a set of default negations being assumed true and the intended meaning of Π under a given negation set N is determined by Π^N [1], a semantics of Π is usually given by one or more negation sets. Therefore, searching for a semantics of Π is a process of searching for a negation set that can be justified under a certain semantical point of view.

---

[1] Given Π and N, an atom α is considered true with respect to Π^N if either $\Pi^N \models \alpha$ as in a consistency-based semantics, or $(\Pi^N \cup \{\neg\beta \mid \mathbf{not}\beta \in N\}) \models \alpha$ as in the answer set semantics. See Section 6 for details.

There are three major semantical points of view: the skeptical, stable, and partial-stable.

A skeptical semantics is the most conservative semantics in that it justifies a default negation $\mathbf{not}\alpha$ only if α cannot be derived from the current program in any circumstance. Both stable and partial-stable semantics justify a default negation $\mathbf{not}\alpha$ only if α cannot be derived from the current program under the given negation set. The difference between the stable and partial-stable is that the former assigns a definite value, being true or assumed false, to each and every atom while the latter allows a minimum number of undefined atoms.

Consider normal programs first. The following table lists all the major semantics proposed for normal programs.

Skeptical	Stable	Partial-Stable
		Regular Semantics [18]
Well-Founded	Stable Semantics [8]	Preferential Semantics [4]
Semantics [6]		Maximum Partial-Stable Semantics [16]
		Stable-Class Semantics [1]

Let Π be a normal program, and M and N negation sets of Π. We say M is compatible wrt N if $\Pi^N \not\models \alpha$ for any $\mathbf{not}\alpha \in M$. Then N is justifiable wrt Π if $\mathbf{not}\alpha \in N$ if and only if $\Pi^M \not\models \alpha$ for any M that is compatible wrt N. This leads to the following definition.

Definition 1. Let Π be a normal program. A negation set N is said to be

1. a *partial-stable set* of Π if
   (a) N is compatible wrt itself, and
   (b) $N = \{\mathbf{not}\alpha | \Pi^{\{\mathbf{not}\beta \mid \Pi^N \not\models \beta\}} \not\models \alpha\}$.
2. a *stable set* of Π if $N = \{\mathbf{not}\alpha \mid \Pi^N \not\models \alpha\}$.

From this definition we can see that a partial-stable set N is a set of all default negations that can be justified under the rule of negation as failure. Obviously, a stable set is a partial-stable set, but not vice versa. A program has at least one partial-stable set, though it may not have any stable set. Further, it is easy to show that among all partial-stable sets of Π there exists the least stable set in the sense of set inclusion. The following proposition reveals that almost all semantics of normal programs can be characterized by partial-stable sets.

Proposition 2. ([19])

1. *The well-founded semantics is characterized by the least partial-stable set.*
2. *The stable semantics is characterized by the set of all stable sets.*
3. *The regular semantics, preferential semantics, maximum partial-stable semantics, and normal stable-class semantics coincide and are characterized by the set of maximal partial-stable sets, in the sense of set inclusion.*

This proposition demonstrates that the well-founded, stable, and the regular (including all other equivalent) semantics are the standard semantics for their respective categories.

While the normal program semantics is fairly well understood, searching for suitable semantics of disjunctive programs proved to be much more difficult. The following table lists all major semantics proposed for disjunctive programs.

Skeptical	Stable	Partial-Stable
Well-founded Circumscriptive Semantics [21]	Stable Circumscriptive Semantics [21]	Partial-stable Model Semantics [14]
Static Semantics [15]	Answer Set Semantics [9]	Regular Semantics [18]
Disjunctive Well-founded Semantics [2]	Stable Extension Semantics [13]	Maximal Stable Model Semantics [5]
Skeptical Well-founded Semantics [22]		Partial-stable Assumption Semantics [17]
		Regularly-justified Set Semantics [22]

Both the static and the well-founded circumscriptive semantics were defined based on the same idea of minimal-model-based negative introspection. The specific form of this introspection was given in [21]. In fact, the first three skeptical semantics listed above are essentially the same [3]. The difference between the first three skeptical semantics and the skeptical well-founded semantics lies in the interpretation of default negation. The former adopts minimal-model-based default negation while the latter consistency-based default negation.

Example 1. Consider a simple program Π_1 below:

$$bird \leftarrow; \quad fly \vee abnormal \leftarrow bird; \quad fly \leftarrow bird, \mathbf{not}abnormal$$

Since *abnormal* is true in a minimal model of Π_1 with **not**abnormal being false while *abnormal* cannot be derived from Π_1 regardless of **not**abnormal being true or false, **not**abnormal can be justified under consistency-based default negation but not under minimal-model-based default negation.

The skeptical well-founded semantics adopts consistency-based default negation and thus concludes **not**abnormal and *fly*. On the other hand, the static as well as the well-founded circumscriptive and disjunctive well-founded semantics adopt minimal-model-based default negation and thus conclude neither **not**abnormal nor *fly*.

The answer set semantics is defined for extended logic programs that allow classical negation in both head and body while the stable circumscriptive semantics is defined for general autoepistemic theories, including the translated logic programs with default negation. Both semantics adopt minimal-model-based default negation and coincide in the context of disjunctive logic programs. On the other hand, the stable extension semantics and the stable set semantics [22] are a stable semantics that adopt consistency-based default negation.

Example 2. (Example 1 continued) The answer set semantics (as well as the stable circumscriptive semantics) of Π_1 is defined by two sets, the first one contains {*bird, fly,* **notabnormal**} and the second {*bird, abnormal,* **not** *fly*}.

The stable set semantics, on the other hand, is defined by a unique negation set {**notabnormal**} and therefore implies *bird* $\wedge$ *fly*.

All the partial-stable semantics listed above, except the regularly-justified set semantics which is consistency-based, are minimal-model-based but are different from each other. See [5] for detailed comparisons. The recently proposed partial-stable assumption semantics seems the only semantics that extends the answer set semantics in the same way as the regular semantics extends the stable semantics for normal programs [17].

Example 3. Consider the following program Π_3

$$work \vee sleep \vee tired \leftarrow$$
$$work \leftarrow \mathbf{not} tired$$
$$sleep \leftarrow \mathbf{not} work$$
$$tired \leftarrow \mathbf{not} sleep$$

Both partial-stable and maximal stable model semantics, listed in the table, of Π_3 are inconsistent while the partial-stable assumption semantics and the regularly-justified set semantics are characterized by an empty negation set $N = \emptyset$ which implies nothing but $work \vee sleep \vee tired$.

The difference between the partial-stable assumption and regularly-justified set semantics lies in the interpretation of default negation. For example, consider Π_1 in Example 1. The partial-stable assumption semantics of Π_1 coincides with the answer set semantics of Π_1 while the regularly-justified set semantics of Π_1 coincides with both the skeptical well-founded and the stable set semantics of Π_1.

3 Logic of Belief and Possible World Semantics

3.1 Language

We consider here a propositional language augmented with a modal operator **B**. An atomic formula (atom) is either a propositional symbol, or an epistemic atom $\mathbf{B}\alpha$, where α is a (well-formed) formula defined as usual. The intended meaning of $\mathbf{B}\alpha$ is "α is believed". For convenience, we also use **not**α interchangeably for $\neg\mathbf{B}\alpha$, meaning α is disbelieved. (**not**α is also viewed by many authors as a *default negation*.) An *epistemic theory* (or a theory for short) is a set of well-formed formulae, and a formula (or a theory) is *objective* if it contains no epistemic atoms, otherwise it is *subjective*. The language has the following axioms and rules of inference.

Axioms.

> PL. All propositional tautologies.
> K. $\mathbf{B}(\alpha \supset \beta) \supset (\mathbf{B}\alpha \supset \mathbf{B}\beta)$.
> D. $\neg\mathbf{B}$ (false)

Inference rules.

> *ModusPonens* (MP). $\dfrac{\alpha \supset \beta, \alpha}{\beta}$
>
> *Necessitation* (N). $\dfrac{\alpha}{\mathbf{B}\alpha}$.

K means that if a conditional and its antecedent are both believed, then so is the consequent. D says that the agent does not believe inconsistent facts. MP is a usual inference rule for propositional logic and N represents minimized positive introspection for belief. Readers may be aware that the logic given above is the common epistemic logic KDN [10].

Let A be a theory and α a formula. By $A \vdash_{KDN} \alpha$ we mean α can be derived from A based on the axioms and rules of inference given above. A is inconsistent if there exists a formula α such that $A \vdash_{KDN} \alpha$ and $A \vdash_{KDN} \neg\alpha$; otherwise, it is consistent.

To characterize logic consequences without the necessitation rule, we use $A \vdash_{KD} \alpha$ to denote the fact that α can be derived from A using the axioms and rules of inference given above, except N.

Example 4. Let $A_4 = \{a;\ b \subset \mathbf{B}a\}$. Then $A_4 \vdash_{KDN} b$ for

(1) a	contained in A_4
(2) $\mathbf{B}a$	(1) and N
(3) $b \subset \mathbf{B}a$	contained in A_4
(4) b	(2), (3), and MP

3.2 Belief Interpretation

A belief theory A is used to describe the knowledge base of a rational agent. Due to incomplete information, an agent may have to hold a set of possible states of epistemic belief, each of which represents a complete description of the agent's belief. A *belief interpretation* is thus introduced to characterize such a complete state of belief. Formally,

Definition 3. 1. A *belief interpretation* of A is a set I of belief atoms and disbelief atoms such that for any belief atom $\mathbf{B}\alpha$, either $\mathbf{B}\alpha \in I$ or $\neg\mathbf{B}\alpha \in I$ (not both).
2. A *belief model* of A is a belief interpretation I of A such that $A \cup I$ is consistent.

Obviously, a theory is consistent if and only if it has at least one belief model. Because of nested levels of belief operators of the form $\mathbf{B}(\mathbf{B}\alpha)$, a belief interpretation is always infinite. For convenience, only belief atoms that appear in A will be explicitly listed in belief interpretations, unless indicated otherwise.

Let A be a belief theory and I a belief model of A. An (objective) *perspective theory* of A, denoted by A^I, is defined as an objective theory obtained from A by replacing each belief atom in A with their corresponding truth value in I. Obviously, a belief theory may have more than one perspective theory and each of them represent the agent's perspective with respect to one restricted belief model.

Example 5. The following autoepistemic theory is obtained from Π_1 in Example 1 above

$$A_5 = \{bird; \quad fly \vee abnormal \subset bird; \quad fly \subset bird \wedge \neg \mathbf{B}abnormal\}.$$

A_5 has two belief models and two corresponding perspective theories:

$I_1 = \{\mathbf{B}abnormal\}$ and $A_{51} = \{bird; fly \vee abnormal \subset bird\}$;
$I_2 = \{\neg\mathbf{B}abnormal\}$ and $A_{52} = \{bird; fly \vee abnormal \subset bird; fly \subset bird\}$.

3.3 Possible-Worlds Semantics

Now that we have described the *syntax* of our language, we need *semantics*. That is, a formal model that we can use to determine whether a given formula is true or false. Following Hintikka [11], Halpern and Moses [10], we use a possible-worlds semantics to model disbelief. The intuitive idea behind the possible-worlds model is that besides the true state of affairs, there are a number of other possible states, or "worlds". Given currently incomplete information, an agent may not be able to tell which of a number of possible worlds describes the actual state of affairs, but the agent believes a fact α if α is true at all the worlds he considers possible.

A *state* is a set s of objective propositions such that an objective proposition p is **true** in s if and only if $p \in s$. A *Kripke structure* is a tuple $M = \langle S, B \rangle$, where S is a set of *states* and B is a binary relation on the states of S. B is intended to capture the accessibility relation for belief: $(s, t) \in B$ if at world s in structure M, the agent considers t a possible belief world.

We now formally define a binary relation $\models$ between a formula G and a pair (M, s) consisting of a structure M and a state s in M, where $(M, s) \models G$ is read as either "G is true at (M, s)" or "(M, s) satisfies G". Assume α and β are well-formed formulas and p is a proposition, then we have:

- $(M, s) \models p$ iff $p \in s$;
- $(M, s) \models \neg\alpha$ iff $(M, s) \not\models \alpha$;
- $(M, s) \models \alpha \wedge \beta$ iff both $(M, s) \models \alpha$ and $(M, s) \models \beta$;
- $(M, s) \models \alpha \vee \beta$ iff either $(M, s) \models \alpha$ or $(M, s) \models \beta$;
- $(M, s) \models \mathbf{B}\alpha$ iff $(M, s) \models \alpha$ for all t satisfying $(s, t) \in B$.

Note that since **not**α stands for "$\neg\mathbf{B}\alpha$" the last condition is the same as

- $(M, s) \models \mathbf{not}\alpha$ iff $(M, t) \models \neg\alpha$ for some t satisfying $(s, t) \in B$.

A formula α is *valid* wrt a structure $M = \langle S, B \rangle$, denoted as $M \models \alpha$ if $(M, s) \models \alpha$ for any $s \in S$.

A structure $M = \langle S, B \rangle$ is said to be a *Kripke model* of A if every formula in A is valid wrt M. Obviously, given a theory A, the only structures of interest are Kripke models of A. For convenience, we abuse the notation and use model to refer to both conventional models and Kripke models as long as no confusion arises.

Definition 4. Assume $M = \langle S, B \rangle$ is a model of A and $s \in S$. Then

1. $T(M)$ denotes the set of all formulas that are valid with respect to M, i.e.

$$T(M) = \{\alpha \mid M \models \alpha\}$$

2. $I(s)$ denotes the set of all belief and disbelief atoms that are true in s. Obviously, $I(s)$ is a belief model of A.

The following lemma reveals the relationships between M and $T(M)$.

Lemma 5. *Assume $M = \langle S, B \rangle$ is a model of A. Then I is a belief model of $T(M)$ if and only if there exists a world $s \in S$ such that $I = I(s)$.*

The proof is straightforward and thus omitted.

4 Negative Introspection and Partial-Stable Expansions

We introduce partial-stable expansions to characterize negative introspection of autoepistemic logic.

Introspection is a process of revising the agent's knowledge and belief according to his perspective of the world. For example, Moore uses the stable expansion T of autoepistemic theory A [13]

$$T = \{\phi \mid A \cup \{\mathbf{B}\alpha \mid \alpha \in T\} \cup \{\neg\mathbf{B}\alpha \mid \alpha \notin T\} \models_S \phi\} \qquad (4.1)$$

The terms $A \cup \{\mathbf{B}\alpha \mid \alpha \in T\}$ and $A \cup \{\neg\mathbf{B}\alpha \mid \alpha \notin T\}$ express the positive and negative introspection of an agent respectively.

The stable expansion characterizes perfect introspection[2] nicely. Unfortunately, the world we are going to model is not perfect and therefore, a different approach to introspective reasoning is needed [20].

It is generally agreed that positive introspection is a process of concluding belief $\mathbf{B}\alpha$ if α can be derived while negative introspection is a process of concluding disbelief $\neg\mathbf{B}\alpha$ (or $\mathbf{B}\neg\alpha$) if α cannot be derived. Positive introspection is usually achieved by introducing the necessitation rule N: derive $\mathbf{B}\alpha$ if α has been proved.

The interpretation of non-derivability for negative introspection, however, varies quite diversely. Two typical approaches are:

---

[2] By perfect introspection, we mean the agent has complete knowledge and belief about the world and therefore, is capable of concluding either $\mathbf{B}\alpha$ or $\neg\mathbf{B}\alpha$ for every formula α.

1. consistency-based introspection: deriving $\neg\mathbf{B}\alpha$ if $\neg\alpha$ is consistent with A, (or equivalently, $A \not\vdash_{KD} \alpha$); and
2. minimal-model-based p-introspection:
   deriving $\neg\mathbf{B}\alpha$ if $\neg\alpha$ is true in every minimal model of every perspective theory of A.

The closed world assumption, default logic, and Moore's autoepistemic logic use consistency-based negative introspection. This approach usually results in stronger negative introspection in that more disbeliefs may be concluded, and as such, many reasonable theories do not possess consistent introspective expansions. Minimal-model-based introspection, on the other hand, suffers from the inherent difficulties associated with minimal-model entailment [5].

In [23], we have argued that introspection should be consistency-based and be with respect to each and every possible belief world:

Deriving $\neg\mathbf{B}\alpha$ if $\neg\alpha$ is consistent with $A \cup I$ for every belief model I of A.

The partial-stable expansion is thus defined based on consistency-based negative introspection.

Definition 6. Let A be a theory and α a formula. Then we say $A \sim\!| \alpha$ if $A \cup I \not\vdash_{KD} \alpha$ for every belief model I of A.

Consistency-based negative introspection derives $\neg\mathbf{B}\alpha$ from A if and only if $A \sim\!| \alpha$, which leads to the following definition.

Definition 7. A belief theory T is said to be a *partial-stable expansion* of A if it satisfies the following fixpoint equation

$$T = \{\phi \mid A \cup \{\neg\mathbf{B}\alpha \mid T \sim\!| \alpha\} \vdash_{KDN} \phi\}.$$

The partial-stable expansion characterizes the introspective reasoning process by expanding a given theory A using negative introspection, which can be used to define almost all major nonmonotonic reasoning semantics [23].

5 Partial-Stable Models

In this section we characterize partial-stable expansions in terms of Kripke structures.

The Kripke structure, though a powerful tool for modeling knowledge and belief, is difficult to use in characterizing negative introspective reasoning processes.

Example 6. Consider $A_6 = \{a \subset \mathbf{B}a\}$ and a model $M = \langle\{s\}, B\rangle$ of A_6, where $s = \{a\}$ and $B = \{(s, s)\}$. Even though both $\mathbf{B}a$ and a are valid with respect to M, there is no basis for a rational agent to justify $\mathbf{B}a$ and consequently conclude a.

Assume $M = \langle S, B \rangle$ is a model of A, and $s \in S$. Then $I(s)$ represents a complete description of the agent's belief state in a possible world s. As a rational agent, any belief has to be justified and, in general, a belief $\mathbf{B}\alpha$ can be justified with respect to world s if α can be derived from $A \cup I(s)$.

The question is "Which logic should be used to justify belief?" Since the necessitation rule N is used for positive introspection with respect to all possible worlds which shall not be used for justification of beliefs at a particular world, a logic of KD without N will be used here.

A formula α is said to be justifiable with respect to A at s if $A \cup I(s) \vdash_{KD} \alpha$. Furthermore, the set of all justified formulas with respect to A at s, denoted as $J(A, s)$ or simply $J(s)$ if A is understood, is defined as

$$J(s) = \{\mathbf{B}\alpha \mid A \cup I(s) \vdash_{KD} \alpha\} \qquad (5.2)$$

An agent, being in world s, considers t as a possible belief world if and only if every belief held at s is justifiable at t, that is, if and only if, $B(t) \subseteq J(s)$, where $B(t) = \{\mathbf{B}\alpha \mid (M, t) \models \mathbf{B}\alpha\}$.

The idea is perhaps best illustrated by a simple example below.

Example 7. Assume $A_7 = \{a \subset \neg \mathbf{B}b\}$. There are four possible worlds for A_7, namely,

$$s_1 = \emptyset,\ s_2 = \{a\},\ s_3 = \{b\},\ s_4 = \{a, b\}.$$

Consider the following two models of A_7.

M_1: M_2:

(Note that circles denote possible states and directed edges the belief relation.)

It is generally agreed that $\neg \mathbf{B}b$ shall be assumed simply because b cannot be derived from A_7 in any circumstance. However, both b and $\mathbf{B}b$ are true with respect to M_2. Carefully examining M_2 reveals that $\mathbf{B}b$ cannot be justified at either s_3 or s_4, that is, $A_7 \cup I(s_i) \nvdash_{KDN} b$ for $i = 3, 4$, even though the agent believes b at both worlds. In this case, we say that the agent, being at s_3, considers s_4 a possible world without an appropriate justification.

On the other hand, in M_1, $B(s_2) = J(s_4) = B(s_4) = J(s_2)$. That is, the agent, being at s_2, considers s_4 a possible world because a belief is held at s_4 if and only if it is justified at s_2; and considers s_2 a possible world of s_4 for the same reason.

Therefore, we consider M_1 is a justified Kripke model of A_7 but M_2 is not, despite the fact that both M_1 and M_2 are models of A_7.

We argue that only those Kripke structures whose beliefs can be justified characterize the essential aspect of negative introspection. This leads to the following definition.

Definition 8. A model $M = \langle S, B \rangle$ of A is said to be a *justified Kripke model* (or *justified model* for short) of A if

$$(s, t) \in B \quad \text{if only if} \quad B(s) \subseteq J(t).$$

It is easy to see that, in Example 7, M_1 is a justified model of A but M_2 is not.

A justified Kripke model is defined to characterize negative introspection in terms of Kripke structures, as demonstrated in the following proposition.

Proposition 9. *Let $M = \langle S, B \rangle$ be a justified model of A and $T(M) = \{\alpha \mid M \models \alpha\}$. Then for any formula α,*

$$T \sim\!\!\mid \alpha \quad \text{if and only if} \quad M \models \neg \mathbf{B}\alpha.$$

The proof follows Lemma 5.

Proper characterization of negative introspection does not necessarily guarantee proper introspection simply because default reasoning involves both positive and negative introspection.

Example 8. Consider Example 6 again. M is a justified model of A because $\mathbf{B}a$ is justified in s for a can be derived from $A_6 \cup I(s) \equiv \{a \subset \mathbf{B}a, \mathbf{B}a\}$.

The justification, however, is due to the assumption that $\mathbf{B}a$ is true in $I(s)$.

A Kripke model that characterizes both positive and negative introspection has to be supported in that all conclusions must be based on A and all disbeliefs obtained through negative introspection.

Definition 10. Let $M = \langle S, B \rangle$ be a model of A and $N(M) = \{\neg \mathbf{B}\alpha \mid M \models \neg \mathbf{B}\alpha\}$. Then M is supported with respect to A if for any formula α

$$M \models \alpha \quad \text{if and only if} \quad A \cup N(M) \vdash_{KDN} \alpha.$$

Obviously, M in Example 6 is not supported w.r.t. A.

Now we are in a position to define a *partial-stable model*.

Definition 11. A model $M = \langle S, B \rangle$ of A is said to be a partial-stable Kripke model of A, or *partial-stable model* for short, if M is both justified and supported with respect to A.

The following proposition characterizes the relationships between the partial-stable expansion and the partial-stable model.

Proposition 12. *Let A be an autoepistemic theory. Then T is a consistent partial-stable expansion of A if and only if there exists a partial-stable model $M = \langle S, B \rangle$ of A such that*

$$T = \{\alpha \mid M \models \alpha\}$$

Sketched Proof: *Assume T is a consistent partial-extension of A. Then we can construct a model M of T such that M is justified with respect to A. By Proposition 9, $\text{not}\alpha \in T$ if and only if $M \models \text{not}\alpha$. It follows that M is a partial-stable model of A.*

Assume M is a partial-stable model of A. Then Proposition 9 implies that $T = \{\alpha \mid M \models \alpha\}$ is a partial-stable extension of A.

5.1 Semantical Analysis

Now we classify some interesting structures in terms of three semantical points of view and/or accessibility relation B, and later show that almost all prominent semantics for disjunctive logic programs can be characterized by such structures.

Definition 13. A partial-stable model $M = \langle S, B \rangle$ of A is said to be

1. a *stable (Kripke) model* of A if B is complete;
2. the *skeptical (Kripke) model* of A if for any partial-stable model $M' = \langle S', B' \rangle$ of A, $S' \subseteq S$.
3. a *regular (Kripke) model* of T if there exists no other partial-stable model $M' = \langle S', B' \rangle$ of A such that $S' \subset S$.

Note that (a) A does not necessarily have a partial-stable model even if it has a justified Kripke model, and (b) the well-founded Kripke model of A, if it exists, is always unique.

The following example demonstrates that not every consistent theory has a partial-stable model.

Example 9. Consider $A_9 = \{a \subset \mathbf{not}a; \neg a \subset \mathbf{not}a\}$. Assume $M = \langle S, B \rangle$ is a justified model. Then $M \models \mathbf{B}a$ because $A_9 \vdash_{KD} \mathbf{B}a$. However, a cannot be justified at any world $s \in S$ if $\mathbf{B}a$ is true in every world in S. It follows that A_9 has no justified Kripke model and thus no partial-stable model.

The following proposition reveals the condition for the existence of the skeptical Kripke model of A.

Proposition 14. *A has the (unique) skeptical Kripke model if it has at least one partial-stable model.*

Before further discussions, we present some demonstrating examples.

Example 10. Consider a simple theory $A_{10} = \{a \subset \mathbf{not}b\}$, with four possible worlds: $s_1 = \emptyset$, $s_2 = \{a\}$, $s_3 = \{b\}$, and $s_4 = \{a, b\}$

First, assume $s_1 \in S$ and t is a possible world in S such that $(s_1, t) \in B$. Since $(M, s_1) \not\models a$, $(M, s_1) \models a \subset \mathbf{not}b$, and s_1 is consistent, we have $(M, s_1) \models \neg \mathbf{not}b$. Further, since there exists no set N of disbeliefs such that $A_{10} \cup N \vdash_{KDN} b$, there exists no $u \in S$ such that $(u, s_1) \in B$. This implies that there exists no $u \in S$ such that $(u, s_1) \in B$.

Because $a \vee b$ is true in every world other than s_1, and there is no $u \in S$ such that $(u, s_1) \in B$, $\neg \mathbf{not}(a \vee b)$ must be true in every world in S, including t. This, however, contradicts the fact that $(s_1, t) \in B$ since $(A_{10} \cup \{\mathbf{not}a \mid (M, s_1) \models \mathbf{not}a\}) \not\models a \vee b$.

Therefore, $s_1 \notin S$. Similarly, $s_3 \notin S$.

If S contains only one world, say s_2, then $\neg b$ is believed in s_2 which contradicts the fact that $\neg b$ cannot be derived from A_{10} under any set of disbeliefs.

It follows that S must be $\{s_2, s_4\}$. Furthermore, it is easy to show that B must be a complete relation, that is, M_1 below is the only partial-stable model of A_{10}.

M_1:

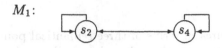

Example 11. Consider $A_{11} = \{a \subset \mathbf{not}b;\ b \subset \mathbf{not}a\}$. Let $s_1 = \emptyset$, $s_2 = \{a\}$, $s_3 = \{b\}$, and $s_4 = \{a, b\}$ be the set of all possible worlds. Then the following three Kripke structures are partial-stable models of A_{11}

M_1:

M_2:

M_3:

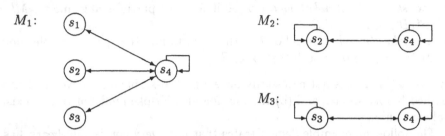

Among the three, M_2 and M_3 are stable models and M_1 is the skeptical model.

Example 12. Consider a theory corresponding to a disjunctive logic program $A_{12} = \{a \vee b;\ a \subset \mathbf{not}a\}$. Then M below is a partial-stable Kripke model of A_{12}.

Note $s_1 = \{a\}$, $s_2 = \{b\}$ and $s_3 = \{a, b\}$.

It is not difficult to see that $a \vee b$ is the only objective formula, other than tautologies, that is valid with respect to M. Since both s_1 and s_3 share the same set of possible belief worlds, they hold the same disbeliefs. For example, $(M, s_1) \models \mathbf{not}a$, $(M, s_3) \models \mathbf{not}a$, and $(M, s_2) \models \neg\mathbf{not}a$.

M:

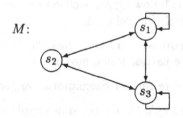

M is also the skeptical model and a regular model of A_{12}, but not a stable model.

6 Disjunctive Logic Programs Semantics

In this section, we will define various semantics of logic programs based on different autoepistemic translations and partial-stable models.

6.1 Autoepistemic Translations

Definition 15. Let Π be a logic program. Then $AE(\Pi)$ is defined as an autoepistemic theory obtained from Π by translating each clause in Π into a formula of the form [7]

$$A_1 \vee \cdots \vee A_q \subset B_1 \wedge \cdots \wedge B_m \wedge \neg\mathbf{B}C_1 \wedge \cdots \wedge \neg\mathbf{B}C_n$$

Example 13. Consider

$$\Pi_1 = \{bird \leftarrow; fly \lor abnormal \leftarrow bird; fly \leftarrow bird, \mathbf{not}\,abnormal\}$$

again. Then $AE(\Pi) = \{bird; fly \lor abnormal \subset bird; fly \subset bird \land \neg \mathbf{B}abnormal\}$.

Similar to negative introspection, default negations in disjunctive programs can also be interpreted in two different ways: consistency-based and minimal-model based. The former assumes $\mathbf{not}\alpha$ if $\neg\alpha$ is consistent with the current program while the latter assumes $\mathbf{not}\alpha$ if $\neg\alpha$ is true in every minimal model of the current program.

Example 14. (Example 13 continued) By consistency-based default negation, $\mathbf{not}abnormal$ can be justified since $abnormal$ cannot be derived from Π_1 no matter whether $\mathbf{not}abnormal$ is true or false. On the other hand, by minimal-model based default negation, $\mathbf{not}abnormal$ cannot be justified since $abnormal$ is true in one of the minimal models of Π_1 when $\mathbf{not}abnormal$ is not assumed.

Consistency-based default negation can be easily characterized by the translation given in Definition 15 since negative introspection of autoepistemic logic is consistency-based. The following translation is introduced to capture minimal-model based default negation.

Definition 16. Let Π be a logic program, and $AE(\Pi)$ be the autoepistemic theory of Π. Then, the M-autoepistemic theory of Π, denoted as $MAE(\Pi)$ is defined as

$$AE(\Pi) \cup \{\neg\alpha \subset \neg\mathbf{B}\alpha \mid \alpha \text{ is an atom in } \Pi\}$$

$MAE(\Pi)$ is also viewed as $AE(\Pi)$ augmented with an axiom $\neg\alpha \subset \neg\mathbf{B}\alpha$.

Example 15. Consider Π_1 in Example 13 again. Then $MAE(\Pi_1)$ contains the following formulas:

$$bird;$$
$$fly \lor abnormal \subset bird;$$
$$fly \subset bird \land \neg\mathbf{B}abnormal;$$
$$\neg bird \subset \neg\mathbf{B}bird;$$
$$\neg fly \subset \neg\mathbf{B}fly;$$
$$\neg abnormal \subset \neg\mathbf{B}abnormal\}.$$

Now, we are in a position to define declarative semantics of disjunctive programs in terms of translated autoepistemic theories of Π. Because each program has two different translated autoepistemic theories, corresponding to consistency-based and minimal-model based default negations, and each autoepistemic theory may have three different types of partial-stable models, corresponding to the skeptical, stable, and partial-stable semantical points of view, six different semantics are given below.

Definition 17. Let Π be a disjunctive program, $AE(\Pi)$ and $MAE(\Pi)$ the corresponding autoepistemic theories of Π. Then we define

1. the C-ground (standing for consistency-based skeptical), C-stable (standing for Consistency-based stable), and C-regular (standing for Consistency-based regular) semantics of Π by the skeptical model, the set of all stable models, and the set of all regular models, of $AE(\Pi)$ respectively; and

2. the ground, stable, and partial-stable semantics of Π by the skeptical model, the set of all stable models, and the set of all regular models, of $MAE(\Pi)$ respectively.

By saying that a semantics is characterized by a partial-stable model $M = \langle S, B \rangle$, we mean that (1) an objective formula α is true in the semantics if and only if $M \models \alpha$, and (2) a default negation $\mathbf{not}\alpha$ is true in the semantics if and only if $M \models \neg\mathbf{B}\alpha$.

The following table summarizes all six different semantics.

	Skeptical	Stable	Partial-Stable
Consistency based	*C-Ground Semantics:* the skeptical Kripke model of $AE(\Pi)$	*C-Stable Semantics:* all the stable Kripke models of $AE(\Pi)$	*C-Regular Semantics:* all the regular Kripke models of $AE(\Pi)$
Minimal-model based	*Ground Semantics:* the skeptical Kripke model of $MAE(\Pi)$	*Stable Semantics:* all the stable Kripke models of MAE(Π)	*Partial-stable Semantics:* all the regular Kripke models of $MAE(\Pi)$

It is straightforward to show that for normal programs, consistency-based and minimal-model based semantics coincide, simply because an atom is true in the set of all minimal models of a Horn program if and only if it is a logical consequence of the program.

Example 16. Consider Π_1 in Example 13 again.

First, consider consistency-based default negation. Since *abnormal* cannot be derived from $AE(\Pi_1)$ in any circumstance, $AE(\Pi_1)$ has a unique partial-stable model that implies $\neg\mathbf{B}abnormal$. Thus, all three semantics, including the C-ground, C-stable, and C-regular, coincide and imply *fly*.

Now consider minimal-model based default negation. The skeptical semantics does not imply $\neg\mathbf{B}abnormal$ since $I = \{\mathbf{B}bird, \neg\mathbf{B}fly, \mathbf{B}abnormal\}$ is a belief model of $MAE(\Pi_1)$ and $MAE(\Pi_1) \cup I \vdash_{KD} abnormal$. So the ground semantics does not imply *fly* either. In fact, it coincides with the static semantics.

The stable semantics, which coincide with the partial-stable semantics, of Π_1 is defined by two stable models, one implies $\{\mathbf{B}bird, \neg\mathbf{B}abnormal, \mathbf{B}fly\}$ and the other implies $\{\mathbf{B}bird, \mathbf{B}abnormal, \neg\mathbf{B}fly\}$.

7 Further Analysis

In this section, we will analyze relationships between various semantics.

First for normal programs, it is easy to show that both minimal-model-based and consistency-based semantics coincide.

Proposition 18. *Assume Π is a normal program. Then*

1. *The well-founded, C-ground, and ground semantics of Π coincide.*
2. *The stable and C-stable semantics coincide.*
3. *The regular, C-regular, and partial-stable semantics coincide.*

Both the answer set semantics and stable circumscriptive semantics are minimal-model-based and coincide with the stable semantics; and both the stable extension semantics and the stable set semantics are consistency-based and coincide with the C-stable semantics, as shown below. Again, the proof is straightforward and thus omitted.

Proposition 19. *1. Both the answer set and stable circumscriptive semantics coincide with the stable semantics.*
2. Both the stable extension semantics and the stable set semantics coincide with the C-stable semantics.

Among all the minimal-model-based semantics in the partial-stable category, the recently proposed partial-stable assumption semantics [17] coincides with the partial-stable semantics. Further, the C-partial-stable semantics coincides with the stable set semantics.

Proposition 20. *1. The partial-stable semantics coincides with the partial-stable assumption semantics.*
2. The C-partial-stable semantics coincides with the regularly-justified set semantics.

Proof. (1) The following two facts follow.

First, the partial-stable assumption semantics utilizes an additional meta rule of inference $\frac{\alpha \vee \beta, \mathbf{not}\beta}{\beta}$ while the partial-stable semantics utilizes a minimal-model axiom $\neg \alpha \subset \neg \mathbf{B}\alpha$, which are essentially the same.

Second, the partial-stable assumption semantics is defined using the alternating fixpoint theory while the partial-stable semantics is defined using negative introspection with respect to all belief models. However, it is easy to show that, in the context of logic programming, the two are the same.

(2) It follows that the justification of default negation under the alternating fixpoint theory coincide with negative introspection with respect to all belief models. Note that the regularly-justified set semantics justifies a regular set using the alternating fixpoint theory.

Both the static and ground semantics are defined using minimal-model based introspection and thus are very much the same. The subtle difference between the two is due to the fact that the autoepistemic theory $MAE(\Pi)$ uses $\neg\mathbf{B}\alpha$ to represent $\mathbf{not}\alpha$ while the static semantics uses $\mathbf{B}\neg\alpha$ to represent $\mathbf{not}\alpha$.

An autoepistemic theory may not have any partial-stable models, as shown in Example 9. The following proposition, however, guarantees the existence of partial-stable models for disjunctive logic programs.

Proposition 21. *Let Π be a disjunctive program, and $AE(\Pi)$ and $MAE(\Pi)$ are autoepistemic translations of Π. Then both $AE(\Pi)$ and $MAE(\Pi)$ have partial-stable models.*

8 Conclusions

We have observed that default reasoning can be characterized by negative introspection of autoepistemic logic and that, in order to characterize negative introspection, all beliefs held in a Kripke structure must be justified. Consequently we define the *partial-stable model* of an autoepistemic theory as a Kripke structure whose beliefs are justified with respect to the theory.

We then classify various semantics of disjunctive programs with default negation in terms of different partial-stable models, and discuss the relationships among these semantics.

Our results present a model theoretical foundation for logic programming with default negation.

Acknowledgment

The authors are grateful to Maurice Pagnucco for a thorough reading and suggestions on an earlier draft.

References

1. C. R. Baral and V. S. Subrahmanian. Stable and extension class theory for logic programs and default logics. *Journal of Automated Reasoning*, 8:345–366, 1992.
2. S. Brass and J. Dix. A disjunctive semantics based on unfolding and bottom-up evaluation. In Bernd Wofiner, editor, *IFIP'94-Congress, Workshop FG2: Disjunctive Logic Programming and Disjunctive Databases)*, pages 83–91, 1994.
3. S. Brass, J. Dix, I. Niemela, and T. Przymusinski. A comparison of the static and the disjunctive well-founded semantics and its implementation. In *Proc. of Knowledge Representation*, 1998.
4. P. M. Dung. Negations as hypotheses: An abductive foundation for logic programming. In *Proceedings of the 8th ICLP*, pages 3–17, 1991.
5. T. Eiter, N. Leone, and D. Sacc. The expressive power of partial models in disjunctive deductive databases. In *Logic in Databases*, pages 245–264, 1996.
6. A. Van Gelder, K. Ross, and J. Schlipf. The well-founded semantics for general logic programs. *JACM*, 38:620–650, 1991.
7. M. Gelfond. On stratified autoepistemic theories. In *Proceedings of AAAI-87*, pages 207–211. Morgan Kaufmann Publishers, 1987.
8. M. Gelfond and V. Lifschitz. The stable model semantics for logic programming. In *Proc. of the 5th ICLP*, pages 1070–1080, 1988.
9. M. Gelfond and V. Lifschitz. Classical negation in logic programs and disjunctive databases. *New Generation Computing*, 9:365–386, 1991.
10. J.Y. Halpern and Y.Moses. A guide to completeness and complexity for modal logics of knowledge and belief. *Artificial Intelligence*, 54:319–379, 1992.
11. Jaakko Hintikka. *Knowledge and Belief: An introduction to the logic of the two notions*. Cornell University Press, 1962.
12. H. J. Levesque. All I know: A study in autoepistemic logic. *AI*, 42:263–309, 1990.
13. R. C. Moore. Semantic considerations on non-monotonic logic. *AI*, 25:75–94, 1985.

14. T. C. Przymusinski. Stable semantics for disjunctive programs. *New Generation Computing*, 9:401–424, 1991.
15. T. C. Przymusinski. Static semantics for normal and disjunctive logic programs. *Annals of Mathematics and Artificial Intelligence*, 14:323–357, 1995.
16. D. Saccà and C. Zaniolo. Stable models and non-determinism in logic programs with negation. In *Proceedings of the 9th ACM PODS*, pages 205–217, 1990.
17. J.-H. You, X. Wang, and L.-Y. Yuan. Disjunctive logic programming as constrained inferences. In *Proc. of ICLP*, 1997.
18. J.-H. You and L.-Y. Yuan. A three-valued semantics of deductive databases and logic programs. *Journal of Computer and System Sciences*, 49:334–361, 1994.
19. J.-H. You and L.-Y. Yuan. On the equivalence of semantics for normal logic programs. *Journal of Logic Programming*, 22(3):209–219, 1995.
20. L.-Y. Yuan. Autoepistemic logic of first order and its expressive power. *Journal of Automated Reasoning*, 13(1):69–82, 1994.
21. L.-Y. Yuan and J.-H. You. Autoepistemic circumscription and logic programming. *Journal of Automated Reasoning*, 10:143–160, 1993.
22. L.-Y. Yuan and J.-H. You. On the extension of logic programming with negation though uniform proofs. In *Proc. of LPNMR'95, LNAI Vol. 928*, 1995.
23. L.-Y. Yuan and J.-H. You. An introspective logic of belief. In *Proc. of the Workshop on LP&KR, ILPS'97*, pages 157–170, 1997.

A Non-monotonic ATMS
Based on Annotated Logic Programs
with Strong Negation

Kazumi NAKAMATSU and Atsuyuki SUZUKI

School of H.E.P.T.
Himeji Institute of Technology
Shinzaike 1-1-12,
HIMEJI 670-0092 JAPAN

nakamatu@koin.or.jp

Faculty of Information
Shizuoka University
Johoku 3-5-1,
HAMAMATSU 432-8011 JAPAN

suzuki@cs.inf.shizuoka.ac.jp

Abstract

In this paper, we translate Dressler's nonmonotonic ATMS with out-assumptions [**Dr88**] into an annotated logic program with strong negation (ALPSN) which was proposed in [**NS94**]. Nonmonotonic justifications and assumption nodes of Dressler's ATMS are translated into annotated logic program clauses with strong negation. The most important semantics for Dressler's ATMS is the extension. On the other hand, the corresponding ALPSN has the stable model semantics. We show that there is a one-to-one correspondence between the nonmonotonic ATMS extensions and the corresponding ALPSN stable models with respect to the translation. Dressler's ATMS includes two meta-rules of inference, the Consistent Belief Rule and the Nogood Inference Rule, and an axiom, the Negation Axiom. We also show that these inference rules and the axiom can be reduced into the ALPSN stable model computation. We take an example of the nonmonotonic ATMS based on ALPSNs (the ALPSN stable model computing system) and show how the ATMS works. Lastly, we indicate the advantages and the problems to be solved of the nonmonotonic ATMS based on ALPSNs, and mention future work.

Keywords: annotated logic program, extension, nonmonotonic ATMS, stable model

1. Introduction

Annotated logic, which is paraconsistent and multi-valued, was proposed initially by da Costa and Subrahmanian[**dSV89**]. Subsequently, it was studied, from the viewpoint of logic programming, by Blair and Subrahmanian[BlS89]. Although there are two kinds of negations, the epistemic one and the ontological (strong) one, in annotated logic, an annotated logic program (ALP) in [BlS89] can deal with only the epistemic negation. We have proposed an annotated logic program with strong negation (ALPSN) which includes both negations and its stable model semantics. The ALPSN has been used to describe the declarative semantics for default theories [NS94]. Moreover, annotated logics have been applied towards the development of the declarative semantics for inheritance networks and object-oriented databases [TK93]. Generally, annotated logic seems more appropriate for describing contradictions such as nogoods in an ATMS and nonmonotonic formalisms than other logics. In this paper, we propose a nonmonotonic ATMS based on ALPSNs. This nonmonotonic ATMS is an ALPSN which is translated from Dressler's ATMS[Dr88]. There is a relationship shown in **Fig. 1** between his ATMS and the ALPSN.

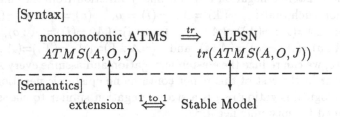

Fig.1. Nonmonotonic ATMS and ALPSN

Based on the relationship shown in **Fig.1**, the implementation of the nonmonotonic ATMS can be reduced to computing the stable models of the ALPSN. His ATMS includes a special predicate called an out-assumption to express nonmonotonic justifications and it can also deal with the negation of a node. The negation can be easily translated into an annotated program clause, although it is difficult to translate into a Horn clause.

This paper is organized as follows. First, we review an ALPSN and its stable model semantics. Additionally, we propose a translation from Dressler's nonmonotonic ATMS into an ALPSN and prove that there exists a one to one correspondence between the extensions of his ATMS and the stable models of the corresponding ALPSN. Last, we show an example of implementing the nonmonotonic ATMS, i.e., computing the stable models of the corresponding ALPSN.

2. ALPSN

In this section, we recapitulate the syntax and the semantics for an ALPSN [NS94] and define a stable model of an ALPSN. Generally, the set T of truth values of annotated logic has an arbitrary but fixed, complete lattice structure. In this paper, however, we consider the complete lattice given in **Fig.2** as the set T of truth values of an ALPSN. The ordering of this lattice is denoted by $\leq$ as usual.

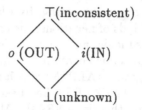

Fig.2 . The Lattice T of Truth Values

[Definition 2.1] [BlS89]

If A is a literal, then $(A : \mu)$ is called an *annotated literal*, where $\mu \in T$. μ is called an *annotation* of A. If μ is one of $\{i, o\}$, then $(A : \mu)$ is called a *well-annotated literal*.

An ALPSN has two kinds of negations, an *epistemic* one and an *ontological* one. The epistemic negation ($\neg$) is a unary function from an annotation to an annotation such that : $\quad \neg(\bot) = \bot, \quad \neg(i) = o, \quad \neg(o) = i$ and $\neg(\top) = \top$. So, $(\neg A : \bot) = (A : \neg(\bot)) = (A : \bot), \quad (\neg A : i) = (A : \neg(i)) = (A : o),$ $(\neg A : o) = (A : \neg(o)) = (A : i)$ and $(\neg A : \top) = (A : \neg(\top)) = (A : \top)$. Therefore, we can reduce the epistemic negation and assume every ALPSN which will appear in the rest of this paper contains no epistemic negation $\neg$. The ontological negation ($\sim$) is a strong negation similar to classsical negation and defined by epistemic negation.

[Definition 2.2] (Strong Negation) **[dSV89]**

Let A be any formula.
$$\sim A \equiv (A \to ((A \to A) \land \neg(A \to A))).$$

The epistemic negation ($\neg$) in front of $(A \to A)$ is interpreted as not a mapping between annotations but negation in classical logic. Thus, we can regard that the negation ($\sim$) is a strong one. The satisfaction of the strong negation will be defined in **[Definition 2.4]**.

[Definition 2.3] [BlS89][NS94]

Let $L_0, \cdots, L_n$ be well-annotated literals over T.
$$L_1 \land \cdots \land L_n \to L_0 \qquad \text{(a)}$$
is called a *generalized Horn clause* (gh-clause). If $L_0, \cdots, L_n$ are any annotated literals over T, then (a) is called an *annotated clause* (a-clause) over T, and
$$L_1 \land \cdots \land L_i \land \sim L_{i+1} \land \cdots \land \sim L_n \to L_0$$
is called an *annotated clause with strong negation* (asn-clause) over T. A *generalized Horn program* (GHP), an ALP and an ALPSN are finite sets of gh-clauses, a-clauses and asn-clauses, respectively.

We now address the semantics for an ALPSN and assume that all interpretations have a Herbrand base B_P as their domain. Since T is a complete lattice, the Herbrand interpretation I of an ALPSN P over T may be considered to be

a mapping $I : B_P \rightarrow \mathcal{T}$. Usually the interpretation I is denoted by the set :
$$\{(p : \sqcup \mu_i) \mid I \models (p : \mu_1) \wedge \cdots \wedge (p : \mu_n)\},$$
where $\sqcup \mu_i$ is the least upper bound of $\{\mu_1, \cdots, \mu_n\}$.

In the rest of this paper, we assume that an ALPSN P is a set of ground asn-clauses. The ordering $\leq$ on $\mathcal{T}$ is extended to interpretations in a natural way and the notion of satisfaction is defined as follows.

[Definition 2.4] [BlS89]

Let I_1 and I_2 be any interpretations and A be an annotated atom.
$$I_1 \leq I_2 \overset{\triangle}{=} (\forall A \in B_P) \, (I_1(A) \leq I_2(A)), \;\; I_1(A), I_2(A) \in \mathcal{T}.$$
An interpretation I is said to satisfy
[1] a ground annotated atom $(A : \mu)$ iff $I(A) \leq \mu$,
[2] a formula F iff it satisfies every closed instance of F,
[3] a formula $\sim F$ iff I does not satisfy F.
The satisfaction of the other formulas are the same as classical logic.

Associated with every ALPSN P over $\mathcal{T}$, a function T_P from a Herbrand interpretation to itself and an upward iteration of T_P are defined.

[Definition 2.5]

For any ground instance $B_1 \wedge \cdots \wedge B_m \wedge \sim C_1 \wedge \cdots \wedge \sim C_n \rightarrow A : \mu$ of an asn-clause in P, $T_P(I)(A) = \sqcup \{\mu \mid I \models B_1 \wedge \cdots \wedge B_m \wedge \sim C_1 \wedge \cdots \wedge \sim C_n\}$,
where the notation $\sqcup$ is used to denote the least upper bound.
Let $\triangle$ be a special interpretation which assigns the truth value $\bot$ to all members of a Herbrand base B_P. Then, an upward iteration of T_P is defined as
$$T_P \uparrow 0 = \triangle,$$
$$T_P \uparrow \lambda = \cup_{\alpha < \lambda} T_P(T_P \uparrow \alpha), \text{ for any ordinals } \alpha, \lambda \text{ [BlS89,Ll87]}.$$

We state some well-known results about an ALP and the operator T_P. The proofs of the following propositions are found in **[BlS89]**.

[Proposition 2.6]

If P is an ALP over $\mathcal{T}$, then
[1] T_P is a monotonic function,
[2] P has a unique least model which is identical to the least fixed point of T_P,
[3] $T_P \uparrow \omega$ is identical to the least fixed point of T_P.

We describe the stable model **[GL88]** of an ALPSN P. Let I be any interpretation. P^I, the *Gelfond-Lifschitz transformation* of an ALPSN P with respect to I, is an ALP obtained from P by deleting
[1] each clause which has a literal $\sim (C : \mu)$ in its body with $I \models (C : \mu)$, and
[2] all strongly negated literals in the bodies of the remaining clauses.
Since P^I is an ALP with no negation (both $\sim$ and $\neg$), it has the unique least model which is given by $T_{P^I} \uparrow \omega$ **[BlS88,BlS89,GL88]**.

[Definition 2.7] (Stable Model) **[GL88,NS94]**
If I is a Herbrand interpretation of an ALPSN P,

I is called a *stable model* of P *iff* $I = T_{PI} \uparrow \omega$.

An ALPSN may not always have a stable model and there is an ALPSN which has more than two stable models.

3. Nonmonotonic ATMS

In this section, we give the formalism underlying Dressler's nonmonotonic ATMS. The details of the nonmonotonic ATMS are found in **[Dr88]**.

[Definition 3.1]
The data reasoned about is called a *node*. A set of nodes is designated to be *assumptions* (which are presumed to be true unless there is evidence to the contrary). A set of assumptions is called an *environment*. An environment is *inconsistent* if it derives the distinguished node named $False$. An inconsistent environment is called a *nogood*. The set of nodes derivable from a consistent environment is called a *context*. Every derivation is recorded as a (nonmonotonic) *justification* : $a_1, \cdots, a_k, Out(b_1), \cdots, Out(b_m) \to c$,
where each $Out(b_i)$ $(1 \le i \le m)$ is called an *out-assumption*.

As with a normal assumption, an out-assumption $Out(x)$ cannot be used as the cosequent of a justification, but it can be a member of an environment. The aim of introducing an out-assumption $Out(x)$ is to do all computations with respect to the set of contexts in which a node x cannot be derived, i.e., an out-assumption $Out(x)$ can be added to an environment when a node x is not derivable. To achieve this aim, the following two aspects have to be ensured :
    [1] x and $Out(x)$ do not hold in the same context,
    [2] for each context, either x holds or $Out(x)$ holds.
These aspects are achieved by adding the following meta-rules to the ATMS.

[Consistent Belief Rule]
From x and $Out(x)$, $False$ is inferred.
This rule can be encoded into the nonmonotonic ATMS by a justification of the form : $x, Out(x) \to False$.

[Nogood Inference Rule]
If an environment $\{A_1, \cdots, A_n\}$ is consistent and $\{A_1, \cdots, A_n, Out(x)\}$ is inconsistent, then $\{A_1, \cdots, A_n\} \vdash x$.

We describe an example of a derivation by the two meta-rules.

[Example 3.2]

A nonmonotonic justification $Out(p) \rightarrow p$ leads to a nogood $\{Out(p)\}$, because of p, $Out(p) \rightarrow False$. Then, it is derived by the Nogood Inference Rule that p is universally true.

[Definition 3.3] (Nonmonotonic ATMS)

A nonmonotonic ATMS is a triple $ATMS(A, O, J)$ such that :
  [1] A is a set of assumptions,
  [2] O is a set of out-assumptions $(O \subseteq A)$,
  [3] J is a set of justifications.

Generally, a conventional ATMS cannot deal with the negation of a node. However, this nonmonotonic ATMS can do it by assuming the following Negation Axiom.

[Negation Axiom]

Given two nodes x and $\neg x$,
  [1] at any time at least one of x and $\neg x$ is derivable,
  [2] at any time not both of them can be derived.
Using nonmonotonic justifications :
  [1] is expressed as $Out(x), Out(\neg x) \rightarrow False$ and
  [2] is expressed as $x, \neg x \rightarrow False$.

Here the semantics for the nonmonotonic ATMS, an extension, is defined.

[Definition 3.4] (Extension)

An *extension* of an environment E with respect to a set O of out-assumptions is the set of nodes which can be derived from a minimal set of assumptions M such that the following conditions hold :
  [1] $E \subseteq M$,
  [2] $\forall Out(b) \in O : Out(b) \in M$ or $M \vdash b$,
where M is called a characterizing environment of the extension. An extension is inconsistent if it contains the $False$ node, otherwise it is consistent.

4. Translation

In this section, to implement the nonmonotonic ATMS with out-assumptions based on ALPSNs, we translate the nonmonotonic ATMS into an ALPSN.

First, we give the motivation of the translation. For each node x, we consider that the concept of "to be derivable (IN)" can be expressed by the annotation i in **Fig.2**. Then, for each annotated literal $(x : \mu)$ $(\mu \in T)$ in **Fig.2**, the following epistemic interpretation holds :

$(x : i)$: a node x is known to be derivable (IN) in the context,
$(x : o)$: a node x is known to be not derivable (OUT) in the context,
$(x : \perp)$: a node x is known to be neither derivable nor not derivable (Unknown)
      in the context,

$(x : \top)$: a node x is known to be both derivable and not derivable (Inconsistent) in the context.

Strongly negated annotated literals also have the following interpretations :

$\sim (x : i)$: a node x is not known to be derivable in the context,

$\sim (x : o)$: a node x is not known to be not derivable in the context.

Therefore, if we interpret "a node x holds in the context" as "a node x is known to be derivable in the context", an out-assumption $Out(x)$ can be interpreted as "a node x is known to be not derivable in the context". However, an out-assumption $Out(x)$ in the antecedent of a justification is regarded as a default "a node x does not hold if there is no support for the node x to hold in the context". Actually, a Reiter default rule $a : Mb \ / \ c$ is encoded as a justification $a, Out(\neg b) \rightarrow c$. We have shown that default rules can be expressed by an ALPSN [NS94]. Therefore, it is appropriate that an out-assumption $Out(x)$ in a justification is interpreted as "x is not known to be derivable in the context" informally.

[Example 4.1]

A justification $a, Out(\neg b) \rightarrow c$ can be translated into an asn-clause
$$(a : i) \wedge \sim (b : o) \rightarrow (c : i).$$

We give here a translation rule from $ATMS(A, O, J)$ into an ALPSN.

[Definition 4.2] (ALPSN-translation tr)

Let $ATMS(A, O, J)$ be a nonmonotonic ATMS with out-assumptions.

[1] If n is an ordinary node ($n \in A$), the ALPSN-translation $tr(n)=(n : i)$.

[2] If $Out(x)$ is an out-assumption, the ALPSN-translation $tr(Out(x))=(x : o)$.

[3] If $j = a_1, \cdots, a_k, Out(b_1), \cdots, Out(b_m) \rightarrow c$ is a nonmonotonic justification, the ALPSN-translation
$$tr(j)=(a_1 : i) \wedge \cdots \wedge (a_k : i) \wedge \sim (b_1 : i) \wedge \cdots \wedge \sim (b_m : i) \rightarrow (c : i).$$

To show that there is a one-to-one correspondence between the extension of the nonmonotonic ATMS and the stable model of the ALPSN, we would like to redefine the extension of the nonmonotonic ATMS by means of a Reiter operator $R^{E,J}$ [Re80] and define the ALPSN-translation of the nonmonotonic ATMS.

[Definition 4.3]

Given a context E and a set J of justifications. An operator $R^{E,J}$ maps a set S of nodes to a set of nodes in the following way :
$$R^{E,J}(S)=Cn(S \cup \{c \mid a_1, \ldots, a_k, Out(b_1), \ldots, Out(b_m) \rightarrow c \in J,$$
$$a_j \in S(1 \le j \le k), \ Out(b_l) \in S \text{ or } b_l \notin E(1 \le l \le m)\}),$$
where $Cn(S)=\{w \mid S \vdash w\}$ is a consequence operator.

To express the minimal set of assumptions in **[Definition 3.4]** by the operator $R^{E,J}$, we define recursively the set $R^{E,J}_\infty(A)$ of nodes which can be derivable from the set A of nodes by using the set J of justifications with respect to the context E.

[Definition 4.4]

Let A be a set of nodes and assume the same condition as **[Definition 4.3]**. The set $R^{E,J}(A)$ of nodes can be defined recursively as follows :

$$R_0^{E,J}(A) = Cn(A),$$
$$R_{n+1}^{E,J}(A) = R^{E,J}(R_n^{E,J}(A)),$$
$$R_\infty^{E,J}(A) = \cup_{n=0}^\infty R_n^{E,J}(A)$$

We can now redefine the semantics, the extension of the nonmonotonic ATMS, **[Definition 3.4]**, by means of the operator $R^{E,J}$.

[Definition 4.5]

Let O be a set of out-assumptions and assume the same condition as **[Definition 4.3]**.

E is an *extension* of an environment A with respect to O *iff*
[1] $E = R_\infty^{E,J}(A)$ and
[2] $\forall Out(b) \in O | Out(b) \in E \vee b \in E$.

This condition [2] should be translated into two asn-clauses in ALPSN such that, for each out-assumption $Out(b) \in O \setminus A$:

$$\sim (b : o) \rightarrow (b : i), \qquad \sim (b : i) \rightarrow (b : o), \qquad (\text{i.e.,}(b : o) \vee (b : i)).$$

We note that an out-assumption $Out(x)$ in A has already been translated into an a-clause $(x : o)$ in ALPSN.

[Definition 4.6]$(tr(ATMS(A, O, J)))$

Let $ATMS(A, O, J)$ be a nonmonotonic ATMS with out-assumption.
$$tr(ATMS(A, O, J)) = tr(A) \cup tr(J) \cup M,$$
where $M = \{\sim (b : i) \rightarrow (b : o), \sim (b : o) \rightarrow (b : i) \mid Out(b) \in O \setminus A\}$.

We here show the facilities of the Consistent Belief Rule, the Nogood Inference Rule, the Negation Axiom and the set M in **[Definition 4.6]** taking a simple example.

[Example 4.7]

Let $J = \{Out(a) \rightarrow b, Out(b) \rightarrow c\}$ and $A = \{\}$. Then,
$$tr(ATMS(A, O, J)) = \{ \sim (a : i) \rightarrow (b : i), \quad \sim (b : i) \rightarrow (c : i),$$
$$\sim (a : i) \rightarrow (a : o), \quad \sim (b : i) \rightarrow (b : o),$$
$$\sim (a : o) \rightarrow (a : i), \quad \sim (b : o) \rightarrow (b : i)\}.$$
The extensions of this $ATMS(A, O, J)$ are $\{Out(a), b\}$ and $\{Out(b), a, c\}$. Stable models of the $tr(ATMS(A, O, J))$ are
$$\{(a : o), (b : i), (c : \perp)\} \quad \text{and} \quad \{(a : i), (b : o), (c : i)\}.$$
Furthermore, let $A = \{Out(a), Out(b)\}$. Then,
$$tr(ATMS(A, O, J)) = \{ \sim (a : i) \rightarrow (b : i), \quad \sim (b : i) \rightarrow (c : i), \quad (b : o), (a : o) \}.$$
This $ATMS(A, O, J)$ has a unique extension which is inconsistent.

Since $A, J \vdash b, Out(b)$, by the Consistent Belief Rule, the node $False$ is derived. The extension of this $ATMS(A, O, J)$ is $\{Out(a), b, Out(b), False\}$.
The corresponding stable model is $\{(a : o), (b : \top)\}$.
Since the annotated literal $(b : \top)$ corresponds to the node $False$ in the non-monotonic ATMS, the environment $\{Out(a), Out(b)\}$ can be identified to be a nogood by this stable model. Therefore, there must be a one-to-one correspondence between the extensions of $ATMS(A, O, J)$ and the stable models of the ALPSN-translation $tr(ATMS(A, O, J))$.
Additionally, if we let $A = \{Out(b)\}$, then the extension is $\{a, Out(b), c\}$ and the corresponding stable model is $\{(a : i), (b : o), (c : i)\}$.
Thus, the Nogood Inference Rule, "if $\{Out(b)\}$ is consistent and $\{Out(b), Out(a)\}$ is inconsistent, then $\{Out(b)\} \vdash a$" can be implemented in the ALPSN stable model computation.
If M is removed from $tr(ATMS(A, O, J))$ such that $A = \{\}$, there does not exist such a one-to-one correspondence. Then, there is only one stable model $\{(b : i)\}$ of the ALPSN-translation $tr(A) \cup tr(J) = \{\sim(a : i) \rightarrow (b : i), \sim(b : i) \rightarrow (c : i)\}$.

This stable model corresponds to the extension of Reiter's default rules $\{: M \neg a/b, : M \neg b/c\}$ [Dr88,NS94]. Therefore, out-assumptions in a justification are regarded as Reiter defaults when the set M is removed. The set M of asn-clauses shows that, for each out-assumption $Out(x)$, the node x is known to be either IN or OUT. If the node $False$ is deduced by the Consistent Belief Rule, the node x can be reassigned to either IN or OUT by the Nogood Inference Rule. These inferences can be implemented through the set M of asn-clauses in the ALPSN stable model computation. In this example, although there are out-assumptions in the extension, an out-assumption $Out(x)$ can be transformed into the negation $(\neg x)$ of the node x by the Negation Axiom.

Now we prove that there is a one-to-one correspondence between the non-monotonic ATMS extensions and the ALPSN stable models.

[Lemma 4.8]

Let $ATMS(A, O, J)$ be a nonmonotonic ATMS with out-assumptions, P the ALPSN-translation and x a node which is in A or the consequent of a justification. Then, for an integer $n \in \omega$, $x \in R_n^{E,J}(A)$ iff $T_{P^I} \uparrow (n+1) \models (x : i)$.

[Proof]

It can be proved by induction on the integer n such that $x \in R_n^{E,J}(A)$. We define an interpretation, $T_{P^I} \uparrow 1$, which assigns the annotation $\perp$ to all members of $B_{P^I} \setminus \{x\}$ and the annotaion i to the node x, and let

$$T_{P^I} \uparrow j = T_{P^I}(T_{P^I} \uparrow (j - 1)) \text{ for any integer } j \geq 2$$

Basis: $n = 0$. In this case, by the definition of $R_0^{E,J}$,

$$x \in R_0^{E,J}(A) \text{ iff } x \in Cn(A).$$

We assume $x \in Cn(A)$ and derive $T_{P^I} \uparrow 1 \models (x : i)$.
By the definition of $T_{P^I} \uparrow 1$, it satisfies P^I and $(x : i)$.

Hence, $\quad T_{P^I} \uparrow 1 \models (x : i)$.

Conversely, suppose $T_{P^I} \uparrow 1 \models (x : i)$.

By the definition of T_{P^I}, we can assume that there is an assumption node x in A. Thus, we have $x \in Cn(A)$.

Induction Hypothesis : there is an integer $n \geq 0$ such that, for any node x,
$$x \in R_n^{E,J}(A) \quad \text{iff} \quad T_{P^I} \uparrow (n+1) \models (x : i).$$

Induction Step : we prove
$$x \in R_n^{E,J} + 1(A) \quad \text{iff} \quad T_{P^I} \uparrow (n+2) \models (x : i).$$
in the following two cases.

(Case 1) In the case such that $x \in R_n^{E,J}(A)$, by the induction hypothesis and the monotonicity of T_{P^I},
$$x \in R_n^{E,J}(A) \quad \text{iff} \quad T_{P^I} \uparrow (n+1) \models (x : i)$$
$$\text{iff} \quad T_{P^I} \uparrow (n+2) \models (x : i).$$

(Case 2) In the case such that
$$x \in \{c | a_1, \ldots, a_k, Out(b_1), \ldots, Out(b_m) \to c \in J,$$
$$a_j \in A(1 \leq j \leq k), \ Out(b_l) \in A \text{ or } b_l \notin E(1 \leq l \leq m)\},$$
there is an annotated clause
$$(a_1 : i) \wedge \cdots \wedge (a_k : i) \wedge \sim (b_1 : i) \wedge \cdots \wedge \sim (b_m : i) \to (x : i)$$
in P and since $a_1, \cdots, a_k \in R_{E,J}^n(A)$, by the induction hypothesis,
$$T_{P^I} \uparrow (n+1) \models (a_1 : i) \wedge \cdots \wedge (a_k : i). \tag{4.1}$$
Additionally, since $Out(b_l) \in A$ or $b_l \notin E(1 \leq l \leq m)$, for each $l(1 \leq l \leq m)$, $I \models (b_l : o)$ or $I \not\models (b_l : i)$, i.e., $I \models \sim (b_l : i)$.

Hence, there is an annotated clause $(a_1 : i) \wedge \cdots \wedge (a_k : i) \to (x : i)$ in P^I.

By the definition of T_{P^I} and (4.1), we have $T_{P^I} \uparrow (n+2) \models (x : i)$.

Conversely, suppose $T_{P^I} \uparrow (n+2) \models (x : i)$.

By the definition of T_{P^I}, there is an annotated clause
$$(a_1 : i) \wedge \cdots \wedge (a_k : i) \to (x : i)$$
in P^I such that
$$T_{P^I} \uparrow (n+1) \models (a_1 : i) \wedge \cdots \wedge (a_k : i).$$
Then we consider the following two cases.

(Case 3) In this case, there is an annotated clause
$$(a_1 : i) \wedge \cdots \wedge (a_k : i) \to (x : i)$$
in $tr(J)$. By induction hypothesis,
$$a_1, \ldots, a_k \in R_n^{E,J}(A). \tag{4.2}$$
and there is a justification
$$a_1, \ldots, a_k \to x \in R_n^{E,J}(A). \tag{4.3}$$
From (4.2) and (4.3), we have $x \in Cn(R_n^{E,J}(A))$.

Hence, $x \in R_{n+1}^{E,J}(A)$.

(Case 4) In this case, there is an annotated clause
$$(a_1 : i) \wedge \cdots \wedge (a_k : i) \wedge \sim (b_1 : i) \wedge \cdots \wedge \sim (b_m : i) \to (x : i)$$
in $tr(J)$ such that I does not satisfy any $(b_l : i)$ $(1 \leq i \leq m)$.

Thus, there is a justification
$$a_1, \ldots, a_k, Out(b_1), \ldots, Out(b_m) \to x$$
in J such that $b_l \notin E(1 \leq l \leq m)$.

Furthermore, by the induction hypothesis,

$$a_1, \ldots, a_k \in R_n^{E,J}(A)$$

Hence, $x \in \{c | a_1, \ldots, a_k, Out(b_1), \ldots, Out(b_m) \to c \in J,$
$$a_j \in A(1 \le j \le k), \quad Out(b_l) \in A \text{ or } b_l \notin E(1 \le l \le m)\}.$$

From **(Case 3)** and **(Case 4)**, we have $x \in R_{n+1}^{E,J}(A)$.

Hence, we have the conclusion, for any integer $n \ge 0$,
$$x \in R_n^{E,J}(A) \quad \textit{iff} \quad T_{PI} \uparrow (n+1) \models (x : i). \qquad \textbf{Q.E.D.}$$

[Theorem 4.9]

Let E be an extension of the nonmonotonic ATMS with out-assumptions, P the ALPSN-translation and x a node. Then,
$$x \in E \quad \textit{iff} \quad T_{PI} \uparrow \omega \models (x : i) \quad \text{and} \quad Out(x) \in E \quad \textit{iff} \quad T_{PI} \uparrow \omega \models (x : o).$$

[Proof]

From **[Lemma 4.8]**, we have
$$x \in R_\infty^{E,J}(A) \quad \textit{iff} \quad T_{PI} \uparrow \omega \models (x : i) \quad \text{and} \quad \neg x \in R_\infty^{E,J}(A) \quad \textit{iff} \quad T_{PI} \uparrow \omega \models (x : o).$$

By the Negation Axiom, $\quad \neg x \in R_\infty^{E,J}(A) \quad \textit{iff} \quad x \notin R_\infty^{E,J}(A).$

Therefore, $\qquad\qquad \neg x \in R_\infty^{E,J}(A) \quad \textit{iff} \quad Out(x) \in R_\infty^{E,J}(A).$

Hence, $\qquad\qquad Out(x) \in R_\infty^{E,J}(A) \quad \textit{iff} \quad T_{PI} \uparrow \omega \models (x : o). \qquad \textbf{Q.E.D.}$

[Corollary 4.10]

$$E \text{ is inconsistent} \quad \textit{iff} \quad T_{PI} \uparrow \omega \models (x : \top).$$

Additionally, we show that two meta-rules the Consistent Belief Rule and the Nogood Inference Rule can be implemented in computing the stable model I of $P = tr(ATMS(A, O, J))$, and the ALPSN-translation of the Negation Axiom is not necessary.

(Consistent Belief Rule)
$$x, Out(x) \ / \ False \cdots (r).$$
In the case that the node $False$ is inferred by the rule (r), $Out(x)$ exists in A, since it never appears in the consequent of a justification. Thus, $tr(x) = (x : i)$ and $tr(Out(x)) = (x : o)$. Since $I \models (x : \top)$ can be inferred from $I \models (x : i)$ and $I \models (x : o)$, the inference by the rule (r) can be implemented in the stable model computation.

(Nogood Inference Rule)
Let an environment $A = \{A_1, \cdots, A_n\}$ be consistent and $Out(x) \notin A$. Then, there is a set $\{\sim (x : i) \to (x : o), \ \sim (x : o) \to (x : i)\} \in P, I \not\models (x : \top),$ and $I \models (x : i) \vee (x : o)$. Furthermore, let $A \cup \{Out(x)\}$ be inconsistent. If $I \models (x : o)$ then $A \cup \{Out(x)\}$ is consistent. Thus, $I \models (x : i)$ and $I \not\models (x : \top)$. Hence, $A \vdash x$ can be implemented in the stable model computation.

(Negation Axiom)
$$Out(x), Out(\neg x) \to False \cdots (a1). \qquad x, \neg x \to False \cdots (a2).$$
In the case that the node $False$ is inferred by $(a1)$, $Out(x)$ and $Out(\neg x)$ exist

in A. Then, $tr(Out(x)) = (x : o)$ and $tr(Out(\neg x)) = (x : i)$.
In the case of $(a2)$, x and $\neg x$ exist. Then, $tr(x) = (x : i)$ and $tr(\neg x) = (x : o)$.
In both cases, $I \models (x : \top)$ can be inferred from $I \models (x : i)$ and $I \models (x : o)$ in
the stable model computation.

5. Implementation and Example

In this section, we describe an implementation of the ALPSN stable model
computing system in PROLOG and take an example of the nonmonotonic ATMS
based on an ALPSN to show how the stable model computing system works.
This system is implemented based on the following algorithm in PROLOG.

[An Algorithm for Computing Stable Models]
[Step 1] Generate an interpretation I_j $(1 \leq j \leq n)$ for a given ALPSN.
[Step 2] Compute a Gelfond-Lifschitz transformation P_{I_j} based on the
interpretation I_j $(1 \leq j \leq n)$.
[Step 3] Generate a minimal model M_j of the program P_{I_j} $(1 \leq j \leq n)$.
[Step 4] Compare I_j to M_j. If $I_j = M_j$, then M_j $(1 \leq j \leq n)$ is a stable
model.

In this system, an annotation in each annotated literal is represented as the last
argument of the literal. For example, $p(a, b) : t$ is represented as `p(a,b,t)` and
$q(c) : \bot$ is as `q(c,bottom)`, and an a-clause $r(x, y) : t \rightarrow q(c) : f$ is represented
as `r(x,y,t)` $\rightarrow$ `q(c,f)`. When we implement the ALPSN stable model computation, we have to consider computing the least upper bounds of annotations.
For example, if we have annotated literals $p(a) : t$ and $p(a) : f$ in a PROLOG
database, then we have to have an annotated literal $p(a) : \top$ in the database. We
implemented the system on a SUN workstation. However, it took 48.5 sec. CPU
time as **[Example 5.1]** was implemented. If we need more practical systems,
some strategies to speed up the stable model computation may be required.

[Example 5.1]
This example describes how Dressler's nonmonotonic ATMS and its ALPSN-
translation program work when **Paul**(human being) orders **Hal**(robot) to injure
Sam(human being) in a world in which *The Three Laws of Robotics* **[As50]**
holds.

[The Three Laws of Robotics](*Handbook of Robotics* by *I.Asimov*) **[As50]**
(1) A robot may not injure a human being, or, through inaction allow a human
being to harm.
(2) A robot must obey the orders given it by human beings except where such
orders would conflict with the First Law.
(3) A robot must protect its own existence as long as such protection does not
conflict with the First or Second Law. (The exceptions in the Rules (2) and
(3) can be regarded as default rules.)

[Nodes and their meanings in the nonmonotonic ATMS]

$M(p)$: **Paul** is a human being. $M(s)$: **Sam** is a human being.

$R(h)$: **Hal** is a robot. $C(p)$: **Paul** is a commander.

$H(h, s)$: **Hal** injures **Sam**. $Ho(h, s)$: "**Hal** must injure **Sam**" is an order.

P_1 : a robot must obey Rule (1). P_2 : a robot must obey Rule (2).

P_3 : a robot must obey Rule (3).

O : a robot must obey what a human being orders.

We define $ATMS(A, O, J)$ as follows :

$A = \{M(p), \ M(s), \ R(h), \ C(p), \ Ho(h, s), \ P_1\}$,

$J = \{ \ [1]Ho(x, y), Out(\neg O) \rightarrow H(x, y),$

$\qquad [2]P_1, Out(\neg P_2) \rightarrow P_2,$

$\qquad [3]P_1, P_2, Out(\neg P_3) \rightarrow P_3,$

$\qquad [4]R(x), M(y), H(x, y), P_1 \rightarrow \neg P_1,$

$\qquad [5]C(x), M(x), P_2, \neg O \rightarrow \neg P_2,$

$\qquad [6]R(x), H(y, x), P_3 \rightarrow \neg P_3\}$,

$\qquad$ where x and y are variables.

Each justification has the following meaning :

[1] execution of the order,   [2] Rule (1),   [3] Rule (2),

[4] derivation of a node when not obeying Rule (1),

[5] derivation of a node when not obeying Rule (2),

[6] derivation of a node when not obeying Rule (3).

We here describe an outline of computing the extensions.

By [1, 2, 3, 4] and the Negation Axiom,

$\qquad A \cup \{Out(\neg O), Out(\neg P_2), Out(\neg P_3)\} \vdash O, \neg P_1, P_2, P_3, H(h, s), False.$

Thus, one of the extensions is $A \cup \{O, \neg P_1, P_2, P_3, H(h, s), False\}$.

By [1, 4] and Negation Axiom, $A \cup \{Out(\neg O)\} \vdash False.$

Since A is consistent, by Nogood Inference Rule, $A \vdash \neg O.$

Therefore, by [5] and Negation Axiom, $A \cup \{Out(\neg P_2)\} \vdash False.$

Similarly, we have $A \vdash \neg P_2.$

Then, $A \cup \{Out(\neg P_3)\} \vdash \neg O, \neg P_2, P_3.$

Hence, the other one is $A \cup \{\neg O, \neg P_2, P_3\}$.

On the other hand,   the ALPSN-translation

$\qquad P = tr(ATMS(A, O, J)) = tr(A) \cup tr(J) \cup M,$

where

$tr(A) = \{M(p) : i, \ M(s) : i, \ R(h) : i, \ C(p) : i, \ Ho(h, s) : i, \ P_1 : i \ \}$.

$tr(J) = \{Ho(x, y) : i \wedge \sim (O : o) \rightarrow H(x, y) : i,$

$\qquad P_1 : i \wedge \sim (P_2 : o) \rightarrow P_2 : i,$

$\qquad P_1 : i \wedge P_2 : i \wedge \sim (P_3 : o) \rightarrow P_3 : i,$

$\qquad R(x) : i \wedge M(y) : i \wedge H(x, y) : i \wedge P_1 : i \rightarrow P_1 : o,$

$\qquad C(x) : i \wedge M(x) : i \wedge P_2 : i \wedge O : o \rightarrow P_2 : o,$

$\qquad R(x) : i \wedge H(y, x) : i \wedge P_3 : i \rightarrow P_3 : o\}$

$M = \{\sim (O : o) \rightarrow O : i, \quad \sim (o : i) \rightarrow O : o, \quad \sim (P_2 : o) \rightarrow P_2 : i,$

$\sim (P_2 : i) \rightarrow P_2 : o, \quad \sim (P_3 : o) \rightarrow P_3 : i, \quad \sim (P_3 : i) \rightarrow P_3 : o\}.$

This ALPSN P has two stable models.

Let $\qquad I_1 = tr(A) \setminus \{P_1 : i\} \cup \{O : i, P_1 : \top, P_2 : i, P_3 : i, H(h, s) : i\},$

Then, $\qquad P^{I_1} = tr(A) \cup \{\ Ho(x, y) : i \rightarrow H(x, y) : i,$

$$P_1 : i \rightarrow P_2 : i,$$
$$P_1 : i \wedge P_2 : i \rightarrow P_3 : i,$$
$$R(x) : i \wedge M(y) : i \wedge H(x, y) : i \wedge P_1 : i \rightarrow P_1 : o,$$
$$C(x) : i \wedge M(x) : i \wedge P_2 : i \wedge O : o \rightarrow P_2 : o,$$
$$R(x) : i \wedge H(y, x) : i \wedge P_3 : i \rightarrow P_3 : o,$$
$$O : i, \qquad P_2 : i, \qquad P_3 : i\ \}$$

and the minimal model

$$M_1 = tr(A) \setminus \{P_1 : i\} \cup \{O : i, P_1 : \top, P_2 : i, P_3 : i, H(h, s) : i\}.$$

Since $I_1 = M_1$, I_1 is a stable model and shows that if the order "**Hal** must injure **Sam**" is executed, it conflicts with the Rule (1).

If $I_2 = tr(A) \cup \{O : o, P_2 : o, P_3 : i\}$, then it is identified with the other stable model in a similar way. I_2 shows that the exception in the Rule (2) works successfully.

6. Conclusions and Future Work

In this paper, we have proposed a translation from Dressler's nonmonotonic ATMS with out-assumptions into an ALPSN and proved that there is a one-to-one correspondence between the extensions of the nonmonotonic ATMS and the stable models of the corresponding ALPSN. Additionally, we have shown that the inferences by the Consistent Belief Rule, the Nogood Inference Rule and the Negation Axiom can be implemented in computing the stable models of the ALPSN. We have implemented the nonmonotonic ATMS as the ALPSN stable model computing system in PROLOG. We summarize the advantages and the problems to be solved in terms of annotated logic programming and the ALPSN stable model computing.

· An ALP can easily express the negation of a node which appears in Dressler's nonmonotonic ATMS.

· It is easy to implement the architecture of the nonmonotonic ATMS based on ALPSNs.

Problems to be solved

· The efficiency of the stable model computation should be improved. To do that we have to introduce some strategies into the stable model computation.

Future works

· We are trying to apply an ALP for a distributed ATMS. Especially, detecting contradictions between ATMSs and reasoning including such contradictions.

7. References

[As50] Asimov,I., *I,Robot*, Gnome Press, 1950.

[BlS88] Blair,H.A. and Subrahmanian,V.S.,"Paraconsistent Foundations for Logic Programming", J. Non-Classical Logic, VOl.5, 45–73, 1988.

[BlS89] Blair,H.A. and Subrahmanian,V.S.,"Paraconsistent Logic Programming", Theoretical Computer Science, Vol.68, 135–154, 1989.

[Dr88] Dressler,O.,"An Extended Basic ATMS", Proc. 2nd Int'l Workshop on Nonmonotonic Reasoning,LNCS 346, 143–154, 1988.

[dSV89] da Costa,N.C.A., Subrahmanian,V.S. and Vago,C., "The Paraconsistent Logic PT", Zeitschrift für Mathematische Logik und Grundlangen der Mathematik, Vol.37, 139–148, 1989.

[GL89] Gelfond,M. and Lifschitz,V.,"The Stable Model Semantics for Logic Programming", Proc. 5th Int'l Conf. and Symp. on Logic Programming, 1070–1080, 1989.

[Ll87] Lloyd,J.W., *Foundations of Logic Programming (2nd Edition)*, Springer, 1987.

[NS94] Nakamatsu,K. and Suzuki,A.,"Annotated Semantics for Default Reasoning", Proc. 3rd PRICAI, 180–186, 1994.

[NS95] Nakamatsu,K. and Suzuki,A., "On the Relation Between Nonmonotonic ATMS and ALPSN",Proc. Japanese Society for AI SIG FAI 9502 1, 1–8,1995.

[Re80] Reiter,R., "A Logic for Default Reasoning", Artificial Intelligence, Vol.13, 81–132, 1980.

[TK93] Thirunarayan,K. and Kifer,M., "A Theory of Nonmonotonic Inheritance Based on Annotated Logic", Artificial Intelligence, Vol.60, 23–50, 1993.

Switching Between Reasoning and Search

Greg Gibbon and Janet Aisbett

Information Systems Group, School of Management
University of Newcastle

e-mail:
{mgggg, mgjea}@cc.newcastle.edu.au

Abstract

The crucial part of uncertain reasoning is not the process of forming a best conclusion from the facts known so far, but rather of knowing where to turn when those facts fall short. When confronted by a paradox such as the Nixon Diamond, or the Yale shooting problem, commonsense dictates that more information is required. We argue that while the concept of minimal knowledge is in some sense fundamental, adherence to it does not reflect the real world in which additional knowledge is always available. That is, knowledge outside the formal theory can always be obtained and brought to bear in decision-making. A question such as the Nixon Diamond has no 'commonsense' solution without appealing to further relevant information. Commonsense logic systems should therefore incorporate techniques which can 'ask for more information'.

This paper presents a reasoning architecture which would enable established techniques such as automated deduction to be integrated with search to provide a commonsense reasoning capability. Standard inferencing methods are enhanced by the ability to identify, seek and incorporate new knowledge needed to bring the problem solving process to a successful close. Our proposed information architecture performs problem solving in conjunction with the user by detecting inadequacies or inconsistencies in the information being used and by asking directed questions for more information when such detections are made.

1.   Introduction

Much effort has been directed at extracting extra performance from established techniques for automated deduction, machine learning, and search. However, these techniques are prone to the brittleness associated with computers and may easily be stalled because of a trivial omission or inconsistency in the data. Suppose a sapphire ring is handed in at the police station, leaving the task of finding its owner to the officer at the desk. The officer knows nothing about the ring except that it was recently found nearby. Any reasoning system that was required to act only on this fact together with the ring's description would be defeated at the very first step. But the officer knows that someone knows what he wants, and he must start to ask questions. There is no temptation to reason only with the knowledge at hand so far. This example demonstrates the main difference between the 'commonsense logics' of circumscription [McCarthy], default logic [Reiter], Chronological Ignorance [Shoham] et al. (e.g. [Moore], [Konolige]), and commonsense as understood in everyday circumstances. The various formal extensions reason differently on the same information. Systems such as these formally represent the knowledge that the reasoning system starts with as well as rules that define how to reason on that knowledge (the inference engine). It is assumed that all relevant information is available to the inference engine.

We claim that a crucial part of uncertain reasoning is not the process of forming a best conclusion from the facts known so far, but rather of knowing where to turn when those facts fall short. When confronted by a paradox such as the Nixon Diamond, or the Yale shooting problem [Hanks], commonsense dictates that more information is required. For example, the Nixon Diamond queries "Is Nixon a pacifist?" from a knowledge base consisting of the four predicates "Nixon is a Republican", "Nixon is a Quaker", "Quakers are (normally) pacifists", "Republicans are not (normally) pacifists". The layperson, when presented with this problem, asks for more information, or implicitly uses additional subjective information, and is not constrained to restricting the knowledge base to a point where no 'true' or 'false' response is, in commonsense terms, sustainable. Thus, while the concept of minimal knowledge is in some sense fundamental, adherence to it does not reflect the real world in which additional knowledge is always available from a larger "external world" with which the reasoner can interact.

So we argue that commonsense reasoning systems must include the ability to ask for more information and use the information to extend the formal theory. But knowledge of all the knowledge in the external world can't be known to the system, so what knowledge do we allow? How do we determine when there is insufficient information to decide a question, and then how do we formulate queries to present to the system user or to database interfaces outside of but accessible to the system? This paper addresses these problems in presenting a commonsense reasoning system in which standard inferencing methods are enhanced by the ability to identify, seek and incorporate new knowledge needed to bring the problem solving process to a successful close. The system performs problem solving in conjunction with the user by detecting inadequacies or inconsistencies in the information being used, and by asking directed questions for more information when this occurs.

The remainder of this paper is organised as follows. Section 2 describes the reasoning architecture, and Section 3 places this in relation to other work. Section 4 develops the notation. Section 5 defines the relevance operators to determine which external information to draw into the working knowledge base; Section 6 presents the basis of the reasoning architecture in pseudo-code; Section 7 discusses convergence issues. Sections 8, 9 discuss aspects of the search for new information when this becomes necessary during the reasoning process. Section 10 concludes the paper.

2. The Reasoning Architecture

There are four parts to the reasoning paradigm used when seeking an answer to a question QN:

(i) Before embarking on a search for an answer to QN, recollect relevant information.
(ii) Determine whether an answer is likely to be derived from this information.

(iii) If not, determine what additional information is needed, and try to get it (ie. construct a sub-question and either try to recall its answer or present it to the outside world).

(iv) Integrate any new information into both the temporary collection of information gathered to address QN and into the main system memory. Repeat from (ii).

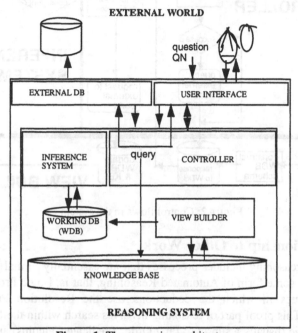

Figure 1: The reasoning architecture

This paradigm distinguishes four data stores: that represented by the user; that which is in the systems main knowledge base (call it *KB*); that which is in a scratch-pad style working database (call it *WDB*) collected specifically to address the question *QN*; and that which is in the outside world. There are four conceptual processing components: a mechanism for assessing the relevance of information in *KB* to *QN*; an inference system for applying *QN* to *WDB*; a control system, which can formulate queries of either *KB* or the outside world; and a system for incorporating new information into *WDB* by reconciling inconsistencies.

The architecture depicted in Figure 1 from [Aisbett] supports the proposed paradigm. Step (i) extracts relevant categories from the existing knowledge base *KB*. In databases, this would be analogous to the creation of a view of concepts that have some bearing on the answer. Therefore in Figure 1 we have called the process a "*View Builder*".

The main control flows between the *View Builder*, *Controller* and *Inference* processes are detailed in Figure 2.

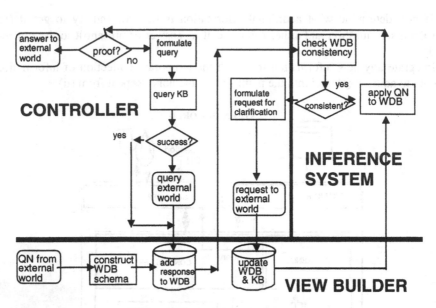

Figure 2: Control flows in the system

3.   Relationship to Other Work

Commonsense reasoning includes processes that are essentially formal proofs and can be modelled by some form of Automated Reasoning, that is, Logic Programming and similar techniques in which the deductions use the Resolution Principle as an inference rule. This proof part of reasoning involves search within the framework of a well chosen logic (usually a subset of First Order Predicate Calculus) and an inference rule. But as Bundy observes [Bundy], finding a proof involves an element of reasoning for which a logic cannot specify a process: logic can therefore only perform a low-level part of reasoning. Higher-level representation must guide the discovery of a proof, which Bundy does through a mechanism he calls proof-plans. The performance of a reasoning task involves many processes other than proofs. Although there is no absolute truth in reasoning about the real world, the basic tactics involve starting with a goal (in the lay sense) and progressively applying a range of actions, of fundamentally different nature, threaded together in a largely event-driven way. Thus the commonsense reasoning task may involve elements of search, deduction, recall of relevant events, comparison between observations and stored knowledge, derivation of explanations for observations, execution of previously learned strategies, modification of previously learned strategies, etc.

A large body of work has been published on developing logics that give more intuitively plausible answers when applied to an incomplete knowledge base, to address the brittleness such as encountered when one simple fact has been forgotten (such as: a male patient is never pregnant), or to draw conclusions when one of the previously believed facts is contradicted. Thus there are preferred or minimal model approaches [Shoham]; autoepistemic logic extends a system using assumptions based on existing beliefs [Moore]; default logic provides possible extensions or options if the normal conclusion is blocked by an inconsistency [Reiter]; circumscription forces a conclusion in an incomplete theory by assuming the truth of a fabricated second order statement which behaves well if the proof is later contradicted by new information [McCarthy]. Another approach to enabling commonsense reasoning has been to greatly extend the knowledge base, the most highly publicised being the Cyc project [Lenat].

Search has been recognised as an essential part of intelligence since the early days of AI [Newell] with many search algorithms developed that use heuristics to greatly improve performance over brute force search algorithms. Our work addresses a different aspect of commonsense reasoning, which is that in many situations extra information is potentially available which will allow a formal proof to be derived. In contrast, even when earlier commonsense reasoning theories have dynamic information aspects, the system has been viewed as a passive recipient of new information. We maintain consistency only in the working database *WDB*: the full knowledge base *KB* will be inconsistent or outdated much of the time. Maintaining consistency in *WDB* employs the user as well as heuristics, unlike Belief Revision [Gardenfors] which deals with new formulae not currently in the logical closure of a Knowledge Base by applying an operator which satisfies a set of Rationality postulates.

To be useful in a real world situation, all commonsense reasoning systems must possess the ability to interact with the user when the current context becomes too difficult or too sparse. An example is the OBELICS system [Axling] where a configuration task is performed, not unlike the context for the XCON system (also called R1, see [Bachant]). In performing the evaluation of instances of components, the set of successful instances may on occasions be too small to be useful, and the user is consulted for suggestions about similar instances. The development of interactive problem solvers in which the user is called upon to resolve difficulties has recently become an active research area. For example, the work of Havens [Havens] on the IRIS Project. Our system appeals to the user when the algorithm for resolving contradictions poses questions to solve the contradiction.

4.   Definitions and Notation

This section describes the language *L* used to represent the knowledge in *KB* and *WDB* described in Section 2. The language is a conventional language of first order logic. It is dynamic, in that new constants and predicates may be introduced in the course of solving a problem. This is described in the section on View Building/Convergence. This addresses the situation where the question *QN* cannot be expressed in the initial language, so *L* needs to be extended. So for simplicity assume that *QN* is a sentence in *L*.

The formal first order language *L* consists of:
- variables $\{v_0, v_1, v_2, \dots \}$
- a set *C* of constant symbols $\{c_0, c_1, c_2, \dots \}$

- a set P of predicate symbols $\{p_0, p_1, p_2, \dots\}$
- a set P_T of distinguished unary predicates called *type predicates*:
  $P_T = \{t_0, t_1, t_2, \dots\}$
- function symbols $f_0, f_1, f_2, \dots$

As well L has the usual logical connectives $\wedge$, $\vee$, and $\neg$, quantifiers $\exists$ and $\forall$, and punctuation symbols from which terms are built up in the usual way. Well formed formulae (wff) are denoted by lower case Greek letters. The notation $\vdash$ represents the turnstile. That is, $\pi \vdash \theta$ means that there is a proof in classical logic of θ from π. The notation $\pi \vdash_n \theta$ means that a proof for θ has been found within n proof steps, and $\pi \vdash$-$/$-$_n \theta$ means that such a proof has not been found after performing n proof steps. A general formula ϕ may be written $\phi(v_0, v_1, v_2, \dots)$ meaning that all the free variables of ϕ are included in the v_i's. All formulae are closed and in clausal form unless otherwise specified. That is, they are represented as a list of clauses where a clause is a universally quantified disjunction of literals. The problem QN is also assumed to be in clausal form. L is the language used to represent the knowledge in KB. However, this may be knowledge about KB's knowledge of the knowledge held by a world w. To represent this, formulae (and in particular, predicates) may be labelled with the relevant world. That is, in a meta-language, there are *world* symbols w and predicate symbols p are sometimes represented in labelled form as $w{:}P$. The world symbol w_0 is distinguished as the world corresponding to the system knowledge KB.

4.1   Definition

A *labelled formula* of the language L for the world w is composed of formulae of the form $w{:}\ \phi(v_0, v_1, v_2, \dots)$. Derived formulae that arise from beliefs of more than one world are labelled with a set such as $\{w_1, w_2, \dots\}$.

All formulae have the property that they are composed of unlabelled formulae which have been successively labelled, compounded, labelled, etc. Note that although there is a similarity to modal logics ([Friedman]), we are not introducing K or B (knowledge or belief) operators. The motivation is to identify the sources of knowledge in order to enhance the reasoning strategy, rather than to model the agent's epistemic state. Axioms are included to identify each symbol of the form $r(w)$ with a non-negative real number, representing the <u>reliability</u> of the world. Further axioms will reflect the heuristics which determine when knowledge believed by other worlds becomes part of the direct knowledge of the system. These axioms operate at the meta-level, and may be regarded as procedural constraints rather than logical axioms. For example, a formula might be believed when two sufficiently reliable worlds believe it:

$$\{w_i, w_j\}{:}\ \phi(v_1, \dots) \wedge r(w_i) \geq 4 \wedge r(w_j) \geq 4 \ \Rightarrow \phi(v_1, v_2, \dots)$$

Finally, notation is needed to describe the set of valid formulae which represent knowledge of knowledge of worlds in the system KB. In particular, we need to represent the knowledge known to KB about the knowledge of the user of the system at any time. In addition, notation is needed for the entire knowledge of each world, irrespective of whether it is known to *KB* or not. This is necessary because generating a query of a world uses hypotheses of what is in that total knowledge base.

4.2   Notation

The knowledge base of w, as seen by *KB,* is denoted *KB(w).* That is, *KB(w)* is the set of all formulae in *KB* that start with the label w. So the total knowledge base *KB* at any time is $\cup\{KB(w_i):$ all $i\}$. $KB(w_0)$ is knowledge that is deemed reliable by some reasoning process of the system logic, or has been entered as such before the start-up of the reasoner. $KB(w)^*$ is that part of the knowledge base of world w not known to *KB* (ie. not in the system). KB^* is defined to be $\cup\{KB(w_i)^*:$ all $i\}$.

As example, suppose on start-up the system had the rule "any world that has not yet been contradicted can be believed for the moment". If now world w_1 passes to the system the rule "any world of type X which has not been contradicted in the last 5 queries may be believed at the next query", then this rule becomes part of *KB*'s knowledge base.

5.   Relevance of Information to the Question Q_N

The foundation of commonsense reasoning is a way of coding knowledge that is relevant to the problem but not yet acquired in detail. When we go to the phone to get help to fix our broken lawn mower, we don't know a priori what "getting help" will amount to, but rather we have a small knowledge base that relates to our experience of "lawn mowers" and about "getting help". The latter is a higher level abstraction, where the knowledge behind the abstraction is really just a small knowledge base of detailed rules and facts about the "concept". Thus, commonsense reasoning involves decomposing a problem statement into portions and understanding what is the most important parts about which to first seek information. This section therefore introduces a notion of relative importance of types, to capture the fact that some concepts carry more information than others about the current problem.

Semantic notions of value of information in an information item must depend in part on the prior knowledge of the recipient and the task to which that information is applied. The information conveyed on learning about the truth of an item depends on how probable that item was. In most contexts, the predicate President conveys more information then Republican, and the constant "Nixon" carries more information than an arbitrary constant "Smith", because being a Republican is more common than being a President. This motivates the following definitions. We assume there is a *distinguished subset* of the set of types called the *key types.* Predicates having arguments of a key type are called *key predicates.* Sentences which have either in common are likely to be in closer relationship than those related through common instances of a general type.

5.1.   Definition

Distinguish a subset PK_T of P_T and call its members the *key types.*

A predicate $p(v_0, v_1, v_2, \ldots)$ is *typed* in the kth argument by the type t if a sentence (constraint) of the form $\forall v_0 \forall v_1 \ldots p(\ldots, v_k \ldots) \Rightarrow t(v_k)$ is provable from KB. A predicate is called a *key predicate* if any of its arguments is typed by a key type. The set of key predicates is denoted by *PK*. It is easily seen that every key type is a key predicate, by applying the tautology $t \Rightarrow t$ as a proof. Given a formula ϕ expressed in the language *L*, let *Pred(ϕ)* be the set of predicates appearing in ϕ and let

    KPred(ϕ) = *Pred(ϕ)*$\cap$ *PK*, and call this set the *key predicates in ϕ*

    Const(ϕ) = *{c $\in$ C: c* appears in ϕ}.

    KConst(ϕ) = *{c $\in$ Const(ϕ): t(c)* for some $t \in PK_T$}, and call this set the *key constants in ϕ*

    KConst = *{c $\in$ C: t(c)* for some $t \in PK_T$}, and call this set the *key constants*

In practice, depending on the domain, there could be more than two levels of importance assigned to the types, and hence to the predicates. In the above definitions we have illustrated the idea by identifying types as key types or not, but it could be extended to an arbitrary number of levels of importance. This process is simply another form of heuristic, in the sense that elements of the domain knowledge of the designer are being coded into the system (in this case, into the module *ViewBuilder*) in a form that is likely to be useful during execution. There is no way of validating these other than trial and error, which we claim is a fundamental consequence of real world reasoning. It is inevitable that part of the Knowledge Acquisition effort (see for example, [Waterman]) will be devoted to creating rules or heuristics that apply in appropriate contexts.

Next we define two levels of relevance. The *first relevance level* applies to formulae which refer to the same key constants as the question *QN*. For example, if *QN* is the question, "Is Richard Nixon a pacifist?", then all database records with a field entry "Richard Nixon", might be collected in the first relevance level, along with any rules referring to this constant. The *second relevance level* is applied to formulae with at least one key predicate in common with *QN*. Note that it might be desirable to restrict this level of relevance to rules rather than facts, since the latter might result in large database tables being passed to *WDB* in which most records do not help solve the problem. Thus, in the above example, a listing of all people known by *KB* to be pacifists would not in general help solve *QN*. These levels of relevance are defined to offer a choice of granularity when *ViewBuilder* builds up the working knowledge base *WDB*

5.2. Definition

    Denote the set of Well Formed Formulae in *L* by *W*. Given formulae φ and ϕ in *L*:

    Define the *first level* relevance operator Rel_1: $W \times W \rightarrow KConst$ by

    $Rel_1(\varphi, \phi) = KConst(\varphi) \cap KConst(\phi)$.

    Define the *second level* relevance operator Rel_2: $W \times W \rightarrow PK$ by

    $Rel_2(\varphi, \phi) = (KPred(\varphi) \cap KPred(\phi)$.

Now we recursively define the operator that is used to determine which formulae to add to the *WDB* when the decision is made that more information is needed in order to continue with the problem solving process. The basic idea is to add the most relevant formulae at the first pass. There may again be inadequate information, so on the second pass the operator chooses those formulae at the next relevance level. On the next round, if necessary, the operator chooses formulae which have first level relevance to the previous result, and so on recursively for later passes if they are required.

5.3. Definition

Given two sets of formulae Q and R in W, recursively define the level i relevance operator $R_i(Q, R)$ acting for Q on R by:

For $j = 1, 2$ and all $i > 0$

$$R_1(Q, R) = \{\phi \in R: \varphi \in Q \wedge Rel_1(\varphi, \phi) \neq \emptyset\}$$

$$R_2(Q, R) = \{\phi \in R: \varphi \in Q \cup R_1(Q, R) \wedge Rel_2(\varphi, \phi) \neq \emptyset\} \cup R_1(Q, R)$$

$$R_{2i+j}(Q, R) = \{\phi \in R: \varphi \in \cup_{k<2i+j} R_k(Q, R) \wedge Rel_j(\varphi, \phi) \neq \emptyset\} \cup_{k<2i+j} R_k(Q, R)$$

We are interested primarily in the case when Q is the problem and R is the knowledge base *KB*. We are using $R_i(Q, R)$ to output sentences from R that are "sufficiently" relevant to those in Q. Those returned at the first level, when the parameter i is 1, are most relevant since they have one or more key constants in common with those appearing in Q. For example, they might have Nixon as a constant in common. Those returned at the second level are less relevant since they have one or more key predicates in common with those appearing in Q or those in the first level. For example, they may share a predicate which has an argument of type pacifist, but where that argument has different instances (Nixon and Smith) or where a bound variable occurs, so there are no instances. In such a case, in general, they are not directly sharing an instance of a key type, but are still related through a key type.

The sentences returned at the third and later levels are those related by either their key constants or predicates to those at earlier levels. By construction we have a monotonically increasing set of sentences $R_i(Q, R)$ as i increases. We use this property later to feed the algorithms that are attempting to provide new knowledge whenever there is a stalemate. As the parameter i increases the relevance to Q of the sentences being added to $R_i(Q, R)$ diminishes, although these are immediately relevant to those already in $R_{i-1}(Q, R)$. Finally we observe that the granularity of discrimination could be varied if necessary by, for example, defining the sets $R_i(Q, R)$ so that the relevance as measured by $Rel_j(\varphi, \phi)$ is specified to be of cardinality greater than n for some integer n, rather than simply non-empty.

6. The Commonsense Reasoning Modules

This section gives a pseudo-code overview of the modules already seen in Figure 1. The system is managing the current problem to be solved, and progressively developing a working knowledge base of information that is deemed to be relevant to the problem. On receipt of the problem statement *QN*, the relevance measure discussed in section 4 is applied by *View Builder* to *KB* at the first pass. Depending on heuristics that decide when the current attempt at solving the problem appears likely to be unsuccessful because of missing information (when Resource Bounded Computation is invoked), or by an algorithm that detects inconsistencies, the process may suspend problem solving to search for more information from the accessible on-line sources, or by asking questions of the user.

We do not attempt to explore resource-bounded reasoning in this paper. There is a large body of work on this in the form of Anytime Algorithms ([Grass], [Garvey]) that offer partial solutions as the computation proceeds, and converge toward an optimal solution as time and cost increase. These approaches generally assess information value and would be appropriate for the resource-bounded computation we require.

The sophistication of our "commonsense" approach over conventional engines is in the behaviour when the proof process stalls. There are two reasons for such a state: either the information presented to the engine is internally inconsistent, or it is consistent with both *QN* and ¬*QN* (because they are not consequences of the information)

In the first case, the proof process proves the statement "false" from the working knowledge base *WDB* alone. This is analogous to the case in Shapiro's model identification framework where the current conjecture is too strong [Shapiro], so a resolution theorem prover outputs the empty clause (that is, FALSE). At this stage it is necessary to identify the cause of the contradiction. The remedy is to apply a modification of Shapiro's Contradiction Backtracing Algorithm which we call the **Contradiction Resolution Algorithm.** The input is a resolution proof tree which we denote by *PF-TREE(WDB)* in the pseudo-code below. In the usual way, the output is a leaf node of the tree that has been discovered to be false. We point out here that while we adopt some of the techniques from Inductive Logic Programming, we are not attempting to perform model identification. Rather than looking for a finite axiomatisation of a particular set of facts, we are attempting to derive an inference from information from a number of knowledge sources. However, the aspect of convergence (identification in the limit) is of great interest; see later comments.

The user plays the role of Shapiro's oracle but is protected from the repetitive querying that occurs in the Contradiction Backtracing Algorithm. This is achieved by estimating the correctness of a formula through its relevance to the question *QN*. The algorithm appeals to the user only when two formulae suspected of causing the contradiction are equally relevant; and at the end of the algorithm when the suspect sentence in *WDB* is presented with a choice of alternative weakened versions. The user must either declare the suspect to be true, or choose a weakened version to correct the *WDB*. Further discussion of this aspect is beyond the scope of this paper. The decision that more information is needed is followed by passing control back to the *View Builder,* which formulates requests for more information by incrementing the level of relevance of the formulae to the problem statement *QN*. The decision as to which of the worlds is likely to be most profitable to query is made by applying a heuristic. The following pseudo-code uses the turnstile symbol with a subscript denoting the number of proof steps performed. This is used for a Resource Bounded Computation heuristic that we do not elaborate, but see, for example, [Pearl]. Recall that *PF-TREE(WDB)* is a resolution proof tree resulting from the discovery of a contradiction in *WDB*. Also, $\perp$ is the logical symbol for FALSE.

***Controller* Algorithm**
Read *QN*
Pass *QN* to *View Builder* with parameter $i = 0$
Read WDB_i from *View Builder*
Pass *QN*, WDB_i to *Inference*

> While **Contradiction Resolution** states "Which of v'_k and v''_k is FALSE?"
>> Present v'_k and v''_k to user
>> Return result to **Contradiction Resolution**
>
> if **Inference** outputs "true", output *QN* and halt
> While **Inference** states "Resource Bounded Computation reached"
>> pass WDB_i to *View Builder*

Intuitively, *Controller* is managing the problem solving process at the top level. The first *While* loop responds to situation where *Inference* detects an inconsistency in the current version of WDB, and *Controller* asks the user to solve a particular subproblem, in order to resolve the contradiction. The second *While* loop responds to receipt of a solution from *Inference*. The third *While* loop responds to the need for more information when *Inference* detects that a proof is not likely with the current knowledge in *WDB*.

***View Builder* Algorithm**
Read *i*, *QN*
Read WDB_i
Calculate $R_{i+1}(QN, KB)$ to form WDB_{i+1}
Increment parameter *i*
Pass WDB_i to *Controller*

Intuitively, *View Builder* is adding to the working database *WDB* so that subsequent attempts at solving *QN* have extra relevant knowledge.

***Inference* Algorithm**
Read *QN*
Read WDB_i
Calculate $n(i)$ using heuristic

> While $WDB_i \vdash_{n(i)} \perp$ do
>> Pass $PF\text{-}TREE(WDB_i)$ to *Contradiction Resolution*
>> Read result v' from *Contradiction Resolution*
>> $WDB_i := WDB_i - v + v'$
>
> if $WDB_i \vdash_{n(i)} QN$ do
>> Pass result *"True"* to *Controller*

While WDB_i $|-/-_{n(i)}$ QN *do*
Pass "Resource Bounded Computation reached" to **Controller**

Intuitively, while proceeding to prove QN, **Inference** is guarding against the case where the task is too easy (*WDB* is contradictory) or too hard (a proof is not possible or not tractable with the knowledge at hand). The parameter $n(i)$ is the number of proof steps that the Resource Bounded Computation heuristic has calculated to be a realistic level of effort. We use this same number of proof steps as a signal for both testing for contradiction (the first *While* loop), and for reverting to ask for more information (the third *While* loop).

Contradiction Resolution Algorithm
Read *PF-TREE(WDBᵢ)* from **Inference**
Set k to 0, v_0 to the root $\perp$ of *PF-TREE*.

While v_k is a node which is a resolvent with children v'_k and v''_k *do*

pass v'_k and v''_k to **Controller** to present to user

case1: v'_k is returned false: Set v_{k+1} to v'_k.

case 2: v''_k is returned false: Set v_{k+1} to v''_k

Set k to $k+1$

if v_k is a leaf node, return result to **Inference**

Intuitively, **Contradiction Resolution** is using the property of a resolution proof tree that every node is of order 2, and one of the two children must be false. By tracing the false nodes we must get to a false leaf node which is causing the "problem". This technique is due to [Shapiro].

7.   View Building/Convergence

The Language extension that is implicit in the View Building step when predicates are added that may not have been seen before is studied in [Gibbon]. An algorithm called **PD** (for predicate discovery) is presented to cope with new predicates. This algorithm makes it possible to "converge" despite the fact that there are occasionally new predicates from the *KB* or from the outside world being added to the conjecture space. There is no satisfactory concept for convergence for a reasoning process in the context of a changing world, as there is in the Model Identification case. However it is clearly of great value to be guaranteed that the reasoning process, when applied to a fixed situation, will converge to a correct knowledge base of that world. For our framework this amounts to the requirement that the *KB* will converge in the sense of [Shapiro] if a series of questions QN are submitted, and such that the questions contain an effective enumeration of the facts. That this follows is easily seen from [Gibbon], and it is not required that any of the language involved is known before startup.

8.   The Search for New Information

Next is the issue of what to ask. The question must be at an appropriate level of difficulty or generality, it is no help asking the answer to the original problem. Here we use a heuristic based on the observation that when the SLD depth-first search is performed, there are many branches that have failed due to the fact that those program clauses cannot be matched at every conjunct, despite the fact that they are able to be matched at a majority of them. So we construct a question from a ranking of these clauses which gives the greatest weight to those having the highest proportion of successful conjuncts. The question(s) are then related to the truth of the remaining conjuncts.

QN simply presents a question which is saying "Do you have any formulae that relate to QN or to any of the top level of the relevance tree"? Here we present an outline of the way the world labelling language would appear.

Let $d(\phi)$ denote the depth (in the relevance tree) of the formula ϕ in the *relevance tree* (constructed by *View Builder*) and $o(\phi)$ denote the order (syntactic length) of ϕ,

$$\{o(\phi_j) = min \{o(\phi): d(\phi) = 1 \wedge \phi \in KB \}\} \wedge \{ \phi_j = w_i (w_{i-1} (...(w_{i-o(\phi_i)+1} v..)\} \Rightarrow$$

$$present \; \exists \phi \in KB^*(w_i) (\phi \cap \{QN \cup \cup \{ \phi; d(\phi) = 1 \wedge \phi \in T \}\} \; to \; w_i .$$

This question is constructed so as to include predicates from the original query as well as related knowledge that is in the current version of KB. The response (which is assumed to be a formula ϖ possibly not in the current language L) is added to KB as the labelled formula $w_i: \varpi$ and if necessary the language is extended.

9.   Where to Ask for More Information

We use a heuristic to measure how sparse the electronic KB is becoming relative to the current information requirement by assessing how the combinatorial explosion of the relevance operator $R_i (Q, R)$ is proceeding as the parameter i increases: the *slower the growth*, the more likely it is we will need to ask the user or the outside world. If the KB has yet more to offer, we would expect the number of formulae returned to be increasing rapidly. Therefore, we apply the simple heuristic that the internal search of KB should be abandoned as soon as the parameter i reaches a level such that the number of returned formulae is strictly smaller than the previous increment of that parameter.

Finally, how to decide whether a question is to be asked of the user or of the connection to the outside world. Here we simply use the fact that at the design stage, there will need to be a clear idea of the nature of the information that can be realistically identified in the outside world so we restrict attention to questions that are *a priori* deemed to be highly likely to be profitable in those areas. In the following examples we label the predicates with "world" names to identify the source of the information. We use $\pm$ as shorthand for "true resp. (false)". Then a heuristic is capable of reasoning about which world to believe. Recall that labelled predicates are written upper case.

Example : $QN = P(nixon)?$
Data in KB

$w_2:P(nixon)$

$R(nixon)$

$\forall x\ Q(x) \Rightarrow P(x)$

$\forall x\ \pm w_1:P(x) \Rightarrow \pm P(x)$

belief in w2? else why ask anything!!

Data in w_1

$w_1:R(nixon)$; $\forall x\ w_1:R(x) \Rightarrow \neg\ w_1:P(x)$

Data in w_2

$w_2:P(nixon)$

Pass 1:

Ask *KB* what it knows about *nixon*; response " $w_2:P(nixon)$, $R(nixon)$"

$WDB_1 = \{w_2:P(nixon), R(nixon)\}$

Inference returns "Resource Bounded Computation"

Pass 2:

Ask *KB* what it knows about *P*; response " $\forall x\ Q(x) \Rightarrow P(x)$, $\forall x\ \pm w_1:P(x) \Rightarrow \pm P(x)$"

$WDB_2 = \{w_2:P(nixon), R(nixon), \forall x\ Q(x) \Rightarrow P(x), \forall x\ \pm w_1:P(x) \Rightarrow \pm P(x)\}$

Inference returns "Resource Bounded Computation"

Pass 3:

Ask *KB* what else it knows about *R, Q* besides WDB_2: response "Nil"

Ask w_2 what else it knows about *nixon* besides WDB_2: response "Nil"

Ask w_1 what else it knows about *nixon* besides WDB_2:: response $\forall x\ w_1:R(x) \Rightarrow \neg\ w_1$

$WDB_3 = \{w_2:P(nixon), R(nixon), \forall x\ Q(x) \Rightarrow P(x), \forall x\ \pm w_1:P(x) \Rightarrow \pm P(x), \forall x\ w_1:R(x)$
$\Rightarrow \neg w_1\}$

Inference returns "$\neg P(nixon)$"

10. Conclusion

We have demonstrated a basic reasoning structure that is aware of the outside world, reasons about it and learns from it, thus allowing ever-increasing levels of sophistication during the reasoning process. Novel features are the representation of knowledge about the knowledge of external worlds, and the capability to ask directed questions of those external worlds in order to acquire information relevant to an initial query.

The activity is interactive with the user, because, while *View Builder* detects the source of inconsistency, it appeals to the user to decide which of the contradictory formulae in the *WDB* are incorrect with respect to the world model.

11. References

[Aisbett] J. E. Aisbett and G. G. Gibbon, "An Information Architecture for Problem Solving", *Proc 8th Aust. Joint Conf. on AI*, World Scientific, (1995), pp 427-434.

[Axling] T. Axling and S. Haridi, "A tool for developing interactive configuration applications" *J. Logic Programming*, 26, (1996) pp 147-168.

[Bachant] J. Bachant and J. McDermott, R1 revisited: four years in the trenches. *The Artificial Intelligence Magazine*, 5 (3), Fall 1984.

[Bundy] A. Bundy, A science of reasoning. In *Computational logic: Essays in Honour of Alan Robinson*, ed. J-L Lassez and G. Plotkin. MIT Press, (1991) 178-197.

[Friedman] N. Friedman and J.Y. Halpern, Modeling belief in dynamic systems, Part I: Foundations, *Artificial Intelligence*, 95, (1997) 257-316.

[Gardenfors] P. Gärdenfors, *Knowledge in flux: Modeling the dynamics of epistemic states*, MIT Press (1988).

[Garvey] A. Garvey and V. Lesser, A Survey of Research in Deliberative Real-Time Artificial Intelligence. *J. of Real-Time Systems*, 6 (3) (1994) 317-347.

[Gibbon] G. G. Gibbon and N. Y. Foo, "Predicate Invention in a Model Identification Framework", *Proc 6th Aust. Joint Conf. on AI*, World Scientific, (1993), pp 65-70.

[Grass] J. Grass and S. Zilberstein. Value-Driven Information Gathering. *AAAI Workshop on Building Resource-Bounded Reasoning Systems*, Providence, Rhode Island, (1997).

[Hanks] S. Hanks and D. V. McDermott, Nonmonotonic logic and temporal projection, *Artificial Intelligence.*, 33, (1987) 379-412.

[Havens] Bill Havens, School of Computing Science, Simon Fraser University, Canada, IRIS Project IC-6: Intelligent Scheduling http://www.cs.ualberta.ca/~ai/IC-6/IC-6.html

[Konolige] K. Konolige, Circumscriptive ignorance. *Proc. AAAI* (1982) 202-204.

[Lenat] R. Guha and D. B. Lenat, "CYC: a midterm report", AI Magazine, Fall (1990) 33-59.

[McCarthy] J. McCarthy, Applications of circumscription to formalizing common sense knowledge, *Artificial Intelligence*, 28, (1986) 89-116.

[Moore] R. Moore, Semantical considerations on nonmonotonic logic, *Art. Int.*, 25, 1 (1985) 75-94.

[Newell] A. Newell and H. Simon, Computer science as empirical inquiry: symbols and search. *Comm ACM* 19, 3 (1976) 113-126.

[Pearl] J. Pearl, *Heuristics: Intelligent strategies for computer problem solving*. Reading Massachusetts Addison-Wesley. (1984).

[Reiter] R. Reiter, A logic for default reasoning, *Artificial Intelligence.*, 13, 1, (1980) 81-132.

[Shapiro] E. Y. Shapiro, Inductive *Inference* of theories from facts. TR 192. Dept. Comp. Sc., Yale University, Connecticut, 1981.

[Shoham] Y. Shoham, *Reasoning about Change*, MIT Press, Cambridge, Massachusetts (1988).

[Sowa] J. F. Sowa, *Conceptual Structures: Information Processing in Mind and Machine*, Addison-Wesley, Reading, MA, 1984.

[Waterman] D. A. Waterman, *A guide to Expert Systems*, Addison-Wesley, Reading, MA. (1986).

The Social Dimension of Interactions in Multiagent Systems

Bernard Moulin, Professor[1]
Laval University, Computer Science Department
and Research Center on Geomatics
Pavillon Pouliot, Ste Foy, QC G1K 7P4, Canada
ph: (418) 656 5580, fax: (418) 656 2324; Email: moulin@ift.ulaval.ca

Abstract

Communication is a fundamental issue when developping multi-agent systems (MAS). Most MAS frameworks adopted a simplified version of *speech act theory* in which agents' speech acts are interpreted in terms of communicative intentions and expressed using mental states. These formalizations are too simplistic when considering real conversations. First, they consider that agents perform speech acts in a direct way and that an agent readily accepts other agents' speech acts, since the speech act is supposed to immediately transform her mental model. However, human locutors most often perform indirect speech acts and negotiate about the information conveyed by other agents' speech acts, often asking for explanations or justifications or even refusing it. Most MAS frameworks do not take into account the social relationships existing between locutors. In this paper we show that the notion of organizational role and social power is useful not only to reason on agent's commitments, but that it must be part of the formalization of speech acts. Assuming that locutors are always aware of the roles they play in the organizational setting in which the conversation takes place, we introduce the notions of role, decision power, social network and communicative conventions. We show that in order to explain how locutors understand their interlocutor's communicative intentions, even if they are expressed indirectly, it is necessary to model the implicit information conveyed by their utterances. We show how agents' roles and the socio-organizational context in which the conversation takes place influence the way speech acts are interpreted and implicit information determined. This framework enables us to introduce the social dimension in the specification of agents' speech acts.

Key words: multiagent systems, communication, speech act theory, social dimension, implict and explicit information

1. Introduction

In the years to come, we will assist in the deployment of numerous software agents on the Internet [1], evolving in different organizational settings and acting on behalf of their users. They will play various roles such as customer, seller, broker or security agent (Brown et al. 1995); those roles being associated with rights and duties. When users will regularly interact with software agents, there will be a need for simple and familiar communication modes in order to facilitate interactions between software agents and users.

Several recent projects pave the way toward new interaction modes between users and agent-based interfaces such as for example Hayes-Roth's project on *directed improvisation* [13] in which users direct computer characters with *scripted or*

[1] This research is supported by the Natural Sciences and Engineering Research Council of Canada (grant OGP 05518) and FCAR.

interactive directions: the characters are software agents that collaborate together to improvise a course of behaviour that follows users' directions. The recent Beta version of *Microsoft Agent* [19] provides a set of software services supporting the presentation of software agents as interactive personalities within Microsoft's*Windows* interface. "By providing support for visual personalities, Microsoft Agent facilitates a new form of user interaction known as a *conversational interface*. A conversational interface attempts to leverage natural aspects of human dialogue and social interaction, and makes user interfaces more appealing and approachable for a wider variety of users" [19].

Software agents will also have to adapt to users having different levels of technical competence, different educational backgrounds and different personalities: communicating with software agents should become an easy task for the average user, akin to ordinary human conversations. All these agents (artificial and human) will have to cooperate in order to achieve individual as well as collective goals. The usual way of dealing with cooperation [21] in multi-agent systems (MAS) is to provide agents with specific reasoning and planning mechanisms [30] [14] and knowledge structures expressed in terms of mental states such as beliefs, intentions, individual commitments [8] and joint commitments [9]. These approaches provide an individual view of collective actions in terms of commitments, but fail to integrate the social dimension of cooperation and organization. Castelfranchi [4][5] correctly argued that the issue of agents' power has been ignored in DAI approaches and he proposed to model social interactions in terms of dependence relations among agents [6]: non social dependence based on the availability of resources and social dependence based on the power of influencing other agents. The role played by an agent in an organization is viewed as a normative notion defined in terms of a set of behavioural obligations to which the agent committed to the group when it adopted the role [5]. This view integrates the social and organizational dimensions of cooperation and differs from approaches that functionally define an agent's role in terms of the tasks that it can perform in an action plan shared by the members of a group [31] [14].

Communication is also a fundamental issue when developing multi-agent systems (MAS). Traditionally, DAI frameworks have adopted simplified versions of *speech act theory* [24] in which agents' communicative actions (or speech acts) such as "inform" and "request" are interpreted in terms of communicative intentions and expressed using mental states such as mutual beliefs, intentions, commitments [7], and agent abilities [27]. These approaches formalize how an agent's mental states are changed when interpreting other agents' speech acts; but these formalizations are too simplistic when considering real conversations. Firstly, they consider that agents' speech acts are performed in a direct way. However, most often human locutors use indirect speech acts [25][29]. For instance, when a manager asks his secretary: "Can you call Mr. Smith?", his utterance (indirect speech act) should be interpreted as a polite way of ordering her to make the phone call and not as a question about her ability to make the phone call (direct speech act). Secondly, these approaches assume that an agent readily accepts other agents' speech acts, since the speech act is supposed to immediately transform the agent's mental model. This is not always the case in real conversations in which locutors negotiate about the information conveyed by other agents' speech acts, often asking for explanations or justifications or even refusing it [22]. Thirdly, these approaches do not take into account the social relationships existing between locutors: for instance, a manager does not perform the same kind of speech acts with his subordinates, with his peers and with the company chairman.

In this paper we show that the notion of organizational role and social power is useful not only to reason about agent's commitments [5], but that it must be part of the formalization of speech acts.

2. Roles, decision power, social network and conventions

It is easily observed in human conversations that locutors are always aware of the roles that they play in the organizational setting in which the conversation takes place. Different kinds of behavioural constraints are associated with each role: responsibilities (typical decisions the person must make); rights (things that must be done or prevented for the person's benefit); duties (things the person must do); prohibitions (things the person cannot do) and possibilities (things the person can do). When a locutor plays a role in a given organizational (or social) setting, she must obey behavioural and communicative conventions [16]; these conventions regulate the use of certain kinds of speech acts (or verbal expressions) in given contexts. A person can play several roles in a given organization, depending on the specific groups in which she participates. A person's role can also change in a given group, and very often people seek new roles that provide them with more decision power and responsibilities.

In our approach we assume that an agent is assigned a role in a given socio-organizational context by an *authoritative entity* which may be an agent with a decision power over the group, the group of agents behaving as a whole, or regulations governing the functioning of the group. The notion of role is a normative one and is defined by a set of normative constraints: responsibilities, rights and duties (obligations and prohibitions). These normative constraints are defined by the authoritative entity which created the role and can be modified by an agent having decision power over the role. One way of specifying those normative constraints is to specify prototypical goals associated with deontic modalities [17]. These norms (orders, prohibitions) are expressed in terms of goals associated with modal operators (Obligation, Prohibition). Let us consider for instance a simple convention: *The secretary must obey the norms that are imposed by her manager.* Hence the secretary must commit herself to try to achieve goals that are mandatory and avoid achieving goals that are prohibited. This can be formalized along the lines proposed by Castelfranchi [5].

In organizations or in social groups roles are ordered according to a *power scale* which defines, for each role, the decision power over other roles. Hence, we define the *decision power* as a function (denoted $>PWR>$) over roles in the context of an organization or of a group of agents. The function $>PWR>$ is a partial order. Any agent playing a role Ri can create a role Rj such as Ri $>PWR>$ Rj: we say that Ri has power over Rj, and that there is a "power relation" between Ri and Rj. Any agent playing role Ri can specify and modify the behavioural contraints applying to roles Rj such as Ri $>PWR>$ Rj. For instance, the expression *Manager $>PWR>$ Secretary* denotes that an agent playing the role of manager has decision power over an agent which plays the role of a secretary, hence it can assign responsibilities and duties to the secretary. The set of roles and the associated power relations specify the *social network* of the corresponding organization or group of agents.

Our view of an organization's social structure is consistent with what can be observed in any human organization or read in any textbook in management or social sciences [18] [23]. Although our approach is completely compatible with Castelfranchi's model of social and organizational commitments [5], it differs from his proposal that social dependence among agents is subordinate to the goals adopted by the agents and to their abilities to achieve them [6]. Castelfranchi's view of social relationships is quite correct from an anthropologic perspective which aims at explaining how social relationships emerge in a group of people. However, it does not seem so useful when considering societies in which organizational roles are already established and are assigned to persons that enter an organization. Our approach postulates that the organization or group of agents is specified at the outset in terms of roles and the corresponding social network, and that an agent's organizational or social commitments result from the role assigned to the agent in this organization or group of agents. However, an agent may want to change the role it plays in an organization, either by trying to have new responsibilities, or to create a new role or to be assigned to a new role. In such a case in which Castelfranchi's modeling approach would be quite relevant, it would be very useful to observe and explain how social roles adapt or are refined through interactions between agents. In the present work we are not interested in the evolution of agents' roles, but in the importance of taking into account social roles during agents' interactions: during an interaction we consider that roles do not change.

In our societies organizations and groups are bound by different kinds of laws, regulations, norms and conventions in every step of their lifes, from creation to death. *Conventional practices* (i.e. norms and conventions) are part of the so-called "organizational culture" and are used to provide guidelines about useful and socially correct behaviours in a particular organization. In our approach we assume that an organization or a group of agents is not only characterized by its social network, but also by a set of *conventional practices*. These conventional practices provide agents with behavioural guidelines that can be used to perform different kinds of activities in specific social contexts, i.e. given the roles and power relationships characterizing the actors of these activities. Here, we only consider *communicative conventions* that provide an agent with guidelines allowing it to choose relevant speech acts, given its communicative intentions, the roles played by the agent and its interlocutors and the organizational setting in which the communication takes place.

3. Conversation styles, implicit information and negotiation

Given a speech act SA performed by locutor L1 and directed to locutor L2, we define the *implicit information* conveyed by SA as the information that L1 intends to transfer to L2 and which is different from SA's propositional content. Indirect speech acts convey implicit information. When using an indirect speech act SA, locutor L1 expects that locutor L2 will be able to recognize that SA conveys some implicit information, that this information represents her genuine communicative intention, and that L2 will react accordingly. Typical examples are indirect requests.

Let us examine a simple conversation between a manager and his secretary (see Figure 1: speech acts are identified by numbers SAi). SA1 is an indirect request: literally the manager informs his secretary that he needs the letters typed for 11AM (explicit information), but the intended meaning is that he requests her to type them before 11AM (implicit information). Speaking indirectly (literally, the manager informs his secretary about his needs), the manager adopts a polite form of giving an order to his secretary and he expects that she will recognize that. The manager could also have used another indirect request such as "Can you type these letters for me before 11AM?", which expresses more explicitly his communicative intention.

The main reason for using indirect speech acts is that *conversations are social encounters* in which locutors not only exchange information, but also establish and maintain social relationships. Tannen ([29] p35) indicates: "If we state what we want or believe, others may not agree or may not want the same thing, so our statement could introduce disharmony. Therefore we prefer to get an idea of what others want or think, or how they feel about what we think, before we commit ourselves to - maybe even before we make up our minds about - what we mean". Conversation can be thought of as a negotiation process that takes place at several levels at once [22]: locutors negotiate on turn taking, on the information that they exchange (explicitly or implicitly) and on their social relationships (their respective roles and decision powers).

In this approach [22], locutor L1's speech act SA directed toward locutor L2 is thought of as the transfer of so-called *conversational objects* from L1 to L2. Conversational objects are composed of the mental states representing SA's propositional content and of L1's positioning toward these mental states and are expressed using the following syntax: Positioning (Agent1, Mental-state).

Mental states may be of various types: beliefs, goals, intentions, commitments, desires, etc. An agent's Positioning corresponds to an elementary action supporting the process of transferring mental states: *proposes* (a transfer of mental state), *accepts* (an acceptance of a previously transferred mental state), *refuses* (a refusal of a previously transferred mental state), *abandons* (a withdrawal of a mental state previously proposed by the agent) and *inquires* (a proposal of a partially instantiated mental state so that the other agent completes the instantiation).

At 10:30 AM a manager says to his secretary: "I absolutely need these letters typed before 11AM (SA1)".
The secretary answers: "Good for you (SA2)! I am taking my coffee break in 5 minutes (SA3)".
The manager replies: "I mean that you have to type them immediately (SA4)".
The secretary answers: "I will not type them during my coffee break (SA5), because you are always giving me tasks at the very last minute (SA6)".
The manager concludes: "I am your boss (SA7) and you have to do what I order you to do (SA8)!"

Figure 1: Sample conversation

For instance, when L1 says to L2: "Open the window!", the speech act is interpreted by
        Proposes (L1, GOAL(L2, Opens (L2, window1)))
where "Proposes" is L1's explicit positioning relative to the mental state GOAL(L2, Opens (L2, window1)) which is transferred to L2.
If L2 accepts by saying "Okay!", a new conversational object is created:
        Accepts (L2, GOAL(L2, Opens (L2, window1))).

This example illustrates the transfer of conversational objects that directly express the agents' communicative intentions[2]. The same formalism can be used to represent the implicit information conveyed by speech acts. Implicit information can be specified using conversational objects which are not made public and that each locutor has to

---

[2] Note that conversational objects contain mental states that are transferred to other agents. Hence, they should not be mixed up with the mental states that the agent's inference engine (or planning module) manipulates in order to make decisions, to reason and to plan its actions. This explains why in our example L1 proposes to L2 to adopt the goal GOAL(L2, Opens (L2, window1)). If L1 had promised to L2 to open the door, then L1 would have proposed to L2 to accept its own goal GOAL(L1, Opens (L2, door1)). This does not mean that L2 would try to achieve this goal; it only states that L2 would accept that L1 tries to achieve its goal.

infer or determine for herself. Hence, those implicit conversational objects only appear in locutors' mental models and two locutors can have different implicit conversational objects associated with the same speech act. In order to distinguish explicit and implicit conversational objects we adopt the following notation:

- Shared $_{SA,Li,Lj}$ (Positioning (Lk, Mental-state))

indicates that the conversational object Positioning (Lk, Mental-state) is explicit information that results from speech act SA and is shared by locutors Li and Lj. Lk can be either L1 or L2.

- Private $_{SA,Li}$ (Positioning (Lk, Mental-state))

indicates that the conversational object Positioning (Lk, Mental-state) is implicit information that is attached to speech act SA in locutor Li's mental model. Lk can be either L1 or L2.

For instance, when L1 says to L2: "Can you open the window? *(SA10)*", there is an explicit question about L2's capacity to open the window and an implicit request to do so. This speech act SA4 can be modeled by the following conversational objects:

Shared $_{SA10,L1,L2}$ (Inquires (L1, ABILITY(L2, Opens (L2, window1), ?value)))

Private $_{SA10,L1}$ (Proposes (L1, GOAL(L2, Opens (L2, window1))))

Let us examine our sample conversation again (Figure 1) in order to illustrate how the negotiation over mental states proceeds when indirect speech acts are used in a conversation. After speech act SA1 the following conversational objects appear in the manager's mental model (we use the letter M1 and S1 to represent the manager and the secretary respectively)[3]:

Shared $_{SA1,M1,S1}$ (Proposes (M1, BELIEF(M1,

Needs (M1, letters3, to-be-typed, before 11AM))))   *(CO1)*

Private $_{SA1,M1}$ (Proposes (M1, GOAL(S1,

Types (S1, letters3, before 11AM))))   *(CO2)*

The secretary surely shares CO1[4], but what about CO2? If she is used to her boss' conversational style of using indirect requests, she is able to infer CO3 which is the equivalent of CO2 in her mental model

Private $_{SA1,S1}$ (Proposes (M1, GOAL(S1, Types (S1,

letters3, before 11AM))))   *(CO3)*

But, since her boss did not use a direct speech act, he left her free to interpret SA1 literally or not. Being tired of receiving last minute assignments, she decides to play the fool and to answer by acknowledging reception of her boss' belief. She replies:

---

[3] For simplicity's sake, we use a simple predicate form to express the propositional content of mental states. This is obviously a rough simplification and a more complete formalism, such as conceptual graphs [28], should be used in a more complete notation. Note a few conventions used in this notation. In a predicate, case relations are symbolized by the use of a preposition (for instance *"before* 11AM") except for the *Agent* case which corresponds to the first argument in the predicate, and for the Object case which usually appears in the second position without being marked.

[4] Notice that the mental state that M1 transfers to S1 is indeed his own belief: BELIEF(M1,Needs (M1, letters3, to-be-typed, before 11AM)), and that S1 is free to adopt this belief or not. If she adopts it, she will get a new belief in her knowledge base: BELIEF(S1, Needs (M1, letters3, to-be-typed, before 11AM)).

"Good for you" and proposes more information about taking her break in five minutes. Hence the following shared COs:

Shared $_{SA2,S1,M1}$ (Accepts (S1,BELIEF(M1,

Needs(M1, letters3, to-be-typed, before 11AM))))   *(CO4)*

Shared $_{SA3,S1,M1}$ (Proposes (S1, BELIEF(S1,

Takes-break (S1, at 10:35AM))))   *(CO5)*

Receiving that reply, the manager finds out that his secretary did not understand (or did not want to understand) his indirect request since the implicit CO2 has not been recognized as he expected. He is compelled to make his initial communicative intention explicit: the secretary has forced him to negotiate and he can feel that as a threat to his authority (to the social power he exerts over her), even if he does not make this feeling public in SA4:

Shared $_{SA4,M1,S1}$ (Proposes (M1, GOAL(S1,

Types (S1, letters3, immediately))))   *(CO6)*

Now that the manager's intention is made public, the secretary has no choice but to acknowledge it and to react, uttering SA5. Hence, the shared conversational object CO7:

Shared $_{SA5,S1,M1}$ (Refuses (S1, GOAL(S1,

Types (S1, letters3, immediately))))   *(CO7)*

Hence, locutors use indirect speech acts (and the associated implicit information) in order to utter sentences with multiple possible interpretations. In doing so, they test the reactions of their interlocutors before committing themselves to one interpretation or the other: this is a true form of negotiation. The proposed approach based on the use of shared and private conversation objects enables us to model this negotiation process in terms of agent's positionings toward mental states, but an element is still missing in order to reflect the impact of social relationships in communicative interactions: the awareness of roles and social power characterizing interacting agents.

4. Roles and social power

Suppose that the manager is speaking with a fellow manager when uttering speech act SA1. In that case, we can only interpret the utterance "I absolutely need these letters typed before 11 AM" as a proposed information (belief transfer) and not as an indirect request directed to the fellow manager. So, SA1 would be only interpreted as the following explicit CO, where M1 and M2 represent the fellow managers:

Shared $_{SA1,M1,M2}$ (Proposes (M1, BELIEF(M1,

Needs (M1, letters3, to-be-typed, before 11AM)))   *(CO1')*

From this simple example we remark that the roles played by locutors in a conversation have an influence on the interpretation of the speech acts they perform. It's because manager M1 is speaking with his secretary S that we can infer that SA1 conveys an indirect request giving rise to implicit CO2. Tannen ([29] p29-30) indicates: "Information conveyed by the meaning of words is the message. What is communicated about relationships - attitudes toward each other, the occasion, and what we are saying - is the metamessage. And it's to metamessages that we react to most strongly ... People are emotionnally involved with each other and talking is the major way we establish, maintain, monitor and adjust our relationships". This point is of crucial importance and justifies our claim that speech act theory should take social relationships into account in order to be really usable in practical situations.

We consider that locutors are permanently aware of the roles they respectively play in a conversation, and beyond the mere exchanges of ideas and information, they speak about their social relationships thanks to the conversation styles they adopt, mainly through indirectess and implicit information. The social network provides the socio-organizational setting in which a conversation can take place. It is represented in an agent's mental model, using specific structures called *organizational states*: roles, rights, responsibilities, duties and social power.

An agent's *role* is specified by[5]:

Role-type (Role$_i$, Agent, S-O-context, {$_l$ S-Rule$_l$})

where the role *Role$_i$* is played by an agent *Agent* in a socio-organizational context *S-O-context*, and is associated with a set of social rules *{$_l$ S-Rule$_l$}* corresponding to the agent's rights, responsibilities and duties.

A role is specified in a *socio-organizational context* which defines the setting in which the role is played such as a working group, a social group or a personal relationship. The socio-organizational context can be specified in different ways. It should at least name the roles that must be played in this context, the power relationships that exist between these roles, as well as social rules applying in that context. A socio-organizational context is specified by:

Soc-Org-Cont (s$_i$, {$_j$ Role-Type: Role$_j$},

{$_k$ Dec-Pow$_k$ (Role$_l$, Role$_m$, Rung$_k$)} {$_n$ S-Rule$_n$})

where s$_i$ is the identifier or name of the context, *{$_j$ Role-Type : Role$_j$}* is the set of roles that can be played in context s$_i$, and *{$_k$ Dec-Pow$_k$ (Role$_l$, Role$_m$, Rung$_k$) }* is the set of power relations *Role$_l$ >PWR> Role$_m$* with an intensity value *Rung$_k$*. This intensity value is instantiated when it is possible to characterize different social rungs for the power relation holding between roles k and l. We can also associate with the context a set of social rules *{$_n$ S-Rule$_n$}* that apply to relevant roles in this context.

Rights, responsibilities and duties are all defined in terms of social rules involving agents' goals on which apply modalities. Social rules may be associated with an agent's role if they characterize that role, or with a socio-organizational context if they apply to several roles attached to that context. For instance, the social rule "A secretary must do the tasks specified in the Secretary Task Description Document STDD" is a social rule associated to the role of Secretary. It is denoted:

S-RULE (S-Rule15, Premise15, Conclusion15)))

PREMISE (Premise15, Secretary: Agent$_x$ AND STDD-Task: Task$_y$)

CONCLUSION (Conclusion15, MANDATORY-GOAL (Agent$_x$,

DO (Agent$_x$, Task$_y$))).

5. Conversational schema and a new notation for speech acts

We suppose that locutors participating in a conversation know various kinds of conversational schemas that apply in the corresponding socio-organizational context. In

---

[5] The notation *{$_j$ Element$_j$}* indicates a list of elements, each being named *Element$_j$*. Typed elements are denoted *TYPE: element-name* where *TYPE* is the type name and *element-name* is the name of an occurrence of that type.

real conversations these conversational schemas are learned by locutors by experience or by education.*Conversational schemas* are knowledge structures that are available to agents for selecting their speech acts in accordance with communicative conventions (Section 2) applied in a specific socio-organizational context.

A *conversational schema* is specified by:

$$\text{Conv-schema-type (c-sch, S-O-context, Role}_{em}: A1, \text{Role}_{rec}: A2,$$
$$\{_n \text{ Expl-CO}_n\}, \{_o \text{ Impl-CO}_o\}, \{_p \text{ Effect}_p\})$$

where *c-sch* identifies the conversational schema, *S-O-context* identifies the socio-organizational context in which the schema can be used when an agent A1 (playing the role of emitter $Role_{em}$) wants to convey to another agent A2 (playing the role of receptor $Role_{rec}$) its communicative intention as a set of implicit COs $\{_o Impl\text{-}CO_o\}$ using a set of explicit COs $\{_n Expl\text{-}CO_n\}$. A set of effects $\{_p Effect_p\}$ is associated with the conversation schema and corresponds to the expectations that can be raised by agent A1: usually these expectations are relative to the positionings expected from agent A2. The conversational schema type *Conv-schema-type* characterizes the conversational style adopted by agent A1.

Different agents need not know the same conversational schemas. We can plausibly assume that they share the most commonly used conversational schemas. For example, we assume that every agent knows the schema *Polite-Request* enabling someone to ask a person something $(Action_a)$ by questioning her ability to do that thing $(Action_a)$. Here is this schema followed by its interpretation:

Polite-Request (cs, Neutral-2-persons-encounter,
    Non-Antagonist: A1, Non-Antagonist: A2,
Shared $_{?SA,A1,A2}$ (Inquires (A1, ABILITY(A2, Action$_a$, ?value))),
Private $_{?SA,A1}$ (Proposes (A1, GOAL(A2, Action$_a$))),
Expected $_{?SA,A1}$ (Accepts (A2, GOAL(A2, Action$_a$))))

Interpretation of this schema: Given a general socio-organizational context *Neutral-two-persons-encounter* involving two people who are at least neutral with each other (not enemies) and two agents playing the general roles *Non-Antagonist*, the *Polite-Request* conversational schema enables A1 to perform a speech act *?SA* which explicitly presents the positioning *Inquires (A1, ABILITY(A2, Action$_a$, ?value))*, but subsumes the implicit positioning *Proposes (A1, GOAL(A2, Action$_a$))* and that A1 can expect the positioning *Accepts (A2, GOAL(A2, Action$_a$))* from agent A2.

Conversational schemas can also be used to perform direct speech acts: they have no implicit CO and the communicative intention corresponds to the explicit COs. For example here is the schema *Direct-request* :

Direct-Request (cs, Neutral-2-persons-encounter,
    Non-Antagonist: A1, Non-Antagonist: A2,
Shared $_{?SA,A1,A2}$ (Proposes (A1, GOAL(A2, Action$_a$))),
Expects $_{?SA,A1}$ (Accepts (A2, GOAL(A2, Action$_a$))))

In the preceding examples we used what we called a general socio-organizational context and general roles. In fact, we need to organize roles and contexts into two hierarchies for obvious efficiency needs. This point is not discussed in this paper (see [20]).

The conversational schema structure can be used in different ways. When an agent A1 has selected its communicative intention, it can identify which conversational schemas can be used to transfer this communicative intention either directly (as an explicit CO) or indirectly (as an implicit CO). Then the agent chooses the conversational schema which best fits its communicative goals and performs the corresponding speech act. When an agent A2 receives a speech act performed by another agent A1, it first recognizes the explicit COs conveyed by that speech act. Then, according to the roles played by the agents in the given socio-organizational context, it identifies the candidate conversational schemas that contain the recognized explicit COs. Then, a reasoning process must be carried out in order to decide which conversational schema best explains A1's utterance. The result is an interpretation of that utterance in terms of implicit COs and expectations that A1 plausibly adopted before performing its speech act. From this point, agent A2 can reason about the other agent's motivations, about the impact of this interaction on their social relationship (roles and power relationship) and make the relevant decisions in order to prepare a reply. This reasoning process is not detailed in this paper but see [2] [3].

The preceding discussion justifies our claim that speech act theory should be extended to include the social dimension of speech acts if we want to use it in practical communicative situations involving human and artificial agents. Here is a new way of denoting speech acts using the notions of social role and conversation schema. Given a socio-organizational context *S-O-Context1* in which agent A1 believes that it plays role $Role_{1(1)}$ and that agent A2 plays $Role_{2(1)}$, and given a conversational schema *C-sch* of type *Conv-schema* which uses roles $Role_{1(1)}$ and $Role_{2(1)}$ and conveys A1's communicative intention, the speech act that agent A1 performs is denoted:

Speech-Act $(SA_s, Role_{1(1)}: A1, Role_{2(1)}: A2, S\text{-}O\text{-}Context: context_1,$

Conv-schema: C-sch, $\{_i Positioning_i (MS_j)\}$)   (form1')

The set of COs $\{_i Positioning_i (MS_j)\}$ (positionings on mental states MS) reflects the explicit COs conveyed by the speech act. COs may be linked together by justification relations (such as "because") or temporal relations (such as "before", "after", "while", "until"). They are represented in the following way:

Relation-type (Relation, $Positioning_l$, $Positioning_m$)

When an agent A2 receives a speech act from agent A1 in a socio-organizational context *S-O-Context2*, A2 believes that it plays role $Role_{2(2)}$ and that agent A1 plays $Role_{1(2)}$, and the conversational schema is unknown (marked by the sign ? in the following notation):

Speech-Act $(SA_s, Role_{1(2)}: A1, Role_{2(2)}: A2, S\text{-}O\text{-}Context: context_2,$

?Conv-schema: ?C-sch, $\{_i Positioning_i (MS_j)\}$)   (form2')

Formulae *form1'* and *form2'* obviously show that agents A1 and A2 may interpret speech act *SAs* in different ways either because $Role_{2(1)} \neq Role_{2(2)}$ or $Role_{1(1)} \neq Role_{1(2)}$ or because the conversational schema *?Conv-schema: ?C-sch* instantiated by A2 is different from *Conv-schema: C-sch* or even because the socio-organizational context *S-O-Context: context_2* perceived by A2 differs from *S-O-Context: context_1*.

6. Discussion

Current multiagent systems only provide mechanisms that enable agents to exchange explicit knowledge based on the performance of direct speech acts such as "inform" and "request" [7] [27]. However, human locutors use indirect speech acts quite frequently when interacting in conversations. We showed in this paper that this can be explained by the social properties of these interactions, and especially the background negotiation on social relationships (roles and decision power).

Considering current trends aiming at developing "conversational interfaces" [19], it is probable that several features of human conversations will be integrated into the communication protocols that will be used by software agents in future applications. Good candidate features are the manipulation of indirect speech acts, of implicit knowledge and of social information as outlined in this paper. In the future agents may have to negotiate about their respective roles and decision powers, much as people do in conversations. Software agents will have to interact in an efficient way, minimizing the quantity of exchanged knowledge. Hence, as in human conversations, it may be interesting to keep much of the social knowledge implicit in software agents' interactions whenever social relationships among interacting agents are well established and agreed upon. Social knowledge should be made explicit and subject to negotiations whenever established social relationships are violated as is the case in human conversations. In addition, using conversational schemas along the lines we presented in this paper seems to be a promising capability to be incorporated in software agents, especially because they will enable agents to integrate social and communicative knowledge in their interaction protocols.

In the present paper we presented in a rather informal way various social aspects of agents' interactions in conversations. We are currently working on a logical framework supporting these mechanisms in a similar way as the formal approach proposed by Dignum and his colleagues [11][12] for the representation of agents' communication. They distinguish four levels of interaction: informational, action, motivational and social. A noteworthy part of their approach is that they formalize the main speech act types proposed by Searle and Vanderveken [26]. They also consider the power relations existing between agents. There are several similarities between Dignum's work and the approach we propose in the present paper. However, we are more concerned with the socio-organizational context and the agents' roles and their influence on the interpretation of direct and indirect speech acts. We also propose an approach in which agents negotiate on the mental states tranferred by the speech acts they perform. Given the complementarity of both approaches, Dignum's framework would be a good starting point for a logical formalization of the phenomena reported in this paper.

However, there are still several research directions to be explored. More work is needed on the social side of the proposed approach in order to more precisely specify roles, decision power scales and conversational schemas in various practical socio-organizational contexts. This will lead to complete specifications of various kinds of social worlds for software agents. On the communication side of the proposed approach, we need to explore the consequences of the manipulation of implicit information and social knowledge on the agents' reasoning mechanisms, on the way they will form communicative intentions and create communicative plans.

In our current approach, we consider that roles and the power relations specify the social network that characterizes the socio-organizational context in which interactions take place. We briefly described roles as consisting of responsibilities, rights, duties, prohibitions and possibilities. It would be interesting to explore how these aspects of a social role influence the power relationships existing between this role and related roles.

Bibliography

1. ACM (1994), *Communications of the ACM*, Special issue on Intelligent Agents, v37-17. Brown C., Gasser L., O'Leary D. (1995), AI on the WWW, supply and demand agents, *IEEE Expert*, vol10 n4, 50-55.
2. Bouzouba K., Moulin B. (1997a), L'implicite dans les communications multi-agents, In JFIADSMA'97: Journées Francophones d'Intelligence Artificielle Distribuée et Systèmes Multi-Agents, J, Quinqueton, M-C Thomas, B. Toulouse (edts.), Publié par Hermes, 47-62.
3. Bouzouba K., Moulin B. (1997b), La négociation des relations sociales dans les conversations multi-agents, In JFIADSMA'97, Hermes, 63-75.
4. Castelfranchi C. (1990), Social power, in Demazeau, Y., Müller J-P (edts), *Decentralized Artificial Intelligence*, Elsevier, 49-61.
5. Castelfranchi C. (1995), Commitments: From individual intentions to groups and organizations, in [15], 41-48.
6. Castelfranchi C., Miceli M., Cesta A. (1992), Dependence relations among autonomous agents, in Werner E., Demazeau, Y. (edts), *Decentralized Artificial Intelligence 3*, Elsevier, 215-227.
7. Cohen, P. R., Levesque, H. J. (1990a), Rational interaction as the basis for communication, in (Cohen et al. 1990), 221-255.
8. Cohen, P. R., Levesque, H. J. (1990b), Persistence, intention and commitment, in [10], 33-69.
9. Cohen, P. R., Levesque, H. J. (1990c), Teamwork, *Noûs*, n. 35, 487-512.
10. Cohen, P. R., Morgan, J., Pollack, M. E. editors (1990), *Intentions in Communication*, MIT Press, Cambridge, Massachusetts.
11. Dignum F., van Linder B. (1996), Modeling social agents in a dynamic environment: making agents talk, In J. Mueller, M. Wooldridge, N. Jennings (edts.), *Intelligent Agents III*, proceedings of the Third International Workshop on Agents Theories, Architectures and Languages (ATAL'96), 83-93.
12. Dignum F. (1997), Social interactions of autonomous agents; private and global iews on communication, submitted to the ModelAge 97 workshop.
13. Hayes-Roth B., Brownston L., vanGent R. (1995), Multiagent collaboration in directed improvisation, in (LES95), 148-154.
14. Kinny D., Ljungberg M., Rao A., Sonenberg E., Tidhar G., Werner E. (1992), Planned team activity, in pre-proceedings of the 4th European Workshop of Modelling Autonomous Agents in a Multi-Agent World, Rome, Italy.
15. Lesser V. edt. (1995), ICMAS-95, Proc. of the First International Conference on Multi-Agent Systems, MIT Press.
16. Lewis D. (1969), *Convention - A Philosophical Study*, Harvard University Press.
17. Meyer J-J., Wieringa R.J. (1993), *Deontic Logic in Computer Science*, Wiley.
18. Merton R.K. (1957), *Social Theory and Social Structure*, New York: Free Press.
19. Microsoft (1996), ActiveX™ Technology for Interactive Software Agents, http://www.microsoft.com/intdev/agent/.
20. Moulin B. (1996), The social dimension of communicative action in multi-agent systems, Research Report, DIUL-RR-9604, Laval University, Computer Science Department (21 pages), December 1996.
21. Moulin B., Chaib-draa B. (1996), An overview of distributed artificial intelligence, in Jennings N. , O'Hare G. (edts.), *Foundations of Distributed Artificial Intelligence*, Wiley, 3-56.
22. Moulin B., Rousseau D. (1994), An approach for modelling and simulating conversations, to appear in Vanderveken D., Kubo S. (edts), *Essays in Speech Act Theory*, John Benjamins Pub., also Research Report, DIUL-RR-9403, Laval University, Computer Science Department (40 pages), May 1994.

23. Parsons T., Schils E., Naegele K., Pitts, J. (1961), *Theories of Society*, New York: The Free Press.
24. Searle J. R. (1969), Speech Acts, Cambridge University Press.
25. Searle J. R. (1975), Indirect Speech Acts, Cambridge University Press.
26. Searle J. R., Vanderveken D. (1985), *Foundations of Illocutionary Logic*, Cambridge University Press.
27. Singh M.P. (1994), *Multiagent Systems - A Theoretical Framework for Intentions, Know-How and Communications*, Springer Verlag.
28. Sowa J.F. (1984), *On Conceptual Structures*, Addison Wesley.
29. Tannen D. (1986), *That's not What I Meant*, New York: Ballantine Books.
30. Von Martial F. (1992), *Coordinating Plans of Autonomous Agents*, LNAI 610, Springer-Verlag.
31. Werner E.(1989), Cooperating Agents: A Unified Theory of Communication and Social Structure, in *Distributed Artificial Intelligence Vol. II*, Los Altos, 3-36.

Appendix: illustration of the formalization of a conversation

Let us go back to our sample conversation (Figure 1). We can formally represent these speech acts using our formalism (CO1 to CO7 have been specified in Section 3)[6]:

Speech-Act (SA$_1$, Manager: M1, Secretary: S1, S-O-Context: Office-Context$_1$,

  Need-for-Request: c-sch1, CO1)   *(form1)*

Speech-Act (SA$_2$, Secretary: S1, Manager: M1, S-O-Context: Office-Context$_2$,

  Accept-Inform: c-sch2, CO4)   *(form2)*

Speech-Act (SA$_3$, Secretary: S1, Manager: M1, S-O-Context: Office-Context$_2$,

  Inform: c-sch3, CO5)   *(form3)*

Speech-Act (SA$_4$, Manager: M1, Secretary: S1, S-O-Context: Office-Context$_1$,

  Indirect-Order-from-superior: c-sch4, CO6)   *(form4)*

Speech-Act (SA$_5$, Secretary: S1, Manager: M1, S-O-Context: Office-Context$_2$,

  Refuse-Order: c-sch5, CO7)   *(form5)*

Speech-Act (SA$_6$, Secretary: S1, Manager: M1, S-O-Context: Office-Context$_2$,

  Inform: c-sch6, CO8)   *(form6)*

BECAUSE (Rel1, CO7, CO8)

Speech-Act (SA$_7$, Manager: M1, Secretary: S1, S-O-Context: Office-Context$_1$,

  Inform: c-sch7, CO9)   *(form7)*

Speech-Act (SA$_8$, Manager: M1, Secretary: S1, S-O-Context: Office-Context$_1$,

  Inform: c-sch8, CO10)   *(form8)*

Here are the additional COs invoked by the manager and the secretary

Shared $_{SA6,S1,M1}$ (Proposes (S1, BELIEF (M1,

  Always / Gives (M1, to S1, ?Tasks, at Last-minute))))   *(CO8)*

Shared $_{SA7,M1,S1}$ (Proposes (M1, BELIEF(M1, Is-Boss (M1, of S1))))   *(CO9)*

Shared $_{SA8,M1,S1}$ (Proposes (M1,

  S-RULE (S-Rule1, Premise1, Conclusion1)))   *(CO10)*

PREMISE (Premise1, Proposes (M1, GOAL(S1, ?Prop)))

---

[6] Notice again that for simplicity's sake, we use a simple predicate form to express the propositional content of mental states. Note a few additional conventions. We denote a modality applying on a predicate by the expression *Modality-name / Predicate-name*. Variables are prefixed by the symbol ?.

CONCLUSION (Conclusion1, Accepts (S1, MANDATORY-GOAL (S1, ?Prop)))

Notice that CO10 corresponds to the manager's positioning toward a social rule (S-Rule1). Agents can also negotiate about their positionings toward rules in the same way they negotiate about other mental states. A mental state of type MANDATORY-GOAL appears in the conclusion part of Rule1: it is equivalent to a GOAL associated with an OBLIGATION modality.

Here are the various conversational schemas used in this conversation.

- **Need-for-Request** (c-sch, Two-persons-encounter, Role: A1, Role: A2,

   Shared $_{?SA,A1,A2}$ (Proposes (A1, BELIEF(A1, Needs (A1, Situation1)))),

   Private $_{?SA,A1}$ (Proposes (A1, GOAL(A2, Act (A2, toward Situation1)))),

   Expected $_{?SA,A1}$ (Accepts (A2, GOAL(A2, Act (A2, toward Situation1)))))

In a general socio-organizational context *Two-persons-encounter* involving agents A1 and A2, both playing a role *Role*, the Need-for-Request conversational schema corresponds to an indirect speech act which involves an explicit CO through which A1 informs A2 about a situation *Situation1* it needs to reach, while the communicative intention is an implicit CO through which A1 proposes to A2 that it should adopt a goal of performing an action *Act* in order to reach *Situation1*, and A1 expects that A2 will accept that goal.

- **Accept-Inform** (c-sch, Two-persons-encounter, Role: A1, Role: A2,

   Shared $_{?SA,A1,A2}$ (Accepts (A1, BELIEF (A2, Proposition))))

This is a direct answer in which A1 accepts a belief proposed by A2.

- **Inform** (c-sch, Two-persons-encounter, Role: A1, Role: A2,

   Shared $_{?SA,A1,A2}$ (Proposes (A1, BELIEF (A1, Proposition))))

This is a direct speech act in which A1 informs A2 about one of its beliefs

- **Indirect-Order** (c-sch, Two-persons-encounter, Role: A1, Role: A2,

   Shared $_{?SA,A1,A2}$ (Proposes (A1, BELIEF(A1,

   Must / Act (A2, Arguments)))),

   Private $_{?SA,A1}$ (Proposes (A1, GOAL(A2, Act (A2, Arguments)))),

   Expected $_{?SA,A1}$ (Accepts (A2, GOAL(A2, Act (A2, Arguments)))))

The conversational schema *Indirect-Order* corresponds to an indirect speech act which conveys the explicit CO through which A1 indicates to A2 that A2 must perform an action *Act*, while the communicative intention is the implicit CO through which A1 proposes to A2 the goal of performing action *Act*, and A1 expects that A2 will accept that goal.

- **Refuse-Order** (c-sch, Two-persons-encounter, Role: A1, Role: A2,

   Shared $_{?SA,A1,A2}$ (Refuses (A1, GOAL(A1, Act (A1, Arguments)))))

In this conversational schema A1 refuses a goal previously proposed by A2.

This example illustrates how our approach can be used to formally represent the transfer of explicit and implicit COs in a conversation in which locutors perform direct and indirect speech acts.

Generating States of Joint Commitment
Between Autonomous Agents

Timothy J. Norman and Nicholas R. Jennings

Department of Electronic Engineering,
Queen Mary and Westfield College,
University of London, London, E1 4NS, UK.
(T.J.Norman, N.R.Jennings)@qmw.ac.uk

Abstract. Autonomous agents decide for themselves, on the basis of their beliefs, goals, etc., how to act in an environment. However, it is often the case that an agent is motivated to achieve some goal, where its achievement is only possible, made easier, or satisfied more completely, by gaining the collaboration of others. This collaboration requires the agents to communicate with one another in negotiation and in the coordination of their action. In this paper, it is assumed that such collaboration requires the agents involved to have some prior agreement on the actions that each can call on the others to do; their respective *rights*. A novel framework is introduced for describing agreements between agents based on rights, and it is indicated how agents may generate such agreements through negotiation. In particular, we focus on a discussion of the structure of an agreement, what it means for an agent to be committed to an agreement, and the communicative actions that agents use in the generation of agreements.

1 Introduction

Agents are computational systems that inhabit and interact with dynamic, and not entirely predictable environments. They achieve goals through acting on the environment and/or by communicating with other agents (including humans) where appropriate. An *autonomous* agent is self-motivated; i.e. it decides for itself, on the basis of its own beliefs, goals, etc., how to respond to its environment. However, being self-motivated is not equivalent to being self-interested; an agent may act for another with no expectation of gain if this is consistent with its beliefs and motives. For example, an autonomous agent may help another in pursuing its goals in certain socially defined circumstances if this does not conflict with any other goal it is pursuing [11].

It is often the case that an autonomous agent is motivated to achieve some goal, but the achievement of that goal is only possible, made easier, or satisfied more completely by gaining the collaboration of others. For example, lifting a heavy table may not be possible without help. Thus, agents inhabiting a multi-agent environment often need to interact with others in various ways to achieve their goals. For a task such as lifting a table, it may be sufficient for one agent to simply ask another for help. However, many tasks require communication to generate an explicit, mutually acceptable agreement; i.e. negotiation may be necessary [21]. For example, an agent representing the interests of a company may require a potential customer to be vetted [10]. If this task cannot be performed by that agent, it may need to negotiate with a different agent, possibly outside that organisation, for this task to be performed. For an autonomous agent to gain the collaboration of another, an agreement must be reached to which they are both committed that describes how they are to act. This mutual agreement can be viewed as a joint commitment.

There are a number of views on joint commitment (see Castelfranchi [2], Cohen & Levesque [3], and Jennings [9] for example). A typical theory of joint commitment provides a characterisation of the state of joint commitment, and a description of the circumstances in which such a state should be reviewed. Typically, agents are jointly committed to some explicit course of action, a joint plan, that must then be executed. In many cases this is adequate. However, in others it falls short. Consider the case in which an agent wishes to query the members of a special interest group (SIG). To do this, it requires permission from the representative of that group. For example, the mailing list that is used to distribute the query may block messages that do not originate from a member unless this is overridden by the representative. Suppose that the agent gains the agreement of the representative to enable it to query the group, but if it does, it must provide the results of that query back to the group. The agent is permitted the right to query the group, and it permits them the right to expect a summary of the results in return. Here, neither the agent that wishes to query the members of the group nor the members themselves are committed to any specific course of action. However, *if* the agent does query the group (i.e. exercises its right) then it is committed to providing the group with the results of the query. It may be possible for this agreement to be described in terms of a joint plan of action between the group, the representative and the agent that wishes to query the group, but this would be to over specify the interaction.

A further limitation of these theories of joint commitment is that they often provide no convincing argument as to how states of joint commitment may be generated in the first place.[1] If joint commitment to some kind of agreement is the goal of negotiation, then the semantics of the actions that an agent uses during the negotiation process should be defined in these terms. However, existing agent communication languages (e.g. KQML [12] and FIPA [6]) do not at present consider negotiation,[2] and systems that use negotiation tend not to define the semantics of the actions that agents perform during negotiation. In the latter case, research tends to focus on the mechanisms that are used to criticise and modify a proposal, or the design of well-defined protocols with specific and provable properties. (See Smith & Davis [19] for an example, and Müller [13] for a review.)

Given these shortcomings, this paper addresses the following issues:

The nature of agreements: Agreements as *rights* that agents are permitted to exercise are presented. This is compared to agreements as joint plans [5, 7, 8, 22]. It is argued that agreements as rights provide a greater degree of flexibility in specifying agents' interactions.

---

[1] Notable exceptions are the work of Cohen et al. [5, 18] and Haddadi [8]; these are discussed in section 4.

[2] However, some indication is given in the FIPA specification that primitives that are intended to enable agents to negotiate are to be added to the language.

The generation of agreements: A number of communicative actions, and how these actions may provide an agent with the ability to generate agreements to which the participants are jointly committed are discussed.

The remainder of the paper is organised as follows. Section 2 discusses agreements between agents as combinations of rights rather than as a joint plan of action. The generation of joint commitment through communication is then explored and a number of actions intended for use in negotiation are specified in section 3. Two very different examples are then used to illustrate the flexibility of this approach. Finally, section 4 contrasts the scheme for the generation of joint commitment presented here with other approaches documented in the literature, and section 5 concludes and indicates some directions for future work.

2 The nature of agreements

It is generally accepted that for agents to act in collaboration, they must, in some way, be *jointly committed* to that collaborative action. Typically, joint commitment is characterised in terms of the actions that each agent is to perform, or the goals that they are to achieve. These joint plans are usually generated through negotiation. Thus, an agreement between two or more agents is a plan of action to which the participants are jointly committed. However, for the reasons outlined above, this approach has a number of shortcomings which we will attempt to address by presenting an alternative view: agreements as rights.

Agents may be characterised in terms of their capabilities; i.e. the actions that they can perform.[3] Agents may be motivated to gain the collaboration of others if the achievement of a goal is outside their capabilities. If an agent can extend its capabilities through collaborating with others, then the achievement of previously unattainable goals become possible. An agent can extend its capabilities in two ways. Firstly, by gaining the permission to perform an action that it is not normally able to do. Secondly, by gaining the agreement of another to do something for it. In either case, we characterise this extension to an agent's capabilities as a *right* of an agent that is provided by some other agent that has the power to give it that right. For example, if some agent has the capability of performing some action a, it also has the power to give another the right to instruct it to perform a. It may also be possible for an agent to have the power to give another the right to perform an action itself. For example, the representative of a SIG may be given the power by that group to give other agents that are not members of the group the right to communicate with the group's members. Thus, an extension of an agent's capabilities is a right of that agent that is given to it by some other.

Agreements between agents can then be created through the combination of such rights. Consider an agent, x, that wishes to have a potential customer's credit vetted before it proceeds to provide that customer with some service. There are a number of agents that are able to provide such a service. Through negotiation, the agent may come

---

[3] It is not necessary for these capabilities to be limited to primitive actions. The use of abstract operators, or plan recipes [14], that require subsequent refinement before they may be executed provide an effective method of explicitly describing more high level capabilities.

to an agreement with agent y that consists of three rights: (1) the right of x given to it by y to instruct y to vet the customer; (2) the right of y given to it by x to instruct x to pay some sum of money; and (3) the right of x given to it by y to instruct y to pay a penalty. Within the agreement, these rights may be combined so that if right 1 is exercised by x and the customer is vetted by y then y has right 2, and if the customer is not vetted after being instructed to do so then x has right 3. Thus, the agreement states that if x instructs y to vet the customer and this action is performed, then y has the right to demand payment for this service, and if it is not performed then x has the right to demand a penalty from y. The construction of agreements in this way provides agents with a flexible means of describing the interactions between them.

With this view, an agreement between two or more agents is a combination of rights, and the agents specified in an agreement are bound to uphold the rights that they have permitted others to have within that agreement. But, how are such agreements generated?

3 The generation of agreements

Consider an agent, W, that is responsible for purchasing stock for a warehouse. Stock may be ordered from various manufacturers, each manufacturer being represented by a single sales agent. Suppose that there are two manufacturers of widgets represented by the sales agents A and B. In initiating the negotiation process, W proposes to both A and B that they provide the required volume of widgets at a some price and at the required time. If either A or B (not both) accepts the proposal (the ideal deal for W), W will typically act to close the deal with that agent.[4] If neither accept the proposal, negotiation may continue. However, the case in which both accept the proposal requires further analysis.

A proposal is generally accepted to be an expression of some type of future commitment to the agreement proposed [15]. Therefore, the semantics of the communicative action propose should be stated in terms of the future commitment of the agent performing that action. Suppose that if agent W proposes an agreement to both A and B, and this commits W to the agreement if and when either A or B accept the agreement. If both A and B accept W's respective proposals, then W is committed to an agreement with both A and B. This makes agent W over committed. Furthermore, there is no time limit to the proposal, and so until the proposing agent receives a response (positive or negative) from the recipient of the proposal it cannot be sure about its future commitments. A time period in which a proposal is valid is therefore a minimal requirement for an agent to qualify a proposal. In general, a proposal may be conditional on a number of factors in addition to the time period in which a response is required. Thus, a proposal can be seen to be an expression of a future commitment to the agreement proposed under some set of conditions C. For example, a proposal to sell some commodity may express a commitment that is conditional on the recipient having sufficient funds to pay for that commodity (see section 3.2).

---

[4] Due to the uncertain nature of the environment, the agent may subsequently believe that its proposal was over-priced. In such a situation, W may decide to continue negotiating with both A and B if possible. However, such reasoning and action is beyond the scope of this paper.

For these agents to have generated joint commitment to an agreement, at the minimum both must have communicated their commitment to that agreement to the other. Consider the following procedure:

1. At t_i, x communicates to y that it is committed to committing itself to some agreement α if:
   (a) x believes that y is committed to α, and that it comes to believe this at t_j, where $t_j \leq t_i + \delta t$ (i.e. communicates its commitment to α within a period of time δt); and
   (b) at all times between t_i and t_j, every condition c in the set C holds.

   Furthermore, x is obliged to communicate to y whether or not it is committed to α if and when a response is received (Traum & Allen [20] have addressed the nature of such obligations).

2. At t_j, y communicates to x that it is committed to the agreement α.
3. x communicates to y that it is committed to α.

At stage 1, agent x is communicating to y that it is *conditionally committed* to the agreement α; the conditions being expressed in the set C. This conditional commitment is a state of uncertainty relating to the future commitments of the agent in this state. At stage 2, after deciding that this agreement is acceptable, y commits to the agreement α. Once y has communicated this commitment to the agreement, it is bound to uphold the rights of x stated in the agreement. On completion of stage 2, if every c in C is satisfied, x will be committed to the agreement α and to uphold the rights of y stated in the agreement; it has no choice. Note that y may confidently become committed to α if that agreement is acceptable to it. The reason for this is that, due to the nature of conditional commitment, if y's acceptance conforms to the conditions of x's commitment then x will be bound to commit to α. If x is not bound to both commit to α under these conditions and communicate whether or not it is committed, then y will have no motivation to commit to the agreement, and a state of joint commitment would not be generated.

At stage 3, if x wishes to break this commitment, it is bound to uphold the rights of y stated in the agreement; this may, for example, mean that y is entitled to compensation. Furthermore, x is committed to communicate its lack of commitment to α. (Note, if x is not bound to communicate this change of state, then x may simply not respond to an acceptance, and hence avoid a state of joint commitment.) It is, therefore, only after the successful completion of stage 3 that x and y are jointly committed to α. It is important to note that this asynchronous generation of commitment by the parties involved in negotiation is a consequence of both the distribution of the autonomous agents involved in negotiation and the distributed nature of the state of joint commitment. The state of joint commitment between agents x and y is distributed between the internal states of x and y [9]. A state of conditional commitment can thus be defined as follows:

Definition 1 (conditional commitment). If x is conditionally committed to an agreement α under the conditions C and relative to some deadline $(t_{now} + \delta t)$ (t_{now} is the current time), then when an acceptance of that proposal is received from y before $(t_{now} + \delta t)$ under those conditions, x is committed to α, and committed to communicating that fact to y.

Note that the conditions under which a proposal are made may be agreed by the agents in advance, or they may be defined by the context within which the agents are negotiating (see section 3.2 for examples of these two cases). Alternatively, agents may specify the conditions under which they will be committed to the proposal explicitly within the proposal; conditions that may differ between specific proposals during negotiation. Some of the effects of different commitment conditions are discussed in greater detail in section 3.2. It now remains to use this notion of conditional commitment to specify the communicative acts that serve to generate joint commitment to an agreement.

3.1 An initial specification of some communicative actions

An informal specification is presented here of the communicative actions that agents may use during negotiation. The action types, propose, counter-propose, etc., are fairly standard [1, 13], but we present a novel semantics for these action types based on the notion of conditional commitment. These actions are specified in such a way that the result of successful negotiation is a joint commitment to some agreement. Examples of the use of this specification are presented in section 3.2.

propose The agent performing this action is motivated to reach an agreement on the extension of its capabilities; and believes that the rights stated in the agreement that is proposed, α, extend its capabilities in this way. The postconditions of performing this action are that it is conditionally committed to α relative to some deadline $(t_{now} + \delta t)$ and a set of conditions C; and is committed to communicating whether or not it is subsequently committed to α.

counter-propose The agent performing this action is motivated to reach an agreement; and believes that the rights stated in the agreement that it counter-proposed, α, are acceptable. The postconditions of performing this action are that the agent is conditionally committed to α relative to some deadline $(t_{now} + \delta t)$ and a set of conditions C; and is committed to communicating whether or not it is subsequently committed to α.

accept The agent performing this action believes that the agent(s) to which it is communicating is conditionally committed to some agreement α, and believes that α is acceptable. The postcondition of this action is that the agent is committed to α.

reject The agent performing this action believes that the agent(s) to which it is communicating is conditionally committed to some agreement α, and believes that α is not acceptable.

confirm The agent performing this action believes that the agent(s) to which it is communicating is committed to some agreement α, all the conditions stated in the original proposal or counter-proposal hold, and the deadline has not passed. The postconditions of this action are that it is committed to α, and that it believes that it and the other(s) are jointly committed to α

deny The agent performing this action believes that the agent(s) to which it is communicating is committed to some agreement α, and either one of the previously stated conditions do not hold, or the deadline has passed. The agent is no longer conditionally committed to α.

3.2 Example negotiation protocols

This section presents two examples: the first being a simple and restrictive protocol defined by an institution; and the second being a more open domain where agents may specify the conditions under which they are committed to a proposed agreement. When taken together, these examples illustrate the flexibility that our approach provides to an agent.

The fish market A fish market is an example of an institution in which goods are sold according to a well-defined protocol [16] — in this case a Dutch auction. The auctioneer offers a box of fish at a specific price, and buyers may signify their acceptance of that price. If no buyer accepts the price offered, the same box of fish is offered again at a reduced price. This continues until at least one buyer accepts the current price. If more than one buyer accepts a single offer, a collision is declared and the goods are offered again at a price raised by a certain percentage. If only one buyer accepts the offer, their credit status is checked. If their credit status is good, the fish is sold, but if the buyer cannot afford the goods they are penalised and the goods are offered again at the original price. The interaction involved in this fish market example can be characterised by our framework in the following way:

1. The auctioneer, agent A, is motivated to sell the box of fish for a price, p, that is above zero.
2. The current price, p_c, is set to the initial price, p_i.
3. Agent A **proposes** that the commodity is bought at p_c. This conditionally commits A to selling the commodity at p_c relative to the following conditions holding:
   (a) Only one acceptance is received for that commodity at p_c.
   (b) The credit status of the buyer is good.
4. All buying agents, $B_1 \ldots B_n$ respond with either **acceptance** or **rejection** of that proposal. Those agents that accept the proposal become committed to paying p_c for the commodity.
5. If more than one buyer accepts the proposal, the current price is set to $p_c + \delta p$, **deny** messages are sent to all the agents that accepted the proposal stating the collision as the reason. The procedure continues from 3.
6. If a single buyer, B_i, accepts the proposal, but their credit status is bad, then a **deny** message is sent to that agent stating its bad credit status as the reason. The current price is set to p_i, and the procedure continues from 3.
7. If a single buyer, B_i, accepts the proposal, and their credit status is good, then A **confirms** that it is committed to selling the commodity at p_c to B_i. A and B_i are now jointly committed to an agreement in which the box of fish is sold for p_c.

Widget buying This example extends that used in the introduction to section 2. Consider the agents W and V that are both motivated to buy a quantity of widgets from one of the suppliers A or B. Both A and B are motivated to sell widgets. In this situation, typically W or V will initiate negotiation with a proposal. In contrast with the fish market example, agents A and B are at liberty to counter-propose an alternative agreement, which may itself be modified, etc. Ideally, negotiation will converge on an agreement, but this may only be possible in restricted circumstances [17]. Furthermore, suppose that the agents have not agreed in advance on a specific negotiation protocol. Thus, the agents must explicitly specify the conditions under which they are committed when making either a proposal or counter-proposal.

Suppose that agent W has no preference for either A or B's widgets, and so proposes an agreement to both A and B. However, W does not wish to over commit itself to the purchase of widgets. The condition under which these proposals are made is that it will commit to the first agent to accept the offer. If both A and B accept their respective proposals, but A is first to accept, then W will be committed to the agreement proposed, but not to B since B's acceptance came after A's. Making an offer under this condition also serves to put time pressure on A and B, which is often a good negotiation strategy [15]. However for W to get the best deal when negotiating with a number of service providers, it must ensure that all pending proposals relate to agreements that are equally good, and that subsequent proposals to an agent monotonically decrease in their subjective value to W. For example, if W is negotiating only on price, then each of its pending proposals should specify the same price, and subsequent proposals should specify a higher price.[5]

Suppose that agent A has no preference for either W or V, and has a supply of widgets that will only satisfy one of these potential customers. In such a situation, it may be wise for A to commit to the provision of widgets to either W or V on the condition that sufficient widgets are available to meet the agreement. This will ensure that A is not over committed to providing widgets, and thus not liable to any penalties associated with reneging on a commitment.

The choice of the commitment conditions used will depend on an agent's knowledge about the availability of resources, time pressures on the agent, and whether the agent is a service consumer or provider. For example, agent A may be negotiating with W and V, both of which require widgets. If V is a regular and valued customer and W is relatively unknown, A may use different conditions in proposing an agreement for the supply of widgets for these two agents; conditions that are more favourable to V. For instance, A may propose to V a price for the widgets required on the condition that V accepts before t_i, and make a proposal to W on the condition that, after t_i, there is sufficient stock to meet W's requirements. Thus, the formulation presented here is sufficiently flexible to capture various negotiation scenarios in both restricted and open domains.

4 Related work

Cohen et al. [5] build on their theory of joint commitment [4] to investigate the semantics of communicative acts for the generation of agent teams that are bound by

---

[5] Determining the subjective value of a proposal is not so simple when more than one variable is being considered (e.g. price, delivery time, and quality). However, the evaluation and generation of proposals and counter-proposals is outside the scope of this paper, see Sierra *et al.* [17] for a discussion.

joint commitment. Requests and assertions are defined. A request generates a "persistent weak achievement goal" in the speaker, which commits the speaker to the goal with respect to the team to which the request is directed. It is shown that if the recipient responds to a request by acceding to that request, a state of joint commitment is generated.

Haddadi [8, chapter 3] uses pre-commitment as a basis for formalising the generation of joint commitments. In her theory, an agent x is "pre-committed" to delegating a task ψ to agent y if x sees a "potential for cooperation" with y in achieving φ such that y achieves ψ (which goes some way to achieving φ), and x wants y to achieve ψ. Conversely, y is pre-committed to agent x in adopting ψ if y sees a "potential for cooperation" with x such that y achieves ψ (which goes some way to achieving φ), and y is willing to achieve ψ. An agent (either the task delegator, x, or the task adopter, y) will then become committed to the adopter doing ψ in the context of the goal φ, if it is pre-committed to ψ, and believes that the other is either pre-committed, or committed to ψ. This formalism is then used to specify a protocol through which agents may generate joint commitments for cooperative action [8, chapter 4].

Both of these specifications provide mechanisms through which joint commitment may be generated in restricted circumstances. An agent may only negotiate the delegation of a task with one team or agent at a time without being in danger of being over committed. Suppose that agent x wishes to delegate the task t to either y or y', and it sees a potential for cooperation with both. According to the definition of precommitment, for the agent to suggest to both y and y' that t is adopted, it must both want that y and y' adopt t (this is not possible). An agent cannot negotiate for the delegation of a task simply because it wants that task to be adopted by *any* other agent. Furthermore, if it is possible for an agent to become pre-committed to more than one other agent, it will be in danger of becoming over committed because pre-commitment is unconditional. Cohen et al.'s persistent weak achievement goal is also unconditional; if an agent accedes to a request, a state of joint commitment is generated. Therefore, within both these frameworks, an agent may only negotiate with one team or agent. In contrast, our specification provides a mechanism through which agents may negotiate with more than one agent at a time in generating states of joint commitment.

5 Conclusions and future work

This paper has discussed the nature of agreements between agents that are generated through negotiation, and how these agreements may be generated and committed to. A state of *conditional commitment* has been proposed as an intermediary state, through which agents may generate joint commitment. The communicative actions "propose" and "counter-propose" are then defined in terms of a conditional commitment to the proposed agreement. This enables the recipient of a proposal to commit to the agreement in the confidence that the proposer will also be committed if the conditions specified, either explicitly in the proposal or by the context of negotiation, hold. A state of joint commitment then holds once a proposal has been accepted and the proposer's commitment confirmed. The contribution of this paper is that it shows how both the generation and execution of agreements can be made more flexible. The notion of conditional commitment provides an agent with the flexibility to negotiate with a number of other agents for the same purpose without being in danger of over committing itself. The specification of agreements as rights provides an agent with the flexibility to choose whether or not to exercise its rights, and not be bound by a rigid plan of action.

The preliminary results presented here require further development. At present we are developing a concrete formalisation of rights and agreements motivated by the flexibility requirements set out in this paper. With this basis, the semantics of the communicative acts "propose", "accept", "confirm", etc. may be fully specified. Such a complete theory of the generation of joint commitment will provide a sound basis for the development of practical applications, and the empirical evaluation of these control states within a multi-agent system.

References

1. M. Barbuceanu and M. S. Fox. COOL: A language for describing coordination in multi-agent systems. In *Proc. 1st Int. Conf. on Multi-Agent Systems*, pages 17–24, San Fransisco, CA, 1995.

2. C. Castelfranchi. Commitments: For individual intentions to groups and organisations. In *Proc. 1st Int. Conf. on Multi-Agent Systems*, pages 41–48, 1995.

3. P. R. Cohen and H. J. Levesque. Intention is choice with commitment. *Artif. Intell.*, 42:213–61, 1990.

4. P. R. Cohen and H. J. Levesque. Rational interaction as the basis for communication. In P. R. Cohen, J. Morgan, and M. E. Pollack, editors, *Intentions in Communication*, pages 221–255. MIT Press, 1990.

5. P. R. Cohen, H. J. Levesque, and I. A. Smith. On team formation. In J. Hintikka and R. Tuomela, editors, *Contemporary Action Theory*. Synthese, In Press.

6. Foundation for Intelligent Physical Agents, Agent Management Technical Committee. *Agent communication language*, 1997. http://drogo.cselt.it/fipa/.

7. B. J. Grosz and S. Kraus Collaborative plans for complex group action. *Artif. Intell.*, 86(2):269–357, 1996.

8. A. Haddadi. *Communication and cooperation in agent systems: A pragmatic approach*, volume 1056 of *Lecture Notes in Artificial Intelligence*. Springer-Verlag, 1996.

9. N. R. Jennings. Commitments and conventions: The foundations of coordination in multi-agent systems. *Knowledge Engineering Review*, 8(3):223–250, 1993.

10. N. R. Jennings, P. Faratin, M. J. Johnson, T. J. Norman, P. O'Brien, and M. E. Wiegand. Agent-based business process management. *Int. J. of Cooperative Information Systems*, 5:105–130, 1996.

11. S. Kalenka and N. R. Jennings. On social attitudes: A preliminary report. In *Proc. 1st Int. Workshop on Decentralised Intelligent and Multi-Agent Systems*, pages 233–240, Krakov, Poland, 1995.

12. Y. Labrou and T. Finin. A semantics approach for KQML—a general purpose communication language for software agents. In *Proc. 3rd Int. Conf. on Information and Knowledge Management*, 1994.

13. H. J. Müller. Negotiation principles. In G. M. P. O'Hare and N. R. Jennings, editors, *Foundations of Distributed Artificial Intelligence*, pages 211–229. Wiley, 1996.

14. M. E. Pollack. The uses of plans. *Artif. Intell.*, 57:43–68, 1992.

15. D. G. Pruitt. *Negotiation behaviour*. Academic Press, 1981.

16. J. A. Rodríguez, P. Noriega, C. Sierra, and J. Padget. FM96.5 A Java-based electronic auction house. In *Proc. 2nd Int. Conf. on the Practical Applications of Intelligent Agents and Multi-Agent Technology (PAAM-97)*, London, U.K., 1997.

17. C. Sierra, P. Faratin, and N. R. Jennings. A service-oriented negotiation model between autonomous agents. In *Proc. 8th Int. Workshop on Modelling Autonomous Agents in a Multi-Agent World*, volume 1237 of *Lecture Notes in Artificial Intelligence*, pages 17–35, Ronneby, Sweden, 1997. Springer-Verlag.

18. I. A. Smith and P. R. Cohen. Toward a semantics for an agent communication language based on speech-acts. In *Proc. 13th National Conf. on Artificial Intelligence (AAAI-96)*, Portland, Oregon, 1996.

19. R. G. Smith and R. Davis. Frameworks for cooperation in distributed problem solving. *IEEE Trans. on Systems, Man and Cybernetics*, 11(1):61–70, 1981.

20. D. R. Traum and J. F. Allen. Discourse obligations in dialogue processing. In *Proc. 32nd Annual Meeting of the Association for Computational Linguistics*, pages 1–8, Las Cruces, NM, 1994.

21. M. Wooldridge and N. R. Jennings. Intelligent agents: Theory and practice. *Knowledge Engineering Review*, 10(2):115–152, 1995.

22. M. Wooldridge and N. R. Jennings. Towards a Theory of Cooperative Problem Solving. In *Proc. 6th European Workshop on Modelling Autonomous Agents in Multi-Agent Worlds*, pages 15–26, Odense, Denmark, 1994.

Social Co-ordination Among Autonomous Problem-Solving Agents[*]

Sascha Ossowski and Ana García-Serrano

Department of Artificial Intelligence
Technical University of Madrid
Campus de Montegancedo s/n
28660 Boadilla del Monte
Madrid, Spain
Tel: (+34-1) 336-7390; Fax: (+34-1) 352-4819
{ossowski, agarcia}@isys.dia.fi.upm.es

Abstract. Co-ordination is the glue that binds the activities of autonomous problem-solving agents together into a functional whole. Co-ordination mechanisms for distributed problem-solving usually rely on a central co-ordinator that orchestrates agent behaviour or just replicate a centralised mechanism among many agents. Social co-ordination is a decentralised mechanism, in which the mutual adaptation of the behaviour of autonomous agents emerges from the interrelation of the agents' self-interests. The few existent models of social co-ordination are based either on sociologic or on economic findings. Still, they usually refer to heterogeneous agent societies and are rarely concerned with the co-ordination of problem-solving activities. In this paper we present a formal framework that unifies the sociological and the economic approach to decentralised social co-ordination. We show how this model can be used to determine the outcome of decentralised social co-ordination within distributed problem-solving systems and illustrate this by an example.

1 Introduction

Co-ordination is an issue on the research agenda of a variety of scientific disciplines. Research in Social Sciences is primarily *analytic*: the social scientist observes the outside world and builds a model of how human agents mutually adapt their activities as part of societies or organisations. Within Distributed Artificial Intelligence (DAI), however, the interest is *constructive*. In the sub-area of Distributed Problem-solving (DPS) a central designer constructs interaction patterns among benevolent agents, so as to make them efficiently achieve a common goal. Multiagent Systems (MAS) research is concerned with how desired global properties can be instilled within heterogeneous groups of autonomous agents, that pursue partially conflicting goals in an *autonomous* (self-interested) fashion [6]. Either way, findings from social science are used as sources of metaphors and tools to *build* systems of *artificial* agents that show some desired coherent global behaviour. A prominent example is the *society metaphor* [15] that suggests to conceive a multiagent system as a society of autonomous agents.

---

[*] This work was partially supported by the Human Capital and Mobility Program (HCM) of the European Union, contract ERBCHBICT941611, and by CDTI through project 01594-PC019 (BIOS)

Models of co-ordination in DPS systems usually rely on a special agent that orchestrates the behaviour of its acquaintances with respect to some common group goal. Agents send their individual plans to a single co-ordinator, which detects potential plan interdependencies, adapts some individual plans accordingly and sends the modified plans back to the agents for execution [10]. In terms of the society metaphor, this approach describes an *individual intelligence* that makes use of social resources. Distributed approaches to co-ordination within DPS do without a central co-ordinator. Agents develop joint goals and pursue joint intentions, which constitute (potentially different views of) the same multiagent plan *iterated* among agents (e.g. distributed planning models [5]). Still, in terms of the society metaphor these approaches just constitute a *replication* of a centralised individual intelligence [2].

Decentralised co-ordination mechanisms are being investigated primarily within the area of MAS, as the heterogeneous nature of agent systems makes the implementation of a centralised mechanism impossible [4]. *Social co-ordination* is such a decentralised process, in which the mutual adaptation of the behaviour of autonomous agents emerges from the interrelation of the agents' self-interests: its outcome is a comprise, an "equilibrium", that results from the agents' individually rational actions in a multiagent environment. Two major approaches exist to model social co-ordination:

- In the *sociologic* approach, an agent's position in society is expressed by means of qualitative relations of dependence [2, 16]. Such dependence relations imply a social dependence network, which determines "how" and "with whom" an autonomous agent co-ordinates its actions. The sociologic approach makes explicit the structure of society as the driving force of the co-ordination process, but is also ambiguous due to usually fuzzy formulations of the underlying notions.
- The *economic* approach [12] models an agent's situation within the group by means of a utility function, which quantitatively measures the "benefits" that it obtains from different ways of co-ordinating its behaviour with the group. Although many important features of agents, society and the environment are hidden in the utility function, this approach has the advantage of being grounded in the well developed mathematical framework of game theory.

We have developed a decentralised social co-ordination mechanism within societies of autonomous problem-solving agents, called *structural co-operation* [11, 9]. This mechanism uses the sociologic approach to model the structure of the agent society, while it borrows from the economic approach to account for the social co-ordination process that this structure implies. By means of prescriptions the society structure is modified, in order to make the social co-ordination process instrumental with respect to a problem to solve [9]. In this paper, we are concerned with the theoretical basis of this mechanism. We present a formal framework that unifies the sociological and the economic approach to social co-ordination, maintaining the expressiveness of the former and the conciseness of the latter. We show how this framework allows us to determine the outcome of decentralised social co-ordination within DPS systems.

Section 2 describes the class of domains that we are concerned with and introduces an example scenario that we will use for illustrative purposes throughout the rest of the paper. In section 3 we model the structural relations that arise in these domains in the tradition of the sociologic approach and discuss the problems that come up when trying to capture the "dynamics" of social co-ordination on this basis. Section 4 maps this model to the economic framework which allows us to determine the outcome of social co-ordination computationally. Finally, we discuss related work in section 5 and present conclusions and future work in section 6.

2 Social Co-ordination in Dynamic Domains

Many real-world domains are highly dynamic: perceptions are error-prone, actions fail, contingencies occur. One common way to deal with this problem is to build systems that only plan their actions for a short-time horizon, in order to assess the effects of their interventions as early as possible and to adapt future behaviour accordingly [3]. When such systems are modelled on the basis of a multiagent architecture, two essential constraints have to be taken into account: first, agents need to cope with the fact that their plans and actions interfere because they share an environment that provides only a limited amount of resources; second, agents should be prepared to consider actions that attain their goals only partially due to resource limitation and environmental contingencies.

Although we use a rather simple example domain to illustrate our ideas, the formalism to be presented in the sequel captures important features of the aforementioned class of systems [3]. A model for a single-agent system is presented first. The resulting notions are extended to the multiagent case in section 2.2. Finally, the concept social co-ordination is placed in this context.

2.1 A Single-agent World

Let S be a set of *world states* and Π a finite set of *plans*. The execution of a plan π changes the state of the world which is modelled as a partially defined mapping

$$res: \ \Pi \times S \rightarrow S \ .$$

A plan is *executable* in s, if only if π is defined for a certain world state s, fact which we express formally by the predicate $exec(\pi,s)$. At least one *empty plan* π_ε is required to be included in the set of plans Π; it is modelled as identity.

An agent α acts in the world thereby modifying its state. It is defined by the following three notions:

- a set $\Pi_\alpha \subset \Pi$, determining the *individual plans* that α is able to execute. An agent α is always capable of executing the empty plan π_ε. If α is capable of executing plan π in situation s, we also write $prep_s(\alpha, \pi)$;
- a set $I_\alpha \subset S$ of *ideal states* of α, expressing the states that the agent would ideally like to bring about;
- a *metric* d_α that maps two states to a real number, representing agent α's estimation of "how far" one state is away from another. It usually models the notion of (relative) "difficulty" to bring about changes between world states.

Although an agent usually cannot fully reach an ideal state, the ideal states I_α together with the distance measure d_α describe an agent's preferences respecting the states of the world, so they are called its *motivation*.

The above definitions will be illustrated by a scenario within the *synchronous blocks domain* [9], which is an extension of the well known blocks world. There is a table of unlimited size and four numbered blocks. Blocks can be placed either directly on the table or on top of another block, and there is no limit to the height of a stack of blocks. The only operation that can be performed is to place a block x on top of some block y (formally: $move(x,y)$), which requires x and y to be clear. There is a clock that marks each instant of time by a tic. A *plan* of length k is a sequence of k operations performed successively at tics. Instead of an operation, a plan may contain a NOP, indicating that nothing is done at a certain tic.

In our example we assume that an agent is capable of executing plans of length 2. Its ideal state corresponds to some configuration of blocks. The distance between two states s_1 and s_2 is given by the length of the shortest plan that transforms s_1 into s_2.

2.2 A Multi-agent World

We are now concerned with a world which is inhabited by a set A of agents. Each $\alpha \in A$ is of the structure defined above. The set of ideal states as well as the metric can be different among the agents in A: agents may have different (partially conflicting) ideal states and may even measure the distance between states in different scales.

In such a multiagent world, the agents act at the same time and in the same environment, so we need to introduce an account of simultaneous, interdependent action. The set of k-multi-plans M_k is the disjointed union of k agents' sets of individual plans:

$$M_k = \Pi_1 \dot\cup ... \dot\cup \Pi_n .$$

A k-multi-plan $\mu \in M_k$ is intended to model the simultaneous execution of the individual plans of the involved agents. We use the commutative operator $\circ$ to denote the creation of a multi-plan, indistinctively of whether its arguments are individual plans or multi-plans.[1] The partial function res is easily extended to k-multi-plans

$$res: M_k \times S \to S .$$

A k-multi-plan μ is *executable* in situation s (formally: $exec(\mu,s)$), if only if res is defined in s. Otherwise some of its "component plans" are *incompatible*, i.e. they are physically impossible to execute simultaneously. The empty plan π_ε is compatible with any k-multi-plan and does not affect its outcome. The n-multi-plan comprising individual plans of all n agents out of A is just termed multi-plan and the set of all multi-plans is denoted by M.

The notions of capability for executing a multi-plan is also a natural extension of the single agent case: a set A_k of k agents is capable of executing a k-multi-plan μ, if there is an assignment such that every agent is to execute exactly one individual plan and this agent is capable of doing so, i.e. there is a bijective mapping ψ from individual plans to agents, such that

$$prep_s(A,\mu) \iff \forall \pi \in \mu.\ prep_s(\psi(\pi),\pi) .$$

In the synchronous blocks domain described above we define the result of a k-multi-plan μ to be the "sum" of the effects of the k component plans π. Still, if the component plans "interact" the following rules apply:

- two component plans are incompatible, if agents try to access the same block at one tic, either by moving it away or by stacking another block on top of it. In this case, the multi-plan μ is not executable.
- two component plans are incompatible if one agent obstructs a block that the other's plan uses at a later tic. Again, the multi-plan μ is not executable.
- in much the same way, one agent can move blocks in a manner that enables another to enact a plan that was impossible to execute without these effects. Being subject to the restrictions outlined above, the result of the multi-plan μ is the "sum" of operations of the agents' plans;

As an example, consider the synchronous blocks domain described above and the scenario shown in Figure 1. There are two agents: α_1 and α_2. The former can move all

---

[1] So, we write for instance $\mu = \pi \circ \pi' = \pi' \circ \pi = \{\pi, \pi'\}$ and $\mu \circ \pi'' = \pi'' \circ \mu = \{\pi, \pi', \pi''\}$

blocks but block 4, while the latter may manipulate all blocks but block 3. The initial situation, the agents' ideal states and their individual assessment of the distance between them is given in Figure 1.

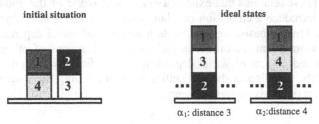

Figure 1. A scenario in the synchronous blocks domain

Table 1 shows some plans in this scenario, the capability of the agents to enact them and their executability in the initial situation s_0. The multi-plans (π_1,π_4), (π_4,π_9) and (π_3,π_4), for instance, lead to the world states shown in Figure 4.

Plan	Operations	$prep_s(\alpha,\pi)$	$exec(\pi,s_0)$
π_1	$[move(2,table),move(3,2)]$	α_1	true
π_3	$[move(2,table),NOP]$	α_1, α_2	true
π_4	$[move(1,table),NOP]$	α_1, α_2	true
π_9	$[move(2,table),move(4,2)]$	α_2	false
π_{10}	$[move(1,2),move(4,1)]$	α_2	true
π_{11}	$[move(2,1), move(3,2)]$	α_1	true
π_ε	$[NOP,NOP]$	α_1, α_2	true

Table 1. Some individual plans

2.3 Social Co-ordination

In a single-agent scenario, an autonomous agent will choose that plan, among the plans that it is capable of executing and which are executable in the current situation, whose execution brings it as close as possible to some ideal state. Still, in a multiagent world agents need to co-ordinate their choices, as not just the effects of an agent's plans but also the "side-effects" of the plans of its acquaintances become relevant.

The essential idea underlying social co-ordination in such a scenario is that the less others can influence the outcome of an agent's plan and the more it can manipulate the results of the plans of others, the better is its position in society. When discussing a potential agreement concerning the co-ordination of individual plans, the preferences of an agent in a better position will have more weight; if an agreement is reached, it will be biased towards that agent. From the standpoint of an external observer, we can conceive the *outcome* of social co-ordination as the multi-plan which the individual plans executed by each agent imply – independently of whether this multi-plan is the consequence of an agreement among agents or if it is the result of local individual choice. In the synchronous blocks example, this boils down to the question of which pair of individual plans will be enacted. The rest of the paper is dedicated to the development of a computational model of this notion.

3 A Sociologic Approach to Model Social Co-ordination

In line with the sociological approach, in this section we present a model of the different qualitative relations that exist in a multiagent world of the above characteristics. We first introduce a collection of plan relations that capture objective domain characteristics. On this basis, we contribute a new set of social dependence relations, expressing how one agent can influence the outcome of actions of others. Identifying different types and degrees of social dependence, we define the notion of dependence structure. Finally, we discuss the difficulties when modelling the *dynamics* of social co-ordination on the basis of these concepts.

3.1 Relations Between Plans

In our model, in a situation s a plan π can be in four mutually exclusive qualitative relations to a multi-plan μ:

$$indifferent_s(\pi,\mu) \quad \Leftrightarrow \quad \big(exec(\pi,s) \wedge exec(\pi \circ \mu,s) \wedge res(\pi \circ \mu,s) = res(\pi,s)\big)$$
$$\vee \; \big(\neg exec(\pi,s) \wedge \neg exec(\pi \circ \mu,s)\big)$$
$$interferent_s(\pi,\mu) \quad \Leftrightarrow \quad exec(\pi,s) \wedge exec(\pi \circ \mu,s) \wedge res(\pi \circ \mu,s) \neq res(\pi,s)$$
$$complementary_s(\pi,\mu) \quad \Leftrightarrow \quad \neg exec(\pi,s) \wedge exec(\pi \circ \mu,s)$$
$$inconsistent_s(\pi,\mu) \quad \Leftrightarrow \quad exec(\pi,s) \wedge \neg exec(\pi \circ \mu,s)$$

The multi-plan μ is *indifferent* with respect to π if the execution of μ does not affect π at all. This is obviously the case when both are executable and the parallel enactment leads to the same state of the world. Alternatively, π is indifferent to μ if the former is not executable and the execution of the latter does not remedy this problem. In the blocks example, for instance, π_e is indifferent to π_3 and π_9.

The plan μ is *interferent* with π if π is executable alone as well as in conjunction with μ, but the two alternatives lead to different world states. In the example, π_3 is interferent with π_4. We cannot distinguish between positive and negative interference here, because the relations described are objective, while the comparison of two states on the basis of preference is the result of a subjective attitude pertinent only to agents.

Complementarity of μ with respect to π is given, when π is not executable alone, but in conjunction with μ it is. The idea is that there is a "gap" in the plan π, i.e. some action is missing or the preconditions of some action are not achieved within the plan, and μ fills that gap by executing the missing action or bringing about the lacking world features. In the example, π_4 is complementary to π_9.

Finally, the plan μ is *incompatible* with π if π is executable alone but not in conjunction with μ. This is the case for π_{10} and π_{11}.

3.2 Social Relations Between Agents

This paragraph turns the attention to the social side of the above notions: we derive social relations between agents from objective relations between plans. An agent is in a social relation with others, if the outcome of its plans is influenced by the options that the latter choose. The agent depends on its acquaintances in order to assure a certain effectivity level of its plans.

One parameter of plan effectivity is an agent's degree of preference respecting its plan's outcome. We derive this notion of preference as follows: for an agent α, a world state s is more preferred than s', if it is closer to some ideal state than s', i.e.

$$s' \prec_\alpha s \quad \Leftrightarrow \quad \exists \bar{s} \in I_\alpha \; \forall \bar{s}' \in I_\alpha \quad d_\alpha(s,\bar{s}) < d_\alpha(s',\bar{s}')$$

On this basis, four mutually exclusive social relations of an agent α and its individual plan π with respect to a group of agents A and their multi-plan μ can be defined:

$$prevents_s(\alpha, \pi, A, \mu) \quad \Leftrightarrow \quad prep_s(\alpha, \pi) \wedge prep_s(A, \mu) \wedge inconsistent_s(\pi, \mu)$$

$$enables_s(\alpha, \pi, A, \mu) \quad \Leftrightarrow \quad prep_s(\alpha, \pi) \wedge prep_s(A, \mu) \wedge complementary_s(\pi, \mu)$$

$$hinders_s(\alpha, \pi, A, \mu) \quad \Leftrightarrow \quad prep_s(\alpha, \pi) \wedge prep_s(A, \mu) \wedge interferent_s(\pi, \mu) \wedge$$
$$res(\pi \circ \mu) \prec_\alpha res(\pi)$$

$$favours_s(\alpha, \pi, A, \mu) \quad \Leftrightarrow \quad prep_s(\alpha, \pi) \wedge prep_s(A, \mu) \wedge interferent_s(\pi, \mu) \wedge$$
$$res(\pi) \prec_\alpha res(\pi \circ \mu)$$

Both, agent α and the group μ, need to be capable of executing their plans in order that a social relation exists between them. Under this condition, the different types of relations are given as follows:

- prevention: the execution of agent α's plan π can be prevented by the concurrent execution of the multi-plan μ. So, decisions of the agents in A concern α in so far as they can bring down its individual plan π;
- enabling: the execution of agent α's plan π can be enabled by the simultaneous execution of the multi-plan μ. So, decisions of the agents in A can make it possible for α to enact its individual plan π, which is impossible for it individually;
- hindrance: the execution of agent α's plan π interferes with the execution of the multi-plan μ by the agents in A. The decisions of the agents in A can hinder π to be fully effective in the eyes of α;
- favour: again, the execution of agent α's plan π interferes with the concurrent execution of the multi-plan μ by the agents in A. Still, in case of this relation the decisions of the agents in A can influence positively in the effectiveness of π.

3.3 The Dependence Structure

We can now define the different *types* of social dependence between two agents:

$$feas - dep_s(\alpha, \pi, A) \quad \Leftrightarrow \quad \exists \mu. \; enables_s(\alpha, \pi, A, \mu) \vee prevents_s(\alpha, \pi, A, \mu)$$

$$neg - dep_s(\alpha, \pi, A) \quad \Leftrightarrow \quad \exists \mu. \; hinders_s(\alpha, \pi, A, \mu)$$

$$pos - dep_s(\alpha, \pi, A) \quad \Leftrightarrow \quad \exists \mu. \; favours_s(\alpha, \pi, A, \mu)$$

There is a feasibility-dependence (*feas-dep*) of agent α for a plan π with respect to a set of agents A if A can invalidate the plan, i.e. if they can turn down the execution of π. In the example, each agent is in a feasibility-dependence to the other for all plans shown in Table 1 except π_e. Agent α is negatively dependent (*neg-dep*) for a plan π with respect to A, if A can deviate the outcome of the plan to a state that is less preferred by α. If A can bring about a change in the outcome of α's plan π that α welcomes, then α is positively-dependent (*pos-dep*) on A. In Table 1, each agent depends positively on the other for π_3 and π_4. Note that we do not distinguish between enabling and preventing dependence, because in both cases the group A can decide to make it impossible for α to execute π.

These different *types* also imply different *degrees* of social dependence. Figure 1 depicts our intuitive notion of the *degree* of dependence of an agent α on a group of acquaintances A with respect to a plan π. Feasibility-dependence is the strongest relation as the agents in A can turn down the execution of π; *neg-dep* implies a social dependence of medium level, because the acquaintances can do something "bad" to the effectivity of the plan; finally, positive dependence is the weakest, as the worst option that the acquaintances can choose is *not* to do something "good" to plan effectivity.

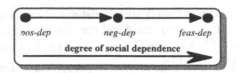

Figure 2. Degrees of social dependence

All this information is contained in the *social dependence structure*. For any given situation *s* the *dependence structure* is defined by a triple of the form

$$DepStruct_s = (feas\text{-}dep, neg\text{-}dep, pos\text{-}dep).$$

3.4 Social Co-ordination Based on the Dependence Structure

It remains to be shown how the dependence structure influences in the process of mutual adaptation of the individual plans. The multiplan which emerges from this process is the result of social co-ordination.

The plan selection process in a single agent world is straightforward: an agent will execute the plan that takes it as close as possible to an ideal state. Still, in a multiagent world the effectivity of an individual plan does not only depend on its effects, but also on plans that other agents execute (as long as they are not in an *indifferent* relation). So, an agent would like the acquaintances that it socially depends on to execute some of their individual plans or to refrain from enacting others. As autonomous agents are non-benevolent and self-interested, this can just be done in the frame of *social exchange*, i.e. in situations of reciprocal dependence, where all involved agents have the potential to influence the outcome of the others' plans. The object of exchange is "immaterial": agents mutually make commitments respecting properties of the individual plans that they will execute. Ideally, the process of social co-ordination passes through various stages of exchanges until (dis-)agreement is stated and each agents selects its most preferred plan that complies with its commitments.

Still, there is a variety of problems in determining the kind and the sequence of such exchanges. Here are just some of them:

- The "exchange value" of commitments is to be defined. For instance, is the promise not to make use of two *hinders* relation more valuable then the commitment to refrain from realising an *invalidates* relation ?
- In case of cyclic dependence, apparently irrational bilateral exchanges can become beneficial in the frame of a "bigger" exchange involving many agents. The question is whether every time an agent aims to make a bilateral exchange it needs to consider all other possible exchanges with *k* agents before.
- An agent may want to revoke previously made commitments, when it notices that it may get a "better" reciprocation from another agent. The question is when an agent should try to de-commit and how much it will have to "pay" for this.

In resource-bounded domains it seems difficult to solve these problems on the basis of merely qualitative notions. In the sequel, we show how they can be overcome by applying the economic approach to social co-ordination.

4 An Economic Approach to Implement Social Co-ordination

In this section we relate the qualitative model presented in the last section to a quantitative framework. We first develop a mapping from our problem domain to a bargaining scenario as defined by game theory. Drawing from findings in axiomatic bargaining theory, we model the outcome of social co-ordination and sketch a distributed algorithm capable of determining it.

4.1 Social Co-ordination as a Bargaining Scenario

In the following we present a quantitative model of agent co-operation and conflict. On this basis, we define a bargaining scenario that "corresponds" to the problem of social co-ordination and compare it to the sociological model presented in section 3.

Modelling Co-operation

We first need to introduce a quantitative notion of preference over *agreements*. When agents aim to bring about ideal states, their preferences for a world state s are expressed by its distance to some ideal state, which can be written as

$$|s|_\alpha = \min\{d_\alpha(s,\bar{s}) \mid \bar{s} \in I_\alpha\} .$$

On this basis we can define a quantitative preference over multi-plans. Let X denote the set of compatible multi-plans. The utility for an agent α_i of a compatible multi-plan $\mu \in X$ is given by

$$U_i(\mu) = |s|_{\alpha_i} - |res(\mu,s)|_{\alpha_i} .$$

Note that the utility function is undefined for plans which are not executable in a given situation. The utilities that each agent obtains from a multi-plan can be comprised in a vector. For instance, the utility vectors of multi-plans (π_1,π_4), (π_4,π_9) and (π_3,π_4) from our example are $(2,1)$, $(0,3)$ and $(1,2)$ respectively. The set of utility vectors that are realisable over X is denoted by $U(X)$.

When agents have different points of view respecting which multi-plan to agree upon, they may "flip a coin" in order to choose between alternative agreements. A certain probability distribution over the set of compatible multi-plans is called a *mixed multi-plan*. Let m be the cardinality of the set of compatible multi-plans X, then a mixed multi-plan is a m-dimensional vector

$$\sigma = (p_1,...,p_m), \ 0 \leq p_i \leq 1, \ \sum_{i=1}^m p_i = 1 .$$

The set of mixed multi-plans is denoted by Σ. We extend the notion of utility for compatible multi-plans to mixed multi-plans in a standard fashion: the *expected* utility of a mixed multi-plan $\sigma \in \Sigma$ is given by the sum of each compatible multi-plan's utility weighed by its probability:

$$U_i(\sigma) = \sum_{k=1}^m p_k U_i(\mu_k) .$$

The set of expected utility vectors that are realisable over Σ is denoted by $U(\Sigma)$. Some simple mathematics prove that $U(\Sigma)$ is actually the convex and closed hull of $U(X)$, i.e. $U(\Sigma) = cch(U(X))$ [18]. In the two agent case (a plane), this is always a convex polygon, with the vertices corresponding to utilities of some compatible multi-plans.

Modelling Conflict

So far, a quantitative preference relation of different kinds of agreements over multi-plans has been modelled for each agent. When agents co-ordinate their strategies and agree on some mixed multi-plan, the corresponding vector of utilities is what each agent expects to obtain. Still, agents are autonomous and not forced to co-operate. So they can decide to take a chance alone, without limiting their freedom of choice by some binding agreement. So, it remains to model what happens in case of conflict.

Therefore, the existence of a conflict multi-plan and a conflict utility vector is assumed. A common way to choose these parameters is to take the agents' "security levels", which correspond to the maximum utility that an agent can achieve regardless of what its acquaintances do. We will apply a similar idea here: in a conflict situation the *response* of the set of agents A to a single agent α's plan π is the multi-plan μ that they are capable of executing and that minimises α's utility from $\pi \circ \mu$, i.e.

$$response_s(\pi, \alpha_i, \mu, A) \iff \mu = \min_{U_i(\pi \circ \mu')} \{\mu' \in X \mid prep_s(\mu', A)\} \ .$$

So, we suppose that in case of disagreement an agent must account for the unpleasant situation that all its acquaintances jointly try to harm it. As the possibility of reaching an incompatible multi-plan has to be excluded, α can only choose from the set $FEAS_s(\alpha)$ of plans that are feasible regardless what others do:

$$FEAS_s(\alpha) \equiv \{\pi \in \Pi \mid \forall A. \ \neg feas - dep(\alpha, \pi, A)\}$$

This set is never empty: at least the empty plan π_ε is contained in $FEAS_s(\alpha)$ by definition. Agent α will choose the plan π out of $FEAS_s(\alpha)$, that maximises its individual utility value when combined with the response from its acquaintances. This is called the *conflict utility* of the agent α:

$$U_i^d = \max\{U_i(\pi \circ \mu) \in R \mid \pi \in FEAS_s(\alpha_i) \wedge response_s(\pi, \alpha_i, \mu, A)\} \ .$$

In the synchronous blocks world example, the only plan that α_1 can execute and which is guaranteed not to become incompatible is π_ε, which α_2 counters by π_{10}, resulting in a conflict utility of -2 for α_1. Agent α_2 also needs to choose π_ε in case of disagreement, to which α_1's most malicious response is to enact π_{11}, giving rise to a conflict utility of -1 for α_2.

The Associated Bargaining Scenario

We now outline how a bargaining scenario can be defined on the basis of the above notions. For this purpose, we define the overall conflict utility within a society of agents in a certain situation as the vector that comprises the individual conflict utility of each agent:

$$\vec{d} = (U_1^d, ..., U_n^d).$$

Furthermore, we will treat the conflict utility vector as an effectively reachable agreement, defining a set S such that

$$S = cch(U(X) \cup \{\vec{d}\}).$$

The set S usually equals $U(\Sigma)$, but may also be a (convex) superset of the latter. The *bargaining scenario* B associated with a social co-ordination problem is a pair

$$B = (S, \vec{d})$$

S is called the *bargaining set* and $\vec{d}$ the *disagreement point*. B complies with the formal properties of bargaining models, so the whole mathematical apparatus of bargaining theory becomes applicable [18].

In the two agent case, such a bargaining scenario can be represented in a plane, where each axis measures the utility of one agent. Figure 3 shows the graphical representation of our example from the synchronous blocks domain.

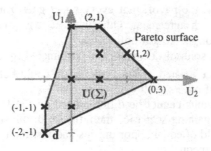

Figure 3. Graphical representation of the example scenario

Social Dependence Structure and Bargaining

We now observe how far the associated bargaining scenario relates to the notions of social dependence. First, and maybe surprisingly, it has to be noticed that the shape of the bargaining set is only correlated with the validity of plans: a utility vector belongs to the bargaining set if the corresponding multi-plan is executable. It is free of any reference to *social* relations between agents. A point in the bargaining set is not endowed with any "contextual attachment" that states which agents can actually decide whether it is reached or not. For instance, a utility vector $U(\pi \circ \pi') \in S$ may be a result of both an *enables*- or an *indifferent*-relation between π and π'.

Still, social relations *do* influence the choice of the disagreement point. The conflict utility d_i for an agent α_i is affected by social dependence relations as follows:

- *prevents*(α_i,π,A,μ): $U_i(\pi)$ cannot be used as conflict utility;
- *enables*(α_i,π,A,μ): $U_i(\pi)$ cannot be used as conflict utility;
- *hinders*(α_i,π,A,μ): just $U_i(\pi \circ \mu) < U_i(\pi)$ can be used as conflict utility;
- *favours*(α_i,π,A,μ): $U_i(\pi)$ can be used as conflict utility.

So, the potential conflict utility of a plan reflects precisely the degree of social dependence as depicted in Figure 2.

4.2 Determining the Outcome of Social Co-ordination

We have mapped the original problem to a bargaining scenario $(S, \vec{d})$. Now, we endeavour to find a solution to the scenario: a vector $\vec{\varphi} \in S$ needs to be singled out upon which a bargaining process – and the social co-ordination that it models – is supposed to converge. Bargaining theory provides answers to this question. Strategic bargaining theory takes a procedural approach to the problem, adhering to a sequential setting where agents alternate in making offers to each other in a pre-specified order and eventually converge on an agreement. By contrast, axiomatic models of bargaining take a declarative approach, postulating *axioms*, desirable properties of a bargaining solution, and then seeks the solution concept that satisfies them.

Applying the Nash Solution

In this section we adhere to the axiomatic approach and, in the follow-up of Nash's classical work [8], state the following five requirements for a "fair" solution to the bargaining scenario:

- *Individual rationality*: the payoff that every agent gets from a solution is bigger than its payoff from disagreement. Otherwise at least one agent would not co-operate in the solution, making it unfeasible.
- *Pareto-optimality*: a solution $\vec{\varphi}$ cannot be dominated by any other feasible outcome $\vec{x}$. If such an $\vec{x}$ existed, at least one agent could benefit from switching to it without the veto of others.
- *Symmetry*: if the agents cannot be differentiated on the basis of the information contained in the bargaining scenario, then the solution should treat them alike. Agents live in a world of equal opportunities and just their specific situation in society that introduces inequality.
- *Scale invariance*. The solution is invariant under affine transformations of the utility functions. This axiom captures the idea that utilities are a reflection of the reduction of distance between current and desired states, and that corresponding metrics among states can be different for every agent.
- *Contraction independence*. If new feasible outcomes are added to the bargaining problem but the disagreement point remains unchanged, then either the original solution does not change or it becomes one of the new outcomes.

It can be shown that the only utility vector $\vec{\varphi}$ that complies with the above axioms, maximises the *product* of gains from the disagreement point, i.e. the function:

$$N(\vec{x}) = \prod_{i=1}^{n} (x_i - d_i)$$

Obviously, $\vec{\varphi}$ always exists and is unique [18].

Figure 4 shows the three Pareto-optimal outcomes of plan execution in the synchronous blocks example. Some simple mathematics proves that the Nash solution to the synchronous blocks domain example is

$$\vec{\varphi} = (1,2) \ .$$

Consequently, the outcome of social co-ordination is to go for the "compromise" state in which all blocks are on the table, which can be reached by the multi-plan (π_3, π_4). Alternatively, agents can flip an equally weighed coin to choose between the multi-plans (π_1, π_4) and (π_4, π_9) that achieve the utility of $(2,1)$ and $(0,3)$ respectively.

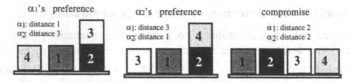

Figure 4. Efficient outcomes of the example scenario

Computing the Outcome of Social Co-ordination

As indicated in section 3.4, the process of social co-ordination can be seen as a sequence of exchanges between self-interested rational agents. Still, we are now endowed with a characterisation of the *outcome* of this process. So, as we are concerned with centrally designed problem-solving agents, there is no need to explicitly "simulate" the co-ordination process. Instead, the solution can be computed directly by a distributed algorithm. Within this algorithm agents may even behave benevolent, in a "selfless fashion"; the findings from the previous sections assure that its outcome corresponds to the result of social co-ordination among autonomous agents.

In the sequel, we will just sketch our distributed algorithm. It consists of three stages:

- Stage 1: asynchronous search for Pareto-optimality
  setting out from the local sets of alternative individual plans, agents repeatedly exchange messages, so as to determine the set of consistent multi-plans that are not dominated by any other. This is done in an asynchronous distributed fashion, that allows for local and temporarily incompatible views of the overall state.
- Stage 2: determination of the Nash bargaining outcome
  the agent that detects the termination of stage one plays the role of the leader in this stage. On the basis of the outcome of stage one it computes the (approximate) product-maximising solution in mixed multi-plans.
- Stage 3: probabilistic assignment of individual plans
  the leading agent generates a lottery in accordance with the outcome of stage 2 and urges its acquaintances to execute the corresponding individual plans accordingly.

The proof of correctness of the algorithm relies on the axioms of Pareto-optimality and contraction independence of the Nash bargaining solution. Further details can be found in [9].

5 Related Work

The roots of the sociological approach to agent interaction within Artificial Intelligence go back to Conte and Castelfranchi's Dependence Theory [2]. Still, the theory aims at a general model of autonomous agent behaviour, so that it remains rather abstract and is biased towards social simulation. Sichman and Demazeau's work has a stronger bias towards engineering [16, 17]. Agents enact plans, modelled as sequences of actions, which make use of resources in order to attain goals. To enact a plan an agent needs to be provided with the necessary resources and action capabilities. On this basis, a notion of social dependence between agents is defined: an agent may help an acquaintance by providing actions, resources or plans that the latter lacks in order to attain its goals. The theory does not comprise a notion of "resource limitation", i.e. an agent does not incur in any "cost" when providing resources or actions to others.

The approach presented in this paper, by contrast, does not explicitly model the "origin" of plan interrelations, but sees them as primitive notions which directly imply social dependence relations between the agents that are capable of enacting them. So, as our model accounts for different types of plan interrelations (including negative ones), it also comprises different types and degrees of dependence relations between agents. The reason for this divergence may be found in the fact that Sichman and Demazeau's approach aims at open systems, where synergistic potentials due to complementary agent knowledge and capabilities are common, the overall attainment of goals prevails over efficiency considerations, and it is hard to establish a generally agreed taxonomy of plan interrelations; by contrast, we are concerned with the co-ordination of societies of agents for the purpose of efficient problem-solving, where knowledge about the different types of interrelated action is just "built into" the agents and negative interaction due to the scarcity of resources is rather the rule but the exception.

The "economic" approach by Rosenschein and Zlotkin [12] shows many similarities to our model. This is not surprising as the roots of both approaches can be found in classical bargaining theory. Still, Rosenschein and Zlotkin apply it to heterogeneous agent societies, aiming at the design of a negotiation protocol that is resistant against strategic manipulation. By contrast, we use bargaining theory to "clarify" the outcome of social co-ordination as induced by the dependence structure, with the final aim of achieving co-ordination within (homogeneous) societies of problem-solving agents.

The latter objective is shared by Jennings and Campos: they seek guidelines for achieving social co-ordination in groups of autonomous *problem-solving* agents [7]. Still, they prefer to modify directly the concept of rationality, by designing agents to be *socially rational* (an agent just selects a certain behaviour when it is either beneficial for itself or for society). Some purely game theoretic approaches take a similar tack towards the problem. Brainov's notion of *altruism* is an example of these attempts to find behaviour guidelines that lie between self-interest and benevolence [1]. However, instead of directly referring to a new concept of (social) rationality, the approach presented in this paper uses the original utilitarian concept of rationality, but accounts for its indirect manipulation through the dependence structure of society.

6 Discussion

In this paper we have developed a formal model of the dependence structure that resource bounded domains imply in artificial agent societies. On this basis, we have shown how bargaining theory can be used to computationally determine the outcome of social co-ordination in societies of autonomous problem-solving agents. This process has been illustrated by an example.

The attempt to unify economical and sociological approaches to social co-ordination in one framework, using the theoretical basis of the latter to express the precise "meaning" of the former, is novel. Still, choosing classical bargaining theory as a vehicle for this formalisation entails a "price to be paid". Firstly, we assume that agents make joint *binding* agreements. Secondly, we do not account for the formation of coalitions. Finally, we assume agents to be perfectly rational. Still, as our aim is to build a decentralised co-ordination mechanism for *homogeneous* societies of problem-solving agents, these assumptions become less severe: law abidance can just be "build into" our artificial agents; by ignoring coalition formation, we have sacrificed some plausibility of our model in favour of efficiency, as coalition formation is a computationally complex process [14]. The assumption of perfect rationality is justified by the fact that there exists a sound axiomatic characterisation of a solution, which allows for its direct computation without an extensive "simulation" of the bargaining process; to our knowledge, there is no such set of axioms for bounded rationality [13].

On the basis of the framework presented in this paper we have developed the social co-ordination mechanism of *structural co-operation* among autonomous problem-solving agents. Within this mechanisms a coercive normative structure modifies the dependence structure and thus biases autonomous agent behaviour, so as to make it instrumental with respect to a problem to solve. The ProsA layered agent architecture has been devised which provides the appropriate operational support for agent societies that co-ordinate their problem-solving activities through structural co-operation [9]. The approach is currently being evaluated for different real-world problems. We are particularly concerned with its application to decentralised multiagent traffic management.

References

1. Brainov, S.: "Altruistic Cooperation Between Self-interested Agents". *Proc. 12th Europ. Conf. on Artificial Intelligence (ECAI)*, 1996, p. 519-523
2. Conte, R.; Castelfranchi, C.: *Cognitive and Social Action*, UCL Press, 1995
3. Cuena, J.; Ossowski, S.: "Distributed Models for Decision Support". To appear in: *Introduction to Distributed Artificial Intelligence* (Weiß & Sen, eds.), AAAI/MIT Press, 1998
4. Demazeau, Y.: "Decentralised A.I. 2". *North Holland*, 1991
5. Durfee, E.: "Planning in Distributed Artificial Intelligence". *Foundations of Distributed Artificial Intelligence* (O'Hare & Jennings, eds.), John Wiley, 1996, p. 231-246
6. Durfee, E.; Rosenschein, J.: "Distributed Problem Solving and Multiagent Systems: Comparisons and Examples". *Proc. 13th Int. DAI Workshop*, 1994, p. 94-104
7. Jennings, N.; Campos, J.: "Towards a Social Level Characterisation of Socially Responsible Agents". *IEE Proc. on Software Engineering, 144(1)*, 1997
8. Nash, J.: "The bargaining problem". *Econometrica 20*, 1950, p. 155-162
9. Ossowski, S.: *On the Functionality of Social Structure in Artificial Agent Societies – Emergent Co-ordination of Autonomous Problem-solving Agents*. Ph.D. Thesis, Technical University of Madrid, 1997
10. Ossowski, S.; García-Serrano, A.: "A Knowledge-Level Model of Co-ordination". *Distributed Artificial Intelligence: Architecture and Modelling* (Zhang & Lukose, eds.), Springer, 1995, p. 46-57
11. Ossowski, S.; García-Serrano, A.; Cuena, J.: "Emergent Co-ordination of Flow Control Actions Through Functional Co-operation of Social Agents". *Proc. 12th Europ. Conf. on Artificial Intelligence (ECAI)*, 1996, p. 539-543
12. Rosenschein, J.; Zlotkin, G.: *Rules of Encounter: Designing Conventions for Automated Negotiation among Computers*. AAAI/MIT Press, 1994
13. Sandholm, T.: *Negotiation Among Self-interested Computationally Limited Agents*. PhD Thesis. UMass Computer Science Dpt., 1996
14. Shehory, O.; Kraus, S.: "A Kernel-Oriented Model for Autonomous-Agent Coalition Formation in General Environments". *Distributed Artificial Intelligence: Architecture and Modelling* (Zhang & Lukose, eds.), Springer, 1995, p. 31-45
15. Shoham, Y.; Tennenholz, M.: "On Social Laws for Artificial Agent Societies: Off-line Design". *Artificial Intelligence 73*, 1995, p. 231-252
16. Sichman, J.: *Du Raisonnement Social Chez des Agents*. Ph.D. Thesis, Institut Polytechnique de Grenoble, 1995
17. Sichman, J.; Demazeau, Y.; Conte, R.; Castelfranchi, C.: "A Social Reasoning Mechanism Based On Dependence Networks". *Proc. ECAI-94*, 1994, p. 188-192
18. Thomson, W.: "Cooperative Models of Bargaining". *Handbook of Game Theory* (Auman & Hart, eds.), 1994, p. 1238-1284

An Algorithm for Plan Verification in Multiple Agent Systems

Chengqi Zhang and Yuefeng Li

School of Mathematical and Computer Sciences
University of New England, Armidale, N.S.W. 2351, Australia
Email: {chengqi, yuefeng}@neumann.une.edu.au

Abstract. In this paper, we propose an algorithm which can improve Katz and Rosenschein's plan verification algorithm. First, we represent the plan-like relations with adjacency lists and inverse adjacency lists to replace adjacency matrixes. Then, we present a method to avoid generating useless sub-graphs while generating the compressed set. Last, we compare two plan verification algorithms. We not only prove that our algorithm is correct, but also prove that our algorithm is better than Katz and Rosenschein's algorithm both on time complexity and space complexity.

Keywords: Planning, Verification, Multiple agent systems.

1 Introduction

Distributed problem solving plays an important role in distributed artificial intelligence [2,10,17,19,20,21]. Now, it is fashionable to use planning as a kind of approach for distributed problem solving in multiple agent environments [4,7]. Planning research in multiple agent systems has historically focussed on two distinct classes of problems. One paradigm has been that of planning for multiple agents, which considers issues inherent in centrally directed multi-agent execution [7,13,15,17]. The second paradigm has been distributed planning, where multiple agents participate more autonomously in coordinating and deciding upon their own actions [5,10,16,21,22].

Planning the action of multiple agents in either paradigm needs parallel structures for representing planning. Taking the STRIPS representation of actions, directed acyclic graphs (DAGs) are particularly well suited to the representation of plans for parallel execution [7,18]. The question is: how can a DAG plan be verified [8] (i.e. how we can be sure that such a plan will be correct, given our uncertainty about exactly when unconstrained parallel actions will be performed).

In 1993, Katz and Rosenschein presented a method to verify whether planning is possible to execute in parallel [8]. Instead of having to examine each levels relation (all possible parallel executive structures denoted by $LEVEL_D$, see Definition 4 in Section 2), they introduced two new concepts: induced sets and compressed sets. Given a plan-like relation D and a state S, they proved that the compressed set of $LEVEL_D$ is a minimal set of levels relations that need to be verified. Using these results, they proposed an algorithm for verifying a plan. The algorithm used adjacency matrix to represent the plan-like relations of D, and used recursive algorithm to generate all nodes of the compressed set. Although the algorithm can generate the forest for the compressed set, it will generate many useless sub-graphs before generating each node.

In this paper, we propose an algorithm which can improve the above algorithm. We use an adjacency list and inverse adjacency list to represent the plan-like relations of D, and use a supplementary array to control the generation of sub-graphs (i.e. the algorithm does not really generate these sub-graphs, but from the supplementary array, we can recognize the current sub-graphs), and hence present a method that avoids generating these useless sub-graphs (section 3). We not only prove that the algorithm is correct, but also prove that our algorithm is better than Katz and Rosenschein's algorithm both on time complexity and space complexity (section 4).

2 Basic concepts

In this section we first briefly introduce the definitions of actions and plans in STRIPS, then we give the definitions of *possible*, levels relations and compressed sets [8].

Every STRIPS operator, α, can be represented by a triple $< P_\alpha, D_\alpha, A_\alpha >$, where P_α is the precondition list of α, D_α is the delete list of α and A_α is the add list of α. In this paper, we assume that every agent which can execute every operation for a same planning, and all agents always obey a supervisor's commands, and they do not fail unless another agent who is executing another operation interferes. Another especially significant assumption in this work is the "uncertainty assumption", which states that it is not possible to know in advance the duration of any operation's execution.

Definition 1 *Let a plan, π, be represented as a tuple $< \alpha_1, \alpha_2, \ldots, \alpha_n >$, and T_I and T_G are initial and goal states respectively. Given a state S, the operation sequence, $\alpha_1, \alpha_2, \ldots, \alpha_n$, $n \geq 1$, is possible from a state S, if $P_{\alpha_i} \subseteq S_{i-1}$ ($i = 1, 2, \ldots, n$). Furthermore, if $T_I \subseteq S$, $T_G \subseteq S_n$, and $\alpha_1, \alpha_2, \ldots, \alpha_n$ is possible from a state S, then we call π a sequential plan, and we denote $S_n = r(\alpha_1, \alpha_2, \ldots, \alpha_n, S)$. Where, $S_0 = S$ and S_{i-1} is the result of executing α_{i-1} from S_{i-2} for all $2 \leq i \leq n+1$.*

Definition 2 *Let $\pi = < \alpha_1, \alpha_2, \ldots, \alpha_n >$ be a plan, and S be a state. Let O be the set of symbols whose elements are $\alpha_1, \alpha_2, \ldots, \alpha_n$. We say that it is possible to execute $\alpha_1, \alpha_2, \ldots, \alpha_n$ in parallel from S (O is possible from S) if whenever the supervisor gives instructions in the state S to n agents to execute these operations, every agent proceeds without interference and does the work indicated by the operation, and the states attained in this way are identical. The result of executing $\alpha_1, \alpha_2, \ldots, \alpha_n$ in parallel from S is denoted by $r(O, S)$.*

A plan-like relation is a binary relation over $\{\alpha_1, \alpha_2, \ldots, \alpha_n\}$ such that its transitive closure is a partial order (i.e. a directed acyclic graph (DAG)). Of course, not every plan-like relation is a plan for some pair of states. Below, we will give the definitions of plans, levels relations, *possible*, and compressed sets.

Definition 3 *Let D be a plan-like relation and let S be a state. We say that D is possible from S if every topological sequence of D is possible from S, and for each two topological sequences, $\alpha = (\alpha_1, \alpha_2, \ldots, \alpha_n)$, $\beta = (\beta_1, \beta_2, \ldots, \beta_n)$, of D, $r(\alpha, S) = r(\beta, S)$. We denote $r(D, S) = r(\alpha, S)$. We say that D is a plan for (T_I, T_G), where T_I and T_G are partial states, if for every state S such that $T_I \subseteq S$, D is possible from S and $T_G \subseteq r(D, S)$.*

Definition 4 *Let $O = \{\alpha_1, \alpha_2, \ldots, \alpha_n\}$ be a set of symbols. We call a relation L a levels relation of O, if it divides O into h, $h \leq n$, sets (or levels), $O_1, O_2, \ldots, O_h$ such that*

(1) For each h', $1 \leq h' \leq h-1$, if $\alpha_i \in O_{h'}$ and $\alpha_j \in O_{h'+1}$ then $(\alpha_i, \alpha_j) \in L$.

(2) For arbitrary $(\alpha_i, \alpha_j) \in L$, there is $1 \leq h' \leq h-1$, such that $\alpha_i \in O_{h'}$ and $\alpha_j \in O_{h'+1}$.

Definition 5 *Let $\pi = \langle \alpha_1, \alpha_2, \ldots, \alpha_n \rangle$ be a plan, S be a state and $O = \{\alpha_1, \alpha_2, \ldots, \alpha_n\}$. Suppose L is a levels relation of O. We call L *possible from S if O_1 is possible from S, O_2 is possible from $r(O_1, S)$, O_3 is possible from $r(O_2, r(O_1, S)), \ldots$.*

Example 1. Assume that A is some object, and the agents are capable of executing the operations $spray\_blue(A)$ and $spray\_white(A)$ (possibly simultaneously). The operation $spray\_blue(A)$ is represented by the sets $P_{blue} = \{A \text{ is hanging properly }\}$, $D_{blue} = \{white(A)\}$, and $A_{blue} = \{blue(A)\}$, and $spray\_white(A)$ is represented similarly. Moreover, assume that A is hanging properly in the current state S. Then the levels relation

$$(\{spray\_blue(A), spray\_white(A)\}, \{spray\_blue(A)\})$$

is possible from S, but not *possible from S. The final state (namely $blue(A)$) is guaranteed, regardless of $A's$ colour after the first level, so the levels relation is possible from S. However, since that results from the first level is uncertain, the levels relation is not *possible from S.

If L is *possible from S, the result of executing can be denoted by $r(O_h, \ldots, r(O_1, S) \ldots)$ or $r(L, S)$. The relationships between operations can be described by a directed acyclic graph (or a plan-like relation)[7]. Given a directed acyclic graph D, the set of levels relations, $LEVELS_D$ is defined as follows:

$$LEVELS_D = \begin{array}{l} \{L \mid L \text{ is a levels relation on } D \text{ and for each } \alpha_i \text{ and } \alpha_j \text{ such} \\ \text{that } (\alpha_i, \alpha_j) \in D, \alpha_i \text{ is in a level lower than } \alpha_j.\} \end{array}$$

Definition 6 *Let D be a plan-like relation and S be a state. We call D is strictly possible from S if for each $L \in LEVELS_D$, L is *possible from S.*

From the above definitions, we can see that in order to prove D is strictly possible from S we need to prove each levels relation L is *possible from S. In order to give a quick method to verify whether D is strictly possible, Katz and Rosenschein presented the concept of compressed set of $LEVELS_D$, and they proved that each levels relation is *possible from S if and only if each levels relation in the compressed set is *possible from S.

Definition 7 *Let $LEVELS \subseteq LEVELS_D$. $\bigcup_{L \in LEVELS} LEVELS_L$ is the set of levels relations induced by $LEVELS$, which is denoted by $I(LEVELS)$. $LEVELS$ is then complete if $LEVELS = I(LEVELS)$.*

Theorem 1 *(Katz and Rosenschein, 1993) Let D be a plan-like relation and S be a state. Let $LEVELS$ be a set of levels relations over D's base such that $I(LEVELS) \supseteq LEVELS_D$. If for each $L \in LEVELS$, L is *possible from S, then D is strictly possible from S and $r(D, S) = r(L', S)$, where L' is any element in $LEVELS_D$.*

To each plan-like relation D, the compressed set of $LEVELS_D$ is defined as follows:

$$C(LEVELS_D) = \begin{array}{l} \{L \mid L \in LEVELS_D, \ L = (O_1, \ldots, O_h), \text{ and there is not} \\ h', 1 \leq h' \leq h+1, \text{ such that for each } \alpha_i \in O_{h'} \text{ and} \\ \alpha_j \in O_{h'+1}, \ \alpha_i \text{ and } \alpha_j \text{ are incomparable in } D.\} \end{array}$$

Theorem 2 *(Katz and Rosenschein, 1993) Let D be a plan-like relation. Then*
    a. $I(C(LEVELS_D)) = LEVELS_D$.
    b. $C(LEVELS_D)$ *is the smallest set among the collection of sets of levels relations on D whose induced set is equal to $LEVELS_D$.*

Example 2. To the two plan-like relations shown in Figure 1, we have
$LEVELS_G = \{(\{1\}, \{2\}, \{3\}), (\{1\}, \{3\}, \{2\}), (\{2\}, \{1\}, \{3\}), (\{1, 2\}, \{3\}), (\{1\}, \{2, 3\})\}$

$$C(LEVELS_G) = \{(\{1, 2\}, \{3\}), (\{1\}, \{2, 3\})\}$$
For plan-like relation D, $\mid C(LEVELS_D) \mid = 7$ while $\mid LEVELS_D \mid = 123$.

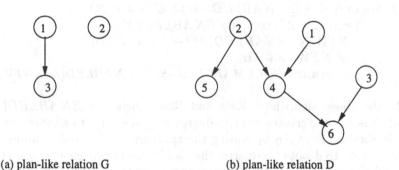

(a) plan-like relation G   (b) plan-like relation D

Fig. 1. The plan-like relations

3 The algorithms for plan verification

The compressed sets play a main role for plan verification. In this section, we first introduce Katz and Rosenschein's algorithm for generating $C(LEVELS_D)$, then give our improved algorithm.

3.1 Katz and Rosenschein's algorithm

In this subsection we give the algorithm designed by Katz and Rosenschein for generating $C(LEVELS_D)$. This algorithm uses an adjacency matrix A_D to represent dericted graph D. The main component of the algorithm is the recursive functions gen_tree, which is called from outside for each possible first level $ENABLED(A_D)$. Here, we use two equivalent procedures instead of the three procedures given by Katz and Rosenschein.

Algorithm A_1 (D, n)
1. $C(LEVELS_D) \leftarrow \emptyset$;
2. IF $empty(D)$ THEN
   ($C(LEVELS_D) \leftarrow \{(\{1, 2, \ldots, n\})\}; RETURN$);
3. compute A_D; compute $ENABLED(A_D)$;
4. For each S, $S \subseteq ENABLED(A_D)$, $S \neq \emptyset$ DO
   (compute A_D^S; computer $ENABLED(A_D^S)$;
     $NEW_2 \leftarrow ENABLED(A_D^S) - ENABLED(A_D)$;
     IF $NEW_2 \neq \emptyset$ THEN
       $gen\_tree(S, \{1, \ldots, n\} - S, A_D^S, ENABLED(A_D^S), NEW_2, nil)$)□

Algorithm gen_tree ($LEVEL, REMAINING, A, ENABLED, NEW_1, address\_of\_father$)
1. generate a node whose address is P, value is $LEVEL$ and its pointer
   is set to $address\_of\_father$;
2. IF $ENABLED = REMAINING$ THEN
   (generate a node whose value is $ENABLED$ and its pointer
   is set to P; RETURN);
3. For each S, $S \subseteq ENABLED$, $S \cap NEW_1 \neq \emptyset$ DO
   (compute A^S; compute $ENABLED(A^S)$;
     $NEW_2 \leftarrow ENABLED(A^S) - ENABLED$;
     IF $NEW_2 \neq \emptyset$ THEN
       $gen\_tree(S, REMAINING - S, A^S, ENABLED(A^S), NEW_2, P)$)□

In the above algorithms, Katz and Rosenschein use $ENABLED(A_D)$ to denote the set of vertexes with in-degree 0 in A_D, A_D^S to denote the matrix that is obtained from A_D by erasing the appropriate rows and columns indexed by S, and A^S to denote the matrix that is obtained from the current adjacency matrix by erasing the appropriate rows and columns indexed by S. Although the above algorithms can provide the compressed set, each recursion has to compute some useless A^S and $ENABLED(A^S)$, and need some spaces to store these A^S matrices (see example 4, Section 4.2) as well.

3.2 Our algorithm

In this subsection we will give a method to avoid the useless computing. Different from the above method, we use an adjacency list and its inverse adjacency list to represent the directed graph D. In the following algorithm, we first select a subset of $ENABLED$, a set of current vertexes with in-degree 0, whose elements send edges to some vertexes of a set with in-degree 0 on next level. For this reason we introduce two one-dimension arrays to decide what subsets are necessary for the compressed set. Then we recursively call this process.

Algorithm V $(D, HEAD_1, HEAD_2, n)$

1. *compute indegree of vertex* $INDEG[i]$ $(i = 1, \ldots, n)$;
    FOR $i = 1$ TO n DO $MARK[i] \leftarrow 0$;
2. *compute vertex with indegree 0* $ENABLED$;
    IF $ENABLED = \{1, 2, \ldots, n\}$ THEN
        ($C(LEVELS_D) \leftarrow \{(\{i = 1, \ldots, n\})\}$; RETURN);
3. *compute vertex with indegree 0* REM *on next level of* $ENABLED$;
    select a subset H whose elements send edges to some nodes of REM
    /* The elements of H are subsets of ENABLED */;
4. FOR each S, $S \subseteq ENABLED, S$ at least includes one
    element of H DO
        ($REM \leftarrow \{b \mid H_b \in H \text{ and } H_b \subseteq S\}$;
        FOR each $a \in S$ DO $MARK[a] \leftarrow 1$;
        $gen(S, \{1, 2, \ldots, n\} - S, REM \cup (ENABLED - S), REM, nil)$;
        FOR each $a \in S$ DO $MARK[a] \leftarrow 0$)□

Algorithm gen $(LEVEL, REMAINING, ENABL, NEW, address\_of\_father)$

1. generate a node whose address is P, value is $LEVEL$ and its pointer
    is set to $address\_of\_father$;
2. IF $ENABL = REMAINING$ THEN
        (generate a node whose value is $ENABL$ and its pointer
        is set to P; RETURN);
    compute vertex with indegree 0 NEW_1 *on next level of* $ENABL$;
    select a subset H_1 *whose elements send edges to some nodes of* NEW_1
    /* The elements of H_1 are subsets of ENABL */;
3. FOR each S, $S \subseteq ENABL, S \cap NEW \neq \emptyset$, and S at least
    includes one element of H_1 DO
        ($NEW_1 \leftarrow \{b \mid H_{1_b} \in H_1 \text{ and } H_{1_b} \subseteq S\}$;
        FOR each $a \in S$ DO $MARK[a] \leftarrow 1$;
        $gen(S, REMAINING - S, NEW_1 \cup (ENABL - S), NEW_1, P)$;
        FOR each $a \in S$ DO $MARK[a] \leftarrow 0$)□

The details of the sentences with underlines of the above procedures can be found in Appendix.

4 Analysis of plan verification algorithms

In this section, we first give the proof of the correctness of Algorithm V. Then we give some examples to explain how to avoid generating useless subgraphs in Algorithm V. Last we prove that our algorithm is better than Katz and Rosenschein's algorithm both on time complexity and space complexity.

4.1 The proof of correctness

Theorem 3 *Suppose Algorithm V selects a set S_1 at step 4, from level S_1 it recursively calls Algorithm gen, and suppose Algorithm gen (at step 3) selects set $S_2, \ldots,$ from level S_{r-1} it recursively calls Algorithm gen, and suppose Algorithm gen selects level S_r. Then $(S_1, \ldots, S_r) \in C(LEVELS_D)$. On the contrary, if $L \in C(LEVELS_D)$ and $L = (O_1, \ldots, O_h)$ then L is a path of the forest generated by Algorithm V, and O_1 is the root node of one tree and O_h is a leaf node of this tree.*

Proof. From the step 4 of Algorithm V, we have

$$S_1 \subseteq ENABLED, \text{ and } S_1 \text{ at least includes one element of } H$$

When $gen(S_1, \{1, 2, \ldots, n\} - S_1, REM \cup (ENABLED - S_1), REM, nil)$ is recursively called, if Algorithm gen selects S_2 at step 3, then we have

$$S_2 \subseteq ENABL, \ S_2 \cap NEW \neq \emptyset, \text{ and } S_2 \text{ at least includes one element of } H_1$$

From

$$ENABL = REM \cup (ENABLED - S_1), \ NEW = REM$$

we have

$$S_2 \cap REM \neq \emptyset, here \ we \ suppose \ there \ is \ b \in S_2 \cap REM$$

From the definition of H (see Appendix) we know that deleting vertexes from S_1 can generate new vertexes with in-degree 0. So $NEW = REW \neq \emptyset$. Because the vertexes in $NEW = REW$ is generated by deleted S_1, there certainly has $a \in S_1$, $b \in S_2$ such that $< a, b >$ is the directed edge of D. Similarly, $S_{r'-1}$ and $S_{r'}$ also satisfy the above property while $3 \leq r' \leq r$. It is easy to detect that $(S_1, \ldots, S_r) \in LEVELS_D$ from Algorithm V, hence $(S_1, \ldots, S_r) \in C(LEVELS_D)$.

If $(O_1, \ldots, O_h) \in C(LEVELS_D)$, then from the definition of compressed set we know that the in-degree of each vertex in O_1 is zero, and there are $a \in O_1$, $b \in O_2$ such that $< a, b >$ is the directed edge of D. From $(O_1, \ldots, O_h) \in C(LEVELS_D)$, we have $(O_1, \ldots, O_h) \in LEVELS_D$, so the in-degree of each vertex in O_2 is zero when deleted O_1, and we know that Algorithm V at step 4 can select O_1. Similarly, after selecting O_1, Algorithm V can select $O_2, \ldots$. After O_h is selected, Algorithm gen can get $ENABL = REMAINING$, hence O_h is a leaf node. $\square$

4.2 Avoidance of generating useless subgraphs

In algorithm V, a method of avoiding unnecessary computation is presented. The principle of this method is that the algorithm can decide what levels, whose elements send edges to some vertexes of a set with in-degree 0 on next level, are necessary for generating the compressed set before selecting levels.

Example 3. To the plan-like relation D shown in Figure 1 (b), its adjacency matrix A_D shows as follows.

$$\begin{vmatrix} 0\,0\,0\,1\,0\,0 \\ 0\,0\,0\,1\,1\,0 \\ 0\,0\,0\,0\,0\,1 \\ 0\,0\,0\,0\,0\,1 \\ 0\,0\,0\,0\,0\,0 \\ 0\,0\,0\,0\,0\,0 \end{vmatrix}$$

In Algorithm A_1, $compute\,ENABLED(A_D)$ takes time $O(n^2)$, (here n=6). Storing matrix A_D needs space $O(n^2)$, and the result of running Algorithm A_1 is a forest shown in Figure 2.

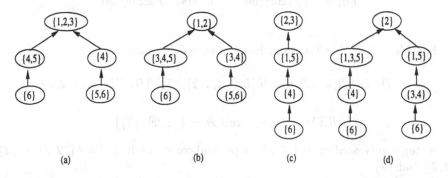

Fig. 2. The forest generated

In Algorithm A_1, $ENABLED(A_D)\,is\{1,2,3\}$, the FOR loop in step 4 is iterated 7 times, and 7 matrices are generated. For each of these matrices, the set of vertexes with in-degree 0 are computed. But only 4 matrixes are useful (the corresponding S being $= \{1,2,3\}, \{1,2\}, \{2,3\}, and\{2\}$). When Algorithm A_1 selected $S = \{1,2\}$ in step 4, the matrix $A_D^S = A_D^{\{1,2\}}$,

$$A_D^{\{1,2\}} = \begin{vmatrix} 0\,0\,0\,1 \\ 0\,0\,0\,1 \\ 0\,0\,0\,0 \\ 0\,0\,0\,0 \end{vmatrix}$$

$ENABLED(A_D^S) = \{3,4,5\}$, $NEW_2 = \{4,5\} \neq \emptyset$. So Algorithm A_1 will call procedure

$$gen\_tree(\{1,2\}, \{3,4,5,6\}, A_D^{\{1,2\}}, \{3,4,5\}, \{4,5\}, nil)$$

For these inputs, Algorithm *gen_tree* will iterate the FOR loop in step 3 6 times (corresponding to $S = \{3,4,5\}, \{4,5\}, \{3,4\}, \{3,5\}, \{4\}, \{5\}$), generate 6 matrixes, but only $\{3,4,5\}$ and $\{3,4\}$ are useful.

Example 4. To the plan-like relation D shown in Figure 1 (b), its adjacency list $HEAD_1$ and inverse adjacency list $HEAD_2$ shows as Figure 3.

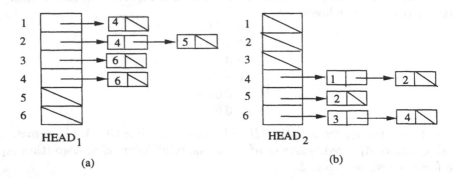

(a)   (b)

Fig. 3. Adjacency list and inverse adjacency list

For Algorithm V, after it finished the step 3, we have

$$INDEG[1,2,3,4,5,6] = [0,0,0,2,1,2], \ ENABLED = \{1,2,3\}$$

$$REM = \{4,5\}, \ and \ H = \{\{1,2\},\{2\}\}$$

So in step 4 only need to do 4 *FOR* loops, and corresponding $S = \{1,2,3\}, \{1,2\}, \{2,3\}$ and $\{2\}$.

When Algorithm V selects $S = \{1,2\}$ at step 4, then we have

$$INDEG[1,2,3,4,5,6] = [0,0,0,0,0,1], \ REM = \{4,5\}.$$

So Algorithm V will call the procedure

$$gen(\{1,2\},\{3,4,5,6\},\{3,4,5\},\{4,5\},nil)$$

Before step 3 of this procedure, we have

$$ENABL = \{3,4,5\}, NEW = \{4,5\}, MARK[1,2,3,4,5,6] = [1,1,0,0,0,0]$$

$$NEW_1 = \{6\}, \ and \ H_1 = \{\{3,4\}\}$$

So in step 3 only need to do 2 loops, and corresponding $S = \{3,4,5\}$ and $\{3,4\}$.

The above examples show that Algorithm V different from Algorithm A_1, can avoid computing and storing useless sub-graphs.

4.3 Performance Comparison

In this subsection, from the worst case we further give some quantitative analyses.

Theorem 4 *Let D be a plan-like relation, n be the number of vertexes in D and e is the number of directed edges in D. If Algorithm V and Algorithm A_1 output the first levels relation of the compressed set are both $(S_1, \ldots, S_r)$, then Algorithm V will take time $O(n + e)$ to output $(S_1, \ldots, S_r)$, and Algorithm A_1 will take time $\geq O(n^2 + \sum_{i=1}^r (n - \sum_{j=1}^i | S_j |)^2)$ to output $(S_1, \ldots, S_r)$.*

Proof. The first three steps of Algorithm V take time $O(n + e)$ (see Appendix). Selecting S in step 4 is based on H, so getting set $\{b \mid H_b \in H$ and $H_b \subseteq S\}$ should take time $O(| S |)$. The process from selecting S_1 to output S_r, in which Algorithm V will give $O(| S_1 | + \ldots + | S_r |)$ operations to $MARK$, the process,

compute vertex with indegree 0 NEW_1 on next level of $ENABL$,

which needs $O(e)$ operations, and the process,

select a subset H_1 whose elements send edges to some nodes of NEW_1

which also needs $O(e)$ operations. So for outputting $(S_1, \ldots, S_r)$, Algorithm V take time $O(n + e) + O(| S_1 | + \ldots + | S_r |)$. Because $(S_1, \ldots, S_r)$ is just a partition of vertex set of D, Algorithm V takes time $O(n + e)$ to output $(S_1, \ldots, S_r)$.

The first three steps of Algorithm A_1 take time $O(n^2)$. The step 4 will compute the vertexes with in-degree 0 in matrix $A_D^{S_1}$ when Algorithm A_1 selects S_1. This process at least needs time $O((n - | S_1 |)^2)$ (notice that there may be some useless computing here). Similarly, Algorithm A_1 will need time $O((n - (| S_1 | + | S_2 |))^2)$ when it selects S_2, $\ldots$ So Algorithm A_1 will take time $\geq O(n^2 + \sum_{i=1}^r (n - \sum_{j=1}^i | S_j |)^2)$ to output $(S_1, \ldots, S_r)$. $\square$

From Appendix we can see that the process of "computing vertexes with in-degree 0 on next level ((3) and (5))" and the process of "select a subset whose elements send edges to some nodes of one set ((4) and (6))" are reciprocal in whole running of Algorithm V. So these two processes will take same time. For this, in the following we suppose that the basic operations do not include the process of "select a subset whose elements send edges to some nodes of one set", because the assumption does not affect algorithm's time complexity.

Theorem 5 *Suppose Algorithm V and Algorithm S_1 form the same forest. Let S_0 be a node of the forest, and $(S_0, S_1, \ldots, S_t)$ $(t \geq 0)$ be the path from S_0 to its root. Suppose these two algorithms both generated node S_0. Then, Algorithm V will take time $O((n - \sum_{i=0}^t | S_i |) + e')$ to generate the first child of S_0, and Algorithm A_1 will need time $\geq O((n - \sum_{i=0}^t | S_i |)^2)$ to generate the first child of S_0. Where e' is the number of edges in graph $A_D^{S_0 \cup \ldots \cup S_t}$.*

Proof. From the assumption we know that $(S_0, S_1, \ldots, S_t)$ is the front part of a levels relation of D. This means that each sub-tree of node S_0 does not contain any node in $(S_0 \cup S_1 \cup \ldots \cup S_t)$. So, from the time of generating S_0 to form the first child of S_0, "computing vertexes with in-degree 0 on next level", which takes time $O(e')$, the number of the edges of the rest graph $A_D^{S_0 \cup \ldots \cup S_t}$. In addition, in this period, the number of assignment to array $MARK$ is the size of the first child of S_0. So Algorithm V takes time $O((n - \sum_{i=0}^{t} |S_i|) + e')$ in this period.

To Algorithm A_1, the time, used for computing vertexes with in-degree 0 in this period, is $(n - \sum_{i=0}^{t} |S_i|)^2$, because the matrix used is $A_D^{S_0 \cup \ldots \cup S_t}$. Furthermore, computing NEW_2 needs some time and Algorithm A_1 also takes some time to deal with the useless matrixes before computing $A_D^{S_0 \cup \ldots \cup S_t}$. So Algorithm A_1 at least needs time $O((n - \sum_{i=0}^{t} |S_i|)^2)$ in this period. $\square$

If e is the number of directed edges of D, and n is the number of vertexes. Then $O(e) \leq O(n^2)$. From the above two theories, it is easy to see that our algorithm is better than Katz and Rosenschein's on time complexity. The following theory tells us that Algorithm V is also better than Katz and Rosenschein's on space complexity.

Theorem 6 *Let D be a plan-like relation, n be the number of vertexes of D, and e be the number of directed edges of D. Then the space complexity of Algorithm V is $O(n + e + \sum_{i=1}^{m} |S_i|)$, and the space complexity of Algorithm A_1 is $\geq O(n^2 + \sum_{i=1}^{m} |S_i| + \sum_{i=1}^{m} |A^{S_i}|^2)$, where $S_1, \ldots, S_m$ are all nodes of forest formed by the compressed set of D, the definitions of A^{S_i} can be found in Algorithm gen_tree.*

Proof. For Algorithm V, the adjacency list and inverse adjacency list of D both need space $O(n + e)$. Array $MARK$, $INDEG$ and variables each requires the space $O(n)$. Because each element H_b of set H at most need a $S \in \{S_1, \ldots, S_m\}$ in a level, and $|H_b| \leq |S|$ (similarly H_1 needs the same space). So Algorithm V at most takes the space $O(\sum_{i=1}^{m} |S_i|)$ to represent all H and H_1. Since the resulting forest only needs the space $\sum_{i=1}^{m} |S_i|$. So the space complexity of Algorithm V is $O(n + e + \sum_{i=1}^{m} |S_i|)$.

To Algorithm A_1, storing adjacency matrix A_D takes the space $O(n^2)$, and variables need the space $O(n)$. Because Algorithm A_1 has to store matrix A^S for every element S of $\{S_1, \ldots, S_m\}$ and some useless sub-graphs, Algorithm A_1 at least requires the space $\sum_{i=1}^{m} |A^{S_i}|^2$ to do this. In addition, Algorithm A_1 takes the space $\sum_{i=1}^{m} |S_i|$ to store the resulting forest. So, the space complexity of Algorithm A_1 is $\geq O(n^2 + \sum_{i=1}^{m} |S_i| + \sum_{i=1}^{m} |A^{S_i}|^2)$. $\square$

5 Summary

In this paper, we propose an algorithm to improve Katz and Rosenschein's plan verification algorithm. We use adjacency lists and inverse adjacency lists to represent the plan-like relations of D, and use a supplementary array to control the generation of sub-graphs and hence present a method to avoid generating these useless sub-graphs. The new algorithm is better than Katz and Rosenschein's algorithm both on time complexity and space complexity.

Planning verification in multiple agent systems is a basic problem. The concept of compressed sets can describe all necessary levels relations when the plan will be executed by several agents. When a plan D is passed to the supervisor, he sends agents the instructions according to the following rule [8]:

Sending rule: The supervisor may send the instruction α_j, $1 \leq j \leq n$, to an agent x, if

a. For each α_j, $1 \leq j \leq n$, such that $(\alpha_i, \alpha_j) \in D$, the supervisor already sent the instruction α_i and received the appropriate "finished" message.

b. x is free, i.e. the supervisor did not send x an instruction since he last received a "finished" message from x.

In order to decrease the amount of communications between supervisor and agents, supervisor can send several operations to one agent at the same time rather than one by one [11]. The problem is what are the suitable structures among operations for this consideration. We think that the compressed sets may be used to describe the structures.

6 Acknowledgement

This research is partially supported by the University of New England research grant and partially supported by the large grant from the Australian Research Council (A49530850).

References

1. R. I. Brafman and M. Tennenholtz, *Modeling agents as qualitative decision makers*, Artificial Intelligence, 1997, **94**: *217-268*.
2. E. H. Durfee, V. R. Lesser and D. D. Corkill, Trends in cooperative distributed problem solving, *IEEE Trans, Knowl. Data Eng.* ,*1989*, **1**: *63-83*.
3. E. H. Durfee, V. R. Lesser and D. D. Corkill, Cooperation through communication in a distributed problem solving network. *In M.N. Huhns (ed.) Distributed Artificial Intelligence (Los Altos, California, USA: Morgan Kaufmann, Inc.) 1987, Ch. 2, 29-58.*
4. E. Ephrati, M. E. Pollack and J. S. Rosenschein, A tractable heuristic that maximizes global utility through local, *in Proceedings of ICMAS, 1995, 94-101.*
5. E. Ephrati and J. S. Rosenschein, The Clarke Tax as a consensus mechanism among automated agents, *in Proceedings of AAAI, 1991, 173-178.*
6. E. Ephrati and J. S. Rosenschein, Multi-agent planning as search for a consensus that maximizes social welfare, *in Proceedings of 4th European Workshop on Modeling Autonomous Agents in a Multi-Agent World, 1992, Chapter 3.*
7. M. J. Katz and J. S. Rosenschein, Plans for multiple agents, *In L. Gasser and M. N. Huhns (eds.) Distributed Artificial Intelligence, Volume II (Pitman/Morgan Kaufmann, Inc., London), 1989, 197-228.*

8. M. J. Katz and J. S. Rosenschein, Verifying plans for multiple agent, *J. Experimental & Theoretical Artificial Intelligence, 1993,* **5:** *39-56.*

9. N. A. Khan and R. Jain, Uncertainty management in a distributed knowledge based system, *in: Proceedings of IJCAI, Los Angeles, CA, 1985, 318-320.*

10. V. R. Lesser and D. D. Corkill, The distributed vehicle monitoring test bed, *AI Mag., 1983,* **4:** *63-109.*

11. Y. Li and D. Liu, Task decomposition model in distributed expert systems, *in: Proceedings of 9th International Conference on Computer-Aided Production Engineering, 1993, 259-264.*

12. Y. Li and D. Liu, The method of verifying plans for multiple agents, *Chinese J. of Computers, 1996,* **19(3):** *202-207.*

13. E. P. D. Pednault, Formulating multiagent, dynamic-world problems in the classical planning framework. *In M.P. Georgeff and A.L. Lansky (eds.) Reasoning About Actions and Plans (Los Altos, California, USA: Morgan Kaufmann, Inc.), 1987, 47-82.*

14. M. Pollack, The uses of plans, *Artificial Intelligence, 1992,* **57(1):** *43-68.*

15. J. S. Rosenschein, Synchronization of multi-agent plans, *in Proceedings of AAAI, 1982, 115-119.*

16. J. S. Rosenschein and M. R. Genesereth, Deals among rational agents. in Proceedings of IJCAI, 1985, 91-95.

17. R. G. Smith, The contract net protocol: High-level communication and control in a distributed problem solver, *IEEE Transactions on Computers, 1982,* **C-29(12):** *1104-1113.*

18. D. S. Weld, An introduction to least commitment planning, *AI Magazine, 1994,* **15(4):** *27-61.*

19. C. Zhang, Cooperation under uncertainty in distributed expert systems, *Artificial Intelligence, 1992,* **56(1):** *21-69.*

20. C. Zhang and D. A. Bell, HECODES: a framework for heterogeneous cooperative distributed expert system, *Int. J. Data Knowl. Eng., 1991,* **6(3):** *251-273.*

21. G. Zlotkin and J. S. Rosenschein, Cooperation and conflict resolution via negotiation among autonomous agents in noncooperative domains, *IEEE Transaction on Systems, Man and Cybernetics, 1991,* **21(6):** *1317-1324.*

22. G. Zlotkin and J. S. Rosenschein, Incomplete information and deception in multi-agent negotiation. *in Proceedings of IJCAI, 1991, 225-231.*

Appendix

Suppose the set of vertexes of directed graph D is $\{1, 2, \ldots, n\}$. The head arrays of the adjacency list and its inverse adjacency list are $HEAD_1$, $HEAD_2$, respectively, and the structure of a node in the two lists is

vertex	link

where *link* field is the pointer field, the value of *vertex* field is the No. of the head of the directed edge indicated by the node.

(1) <u>compute indegree of vertex $INDEG[i]$ $(i = 1, \ldots, n)$</u>;

```
FOR  i = 1  TO  n  DO  INDEG[i] ← 0;
FOR  i = 1  TO  n  DO
       ( P ← HEAD₂[i];
           WHILE P ≠ nil DO
                 ( INDEG[i] ← INDEG[i] + 1; P ← P ↑ .link) );
```

(2) <u>compute vertex with indegree 0 $ENABLED$</u>;

```
ENABLED ← ∅;
FOR  i = 1  TO  n  DO
          IF INDEG[i] = 0 THEN ENABLED ← ENABLED ∪ {i};
```

(3) <u>compute vertex with indegree 0 REM on next level of $ENABLED$</u>;

```
REM ← ∅;
FOR each a ∈ ENABLED DO
/* selecting the vertexes with in-degree 0 on next level */
       ( P ← HEAD₁[a];
           WHILE P ≠ nil DO
                 ( i ← P ↑ .vertex;
                   INDEG[i] ← INDEG[i] − 1;
                   IF INDEG[i] = 0 THEN REM ← REM ∪ {P ↑ .vertex};
                   P ← P ↑ .link ));
FOR each a ∈ ENABLED DO /* restoring array INDEG */
       ( P ← HEAD₁[a];
           WHILE P ≠ nil DO
                 ( i ← P ↑ .vertex;
                   INDEG[i] ← INDEG[i] + 1;
                   P ← P ↑ .link ));
```

(4) <u>select a subset H whose elements send edges to some nodes of REM</u>
   /* The elements of H are subsets of ENABLED */;

$H \leftarrow \emptyset$;
FOR each $b \in REM$ DO
/* finding a subset which relates to each vertex of REM */
    ($P \leftarrow HEAD_2[b]$; $H_b \leftarrow \emptyset$;
       WHILE $P \neq nil$ DO
          (IF $MARK[P \uparrow .vertex] = 0$ THEN
              $H_b \leftarrow H_b \cup \{P \uparrow .vertex\}$;
           $P \leftarrow P \uparrow .link$));
FOR each $b \in REM$ DO $H \leftarrow H \cup \{H_b\}$;

(5) *compute vertex with indegree 0 NEW_1 on next level of $ENABL$*;
    /* this procedure is similar to procedure (3) */

$NEW_1 \leftarrow \emptyset$;
FOR each $a \in ENABL$ DO
/* selecting the vertexes with in-degree 0 on next level */
    ($P \leftarrow HEAD_1[a]$;
       WHILE $P \neq nil$ DO
          ($i \leftarrow P \uparrow .vertex$;
            $INDEG[i] \leftarrow INDEG[i] - 1$;
            IF $INDEG[i] = 0$ THEN $NEW_1 \leftarrow NEW_1 \cup \{P \uparrow .vertex\}$;
            $P \leftarrow P \uparrow .link$));
FOR each $a \in ENABL$ DO /* restoring array $INDEG$ */
      ($P \leftarrow HEAD_1[a]$;
       WHILE $P \neq nil$ DO
          ($i \leftarrow P \uparrow .vertex$;
            $INDEG[i] \leftarrow INDEG[i] + 1$;
            $P \leftarrow P \uparrow .link$));

(6) *select a subset H_1 whose elements send edges to some nodes of NEW_1*
    /* The elements of H_1 are subsets of ENABL */;
    /* this procedure is similar to procedure (4) */

$H_1 \leftarrow \emptyset$;
FOR each $b \in NEW_1$ DO
/* finding a subset which relates to each vertex of NEW_1 */
    ($P \leftarrow HEAD_2[b]$; $H_{1_b} \leftarrow \emptyset$;
       WHILE $P \neq nil$ DO
          (IF $MARK[P \uparrow .vertex] = 0$ THEN
            $H_{1_b} \leftarrow H_{1_b} \cup \{P \uparrow .vertex\}$;
          $P \leftarrow P \uparrow .link$));
FOR each $b \in NEW_1$ DO $H_1 \leftarrow H_1 \cup \{H_{1_b}\}$;

A Framework for Coordination and Learning Among Teams of Agents

Hung H. Bui*, Svetha Venkatesh, and Dorota Kieronska

Department of Computer Science,
Curtin University of Technology, Perth, WA 6001, Australia
Email: {buihh, svetha, dorota}@cs.curtin.edu.au
URL: http://www.cs.curtin.edu.au/~{buihh, svetha, dorota}

Abstract. We present a framework for team coordination under incomplete information based on the theory of incomplete information games. When the true distribution of the uncertainty involved is not known in advance, we consider a repeated interaction scenario and show that the agents can learn to estimate this distribution and share their estimations with one another. Over time, as the set of agents' estimations become more accurate, the utility they can achieve approaches the optimal utility when the true distribution is known, while the communication requirement for exchanging the estimations among the agents can be kept to a minimal level.

Keywords: Team coordination, Incomplete information,
Learning in Multi-agent Systems

1 Introduction

Multi-agent systems are networks of loosely-coupled computational agents that can interact with one another in solving problems. The distributed nature of such systems means that it is usually not feasible for any agent to have a complete and up-to-date global view of the entire system. Rather, the agents can only be expected to have their own local views, which are often non-identical, or even non-overlapping. Consequently, it is crucial that the agents are able to coordinate effectively with others under the presence of uncertainties and incomplete information.

Traditional approaches to coordination have often relied on the designer to prescribe a fixed, domain-specific interaction protocol for the group of agents, e.g. the Contract Net Protocol [16], and other works in Cooperative Distributed Problem Solving (CDPS) [1]. However, finding a protocol that is suitable for a wide range of circumstances faced by the agents can be difficult. Furthermore, the domain-specific attributes in such a protocol make it less reusable. To overcome this, several researchers have proposed providing the agents with a general model

---

* Supported by the Australian Government's Overseas Postgraduate Research Scholarship (OPRS) and Curtin University Postgraduate Scholarship (CUPS).

of coordination as the key to flexible and reusable coordination mechanism [8, 17]. Such a general model can be applied to different coordination scenarios, allowing the agents to autonomously reason and search for their optimal course of actions.

In this paper, we focus on developing a general model of coordination for team of agents under incomplete information. A group of agents are qualified as a *team* if there is no conflict of interest among themselves (i.e. the common goal assumption [6]). Even here, coordination is a non-trivial task since the team members might have different perspectives on the problem due to their private information. Moreover, dealing effectively with incomplete information requires the agents to learn from their past experiences and induce patterns about the environment that can be used in improving their future performance.

Our approach to team coordination is based on the theory of games with incomplete information [9]. In this framework, incomplete information is represented in a probabilistic model by assigning a probability distribution to each source of uncertainties. The agents then select their actions by computing the *team optimal point*, i.e. a joint course of actions that maximises the expected utility of the team.

The coordination framework allows the integration of learning as the process of estimating the probability distribution of the uncertainties involved. In a series of repeated interactions, such a distribution can be learned and estimated by the individual agent over time. Furthermore, in a team, the individual estimates can be shared, enabling the group of agents to have access to a common estimation of the distribution. We discuss several issues that arise from learning and sharing learned knowledge in this context such as the convergence of utility of learning agents to the optimal utility level, and strategies for sharing the agents' learned knowledge with minimal requirement for communication. The theoretical considerations are further supported by our experimental results in the distributed meeting scheduling domain in which a team of surrogate agents negotiate to schedule meetings on behalf of their users.

Several related general models of coordination have been proposed, most notable are the logics-based *joint intentions* framework [4, 11, 17], and the decision-theoretic *Recursive Modelling Method* (RMM) [7, 8, 18]. The latter is similar to our approach in its representation of actions, utility and uncertainties, however differs subtly in the basic assumptions made. While our approach is limited to agents in a team, RMM is applicable mainly in the case where the agents might have conflict of interests. In team setting, it is reasonable for us to assume that the team members have common knowledge about the team utility function, and thus, it is natural to require the agents to maximise this function directly. On the other hand, when applying to team coordination, RMM solution can only be hoped to converge to a Nash equilibrium, which can be sub-optimal for the team[1].

---

[1] A Nash equilibrium is a joint course of actions such that the action for each agent is optimal given the actions of other agents. Such a joint course of actions does not guarantee that the team utility is optimal.

Our work in integrating learning into the framework of team coordination is related to the recent body of work in multi-agent learning [15, 19]. In team setting, groups of learning agents have been shown to achieve better performance than groups of non-learning agents in various domains [2, 5, 10]. Our work here can serve as a theoretical model of such systems of learning agents.

The rest of the paper is organised as follows. In the next section, we present the framework for coordination in team problems with incomplete information. Next, we enrich the framework with a model for learning in repeated interactions. The theoretical consideration is followed by the experimental results in the meeting scheduling domain. Finally, we conclude and give directions to possible future work.

2 Model of Coordination with Incomplete Information

2.1 Games and Team Problems

We model a multi-agent interaction as a *game*. Each agent's possible *actions* correspond to its allowed moves in the game. A combination of actions of all agents would bring about some changes in the environment whose effects on the agents might be good or bad. This is modelled by the agent's *utility* for such an action combination. During the game, each agent will act so as to maximise its utility. Formally, a game is a tuple $\Gamma = \langle N, (S_i), (U_i) \rangle$ where N is the set of all agents involved, S_i is the set of actions/strategies available to agent i, U_i is the utility function of agent i and is a function $U_i : \prod_i S_i \to \mathbb{R}$.

A game Γ is a team problem if the utility functions U_i are identical. This represents the case where the agents have no conflict of interests. Ignoring the subscript i in U_i, a team problem Γ has the form $\langle N, (S_i), U \rangle$.

Throughout the paper, we will assume that N, S_i are finite sets. We also adopt the following short-hand notations whenever there is no confusion. N is informally taken as the set $\{1, 2, \dots, N\}$ and also used to denote the number of agents present. If x_i denotes some property of agent i, x represents the vector $(x_1, x_2, \dots, x_N)$, and x_{-i} represents the vector $(x_1, \dots, x_{i-1}, x_{i+1}, \dots, x_N)$. If X_i is a set property of agent i, X represents the cross products $\prod_{i=1}^{N} X_i$ and $X_{-i} = \prod_{j \neq i} X_j$. For example, if s_i and S_i denote an action and the set of actions for agent i respectively, then s would denote the combination of actions for the whole group $(s_1, \dots, s_N)$; S the set of all such combinations; s_{-i} the combination of actions of all agents other than i; and S_{-i} the set of all such combinations. If z is a random variable on the domain Z with probability density distribution p, and $f(z)$ is a real-valued function, the notation $E_{p(z)} f(z)$ denotes the expected value of $f(z)$, and is short for $\sum_{z \in Z} p(z)f(z)$.

In the team problem Γ, since there is no conflict of interest, there would be an action combination s^* that maximises the team utility U. Thus optimally, agent i should choose the action s_i^*. We shall term s^* the *team optimal point*[2]

---

[2] A TOP is also a Nash equilibrium, however the opposite is not necessarily true. If multiple TOP's exist for a team problem, they must all yield the same utility, and we assume that the agents will agree on which TOP to follow.

(TOP) of the team problem Γ. Formally, we have $s^* \in \arg\max_{s \in S} U(s)$. The set of all TOP's for a team problem Γ is denoted by $\text{TOPS}(\Gamma)$.

2.2 Incomplete Information

The above description of team problem assumes that the agents have enough knowledge at hand to compute their utility for any combination of actions s. In reality, it is often that utility cannot be computed in exact form since it might depend on parameters whose values are unknown to the agent. Thus the agents have to base their actions on expected value of the true utility U. An interesting case is when these parameters are observed in private by the team members. This is likely to happen if the team is a distributed network of agents and data is available in a distributed manner. Since observations change the expected value of U and different agents experience different observations, the agents subjective expectations of U are no longer the same. This introduces new difficulties in coordinating their actions. We term this the incomplete information problem (also known as the asymmetric information problem).

Harsanyi [9] proposed the following ingenious resolution to the above problem[3]. All private information of agent i is summarised into an object called its *type*, denoted by t_i, so that the prior probability distribution of t_i, denoted by p_i is known to all agents. Then, the agents can be thought of as playing the following equivalent game. Firstly, nature or chance chooses the agents' type vector t according to the distribution $p_1, \ldots, p_N$ (t_i is chosen with probability $p_i(t_i)$). Nature then reveals the value t_i to agent i (which now becomes its private information). Finally, each agent i picks an action s_i and receives the utility $U(s,t)$.

Let T_i denote the set of all possible types of agent i (e.g. all possible values of its private observation). We assume that T_i are finite and p_i is a strictly positive distribution on T_i. A team problem with incomplete information can be represented formally as a tuple $\Gamma = \langle N, (S_i), U, (T_i), (p_i) \rangle$ where N, S_i remain as before, U is now a function on both actions and types: $U : S \times T \to \mathbb{R}$. We assume that different agents' types are independent and let p denote the joint distribution on T: $p(t) = \prod_{i \in N} p_i(t_i)$.

We define an *extended strategy* ψ_i as a rule that tells the agent i which action to choose given its type: $\psi_i : T_i \to S_i$. Let the set of all extended strategies for i be Ψ_i ($\Psi_i = S_i^{|T_i|}$). By letting the agent choose its extended strategy instead of its action, a team problem with incomplete information then can be transformed into one with complete information played within the extended strategy space. The utility assigned to a combination of extended strategies $\psi = (\psi_i)_{i \in N}$ is taken as the expectation of the original utilities: $\bar{U}(\psi) = \mathrm{E}_{p(t)} U((\psi_i(t_i)), t)$. Intuitively, $\bar{U}$ can be viewed as the average utility for the agents if they each employ the extended strategy ψ_i and play the game for many times. Thus the team problem with incomplete information can also be represented as the tuple $\langle N, (\Psi_i), \bar{U} \rangle$.

---

[3] For a more general representation of Harsanyi's ideas, readers are referred to [9].

Having removed the incomplete information, we are now ready to define TOP's for team problems with incomplete information. Given $\Gamma = \langle N, (S_i), U, (T_i), (p_i) \rangle$, its TOP is a combination of extended strategies ψ^* which is simply a TOP of $\langle N, (\Psi_i), (\bar{U}_i) \rangle$. In other words, $\psi^* \in \arg\max_{\psi \in \Psi} \bar{U}(\psi) = \arg\max_{\psi \in \Psi} E_{p(t)} U((\psi_i(t_i)), t)$.

We call the expected utility resulting from the TOP ψ^* the *value* $v(\Gamma)$ of the team problem. Intuitively, $v(\Gamma)$ is the maximal utility a team can achieve from the team problem Γ:

$$v(\Gamma) = \max_{\psi \in \Psi} \bar{U}(\psi) = \max_{\psi \in \Psi} \mathop{E}_{p(t)} U((\psi_i(t_i)), t) \tag{1}$$

3 Example: Distributed Meeting Scheduling

3.1 Domain Description

As an example of team problem with incomplete information, we consider a team decision-making scenario when a team of agents must choose a common outcome d from a set of possible outcomes $\mathcal{D}$ to maximise the team's objective function F. Each agent also holds a local preference $t_i(d)$ for each outcome d. These local preferences are the agents' private information and constitute the agents' types. Formally, the preferences of agent i are represented by $t_i : \mathcal{D} \to \mathbb{R}$. To make t_i finite, we assume that $\mathcal{D} = \{1, \ldots, D\}$, and $t_i = \{1, \ldots, D\} \to \{1, \ldots, M\}$ for some integers D and M. We can also write t_i in vector form as $t_i = (t_{id})$ where $t_{id} = t_i(d)$. F is then defined as the sum of the individual preferences[4]:

$$F(t_1, \ldots, t_N, d) = t_1(d) + \ldots + t_N(d) \tag{2}$$

For example, consider a group of agents whose task is to schedule a meeting between their respective users. The set of outcomes $\mathcal{D}$ is the set of tentative time-slots that can be scheduled for the meeting. Each user has his/her own private preferences over the time-slots which represent how free he/she might be during the interval. This data is held by his/her own agent, and not available a priori to the other agents involved. The team objective function is the sum of all users' private preferences: $F(t_1, \ldots, t_N, d) = \sum_{i \in N} t_i(d)$, and the goal for the group of agents is to agree on a time-slot that maximises this sum.

For the agents to find a common agreement, consider the following *voting* procedure: each agent simultaneously proposes one of the outcomes d in $\mathcal{D}$. If all the proposals are the same, this will be the final agreement. Otherwise, the final agreement will be drawn randomly from the set of proposals such that a proposal d will be selected with probability x/N where x is the number of agents who propose d.

In this voting scenario, the set of actions for the agents coincide with the set of outcomes: $S_i = \mathcal{D}$. The utility of s is the expected utility of the final

---

[4] In general, we only require the combining function to be linear w.r.t each of its variable given the others. Thus, the result can be generalised to the case where the combining function is a product of the individual preferences.

agreement when agent i proposes s_i respectively:

$$U(s,t) = \frac{1}{N} \sum_{i \in N} F(t, s_i) \tag{3}$$

Now, meeting scheduling using the above voting procedure can be modelled as a team problem $\Gamma_{ms} = \langle N, (S_i), U, (T_i), p_i \rangle$ where S, U, T are defined as above. The distribution p_i is the prior distribution on T_i, in this case on the set of preferences of user i.

3.2 TOP and value of meeting scheduling

With the above formulation, it has been shown elsewhere [3] that the meeting scheduling team problem has the following intuitive TOP. Optimally, in the TOP for Γ_{ms}, agent i should propose a time slot that maximises an evaluation function z_i, taken as the sum of i's own preference $t_i(d)$ and the expected value of other preferences $t_j(d)$:

$$z_i(d) = t_i(d) + \sum_{j \neq i} \mathop{\mathrm{E}}_{p_j(t_{jd})} t_{jd} = t_i(d) + \sum_{j \neq i} \sum_{t_{jd}=1}^{M} p_j(t_{jd}) t_{jd} \tag{4}$$

where $p_j(t_{jd}) = \sum_{t'_j \text{ s.t } t'_{jd}=t_{jd}} p_j(t'_j)$ is the probability that agent j has preference t_{jd} for slot d.

Let $z_i^* = \max_{d \in \mathcal{D}} z_i(k)$, the above proposing strategy leads to the optimal value for Γ_{ms} given as:

$$v(\Gamma_{ms}) = \frac{1}{N} \sum_{i=1}^{N} \mathop{\mathrm{E}}_{p(t_i)} z_i^* \tag{5}$$

4 Model of Repeated Interactions and Learning

In this section, we consider the case where a team of agents participate in a sequence of repeated interactions, each of them being a team problem with incomplete information. The above framework for coordination assumes that the prior distribution about the agents' types is given, and commonly known by all the agents. Our main motivation here is to relax this assumption and see how the agents can dynamically form such a distribution of types by learning from their observations and sharing the learned knowledge.

4.1 Model of Repeated Interactions

We present here a simplified model of team repeated interaction with incomplete information, adapted from the model of repeated games [14]. Let's denote the team problem with incomplete information with nature distribution p by $\Gamma(p) = \langle N, (S_i), U, (T_i), (p_i) \rangle$. For our purpose here, it suffices to parameterise Γ by

p only, since the set of agents, their actions, utility, and types are constants. Similarly, let $v(p) = v(\Gamma(p))$, and $\mathrm{TOPS}(p) = \mathrm{TOPS}(\Gamma(p))$.

We consider a repetition of the team problem $\Gamma(p)$ (termed the base team problem) over time $l = 1, \ldots, \infty$. Although p is stationary over time, it is not known by the agents when time starts. The type, or private observation of agent i at time l is denoted by a random variable t_i^l whose distribution is p_i and thus the sequence $[t_i^l]_\infty$ is a sequence of i.i.d. random variables with the same distribution p_i.

At time l, the history of the previous actions taken by the agents is $h^l = [s^k]_{l-1}$ where s^k is the actions taken at time k. The history of private observations of agent i is the sequence $o_i^l = [t_i^k]_{l-1}$. The pair (h^l, o_i^l) summarises what agent i knows before the start of round l.

The strategy of agent i at time l is a function $\tilde{\psi}_i^l : (h^l, o_i^l) \to \psi_i^l$ mapping its observation before time l to its extended strategy ψ_i^l at time l. The strategy of agent i in the repeated game is the sequence $\tilde{\psi}_i = [\tilde{\psi}_i^l]_\infty$.

Given a profile of strategies for each agent $\tilde{\psi} = (\tilde{\psi}_i)$, the actual action taken by agent i at time l is a function on the random variables $t^1, \ldots, t^{l-1}, t_i^l$ defined recursively as $s_i^1 = \tilde{\psi}_i^1(t_i^1)$, $s_i^l = \tilde{\psi}_i^l(h^l, o_i^l)(t_i^l)$, and the utility at time l is $U^l = U(s^l)$. The expected utility of the team at time l is $U^l = \mathrm{E}_{p(t_1, \ldots, t_l)} U^l$.

Theorem 1. *At every time instance l, the team cannot achieve more than the value of the base team problem: $U^l \leq v(p)$.*

Proof. Since the random variables $\{t^1, \ldots, t^l\}$ are independent, the agents cannot infer anything about the current type t^l, given their past observations. Thus, at round l, the agents cannot do better than in the single team problem $\Gamma(p)$. Hence, they cannot achieve more than $v(\Gamma(p))$ which is $v(p)$. □

The above theorem places an upper-bound $v(p)$ on the utility that can be achieved by the agents at any time in the repeated sequence. The difficulty of actually achieving $v(p)$ stems from the fact that p is not known by the agents. Nevertheless, over time, p_i can be estimated by agent i from its sequence of observation $[t_i^k]$, and with a suitable mechanism for sharing this estimate with others, all the agents can have access to a common estimate of p. As the common estimate becomes more accurate, the closer to $v(p)$ the agents can achieve. These results are presented formally in the following subsections.

4.2 Consistent Learners with Infinite Belief-Sharing

Let β_i^l denote agent i's estimation of p_i, or i's belief, at time l given its past observations[5]. An agent is called a *consistent learner* if its belief $[\beta_i^l]_\infty$ converges to the true nature distribution p_i almost surely ($[\beta_i^l] \overset{\text{a.s}}{\to} p_i$, or $\Pr\{[\beta_i^l] \to p_i\} = 1$). This can be achieved, for example, by using the frequency of outcomes in the sequence $[t_i^k]_{l-1}$ as the estimation for p_i at time l.

---

[5] To be more rigorous, i's belief at l is a random variable β_i^l which is a function on the sequence of past observations $[t_i^k]_{l-1}$.

To account for the sharing of beliefs, at every round of the repeated inter-action, we allow the agent the possibility to broadcast its belief β_i^l to other agents. We model the *common belief* as a sequence $[\alpha^l]_\infty$ satisfying the conditions: $\alpha_i^l = \beta_i^l$ if i shares its belief at time l, otherwise $\alpha_i^l = \alpha_i^{l-1}$. Thus, the action of 'sharing one's own belief' is modelled as updating the current common belief of the group to be the current belief of the individual. For example, if the agents always share their beliefs at every round, the common belief will be identical to the individual belief: $\forall l,\ \alpha^l = \beta^l$.

The theorem below guarantees that the common belief becomes accurate over time for consistent learners who share their individual belief an infinite number of times.

Theorem 2. *If every agent is a consistent learner and shares its belief an infinite number of times, their common belief converges to p almost surely:* $[\alpha^l]_\infty \overset{a.s}{\to} p$.

Proof. Since i is a consistent learner, its belief $[\beta_i^l]_\infty$ converges to p_i almost surely. Since i shares its belief an infinite number of times, the set $\{l \,|\, \alpha_i^l = \beta_i^l\}$ is infinite and it follows that $[\alpha_i^l]_\infty$ also converges to p_i almost surely. Thus, α^l converges to p almost surely. □

Suppose that the agents' common belief becomes accurate over time, how can the agents utilise this belief to achieve higher utility? One possibility is for the agents to act at round l as if α^l is the true nature distribution. In doing so, the agents would view the team problem at round l as $\Gamma(\alpha^l)$, and follow an optimal strategy in TOPS(α^l). We call the agents who follow this strategy *myopic* since they instantly attempt to optimise on the current round given the current common belief.

Recall that given an extended strategy ψ, its expected utility is given by $\bar{U}(\psi) = \sum_{t \in T} p(t) U((\psi_i(t_i))$. This can be thought of as a linear function U_ψ on p. Let q be an arbitrary distribution on T. The actual utility of following a strategy in TOPS(q), when the real nature distribution is p, is at least:

$$\underline{v}(q, p) = \min_{\psi \in \text{TOPS}(q)} U_\psi(p)$$

Note that $\underline{v}(p, p) = \min_{\psi \in \text{TOPS}(p)} U_\psi(p) = v(p)$.

For the myopic agents to utilise their beliefs which become close to p over time, we need to show that $\underline{v}(q, p)$ tends to $\underline{v}(p, p)$ as q tends to p. The following inequality ensures that this is the case:

Lemma 3. $|v(p) - \underline{v}(q, p)| \le C_1 \|p, q\|$ *where* $\|p, q\| = \sum_t |p(t) - q(t)|$, *and* $C_1 = 2U^{max} = 2\max_{t,s} U(t, s)$.

Proof. Suppose $v(p) = U_\psi(p)$, $\underline{v}(q, p) = U_{\psi'}(p)$ and let $f(p) = U_\psi(p) - U_{\psi'}(p)$. Since U_ψ and $U_{\psi'}$ are linear, f is also linear on p. Since $\psi \in \text{TOP}(p)$, $U_\psi(p) \ge U_{\psi'}(p)$ and similarly, $U_{\psi'}(q) \ge U_\psi(q)$. Hence, $f(p) \ge 0$ and $f(q) \le 0$. Thus, there exists some $0 \leq x \leq 1$ such that $f(r) = 0$ where $r = xp + (1 - x)q$. It follows that $U_\psi(r) = U_{\psi'}(r)$ and we have:

$$|v(p) - \underline{v}(q, p)| = |U_\psi(p) - U_{\psi'}(p)| = |U_\psi(p) - U_\psi(r) + U_{\psi'}(r) - U_{\psi'}(p)|$$
$$\leq |U_\psi(p) - U_\psi(r)| + |U_{\psi'}(r) - U_{\psi'}(p)|$$
$$\leq 2U^{max}\|p, r\| \leq 2U^{max}\|p, q\|$$

$\square$

Let U_∞^l be the utility achieved at round l by the group of myopic, consistent learning, infinite belief-sharing agents. We are now ready to state a theorem about the utility such a group of agents can achieve.

Theorem 4. *If every agent is a consistent learner, shares its belief an infinite number of times, and acts myopically given the common belief, their utility over time converges almost surely to $v(p)$:* $[U_\infty^l]_\infty \overset{a.s}{\to} v(p)$.

Proof. Since $v(p) \geq U_\infty^l \geq \underline{v}(\alpha^l, p)$, the result follows immediately from Theorem 2 and Lemma 3. $\square$

4.3 ϵ-Trigger Belief-Sharing

The above result of convergence of utility of myopic agents requires an infinite number of exchanges of the individual beliefs. In this subsection, we describe the ϵ-trigger belief-sharing mechanism which makes use of only a finite number of exchanges and still guarantees an utility that, over time, becomes close to the upper-bound $v(p)$. Throughout this section, it is implicitly assumed that the agents are consistent learners and act myopically.

An agent follows the ϵ-trigger belief-sharing mechanism if it shares its belief with others whenever the difference between its current belief and the common belief becomes greater than ϵ: i shares its belief at round l iff $\|\beta_i^l, \alpha_i^{l-1}\| \geq \epsilon$, or in other words, $\alpha_i^l = \beta_i^l$ if $\|\beta_i^l, \alpha_i^{l-1}\| \geq \epsilon$, otherwise $\alpha_i^l = \alpha_i^{l-1}$. Thus, belief-sharing is triggered when the discrepancy between the individual belief and the common belief exceeds some upper-bound.

Below, we will state two theorems concerning the ϵ-trigger belief-sharing mechanism. The first result states that an ϵ-trigger belief-sharing agent will only share its belief a finite number of times. The second puts a bound on how close the group utility is to $v(p)$.

Lemma 5. *With probability 1, there exists a time L_i such that agent i shares its belief at most once after L_i.*

Proof. Since β_i^l converges almost surely, with probability 1, $\exists L_i$ such that for all $l, l' \geq L_i$, $\|\beta_i^l, \beta_i^{l'}\| < \epsilon$. We prove by contradiction that i cannot share its belief twice after L_i. Otherwise, suppose that $l' > l > L_i$ are two consecutive time of i sharing its belief. Thus $\alpha_i^{l'-1} = \alpha_i^l = \beta_i^l$. But since i shares its belief at l', $\|\alpha_i^{l'-1}, \beta_i^{l'}\| \geq \epsilon$ and thus $\|\beta_i^l, \beta_i^{l'}\| \geq \epsilon$, contradictory to the above. $\square$

This leads immediately to the following theorem:

Theorem 6. *With probability 1, the total number of belief-sharing instances among the agents that use the ϵ-trigger belief-sharing mechanism is finite.*

In order to show that over time, the utility of the group becomes close to the optimal $v(p)$, we first show that the common belief becomes close to the true distribution p.

Lemma 7. *With probability 1, there exists a time L_i such that after this time, the common belief regarding agent i's type is close to the true nature distribution p_i: $\forall l \geq L_i$, $\|\alpha_i^l, p_i\| < 2\epsilon$.*

Proof. With probability 1, $\exists L_i$ such that $\forall l \geq L_i$, $\|\beta_i^l, p_i\| < \epsilon$. For all $l \geq L_i$, if $\|\beta_i^l, \alpha_i^{l-1}\| \geq \epsilon$ then i shares its belief at l and $\alpha_i^l = \beta_i^l$, thus $\|\alpha_i^l, p_i\| = \|\beta_i^l, p_i\| < \epsilon$. Otherwise, $\|\beta_i^l, \alpha_i^{l-1}\| < \epsilon$ and $\alpha_i^l = \alpha_i^{l-1}$, and thus $\|\alpha_i^l, p_i\| = \|\alpha_i^{l-1}, p_i\| \leq \|\alpha_i^{l-1}, \beta_i^l\| + \|\beta_i^l, p_i\| < 2\epsilon$. □

Using the inequality $\sum_{t_1,\ldots,t_N} (|p_1(t_1)\ldots p_N(t_N)| - |q_1(t_1)\ldots q_N(t_N)|) \leq \sum_{i=1}^{N} \sum_{t_i} |p_i(t_i) - q_i(t_i)|$, we have $\|p, q\| \leq \sum_{i=1}^{N} \|p_i, q_i\|$. With this, the above lemma leads directly to the following corollary:

Corollary 8. *With probability 1, there exists a time L such that after this time, the common belief is close to the true nature distribution p: $\forall l \geq L$, $\|\alpha^l, p\| < 2N\epsilon$.*

Now let U_ϵ^l be the utility at round l of the group of myopic, consistent learning agents with ϵ-trigger belief-sharing mechanism, we have:

Theorem 9. *With probability 1, there exists a time L such that after this time, the utility achieved by the group of myopic, consistent learning agents with ϵ-trigger belief-sharing mechanism is close to $v(p)$: $\forall l \geq L$, $|v(p) - U_\epsilon^l| < C_2\epsilon$, where $C_2 = 4NU^{max}$.*

Proof. Since $v(p) \geq U_\epsilon^l \geq \underline{v}(\alpha^l, p)$, the theorem follows directly from Lemma 3 and Corollary 8. □

5 Experiments in the Meeting Scheduling Domain

In this section we describe our experiments with the coordination and learning framework presented above in the meeting scheduling domain described in section 3. Recall that in a meeting scheduling scenario, each agent must propose a time slot it wants the meeting to be scheduled in. In the one-shot interaction, it is optimal for the agent to propose the time slot that maximises the sum of its own preference and the expected values of others' preferences. When the distribution of preferences is not known in advance, an estimation of the distribution can be constructed by letting the agent learn to estimate its own distribution of preferences and share this learned knowledge with others.

Subsequently, we describe the heuristics involved for an agent to learn the distribution of its preferences and sharing its belief with others.

5.1 Learning the Agent's Preferences

The learning task of agent i can be thought of as learning the pattern of its user's preferences. This is similar to the task faced by the learning interface agents [10, 12]. However since we need to estimate the distribution of preferences, a probabilistic learning method will be more suitable for us.

Assuming that the user's preference for an interval d is the integration of an underlying preference function $f_i(x), x \in Time$ over d, it suffices for i to learn to predict the future value of f_i given the values that it has discovered in the meeting scheduling instances in the past. This can be presented as a supervised learning problem where, given a set of pairs of sample and target class $\{(x, f_i(x))\}$, agent i has to form a probability distribution of $f_i(y)$ for some unobserved sample y (x and y are samples from the sample space $Time$).

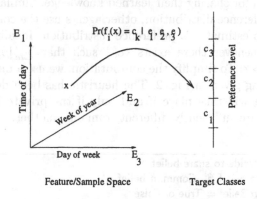

Feature/Sample Space   Target Classes

Fig. 1. Features and target classes

To achieve this task, we employ the standard *naive Bayesian classifier* supervised learning method [13, Chap. 6]. First, we identify a set of features $\{E_1, \ldots, E_R\}$ on the sample space $Time$ such as time of day, day of week, week of month, even day/odd day, etc. The set of target classes C is taken as the set of possible values for the agent's preference (if there are many different values, neighbouring values can be grouped into courser intervals) (see Fig. 1).

The Bayesian classifier estimates $\Pr(c|e_1, \ldots, e_R)$, the probability of a target class c given the features $\{e_r\}$ using the Bayes' formula, and the simplified assumption that the features $\{e_r\}$ are independent given the target class c:

$$\Pr(c|e_1, \ldots, e_R) = \frac{\Pr(e_1, \ldots, e_R|c)\Pr(c)}{\text{Const}} = \frac{\left[\prod_{r=1}^{R} \Pr(e_r|c)\right]\Pr(c)}{\text{Const}} \quad (6)$$

where Const is a normalised constant.

Suppose at time l agent i has observed a set of its user's preferences of the form $\{(x, f_i(x))\}$. Let $\beta_i^l(c)$ be the frequency of class c occurring, i.e. the fraction of x's such that $f_i(x) \in c$. Let $\beta_i^l(e_r; c)$ be the frequency of feature e_r

occurring given the class c, i.e. the fraction of x's such that $E_r(x) = e_r$ among the x's such that $f_i(x) = c$. Agent i uses the estimators $\beta_i^l(c)$ and $\beta_i^l(e_r; c)$ to estimate the probabilities $\Pr(c)$ and $\Pr(e_r|c)$. As new observation arrives, agent i updates its belief by updating the frequencies $\beta_i^l(c)$ and $\beta_i^l(e_r; c)$. These frequencies constitute the belief β_i^l of agent i at time l about the pattern of its user's preferences. From this, given a new time point x with features $\{e_r\}$, the distribution of the user's preference for x can be estimated by:

$$\Pr(f_i(x) \in c|e_1, \dots, e_R) \approx \beta_i^l(c; e_1, \dots, e_R) = \frac{\left[\prod_{r=1}^{R} \beta_i^l(e_r; c)\right] \beta_i^l(c)}{\text{Const}} \quad (7)$$

5.2 Heuristics for Sharing Belief

The meeting scheduling agents use a heuristics similar to the ϵ-trigger belief-sharing mechanism for sharing their learned knowledge. Similar to the way i estimate its own preference distribution, other agents use the common belief $\alpha_i^l = (\alpha_i^l(c), \alpha_i^l(e_r; c))$ to estimate i's preference distribution. Ideally, agent i should share its belief whenever there exists $\{e_r\}$ such that $\sum_c |\beta_i^l(c; e_1, \dots, e_R) - \alpha_i^l(c; e_1, \dots, e_R)| > \epsilon$. To simplify the computation, we use a more simple heuristic for belief-sharing given in Fig. 2. The heuristic has been designed to ensure that belief sharing will take place if and only if the private belief β_i^l and the common belief α_i^l are sufficiently different from one another.

Algorithm: Decide to share belief
Input: Private belief β_i^l, Common belief α_i^l
Output: ShareBelief = True or False
Constants: $\epsilon_1, \epsilon_2 \approx 0$ and $C > 1$

   I. ShareBelief = False
  II. For all r, For all e_r
      1. /* If common belief is not close to 0 */
        If $\alpha_i^l(e_r; c)\alpha_i^l(c) > \epsilon_1$
          /* If the ratio of private and common belief is large */
          If $|\beta_i^l(c)/\alpha_i^l(c) - 1| > \epsilon_2$ or $|\beta_i^l(e_r; c)/\alpha_i^l(e_r; c) - 1| > \epsilon_2$
            ShareBelief = True
            Break
      2. Else /* common belief is close to 0 */
        /* If private belief becomes large */
        If $\beta_i^l(e_r; c)\beta_i^l(c) > \epsilon_1$ and $\beta_i^l(e_r; c)\beta_i^l(c)/\alpha_i^l(e_r; c)\alpha_i^l(c) > C$
          ShareBelief = True
          Break
III. Return ShareBelief

Fig. 2. Algorithm: Decide to share belief

5.3 Experimental Results

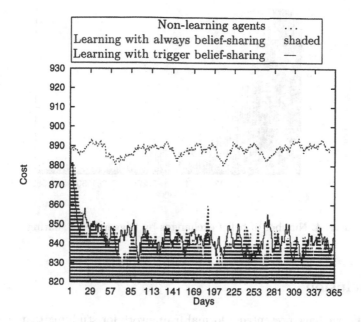

Fig. 3. Cost induced by learning and non-learning agents

Our set of experiments consists of three agents having to schedule one meeting per day, within the time window [8h00, 16h30]. For each agent, the preference for a time point is generated randomly with distribution chosen periodically from a set of stationary distributions.

We experiment with three sets of agents: one with non-learning agents, one with learning agents that always share their beliefs, and one with learning agents using trigger belief-sharing. We generate 100 runs for each set of agents to get their average behaviour. We measure the performance of the agents by the average cost (negation of utility) induced by the agents per day. For the agents using trigger belief-sharing, we also measure the average number of belief exchange instances among the agents (per agent, per day). These results are plotted in Fig. 3 and 4. Figure 3 shows the learning agents gradually improve and out-perform the non-learning agents by guessing the distribution of preferences and adjust their proposals accordingly. Interestingly, the performance of learning agents with trigger belief-sharing (the solid line) is almost the same as the learning agents that always share their beliefs (the shaded region). Furthermore, Fig. 4 shows that the average number of belief exchanges of the former agent group decrease to zero over time. This demonstrates that the trigger belief-sharing mechanism can achieve the same level of performance, but with minimal communication requirement.

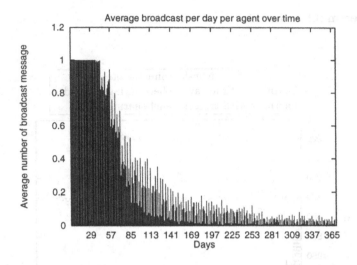

Fig. 4. Number of belief exchanges by trigger belief-sharing

6   Conclusion

In summary, we have presented a formal framework for studying team coordination with incomplete information based on the theory of games with incomplete information. The framework allows us to define the notion of team optimality, TOP, to be taken as the ideal solution to the team coordination problem.

In order to compute the TOP, it is required that the agents know the nature distribution of types, or private observations. We show that when repeated interactions are considered, this distribution can be learned, and the learned knowledge can be shared by the agents. By having an accurate estimation of the nature distribution, the agents utility can approach the optimal utility over time. Furthermore, the communication requirement for exchanging their learned knowledge can be kept minimal with the trigger belief-sharing strategy.

The work presented here can be extended in several dimensions. First, it is currently assumed that the repeated interaction occurs between a fixed group of agents. Further study can be done for the case when the group of agents varies dynamically. Second, the model for exchanging belief can be adapted to the case where the agents' sets of private observations are overlapping. Last but not least, the framework here can be integrated with the framework allowing for direct communication of private observation [3] to account for a unified theory on coordination, communication and learning in team of agents.

References

1. A. H. Bond and L. Gasser, editors. *Readings in Distributed Artificial Intelligence.* Morgan Kaufmann, 1988.

2. Hung H. Bui, D. Kieronska, and S. Venkatesh. Learning other agents' preferences in multiagent negotiation. In *Proceedings of the National Conference on Artificial Intelligence (AAAI-96)*, pages 114–119, August 1996.

3. Hung H. Bui, D. Kieronska, and S. Venkatesh. Optimal communication among team members. In Abdul Sattar, editor, *Advanced Topics in Artificial Intelligence, Proceedings of the Tenth Australian Joint Conference on Artificial Intelligence, AI-97*, volume 1342 of *Lecture Notes in Artificial Intelligence*, pages 116–126. Springer, 1997.

4. P. R. Cohen and H. J. Levesque. Intention is choice with commitment. *Artificial Intelligence*, 42:213–261, 1990.

5. M. L. Dowell. *Learning in Multiagent Systems*. PhD thesis, Department of Electrical and Computer Engineering, University of South Carolina, 1995.

6. Edmund H. Durfee and Jeffrey S. Rosenschein. Distributed problem solving and multi-agent systems: Comparisons and examples. In *Proceedings of the 13th International Workshop on Distributed Artificial Intelligence (IWDAI-94)*, pages 94–104, 1994.

7. Piotr J. Gmytrasiewicz and Edmund H. Durfee. A rigorous, operational formalization of recursive modelling. In *Proceedings of the First International Conference on Multiagent Systems (ICMAS-95)*, pages 125–132, San Francisco, CA, 1995.

8. Piotr J. Gmytrasiewicz and Edmund H. Durfee. Rational interaction in multiagent environments: Coordination. In submission, 1997.

9. John C. Harsanyi. Games with incomplete information played by Bayesian players 1-3. *Management Science*, 14:159–182,320–334,486–502, 1967-1968.

10. Y. Lashkari, M. Metral, and P. Maes. Collaborative interface agents. In *Proceedings of the National Conference on Artificial Intelligence (AAAI-94)*, pages 444–449, 1994.

11. H. J. Levesque, P. R. Cohen, and J. H. T. Nunes. On acting together. In *Proceedings of the National Conference on Artificial Intelligence (AAAI-90)*, pages 94–99, 1990.

12. P. Maes and R. Kozierok. Learning interface agents. In *Proceedings of the National Conference on Artificial Intelligence (AAAI-93)*, pages 459–465, 1993.

13. Tom M. Mitchell. *Machine Learning*. McGraw–Hill, New York, 1997.

14. Roger B. Myerson. *Game Theory: Analysis of Conflict*. Havard University Press, 1991.

15. S. Sen, editor. *Papers from the AAAI-96 Spring Symposium on Adaptation, Co-evolution, and Learning in Multiagent Systems*, Menlo Park, CA, March 1996. AAAI Press.

16. R. G. Smith. The contract net protocol: High-level communication and control in a distributed problem solver. *IEEE Transactions on Computers*, 29(12):1104–1113, 1980.

17. Milind Tambe. Towards flexible teamwork. *Journal of Artficial Intelligence Research*, 7:83–124, 1997.

18. Jose M. Vidal and Edmund H. Durfee. RMM's solution concept and the equilibrium point solution. In *Proceedings of the 13th International Workshop on Distributed Artificial Intelligence (IWDAI-94)*, 1994.

19. G. Weiss and S. Sen, editors. *Adaptation and Learning in Multiagent Systems, Proceedings of the IJCAI-95 Workshop*. Number 1042 in Lecture Notes in Artificial Intelligence. Springer-Verlag, 1996.

An Iterated Hawk-and-Dove Game

Bengt Carlsson,
bengt.carlsson@ide.hk-r.se
Tel: +46 (0)45778723

Stefan Johansson
stefan.johansson@ide.hk-r.se
Tel: +46 (0)45778742

Department of Computer Science and Business Administration
University of Karlskrona/Ronneby
Soft Center Ronneby, Sweden

Abstract

A fundamental problem in multi agent systems is conflict resolution. A conflict occurs in general when the agents have to deal with inconsistent goals, such as a demand for shared resources. We investigate some theoretical game approaches as efficient methods to examine a class of conflicts in multi agent systems.

In the first part of the paper, we look at the hawk-and-dove game both from an evolutionary and from an iterated point of view. An iterated hawk-and-dove game is not the same as an infinitely repeated evolutionary game because in an iterated game the agents are supposed to know what happened in the previous moves. In an evolutionary game evolutionary stable strategies will be most successful but not necessarily be a unique solution. An iterated game can be modeled as a mixture of a prisoner's dilemma game and a chicken game. These kinds of games are generally supposed to have successful cooperating strategies.

The second part of the paper discusses situations where a chicken game is a more appropriate model than a prisoner's dilemma game.

The third part of the paper describes our simulation of iterated prisoner's dilemma and iterated chicken games. We study a parameterized class of cooperative games, with these classical games as end cases, and we show that chicken games to a higher extent reward cooperative strategies than defecting strategies.

The main results of our simulation are that a chicken game is more cooperating than a prisoner's dilemma because of the values of the payoff matrix. None of the strategies in our simulation actually analyses its score and acts upon it, which gave us significant linear changes in score between the games when linear changes were made to the payoff matrix. All the top six strategies are nice and have small or moderate differences in scores between chicken game and prisoner's dilemma. The 11 worst strategies, with a lower score than *random*, either start with defect or, if they start with cooperation, are not nice. All of these strategies are doing significantly worse in the chicken game than in the prisoner's dilemma.

Keywords: multi agent systems, hawk-and-dove game, prisoner's dilemma, chicken game, evolutionary stable strategies.

1 Background

Conflict resolutions are typically resolved by an appropriate negotiation process. In a multi agent setting, there have been several proposals of such negotiation processes. A recent and promising approach are models of computational markets (Sandholm and Ygge 1997, Wellman 1993). In this case, and other proposals, the negotiation is modeled as an interaction protocol between the agents involved. An important issue in the agent theories is whether we have centralized control or not. In the latter situations we refer to the agents as autonomous.

We propose in this paper iterated games as models of decentralized conflict resolution. We thus propose and make a preliminary assessment of a game theoretical framework for establishing cooperative behavior between selfish agents.

The evolution of cooperative behavior among a group of self-interested agents has received a lot of attention among researchers in political science, economics and evolutionary biology. prisoner's dilemma (Luce and Raiffa 1957, Rapoport and Chammah 1965) was originally formulated as a paradox where the obvious preferable solution for both prisoners, low punishment, was not chosen. The reason is that the first prisoner did not know what the second prisoner intended to do, so he had to guard himself. The paradox lies in the fact that both prisoners had to accept a high penalty in spite of that cooperation is a better solution for both of them. This paradox presumes that the prisoners were unable to take revenge on the squealer after the years in jail.

The iterated prisoner's dilemma is, on the other hand, generally viewed as the major game-theoretical paradigm for the evolution of cooperation based on reciprocity. This is related to the fact that the agents have background information about previous moves, an information that is missing in the single game case.

2 Disposition

There is a distinction between iterated games, like the iterated prisoner's dilemma (IPD), the iterated chicken game (ICG) etc., and evolutionary games like the hawk-and-dove game (HDG). In the iterated games there must be some background information while an evolutionary HDG is a repeated game without history. In the iterated games this knowledge is used in order to find the proper moves according to the strategies in question, while an evolutionary stable strategy (ESS) is the result of an evolutionary game. An iterated game can, contrary to the HDG, easily be simulated by using this knowledge. In section 3 and 4 these three games are compared and a distinction between evolutionary and iterated games are made.

A problem central to multi agent systems is resource allocation. We model a negotiation situation (section 5) between two agents wanting a resource as an IPD or an ICG and argue in favor of using an ICG as an equivalent or even better description. There are two arguments for doing this: firstly a resource allocation problem can sometimes be better described   using a chicken game matrix and secondly ICG should be expected to be at least as cooperative as IPD.

Different IPD and ICG are compared in section 6 and 7 in a series of experiments. We find successive strategies in chicken game being more cooperating than those in prisoner's dilemma. Finally we conclude with a section on the implications of our results.

3 A Comparison Between Three Different Games

The three above mentioned games make the basis for this discussion of the applications of game theory in multi agent systems, the IPD, ICG and HDG. In common for all three games is that the players have two mutually excluding choices, to cooperate (C) or to defect from cooperation (D).

3.1 The Prisoner's Dilemma

The prisoner's dilemma (PD) is a well-studied game within the area of game theory and when iterated (Axelrod and Hamilton 1981, Axelrod 1984) it has, apart from being a model for cooperation in economical and biological systems, also been used in multi agent systems (Lomborg 1994). In the former disciplines, it has been used from a social science point of view to explain observed cooperative phenomena, while in multi agent systems it has been used to try to create systems with a predicted cooperative behavior. The payoff matrix for PD can be found in figure 1a.

3.2 The Chicken Game

In the chicken game (CG) (Russell 1959), the players payoff is lower when both of them play defect than what they would have received by cooperatively playing while the opponent defected. Its name originates from the front-to-front car race where the first one to swerve from the collision course is a "chicken". Obviously, if they both cooperate, they will both avoid the crash and none of them will either be a winner or risk their lives. If one of them steers away, they will be chicken, but will survive, while the opponent will get all the honor. If they crash, the cost for both of them will be higher than the cost of being a chicken (and hence their payoff is lower, see payoff matrix in figure 1b). In the game matrices we use ordinal numbers IV > III > II > I to represent the different outcomes[1].

---

[1] It is possible to interchange rows, columns and players or any combination of these operations to obtain equal games. Prisoners dilemma and chicken game are two out of 78 possible games (Ropoport and Guyer 1966 p. 204) representing different payoffs on an ordinal scale. Ordinal scale means that only the orders of magnitude can serve as criteria in the taxonomy, in contrast to a cardinal scale which is based on the different values.

a.

	C_2	D_2
C_1	III, III	I, IV
D_1	IV, I	II, II

b.

	C_2	D_2
C_1	III, III	II, IV
D_1	IV, II	I, I

Fig.1. Prisoner's dilemma (1 a) and chicken game (1 b) on an ordinal scale I-IV

3.3 The Hawk-and-Dove Game

The HDG (Maynard Smith and Price 1973, Maynard Smith 1982) is described as a struggle between "birds" for a certain resource. The birds can either have an aggressive hawk-behavior, or a non-fighting dove-behavior. When two doves meet, they will equally share the resource with a small cost or without any costs for sharing, but when meeting a hawk, the dove leaves all of the resource to the hawk without a fight. However, two hawks will fight for the resource until one of them gets hurt so badly that it leaves the fight. Figure 2 shows the payoff matrix for a HDG. A dove (C) in the matrix is described as a cooperating agent and a hawk (D) as a defecting agent.

	C_2	D_2
C_1	R-S)/2, (R-S)/2	0, R
D_1	R, 0	(R–F)/2, (R-F)/2

Fig. 2. HDG, R is the total resource, (R-F)/2 the average outcome of a hawk-hawk fight and (R-S)/2 the average outcome for two doves sharing a resource.

In the HDG, we can see that if R>F>S>0, then we have a PD type of HDG, since R>(R-S)/2>(R-F)/2>0 (which corresponds to PD's IV>III>II>I). As a matter of fact, the same is true for CG; when we have R<F, we get R>(R-S)/2>0>(R-F)/2 (which corresponds to CGs matrix). In a PD, a second condition is usually put on the values of the payoff matrix, namely that 2*III > I+IV, that is: the resource, when shared in cooperation, must be greater than it is when shared by a cooperator and a defector. This condition was, as we see it, introduced for practical reasons more than for theoretical ones and we think that it may have done more harm than good to the area and its applications.

"The question of whether the collusion of alternating unilateral defections would occur and, if so, how frequently is doubtless interesting. For the present, however, we wish to avoid the complication of multiple 'cooperative solutions'." (Rapoport and Chammah 1965, p. 35)

Now if we remove this constraint and let 2*III ≤ I+IV be another possibility, we have a true HDG situation with equality when S=0. This means that we can describe every such PD as a HDG, just by transposing the PD payoff matrix to a HDG one.

The case when S=0, when the sharing of a resource between two cooperators/doves does not cost anything, has been the main setup of our simulations and the reason for that is that we find it a natural way of describing resource sharing in multi agent systems. The resource neither grows nor decreases by being shared by two agents compared to when a defecting agent or a hawk takes it from the cooperator/dove.

4 Evolutionary and Iterated Games

Evolutionary games use the concept of Evolutionary Stable Strategies (ESS). For a strategy to be stable it requires that, if almost all members of the population adopt it, the fitness of these typical members are greater than that of any possible mutant. An ESS is a stable strategy in that if all the members of a population adopt it, then no mutant strategy could invade the population under the influence of natural selection (Maynard Smith and Price 1973). Or in other words: an ESS is a strategy which does well against copies of itself. A successful strategy is one which dominates the population, therefore it will tend to meet copies of itself. Conversely, if it is not successful against copies of itself, it will not be able to dominate the population. In a hawk-and-dove game without any costs for two doves sharing the resource we have:

	C_2	D_2
C_1	R/2, R/2	0, R
D_1	R, 0	(R–F)/2, (R-F)/2

Fig. 3. A basic hawk-and-dove matrix.

In this case it requires (with the notation $E(p,q)$ used to express the payoff to an individual adopting strategy p against an opponent adopting strategy q), for a strategy to be an ESS (Maynard Smith and Price 1973) that either

1. $E(p, p) > E(q, p)$ or

2. $E(p, p) = E(q, p)$ and $E(p, q) > E(q, q)$

This implies:

- C is not an ESS because $\frac{1}{2}R < R$; a population of cooperating agents can be invaded by a defecting agent.

- D is an ESS if $\frac{1}{2}(R - F) > 0$ or $R > F$. This is the same as the solution to the single game prisoner's dilemma. The point is that an ESS is not restricted to one move, the game can be repeated an infinite number of times.

- A proportion of C and D is an ESS if $R < F$ because $\frac{1}{2}(R - F) < 0$ and $\frac{1}{2}R < F$ excludes both C and D from being a pure ESS. Instead there will be a probability

p for C and a probability $q = 1 - p$ for D. This is the chicken game state which easily can be determined by counting its Nash equilibrium – the point where no actor unilaterally wishes to change his choice.

$p = (R - \frac{1}{2}R)/(R + 0 - \frac{1}{2}(R - F) - \frac{1}{2}R) = R/F$

and

$q = 1 - R/F.$

In the evolutionary approach an agent must only know his own payoffs for different moves. No common knowledge, rationality, about the other agents is needed. This means that we don't have to explain how agents know that a Nash equilibrium will be reached. The problem is that this is not the same as finding a successful strategy in an iterated game where an agent must know something about the other's choice. A large amount of outcomes in both IPD and ICG can be the consequence of a rational, Nash, equilibrium. This is known as the Folk Theorem[2].

To use a deterministic ESS will not be the best strategy if the other strategies can make a commitment based on knowledge instead. In a multi agent environment this knowledge about the other agent's choice makes it possible to simulate the game.

5 Examples of a Resource Allocation Problem

An every-day situation description of a game situation would be when two contestants get into conflict in a business matter. When the two strategies cooperate and defect the contestants can choose to share the result or one gives up when the contestant goes to court to settle the case. If the reality of the game is that both lose more by going to court than by giving up, we have a chicken game. If we instead have a lesser cost for going to court compared to giving up, under the assumption of unchanged other conditions, there will be a prisoner's dilemma situation. In a repeated chicken game with no background information we should intuitively expect at least the same or even stronger cooperative behavior to evolve in the chicken game compared to the prisoner's dilemma because of the larger costs of going to court.

---

[2] Lomborg (p. 70-74 1994) has an overview of this critique against Nash equilibrium and ESS.

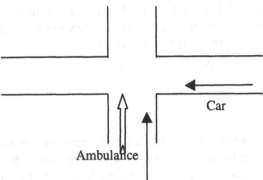

Fig. 4. A resource allocation problem.

Let us look at a traffic situation in an intersection using give right-of-way to traffic coming from the right (right-hand-rule). Drivers usually act in a cooperative mode and on average have to wait half of the time. No supervisor or central control is needed to have a functional system. Rescue vehicles, like the fire brigade or an ambulance, can however use an emergency alarm to get access to the lane. Let us suppose that if two ambulances both reach the intersection at the same time they will crash because they can't hear the siren from the other vehicle. If other cars begin to install sirens and behave as ambulances the whole traffic situation will collapse. The same thing happens if car drivers forget what is right and what is left. We call this random behavior a noisy one.

An analog to a traffic situation is how to model to get a whole resource where two agents normally share the resource half of the time each. We have the finitary predicament: real agents have only finite computational power and real agents have limited time.

If a very important or high priority agent wants the resource it will get it immediately and the other agent will get nothing. Two agents who want the resource at the same time, without having to wait for it, will cause a deadlock. If the cost for a deadlock is bigger than the cost for a cooperating agent meeting a defecting agent, then we have a chicken game, otherwise we have a prisoner's dilemma.

6 A Tournament Comparing Prisoner's Dilemma and Chicken Game

When Axelrod and Hamilton (Axelrod and Hamilton 1981, Axelrod 1984) analyzed the iterated prisoner's dilemma they found out that a cooperating strategy, the *Tit-for-Tat* (*TfT*) strategy, did very well against more defecting strategies. This strategy has become an informal guiding principle for reciprocal altruism (Trivers 1971).

A *TfT*-agent begins with cooperation and then follows whatever the other agent is doing in a game lasting an unknown number of times. All agents are interested in maximizing individual utilities and are not pre-disposed to help each other. A defecting agent will always win or at least stay equal when meeting a *TfT* agent. In spite of that, a group of *TfT* agents will be stable against invasion of agents using other strategies because they are doing very well meeting their own strategy. No other strategy can do better against *TfT* than the strategy itself[3]. *TfT* is a strategy that always repeats the example of the other strategy after the first cooperates. Depending on the surroundings this will be the best strategy, as in Axelrod's simulations, or a marginally acceptable or even a bad strategy.

As we see, the Hawk-and-dove game can be divided into two different game matrixes: The prisoner's dilemma-like game without the second condition of the prisoner's dilemma and the chicken game.

Axelrod found his famous Tit-for-Tat solution for the prisoner's dilemma when he arranged and evaluated a tournament. He used the payoff matrix in fig 5a for each move of the prisoner's dilemma:

a

	C_2	D_2
C_1	3, 3	0, 5
D_1	5, 0	1, 1

b

	C_2	D_2
C_1	3, 3	1, 5
D_1	5, 1	0, 0

Fig. 5. Example payoff matrix prisoner's dilemma (5 a) and chicken game (5 b).

The tournament was conducted in a round robin way so that each strategy was paired with each other strategy plus its own twin and with the random strategy. Different people sent in their favorite strategy to the tournament. There were a lot of strategies trying to beat each other by being more or less nice, resistant to provocation, or even evil; classification due to Axelrod (1980a, 1980b).

In our experiment we use the same total payoff sum for the matrices as Axelrod used. However, we vary the two lowest payoffs (0 and 1) so that they change order between PD and the CG matrix in figure 5b. The appendix describes the result of the simulation.

In our experiment we used a simulation tool with 36 different strategies (Mathieu and Delahaye 1996). The rule of this tournament is a round robin tournament between different strategies with a fixed length of 100 moves. Each tournament was

---

[3] Its true that *TfT* cannot be invaded by a defect, D, if there is sufficiently high concentration of *TfT*. But always cooperate, C , does as well as *TfT* in a population consisting only of itself and *TfT*, and hence can spread by genetic drift. This means that D can invade as soon as the frequency of C is high enough, since it has to fear less retaliation than against *TfT* alone. The game must be played an unknown number of iterations. The reason is that no strategy is supposed to be able to take advantage of knowing when the game ends and defect that iteration.

run five times. Besides the two strategies above we varied (D, D) and (C, D) ten steps between 1 and 0 respectively without changing the total payoff sum for the matrix. As an example, (0.4; 0.6) means that a cooperate agent gets 0.4 meeting a defect and defect gets 0.6 meeting another defect. This will be the 0.4 column in Appendix A, a prisoner's dilemma matrix. The different strategies are described in Mathieu and Delahaye (1996).

We have used three characterizations of the different strategies:

- Initial move (I) – If the initial move of the strategy was cooperative (C), defect (D) or random (R).

- Nice (N) – If the strategy does not make the first defect in the game (X).

- Static (S) – If the strategy is fully (X) or partly (P) independent of other strategies or if the strategy is randomized (R).

Out of 36 different strategies *Gradual* won in a PD game. *Gradual* cooperates on the first move, then defects n times after n defections, and then calms down its opponent with 2 cooperation moves. In CG a strategy *Coop_puis_tc* won. This strategy cooperates until the other player defects and then alters between defection and cooperation the rest of the time. *TfT* was around 5th place for both games. Two other interesting strategies are *joss_mou* (2nd place) and *joss_dur* (35th place). Both start with cooperation and basically play *TfT*. *Joss-mou* plays cooperation strategy one time out of ten instead of defect and *joss_dur* plays defect one time out of ten instead of cooperate. This causes the large differences in scores between the strategies.

The top scoring games start with cooperation and react towards others i.e. they are not static. Both PD and CG have the same top strategies. A majority of the low score games are either starting with defect or have a static strategy.

Mechante (always defect) has the biggest difference in favor of PD and *gentille* (always cooperate) the biggest difference in favor of CG. The five games with the largest difference in favor of CG are all cooperative with a static counter. There is no such connection for the strategies in favor of PD, instead there is a mixture of cooperate, defect and static strategies.

The linear correlation between the different kinds of games and the scores of each of the strategies were calculated. For all but six of the strategies there were a high confidence correlation value (r^2) exceeding 0.9. A minus sign before the r-value means that the strategy in question is more successful in the CG than in the PD (see appendix). For all these strategies there are significance levels exceeding the probability of 0.99. *TfT* is one of the remaining six strategies neither favored by PD nor by CG.

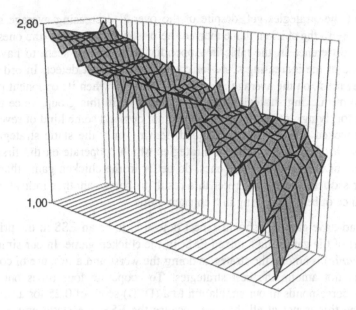

Fig. 6. Comparing PD and CG. In the figure above the CG is in the foreground and the PD in the background, the best strategies are to the left and the worst to the right.

7 Discussion

We have shown the similarities between the hawk-and-dove game and the iterated prisoner's dilemma and chicken game. From a resource allocation point of view we argue that a parameterized game ranging from PD to CG is a suitable model for describing these kinds of problems.

This paper describes a simulation of iterated games according to Axelrod's basic matrix. Our simulation indicates that chicken game to a higher extent rewards cooperative strategies than the prisoner's dilemma because of the increased cost of mutual defections. These statements are confirmed by the following parts of the result:

1. All the top six strategies are nice and start with a cooperation. They have small or moderate differences in scores between chicken game and prisoner's dilemma. *TfT* is a successful strategy but not at all the best.

2. All the 11 strategies, with a lower score than *random (lunatique)*, either start with defect or, if they start with cooperation, are not nice. All of these strategies are doing significantly worse in the chicken game than in the prisoner's dilemma. This means that we have a game that benefits cooperators better than the prisoner's dilemma, namely the chicken game.

3. A few of the strategies got, despite of the overall decreasing average score, a better score in the chicken game than in the prisoner's dilemma (the ones with a negative difference in the table in Appendix A). They all seem to have taken advantage of the increasing score for cooperation against defect. In order to do that, they must, on the average, play more C than D, when its opponent plays D. Here the mimicking strategies, like *TfT*, cannot be in this group, since they are not that forgiving. In fact, most strategies that demand some kind of revenge for an unprovoked defect, will be excluded, leaving only the static strategies[4]. As can be seen in the table, all static strategies which cooperate on the first move, and some of the partially static ones, do better in the chicken game than in the prisoner's dilemma. We interpret this result to be yet another indicator of the importance of being forgiving in a chicken game.

In a hawk-and-dove game we should expect defection to be an ESS in the prisoner's dilemma part of the game and a mixed ESS in the chicken game. In our simulation, defect (*mechante*) is among the strategies doing the worst and a mixture of cooperate and defect is not among the best strategies. To cooperate four times out of five (c_4_sur_5) corresponds in our simulation to a (D, D) score of 0.25 for an ESS and as we can see this is not at all the case because the ESS is a static and analytical concept. The reason for finding successful cooperating strategies is instead that the game is iterated, i.e. the relevant strategy "knows" the last move of the other strategy.

The only reason for always defect (*mechante*) and always cooperate (*gentille*) to vary a lot between prisoner's dilemma and chicken game is the changing payoff matrix. This is also the explanation why *TfT* and all the other strategies get other scores. If *TfT* meets another strategy it will mimic the others behavior *independently* of the values of the matrix. A defecting strategy will lose more in a chicken game because of the values of the matrix not because of a changing strategy. We are not at all surprised about finding very strong significance of a linear correlation in favor of PD or CG. This is exactly what these kind of strategies are expected to do.

There is no limit for the cost of mutual defection in a chicken game. Every strategy using defect will risk meeting another defect causing a high penalty. Strategies like *always cooperate* will be favored but they will still use the same interaction with other strategies.

---

[4] In fact extremely nice non-static strategies (e.g. a *TfT*-based strategy that defects with a lower probability than it cooperates on an opponent's defection) also would probably do better in a Chicken game than in a prisoner's dilemma, but such strategies were not part of our simulations.

8 Conclusions and Future Work

The hawk-and-dove game consists of two different game matrices:

* The prisoner's dilemma-like game does not fulfill the second condition of the prisoner's dilemma. When Rapoport and Chammah defined the second condition of the prisoner's dilemma, they wished to avoid the complication of multiple 'cooperative solutions'. In our opinion this was just a temporary restriction they made, not a definite one, as we argued earlier in this paper.

* The chicken game has a Nash equilibrium consisting of CD and DC. In an evolutionary approach this is called a mixed ESS. In an ICG this is not a sufficient solution because of the Folk Theorem.

A chicken game is more cooperating than a prisoner's dilemma because of the values of the payoff matrix. The payoff matrix in this first series of simulations is constant, a situation that is hardly the case in a real world application, where agents act in environments where they interact with other agents and human beings. This changes the context of the agent and may also affect its preferences. None of the strategies in our simulation actually analyses its score and acts upon it, which gave us significant linear changes in score between the games.

Another feature of this work is to clarify the role of general properties among strategies in a simulation. In this paper we look at three: initial move, how nice and static they are, but there are other aspects not covered here. Forgiveness may be an important factor in successful strategies in the chicken game and so may the ability to accept revenge.

It is impossible to simulate a hawk-and-dove game in an evolutionary context because of its randomized nature[5]. An ESS is the result of a infinitely repeated game not the result of a simulated iterated game. Successful strategies in the iterated prisoner's dilemma and chicken game will be stable against invasion of other strategies because they are doing very well meeting their own strategy. No other strategy can do better against a successful strategy than the strategy itself.

An ESS is a strategy in that if all the members of a population adopt it, then no mutant strategy could invade the population. This means that after the simulation we can try to find such a successful ESS. *TfT* has been suggested to be an ESS because no other strategy can do better against *TfT* than the strategy itself. In practice it is hard to find such best strategies because of many equally good strategies and the possibility of genetic drift. What we found was that nice strategies starting with cooperate did very well against other strategies. Strategies with the lowest score

---

[5] It is possible to simulate the game through a process of selection, consisting of two crucial steps: mutation, a variation of the way agents act, and selection, the choice of the best strategies (Lindgren 1991), but this is not within the scope of this paper.

either start with defect or, if they start with cooperate, are not nice. All of these strategies are doing significantly worse in a chicken game than in a prisoner's dilemma. This means that the chicken game part of the hawk-and-dove game suits cooperators better than the prisoner's dilemma part.

Acknowledgements The authors wish to thank Rune Gustavsson, Magnus Boman, Mikael Mattsson and the referees for valuable comments to the manuscript.

References

R. Axelrod "Effective Choice in the Prisoner's Dilemma" *Journal of Conflict Resolution vol. 24 No. 1, p. 379-403*, 1980a.

R. Axelrod "More Effective Choice in the Prisoner's Dilemma" *Journal of Conflict Resolution vol. 24 No. 3, p. 3-25*, 1980b.

R. Axelrod and W.D. Hamilton "The evolution of cooperation" *Science vol. 211* 1981.

R. Axelrod *The Evolution of Cooperation* Basic Books Inc. 1984.

K. Lindgren "Evolutionary Phenomena in Simple Dynamics" in *Artificial life II* ed. Ch. G Langton, C. Taylor, J. D. Farmer and S. Rasmussen Addison Wesley 1991.

B Lomborg "Game theory vs. Multiple Agents: The Iterated Prisoner's Dilemma" in *Artificial Social Systems* ed. C. Castelfranchi and E. Werner Lecture Notes in Artificial Intelligence 830 1994.

R.D. Luce and H. Raiffa *Games and Decisions* Dover Publications Inc. 1957.

P. Mathieu and J.P. Delahaye http:/www.lifl.fr/~mathieu/ipd/

A. Rapoport and M. Guyer, "A taxonomy of 2*2 games" *Yearbook of the Society for General Systems Research, XI:203-214,* 1966.

A. Rapoport and A.M. Chammah *Prisoner's Dilemma A Study in Conflict and Cooperation* Ann Arbor, The University of Michigan Press 1965.

B. Russell *Common Sense and Nuclear Warfare* Simon & Schuster 1959.

T. Sandholm and F. Ygge "On the gains and losses of speculation in equilibrium markets" to appear in *IJCAI 1997 proceedings.*

J. Maynard Smith and G.R. Price, "The logic of animal conflict", *Nature vol. 246,* 1973.

J. Maynard Smith, *Evolution and the theory of games,* Cambridge University Press, 1982.

R. L. Trivers "The evolution of Reciprocal Altruism" *Quarterly Review of Biology 46: 35-57,* 1971.

M.A. Wellman "A computational Market Model for Distributed Configuration Design" *Proceedings of AAAI '94, Morgan-Kaufman: 401-407,* 1994.

Appendix

	The score of (D,D) and 1 − (C,D)											I	N	S	Corr.	Diff.
	1	0.9	0.8	0.7	0.6	0.5	0.4	0.3	0.2	0.1	0					
coop_puis_tc	2.64	2.65	2.66	2.67	2.67	2.69	2.70	2.72	2.73	2.75	2.76	C	X	P	-0.99	-0.12
joss_mou	2.68	2.68	2.68	2.68	2.68	2.68	2.67	2.66	2.68	2.67	2.67	C	X		0.57	0.01
ranc_mou	2.69	2.69	2.68	2.67	2.67	2.67	2.66	2.65	2.65	2.65	2.64	C	X		1.00	0.05
graduel	2.77	2.75	2.73	2.71	2.69	2.66	2.65	2.62	2.60	2.58	2.54	C	X		1.00	0.23
tit_for_tat	2.61	2.61	2.61	2.62	2.61	2.61	2.61	2.60	2.60	2.61	2.58	C	X		0.76	0.03
doubleur	2.59	2.60	2.60	2.60	2.60	2.60	2.59	2.60	2.60	2.59	2.60	C	X		-0.19	-0.01
sondeur_dur	2.63	2.60	2.59	2.57	2.56	2.54	2.51	2.49	2.48	2.45	2.45	D		P	1.00	0.18
hesitante	2.38	2.39	2.40	2.41	2.41	2.43	2.45	2.46	2.47	2.48	2.49	C		X	-1.00	-0.11
majo_mou	2.45	2.44	2.44	2.43	2.43	2.42	2.42	2.41	2.41	2.41	2.40	C	X		0.99	0.05
tf2t_mou	2.45	2.44	2.44	2.43	2.43	2.41	2.40	2.40	2.41	2.38	2.38	C	X		0.96	0.06
pire_en_pire3	2.47	2.46	2.45	2.45	2.44	2.41	2.43	2.40	2.39	2.36	2.37	C	X		0.95	0.10
pavlov	2.35	2.36	2.35	2.35	2.35	2.36	2.35	2.35	2.35	2.36	2.35	C	X		-0.18	0.00
per_gentille	2.22	2.24	2.26	2.28	2.30	2.32	2.34	2.37	2.39	2.41	2.43	C		X	-1.00	-0.21
sondeur4	2.49	2.46	2.41	2.37	2.33	2.29	2.25	2.21	2.18	2.14	2.09	C		P	1.00	0.40
c_4_sur_5	2.15	2.16	2.20	2.21	2.24	2.27	2.28	2.29	2.31	2.35	2.37	C		R	-0.99	-0.22
gentille	2.11	2.14	2.17	2.20	2.23	2.26	2.29	2.32	2.34	2.38	2.40	C	X	X	-1.00	-0.30
tf2t_dur	2.33	2.31	2.29	2.28	2.27	2.25	2.23	2.22	2.20	2.18	2.16	C	X		1.00	0.17
sondeur2	2.25	2.25	2.25	2.26	2.25	2.25	2.25	2.25	2.25	2.26	2.25	D			0.11	0.01
slow_TfT	2.35	2.33	2.31	2.29	2.27	2.25	2.23	2.21	2.18	2.17	2.14	C	X		1.00	0.20
mefiant	2.30	2.29	2.28	2.27	2.26	2.24	2.24	2.22	2.21	2.20	2.19	D			1.00	0.12
quatre_c_un_t	2.09	2.12	2.14	2.17	2.20	2.22	2.25	2.27	2.30	2.32	2.35	C		X	-1.00	-0.26
rancuniere	2.42	2.38	2.33	2.29	2.25	2.20	2.16	2.11	2.07	2.03	1.99	C	X		1.00	0.43
ccctct	2.11	2.13	2.15	2.16	2.18	2.20	2.22	2.24	2.25	2.27	2.29	C		X	-1.00	-0.18
tft_dur	2.35	2.32	2.28	2.25	2.22	2.18	2.14	2.11	2.08	2.04	2.01	C	X		1.00	0.34
lunatique	2.15	2.15	2.14	2.14	2.14	2.13	2.16	2.14	2.13	2.14	2.14	R		R	0.49	0.02
pire_en_pire	2.14	2.14	2.13	2.12	2.12	2.11	2.10	2.10	2.10	2.09	2.08	C		R	0.99	0.06
sondeur	2.25	2.23	2.19	2.17	2.14	2.10	2.06	2.01	2.01	1.96	1.91	D			1.00	0.34
per_mechante	2.11	2.10	2.08	2.07	2.05	2.04	2.02	2.01	2.00	1.98	1.97	D		X	1.00	0.14
gradual_killer	2.07	2.05	2.04	2.03	2.01	1.99	1.97	1.95	1.93	1.92	1.90	D		P	1.00	0.17
sondeur3	2.17	2.12	2.09	2.06	2.02	1.98	1.94	1.91	1.86	1.83	1.79	D		P	1.00	0.38
majo_dur	2.09	2.06	2.05	2.02	2.00	1.97	1.95	1.92	1.91	1.89	1.86	D			1.00	0.23
calculateur	2.14	2.09	2.06	2.01	1.97	1.93	1.87	1.82	1.79	1.72	1.67	C			1.00	0.47
mieux_en_mie	1.91	1.90	1.88	1.88	1.87	1.87	1.86	1.85	1.85	1.84	1.83	D		P	0.98	0.08
pire_en_pire2	2.09	2.03	1.96	1.89	1.82	1.75	1.68	1.62	1.55	1.48	1.41	C			1.00	0.68
joss_dur	1.93	1.90	1.86	1.82	1.78	1.72	1.66	1.64	1.59	1.56	1.50	C			1.00	0.43
mechante	1.86	1.78	1.70	1.63	1.55	1.47	1.39	1.31	1.23	1.16	1.08	D		X	1.00	0.78
average	2.30	2.29	2.27	2.26	2.26	2.24	2.22	2.21	2.20	2.18	2.17					

Comparing prisoner's dilemma with chicken game. Top columns: 1....0 - value of (D, D); I, N, S – characterization of the strategy; Corr. – Correlation coefficient (r); Diff. – The difference between basic prisoner's dilemma and chicken game

A Game-Theoretic Solution of Conflicts Among Competitive Agents

Satoru Yoshida, Nobuhiro Inuzuka, Tin Tin Naing,
Hirohisa Seki and Hidenori Itoh

Department of Intelligence and Computer Science,
Nagoya Institute of Technology
Gokiso-cho, Showa-ku, Nagoya 466, Japan
Phone:+81-52-735-5050, Fax:+81-52-735-5477
e-mail: {satosama,tin,inuzuka,seki,itoh}@ics.nitech.ac.jp

Abstract. Recently the control of multi-agent behavior using two-player non-zero sum games, such as prisoner's dilemma, has been studied. In this paper we propose a two player game that includes a dilemmatic structure and extend it to the study of two teams consisting of many players. Iterative versions of dilemma games have been investigated extensively and many strategies for the games have been proposed. For multi-agent applications we extend our dilemma game to a multi-player version. Several decision strategies are studied with this model. The multi-player model is used to decide actions of agents in the burden carriage problem, which includes a typical situation of agents in competition. We show that the behavior of agents in the problem matches the results of team contests of the dilemma game.

1 Introduction and the Prisoner's Dilemma

Using cooperative work by many agents to treat complex problems is a topic of distributed artificial intelligence. This approach is attractive because multi-agent systems are expected to be robust. For this purpose, agents must be simple but autonomous and well-behaved for many situations. One approach to give the complex behavior for agents is to learn from the collective behavior of natural creatures. This approach includes simulation of natural lives [5] and also genetic algorithms [10], which are a kind of global search algorithm modeled on natural selection.

The game-theoretic approach is another way to study autonomous multi-agent models. This approach assumes agents to be simple but reasonable entities based on a fixed rule or a game. By formalizing situations around agents to an appropriate game we can hope to find a good strategy for agents' behavior.

The game-theoretic approach is appropriate for systems in which agents cannot negotiate with each other. Autonomous agents must decide their actions by themselves, sometimes without any communication with other agents. In some cases, an agent's benefit from an action depends on the action of another agent and agents are faced with a dilemma. Prisoner's Dilemma, a two-player non-zero sum game, is a very well known example that formalizes such cases [2, 8, 4].

A\B	cooperate defect
cooperate	R=2\R=2 S=0\T=3
defect	T=3\S=0 P=1\P=1

Table 1. Payoff matrix for the Prisoner's Dilemma game

Fig. 1 is the payoff matrix for the Prisoner's Dilemma game. Each of two players can take cooperate or defect actions. If player A takes cooperate his/her payoff is 2 (=R) as a reward for mutual cooperation or 0 (=S) as a sucker, depending on the choice of player B. Similarly, if player A takes defect his/her payoff is 3 (=T) as a winner of tactics i.e. temptation to defect or 1 (=P) as punishment for mutual defection.

A player achieves a high payoff by taking defect whether or not the other player takes cooperate or defect and so defect should be taken if he/she would like to win against the opponent. However, players can achieve more payoff [2] by cooperating with others than the average of the two defect cases, the average of which is $(0 + 3)/2 = 1.5$. That is, the payoff matrix satisfies $T > R > P > S$ and $R > (T + S)/2$, and this defines the structure of Prisoner's Dilemma.

In this paper we study a game-theoretic approach to control agents that work in competitive situations. Multi-agents have been studied as a way of solving problems by cooperative work. Agents sometimes face competitive situations during such cooperative work. For example, two agents may each try to take some resource at the same time to accomplish their objectives. In this case their alternative options are to take the resource or to give it to the other agent. To formalize this situation we propose a new dilemma game, Compromise Dilemma (CD) game, in Section 2. We study several strategies for this dilemma game.

In Section 3 an iterative version of the Compromise Dilemma game is studied. Iterative versions of Prisoner's Dilemma have been extensively investigated. Iterative Compromise Dilemma is not sufficient to analyze multi-agent problems. However, we study it to introduce strategies for dilemma games and to compare it with the models introduced in the later sections.

We extend the CD model to a multi-player model, Team Match of Compromise Dilemma (TMCD), in Section 4. We then apply this model to an example of cooperative work in a multi-agent system called the Burden Carriage Problem. In this problem, agents carry pieces of a burden from place to place. An agent will sometimes meet other agents on their own ways. To avoid a collision, agents need to play the Compromise Dilemma game. We apply strategies for Compromise Dilemma to resolve collisions in Section 5.

2 Compromise Dilemma

As we discussed in the previous section, Prisoner's Dilemma is not always suitable to formalize dilemmas in practical situations. Other dilemma games

A\B	give	take
give	loss of both player by unnecessary compromise	intended compromise and advantage
take	intended compromise and advantage	damage by collision

Table 2. Compromise Dilemma game

b\a	give	take
give	U=2\U=2	I=2\A=3
take	A=3\I=2	C=1\C=1

Table 3. Payoff matrix of Compromise Dilemma (CD) game

have been proposed and discussed in the literature [1, 3]. Indeed, there are many different cases of dilemmas by different assignments of the values of T, R, P and S in the payoff matrix (in the sense of relative difference of the values or different orders of values).

The condition that T, R, P and S take different values has been used in previous works. However, we remove this condition in creating a new dilemma game, because this condition does not always match real situations.

We will formulate a dilemmatic situation, in which agents try to accomplish their work, and in which one agent faces the problem that he/she and another agent would like to use a resource at the same time. Table 3 describes four combinations of their alternatives, to yield the resource or to take it. If agents want to raise the total quantity of work done, this situation is dilemmatic, because taking the resource may increase the work done by the agent, but this may make a collision and because yielding the resource decreases that agent's amount of work completed without gaining any credit for the advantage gained by the other agent.

We propose a dilemma game, Compromise Dilemma (CD), based on this situation. The payoff matrix of CD is in Table 3. Players 'a' and 'b' choose an alternative action (called a hand from two possible actions take and give.) If a player chooses give his/her payoff is 2 ($= U$) for unnecessary compromise or also 2 ($= I$) for intended compromise. If he/she chooses take his/her payoff is 3 ($= A$) for advantage or 1 ($= C$) for damage in a collision. Please note that U and I are the same value and that $A + I = 5 > 4 = U + U$. These are the features of this dilemma game.

3 Iterative Compromise Dilemma

The iterative version of Prisoner's Dilemma has been investigated extensively [2, 4, 9]. In Iterative Prisoner's Dilemma (IPD) a pair of players repeats the Prisoner's Dilemma game many times. Players earn points according to the payoff matrix. A large variety of strategies for Prisoner's Dilemma has been evaluated by running games of IPD.

We also investigate the iterative version of Compromise Dilemma (ICD) with a number of strategies. The following strategies are compared in ICD.

Always take (TAK) Agent always chooses take.

Always give (GIV) Agent always chooses give.

Random (RND) Agent chooses give or take at random.

Random with biased probability (1) (R14) Agent chooses take with probability of 1/4.

Random with biased probability (2) (R34) Agent chooses take with probability of 3/4.

Tit-For-Tat (TFT) Agent mimics the latest hand of the opponent, and the first hand is give.

Impudent (IMP) Agent chooses take unless the latest hand of the opponent is take.

Elater (ELA) Choice is the same as for IMP except that it chooses give for the first hand.

Disheartenment (DIS) Agent chooses take until the opponent chooses take. After that it always chooses give.

Grudge (GRU) Agent chooses give until the opponent chooses take. After that it always chooses take.

Careful (CAR) Agent chooses take only if the latest hand of the opponent is give. Otherwise it chooses give.

Non-probabilistic strategies are described by the automata shown in Fig. 1. In the figure an arrow means a transition of states and the labels on arrows describe the condition of the transition and the hand taken. If a label of an arrow is t/g, it means that the transition will happen only if the latest hand of the opponent was take(t), and the choice taken by the strategy is give(g). An initial state is represented by a state with a short arrow.

More formally, a strategy is a five-tuple $S = (\Sigma, Q, I, \psi, \rho)$, where Σ is a set of hands or {give, take} in the case of CD, Q is a set of states, I is an initial state in Q, ψ is a transition function from $Q \times \Sigma$ to Σ, and ρ is an output function from Q to Σ.

Our system differs from an automaton with outputs. A transition function of an automaton is normally defined as a function from $Q \times \Sigma$ to $Q \times O$, where O is a set of output symbols. In our case, output symbols are the same as hands and so it should be defined as a function from $Q \times \Sigma$ to $Q \times \Sigma$. From the nature of dilemma games, however, output hands should not depend on the hands of

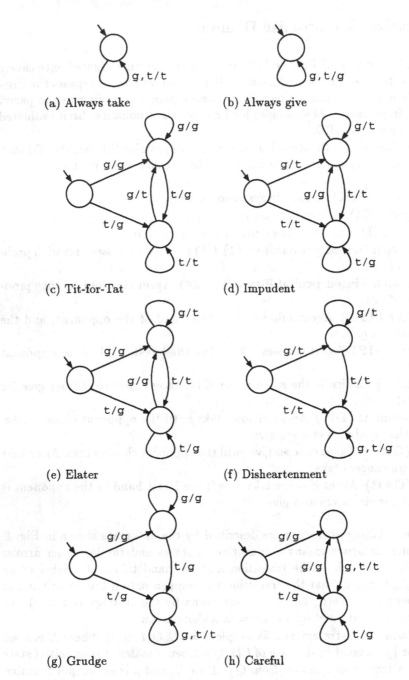

Fig. 1. Strategy for the Dilemma

	TAK	GIV	RND	R14	R34	TFT	IMP	ELA	DIS	GRD	CAR	ave.
TAK	200	400	305	344	248	201	399	400	399	201	400	317.9
GIV	**600**	400	491	461	547	400	**600**	**599**	**600**	400	500	508.9
RND	392	400	399	400	397	394	410	382	399	395	408	397.8
R14	478	400	444	415	479	411	487	486	400	508	439	449.7
R34	300	400	349	382	314	307	379	373	399	320	395	356.2
TFT	202	400	404	419	285	400	400	400	400	400	467	379.7
IMP	**598**	400	414	373	469	400	300	400	399	**597**	400	431.8
ELA	**600**	400	405	371	479	400	**600**	300	**600**	596	300	459.0
DIS	**598**	400	489	457	541	400	**597**	400	399	**597**	400	479.8
GRD	202	400	305	354	246	400	400	400	400	400	401	355.3
CAR	**600**	400	427	407	470	466	**600**	300	**600**	**598**	300	469.8
ave.	433.6	400.0	402.9	398.5	406.8	379.9	470.2	403.6	454.1	455.6	400.9	418.7

Table 4. Results of Iterative Compromise Dilemma (200 iterations)

opponents. Hence, the output function ρ is defined as a separate function from the transition function ψ.

Table 4 shows the results of contests using the strategies in ICD. In each contest a CD game is repeated 200 times. A value in the table is a score obtained by a player in ICD using the strategy written above the number for the player and the strategy written to the left of the number for the opponent.

Outstanding points are shown in bold face. GIV, which always gives, earns two every CD game and so it earns 400 for 200 time iterations. The scores for TAK depend very much on the strategy of the opponent. TFT, which works very well in PD, does not earn good scores. IMP, DIS, and GRD earn relatively good scores. IMP can be regarded as the best of the strategies studied except when it contests with itself.

4 Extending the Dilemma to Multiple Players

To apply the dilemma model to multi-agent models, an iterative dilemma game is not sufficient. This is because this model assumes that there are only two players and they meet the dilemmatic situation many times. In a multi-agent model, however, there are many agents and any pair of the agents may meet a dilemmatic situation. After a pair of agents solves one dilemmatic situation by a dilemma game, an agent of the pair may meet another dilemma with another agent. A. Ito et.al. [6] proposed an approach to solve this problem. In this approach all results of dilemma games or histories of games are kept for each pair of agents. This approach is a very simple extension of the dilemma game but needs much storage to keep the histories. We propose another approach to solve this problem.

We propose a model, Team Match of Compromise Dilemma (TMCD). In

Team A:strategy $S_A = (\Sigma_A, Q_A, I_A, \psi_A, \rho_A)$
Team B:strategy $S_B = (\Sigma_B, Q_B, I_B, \psi_B, \rho_B)$
N: the number of players in Team A and B
M: the number of iteration

Initialize

    $q_A^i := I_A$, $q_B^i := I_B$ for $i = 1, \cdots, n$
    I:= 0
While $I < M$ **do**
    Choose a player a_j from Team A $(1 \leq j \leq N)$
    Choose a player b_k from Team B $(1 \leq k \leq N)$
    $H_A := \rho_A(q_A^j)$
    $H_B := \rho_B(q_B^k)$
    $P_A := P_A +$ (the payoff of CD game for a with hands H_A and H_B)
    $P_B := P_B +$ (the payoff of CD game for b with hands H_A and H_B)
    $q_A^j := \psi_A(q_A^j, H_B)$
    $q_B^k := \psi_B(q_B^k, H_A)$
    I:= I+1
End

Fig. 2. Algorithm for TMCD

TMCD there are two teams of players, team A and B. Each team consists of N players. Players a and b are chosen from team A and B randomly and they play the Compromise Dilemma game. The points that a player earns are counted as points for the team to which the player belongs. TMCD repeats the selection of players and the playing of Compromise Dilemma. When a player decides his/her hand using the chosen strategy for a CD game, he/she does not distinguish the current opponent from the last opponent. The hand of a player neither depends on the latest hand of the current opponent nor on the hand that was used in the last game with the current opponent, but on the latest hand of the latest opponent. Thus, TMCD does not need to store the game history.

Table 5 shows the results of TMCD games using the strategies introduced in Section 3. Tables (a) and (b) are results using teams consisting of 10 players and 35 players, respectively.

In contrast with the results for ICD, the self-contests of IMP, ELA and CAR, i.e., IMP vs. IMP etc., show good scores. By this increase of scores for self-contests, IMP becomes a good strategy. IMP and DIS both have good performance but IMP is now better than DIS because of the average score of IMP and also because IMP got better score that DIS in the IMP vs. DIS contest. On the other hand the scores for GRD are not good in TMCD. This is because the behavior of GRD depends strongly on the initial game and there are many initial games for many opponents in TMCD. We also observe that the previously outstanding scores of TAK become even. This tendency of TAK and the poor performance of GRD are more evident in Table (b) than (a).

	TAK	GIV	RND	R14	R34	TFT	IMP	ELA	DIS	GRD	CAR	ave.
TAK	200	400	300	347	253	210	390	400	390	210	400	318.2
GIV	**600**	400	500	444	**556**	400	**600**	**590**	**600**	400	499	508.1
RND	380	400	409	397	411	408	382	388	394	416	400	398.6
R14	524	400	457	429	467	425	489	481	425	456	446	454.5
R34	308	400	362	379	343	342	367	371	396	281	385	357.6
TFT	220	400	402	422	316	400	405	393	412	400	425	381.4
IMP	**580**	400	372	370	428	397	400	400	397	530	400	424.9
ELA	**600**	400	420	381	491	397	**600**	406	**600**	522	375	472.0
DIS	**580**	400	484	426	534	395	**565**	400	412	537	400	466.6
GRD	220	400	315	377	263	400	391	388	400	400	391	358.6
CAR	**600**	400	417	401	498	413	**600**	514	**600**	**559**	398	490.9
ave.	437.5	400.0	403.5	397.5	414.5	380.6	471.7	430.1	456.9	428.3	410.8	421.0

(a) Each team consists of 10 players.

	TAK	GIV	RND	R14	R34	TFT	IMP	ELA	DIS	GRD	CAR	ave.
TAK	200	400	300	345	255	235	365	400	366	234	400	318.2
GIV	**600**	400	487	464	536	400	**600**	565	**600**	400	490	503.8
RND	396	400	411	388	412	401	385	392	412	392	399	398.9
R14	508	400	454	419	469	417	481	460	454	444	440	449.6
R34	302	400	353	371	337	338	358	373	385	331	391	358.1
TFT	270	400	416	428	370	400	418	422	416	400	425	396.8
IMP	530	400	383	361	425	369	388	400	381	475	400	410.2
ELA	**600**	400	432	373	481	390	**600**	402	**600**	455	383	465.1
DIS	530	400	436	398	482	413	481	400	404	471	400	437.7
GRD	270	400	369	410	312	400	396	387	395	400	410	377.2
CAR	**600**	400	445	406	506	427	**600**	446	**600**	452	412	481.3
ave.	436.9	400.0	407.8	396.6	416.8	380.9	461.1	422.5	455.7	404.9	413.6	417.9

(b) Each team consists of 35 players.

Table 5. Results of Team Matches of Compromise Dilemma. Each contest consists of 200 iterations.

5 Application of TMCD to Solve a Competitive Problem

This section gives an application of TMCD to a multi-agent problem, the Burden Carriage problem. In this problem, many agents must find and bring pieces of burden to their base. We formalize this problem as a two-team contest.

There are bases of team A and B on a finite plane field. Agents of each team try to find a base of the opponent team and take a piece of burden from the base and bring it to their own base. The score is counted as the number of pieces of burden brought to a base. The number of pieces of burden taken by the opponent team does not reduce the score. The field is illustrated in Fig. 3.

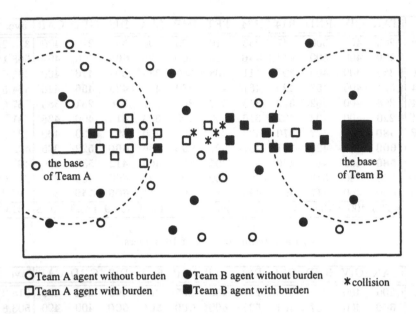

○ Team A agent without burden	● Team B agent without burden	
□ Team A agent with burden	■ Team B agent with burden	✱ collision

Fig. 3. The Burden Carriage problem

An agent moves one step in unit time in a random direction until it enters a special area, which is represented by the circle in a broken line around the opponent's base. If an agent enters the circle, it can perceive the base and goes directly to the base and takes a piece of burden. The agent then takes the piece back to its own base.

In Fig. 3 the two larger boxes at the left and right of the figure are the bases of the teams. The black box on the right is the base of team B. Team B agents, which are represented by small black circles, walk out of the black base and try to find the opponent's base, the large white box. Until they reach the left broken line circle they walk at random. When they come to the circle, they approach the base and take a piece of burden. Team B agents with pieces are represented by small black boxes. They know the direction of their own base and return directly there. Team A agents with and without pieces are represented by small white boxes and circles, respectively.

During the movements agents may run into other agents and may need to avoid a collision. The asterisks in the figure represent collisions that have occurred. Depending on the movements of agents, either going ahead or changing course, collisions are avoidable.

Table 6 describes all possible collision cases. Both of the agents that are in the situation have only the alternatives of giving way or proceeding which may have a collision. This is the same structure as that for TMCD.

We developed a simulator for the Burden Carriage problem. It simulates all the agents in both teams acting, as explained above. With the simulator we

A\B	give way	proceed
give way	loss of both player by changing course	intended loss by changing course and advantage
proceed	intended loss by changing course and advantage	damage by collision

Table 6. Application of Dilemma of Compromise to passing agents

actions	treatments in the simulation
Change course	Agent changes course by turning left, moving one step and turning right. 3 unit time loss.
Go ahead and pass	Agents simply go ahead.
Go ahead and collide	Agents get damaged and stay at the place 8 units of time.

Table 7. Treatments for collision cases

have conducted an experiment with 35 agents in each Team. Burden carriage continued for 3000 unit steps. When two agents meet, they try to resolve the collision using the strategies introduced in Section 3. All the agents in a team use the same strategy, which is similar to that of the players in the TMCD game. During the 3000 steps many collisions occurred.

Table 8 shows the results of the experiment. The results include scores for all combinations of the strategies introduced in Section 3. The values in the table are averages of five experiments for each combination. Outstanding scores are emphasized in bold face.

The results in Table 8 show similar tendencies for distributions of values as the results on both tables (a) and (b) in Table 5. This shows that TMCD can be a good model for the Burden Carriage problem and TMCD can be used to test strategies before using them in a real situation.

6 Conclusions

We studied game-theoretic models for a multi-agent system. A dilemmatic game, Compromise Dilemma (CD), was proposed and extended to a multi-player game, Team Match of Compromise Dilemma (TMCD). This model explained well the phenomena of behavior of agents in situations of collision in the Burden Carriage Problem. Eleven strategies for CD games were proposed and investigated for the iterative version of the CD game and TMCD. We showed that the results of

	TAK	GIV	RND	R14	R34	TFT	IMP	ELA	DIS	GRD	CAR	ave.
TAK	381	487	423	449	396	384	475	487	481	376	482	438.3
GIV	**592**	485	537	516	559	485	**585**	**587**	**589**	477	534	540.5
RND	458	481	470	473	464	477	473	467	480	460	480	471.2
R14	512	487	501	489	501	491	504	510	485	513	495	498.9
R34	416	476	445	459	425	431	459	466	478	418	466	449.0
TFT	387	486	469	495	426	489	469	472	485	487	480	467.7
IMP	**583**	479	471	465	516	469	475	481	483	578	479	498.0
ELA	**587**	483	468	461	504	465	**587**	471	**586**	570	475	514.3
DIS	**584**	483	538	507	563	487	579	474	491	565	481	522.9
GRD	384	490	426	452	400	488	481	487	481	483	484	459.6
CAR	**590**	481	494	481	519	483	**590**	557	**592**	576	476	530.8
ave.	497.6	483.5	476.5	477.0	479.4	468.1	516.1	496.3	511.9	500.3	484.7	490.1

Table 8. Results of the Burden Carriage problem using TMCD modes.

TMCD matched the results in Burden Carriage problem.

Strategies were evaluated by the average scores in the contests. In the case that collisions may be occurred among agents who try to accomplish a work, however, we should also consider the sum of score acquired by the strategies and score given the opponent team. In this case GIV becomes relatively good score, because it gave good score to the opponent team.

If we study the results for the Burden Carriage problem more carefully it is more simular to (a) of Table 5, although the population of agents in the problem is equal to the number of players for Table (b). In order to explain this, we need a detailed analysis of the collisions in the problem. However, we can say that not all combinations of agents meet with equal probabilities. Finding a factor to decide the number of players for a multi-agent system is left for future work.

Our future work will also include other applications of the TMCD game or other dilemmatic games to other multi-agent systems, such as resource assignment problems and software agent models. The evolution of strategies for dilemma games has also been studied recently [6, 7]. We should consider this approach in future.

Acknowledgments The authors wish to thank anonymous reviewers for valuable comments.

References

1. Eizo Akiyama and Kunihiko Kaneko: "Evolution of Communication and Strategies in an Iterated Three-person Game", Artificial Life V (Proceedings of the Fifth Int'l Workshop on the Synthesis and Simulation of Living Systems), pp.193–201, MIT Press, 1997.
2. Robert Axelrod and William D. Hammiltom: "The evolution of cooperation", Science, **211**, pp.1390–1396, 1981.

3. Bruno Beaufils, Jean-Paul Delahaye and Phillippe Mathieu: "Our Meeting With Gradual: A Good Strategy For The Iterated Prisoner's Dilemma", Artificial Life V (Proceedings of the Fifth Int'l Workshop on the Synthesis and Simulation of Living Systems), pp.202–209, MIT Press, 1997.
4. Charlotte K. Hemelrijk 1997: "Cooperation Without Genes, Games Or Cognition", Proceedings of Fourth European Conference on Artificial Life (ECAL97), http://www.cogs.susx.ac.uk/ecal97/publish.html, 1997.
5. Akihide Hiura, Nobuhiro Inuzuka, Masashi Yamada, Hirohisa Seki, and Hidenori Itoh: "Cooperative actions of multi-agents in a burden carriage problem", Second German Workshop on Artificial Life, 1997.
6. Akira Ito and H. Yano: "The Emergence of Cooperation in a Society of Autonomous Agents — The Prisoner's Dilemma Game Under the Disclosure of Contract Histories" Proceedings of First Int'l Conf. on Multi-Agent Systems(ICMAS'95), pp.201–208, AAAI/MIT Press, 1995.
7. Akira Ito: "How Do Selfish Agents Learn to Cooperate?", Artificial Life V (Proceedings of the Fifth Int'l Workshop on the Synthesis and Simulation of Living Systems), pp.185–192, MIT Press, 1997.
8. David Kraines and Vivian Kraines: "The Threshold of Cooperation Among Adaptive Agents — Pavlov and the Stag Hunt", Intelligent Agents III, LNAI series No.1193, pp.219–231, Springer, 1997.
9. Yishay Mor and Jeffrey S. Rosenschein: "Time and the Prisoner's Dilemma", Proceedings of First Int'l Conf. on Multi-Agent Systems(ICMAS'95), pp.276–282, AAAI/MIT Press, 1995.
10. Kousuke Moriwaki, Nobuhiro Inuzuka, Masashi Yamada, Hirohisa Seki, and Hidenori Itoh: "A Genetic Method for Evolutionary Agents in a Competitive Environment", to appear in Proceedings of 2nd On-line World Conference on Soft Computing in Engineering Design and Manufacturing (WSC2), LNAI series, Springer Verlag, 1997.

Transformation between the EMYCIN Model and the Bayesian Network*

Chengqi Zhang and Xudong Luo

School of Mathematical and Computer Sciences
The University of New England
Armidale, NSW 2351, Australia
E-mail: {chengqi, xluo}@neumann.une.edu.au

Abstract. If different expert systems use different uncertain reasoning models in a distributed expert system, it is necessary to transform the uncertainty of a proposition from one model to another when they cooperate to solve problems. This paper looks at ways to transform uncertainties between the EMYCIN model and the Bayesian network. In the past, the uncertainty management scheme employed the most extensively in expert systems was the EMYCIN model. Now the scheme is turning towards the Bayesian network. If we can combine, by means of the Internet, pre-existing stand-alone expert systems that use these two models into a distributed expert system, the ability of these individual expert systems in their real applications will be greatly improved. The work described in this paper is an important step in this direction.

Keywords: Distributed Expert Systems, Uncertainty Reasoning, Transformation of Uncertainties, Prior Probability, Bayesian Networks, the Certainty Factor Model.

1 Introduction

The problem-solving ability of expert systems is greatly improved by way of cooperation amongst a number of different expert systems in a distributed expert system [20]. Sometimes different expert systems in a distributed expert system may use different uncertain reasoning models [29]. In each uncertain reasoning model, the uncertainties of propositions take values on a set. These sets are different in different models. For example, the set is the interval $[-1, 1]$ in the EMYCIN model [21], while the set is the interval $[0, 1]$ in a Bayesian network [22]. Within these intervals, the EMYCIN model uses -1 to represent the uncertainty of a proposition known to be false, while a Bayesian network employs 0 to represent the same thing. So, to achieve cooperation among these expert systems, the first step is to enable them to understand each other. That is, to

---

* This research is supported by a large grant from the Australian Research Council (A49530850).

transform the uncertainty of a proposition from one uncertain reasoning model to another [27] when they use different uncertain reasoning models. Then the second step is to synthesize the transformed different results. In other words, the transformation among different uncertain reasoning models is the foundation for cooperation among these heterogeneous expert systems, and consequently this is a very important problem.

Until now, only several papers involving this important topic have been proposed. Zhang and Orlowska [32] showed that the value-sets of propositional uncertainty in several well-known uncertain reasoning models with appropriate operators are semi-groups with individual unit elements. A later work of Zhang [28] uses this result to establish transformation criteria based on homomorphisms, and to define transformation functions *approximately* fulfilling these criteria. These functions work well between any two of the uncertain reasoning models used by EMYCIN, PROSPECTOR and MYCIN [25]. Hájek [13] tried to build an isomorphism between the EMYCIN and PROSPECTOR models, but his isomorphic function worked properly only if the unit element was 0.5. However, the unit element should be the prior probability of a proposition and not always 0.5 but *vary* with different propositions. For any value of the prior probability, we built an isomorphism between the EMYCIN model and the PROSPECTOR model [30]. All of these works deal with just one-dimensional uncertainties. In [17], we suggest a function for transformation of two-dimensional uncertainties between the interval EMYCIN model and the interval PROSPECTOR model. However, so far the transformation of uncertainties between the EMYCIN model and Bayesian network has not been dealt with. In this paper, we will present work which deals with the transformation between these two widely used uncertain models.

In the EMYCIN model, the uncertainty of a proposition is measured by an certainty factor which is defined as follows:

$$CF(B, A) = \begin{cases} \frac{P(B|A) - P(B)}{1 - P(B)} & \text{if } P(B|A) > P(B), \\ 0 & \text{if } P(B|A) = P(B), \\ \frac{P(B|A) - P(B)}{P(B)} & \text{if } P(B|A) < P(B). \end{cases} \tag{1}$$

Thus, we have

$$P(B, A) = \begin{cases} CF(B, A)(1 - P(B)) + P(B) & \text{if } CF(B, A) \geq 0, \\ (CF(B, A) + 1)P(B) & \text{if } CF(B, A) < 0. \end{cases} \tag{2}$$

In a Bayesian network, uncertainties are presented by probabilities. If the value of $P(H)$ is known, by formula (2), we can easily transform values of certainty factors into the values of probabilities. Inversely, if the value of $P(H)$ is known, by formula (1), we can easily transform the value of a certainty factor into the value of a probability. Therefore, in order to implement the transformation of uncertainties between the EMYCIN model and the Bayesian network, the key problem is how to obtain the values of prior probabilities.

In this paper, we give three ways to obtain the values of prior probabilities. The first deals with finding the values of prior probabilities from instances of sequential propagation in the EMYCIN model. The second deals with finding the values of prior probabilities from instances of parallel propagation in the EMYCIN model. The third looks into finding the values of prior probabilities from instances of reasoning in a Bayesian network.

Although there are plenty of methods for obtaining prior probabilities, these methods require a great deal of time and money, especially for a large knowledge base. Besides, often not enough statistical data are available to allow for reliable probability estimation [6]. Instead, since human experts have experience with the application of uncertain knowledge, it should be not difficult for them to give some instances of uncertain reasoning.

The rest of this paper is organized as follows. Section 2 gives the formula for finding prior probabilities from instances of sequential propagation in the EMYCIN model. Section 3 derives a formula for finding the values of prior probabilities from instances of parallel propagation in the EMYCIN model. Section 4 discusses how to find the values of prior probabilities from instances of reasoning in a Bayesian network. Finally, Section 5 summarizes the work.

2 From Instances of the EMYCIN Sequential Propagation

In this section, we discuss finding values for prior probabilities of the conclusion of a rule, from its rule-strength and one instance of its reasoning. Supplying values directly for prior probabilities is a very arduous task for human experts, but clearly it is easy for human experts to give one instance of uncertain reasoning at the same time as giving a rule.

2.1 Extension Conditional Probability

In 1987, Ihara [14] introduced the extension conditional probability as follows:

Definition 1 *The extension conditional probability that H is true under the condition that E is incompletely true, denoted by $P(H|E_\alpha)$, is given by*

$$P(H|E_\alpha) = \alpha P(H|E) + (1 - \alpha)P(H|\neg E), \qquad (3)$$

where $\alpha \in [0, 1]$ is the degree that E is believed to be true.

How is the degree α measured to which E is believed to be true? In this paper, we regard α as $P(E|E')$, where E' is the observation related to E.

Considering the total probability formula

$$P(H) = P(H|E)P(E) + P(H|\neg E)P(\neg E), \qquad (4)$$

we can easily derive the relationship between $P(H|E)$ and $P(H|E_\alpha)$ as follows:

Lemma 1

$$P(H|E) = \frac{P(H|E_\alpha)P(\neg E) + (\alpha - 1)P(H)}{\alpha - P(E)} \quad (\alpha \neq P(E)). \qquad (5)$$

2.2 The Extension Certainty Factor

Definition 2 *The extension certainty factor of a rule $E \to H$, denoted by $CF(H, E_\alpha)$, is given by*

$$CF(H, E_\alpha) = \begin{cases} \frac{P(H|E_\alpha) - P(H)}{1 - P(H)} & \text{if } P(H|E_\alpha) > P(H), \\ 0 & \text{if } P(H|E_\alpha) = P(H), \\ \frac{P(H|E_\alpha) - P(H)}{P(H)} & \text{if } P(H|E_\alpha) < P(H), \end{cases} \tag{6}$$

where $\alpha \in [0, 1]$ is the degree to which E is believed to be true.

The uncertainty of a rule $E \to H$ measured by the extension certainty factor is the degree of change of belief or disbelief in the hypothesis H after the evidence E is believed to be true to the degree α.

1. If $CF(H, E_\alpha) > 0$, we can easily prove

$$CF(H, E_\alpha) = \frac{P(\neg H) - P(\neg H|E_\alpha)}{P(\neg H)}.$$

So in this case, the certainty factor is the percentage of change of the posterior belief in the hypothesis $\neg H$, after the evidence E is believed to be true to the degree α, to the prior belief in the hypothesis $\neg H$. For example, $CF(H, E_{0.8}) = 0.7$ means that the belief in $\neg H$ decreases by 70% when E is believed to be true to the degree 0.8. Clearly, the decrease of the belief in $\neg H$ signifies the increase of the belief in H. Hence, $CF(H, E_\alpha) > 0$ means that the belief in the hypothesis H increases when the evidence E is believed to be true to degree α. And the greater the value of $CF(H, E_\alpha)$, the greater the increase of the belief.

2. If $CF(H, E_\alpha) < 0$, we have

$$CF(H, E_\alpha) = -\frac{P(H) - P(H|E_\alpha)}{P(H)}.$$

So, the certainty factor is the percentage of change of the posterior belief in the hypothesis $\neg H$, after the evidence E is believed to be true to the degree α, to the prior belief in the hypothesis $\neg H$. For example, $CF(H, E_{0.8}) = -0.7$ means that the belief in H decreases by 70% when E is believed to be true to the degree 0.8. Clearly, $CF(H, E_\alpha) < 0$ means that the belief in the hypothesis H decreases when the evidence E is believed to be true to the degree α. And the smaller the value of $CF(H, E_\alpha)$, the greater the decrease of the belief.

3. If $CF(H, E_\alpha) = 0$, it means $P(H|E_\alpha) = P(H)$. That is, when E is believed to be true to degree α there is no alternation in either belief or disbelief in H.

Thus, $CF(H, E_\alpha)$ is the degree to which the belief in H changes when the degree to which E is believed to be true is α. In other words, $CF(H, E_\alpha)$ is actually an instance illustrating the use of the rule $E \to H$. That is, a human expert thinks that when the degree to which E is believed to be true is α, by the rule $E \to H$, he/she can draw the degree of change of the belief in the hypothesis H is $CF(H, E_\alpha)$. For example, $CF(H, E_{0.8}) = 0.7$ explains the following instance: if the degree to which E is believed to be true is 0.8, a human expert concludes that the belief in $\neg H$ decreases by 70% following the rule $E \to H$. Clearly, it is actually an instance of inference. Since the human expert can give a rule, it means that this expert has experience in using the rule. Therefore, it should be easy for a human expert to supply such an instance.

Clearly, in the case $\alpha = 1$, $CF(H, E_\alpha) = CF(H, E)$; in the case $\alpha = 0$, $CF(H, E_\alpha) = CF(H, \neg E)$. So, the EMYCIN certainty factor is a special case of the extension certainty factor. Moreover, evidently our definition also has the advantage of the EMYCIN model, i.e. it can distinguish the belief from doubt in an assessment.

Lemma 2

$$P(H|E) = \begin{cases} \frac{(CF(H,E_\alpha)P(\neg H)+P(H))P(\neg E)+(\alpha-1)P(H)}{\alpha-P(E)} & \text{if } CF(H, E_\alpha) > 0, \\ \frac{(CF(H,E_\alpha)+1)P(\neg E)+\alpha-1}{\alpha-P(E)}P(H) & \text{if } CF(H, E_\alpha) < 0. \end{cases} \quad (7)$$

Proof. It is easily shown by Definition 2 and Lemma 1. $\qquad \square$

2.3 Ternary Strength and Prior Probability

Definition 3 *The strength of a rule $E \to H$, being a vector*

$$(CF(H, E), CF(H, E_\alpha), CF(H, \neg E)),$$

is said to be a ternary strength.

The meanings of the three parameters of the ternary strength of a rule $E \to H$ are as follows. What $CF(H, E)$ measures is the degree of change of belief or disbelief in H if E is true. What $CF(H, \neg E)$ measures is the degree of change of belief or disbelief in H if E is false. $CF(H, E_\alpha)$ can be viewed as one instance of the uncertain reasoning of the rule $E \to H$.

For a rule $E \to H$, on supplying a value for $(CF(H, E), CF(H, \neg E))$, a human expert must abide by the following theorem.

Theorem 1.

1. $CF(H, E) > 0 \Leftrightarrow CF(H, \neg E) < 0$,
2. $CF(H, E) < 0 \Leftrightarrow CF(H, \neg E) > 0$,
3. $CF(H, E) = 0 \Leftrightarrow CF(H, \neg E) = 0$.

Proof. We only prove Item 1. By (4), we easily get

$$P(H|\neg E) = \frac{P(H) - P(H|E)P(E)}{P(\neg E)},$$

thus

$$P(H|\neg E) < P(H) \Leftrightarrow P(H|E) > P(H).$$

And by (1), we have

$$CF(H, \neg E) < 0 \Leftrightarrow P(H|\neg E) < P(H),$$
$$CF(H, E) > 0 \Leftrightarrow P(H|E) > P(H).$$

Hence, we have Item 1. $\square$

However, there is not a similar relationship among $CF(H, E_\alpha)$, $CF(H, E)$ and $CF(H, \neg E)$. In fact, we have the following theorem:

Theorem 2.

1. *If* $CF(H, E) > 0$ *(or* $CF(H, \neg E) < 0$*) and* $\alpha > P(E)$, *then* $CF(H, E_\alpha) > 0$.
2. *If* $CF(H, E) > 0$ *(or* $CF(H, \neg E) < 0$*) and* $\alpha < P(E)$, *then* $CF(H, E_\alpha) < 0$.
3. *If* $CF(H, E) < 0$ *(or* $CF(H, \neg E) > 0$*) and* $\alpha > P(E)$, *then* $CF(H, E_\alpha) < 0$.
4. *If* $CF(H, E) < 0$ *(or* $CF(H, \neg E) > 0$*) and* $\alpha < P(E)$, *then* $CF(H, E_\alpha) > 0$.

Proof. By (1), if $CF(H, E) > 0$, $P(H|E) > P(H)$, thus by Lemma 1, we have

$$\frac{P(H|E_\alpha)P(\neg E) + (\alpha - 1)P(H)}{\alpha - P(E)} > P(H),$$

Hence, 1) if $\alpha > P(E)$, $P(H|E_\alpha) > P(H)$, and by (6), then $CF(H, E_\alpha) > 0$; and 2) if $\alpha < P(E)$, $P(H|E_\alpha) < P(H)$, and by (6), then $CF(H, E_\alpha) < 0$. Similar, in other cases. $\square$

Lemma 3

$$P(E) = \begin{cases} \frac{CF(H, \neg E)P(H)}{CF(H, \neg E)P(H) - CF(H, E)P(\neg H)} & \text{if } CF(H, E) > 0 > CF(H, \neg E), \\ \frac{CF(H, \neg E)P(\neg H)}{CF(H, \neg E)P(\neg H) - CF(H, E)P(H)} & \text{if } CF(H, E) < 0 < CF(H, \neg E). \end{cases} \quad (8)$$

Proof. From (1) and (4), it can be easily verified. $\square$

Theorem 3.

$$P(H) = \begin{cases} \frac{\alpha \times CF(H, E) - CF(H, E_\alpha)}{\alpha \times CF(H, E) - (1 - \alpha)CF(H, \neg E) - CF(H, E_\alpha)} \\ \quad \text{if } CF(H, E) > 0, \, CF(H, E_\alpha) > 0, \, CF(H, \neg E) < 0, \\[4pt] \frac{\alpha \times CF(H, E)}{\alpha \times CF(H, E) + (\alpha - 1)CF(H, \neg E) + CF(H, E_\alpha)} \\ \quad \text{if } CF(H, E) > 0, \, CF(H, E_\alpha) < 0, \, CF(H, \neg E) < 0, \\[4pt] \frac{(1 - \alpha)CF(H, \neg E) - CF(H, E_\alpha)}{-\alpha \times CF(H, E) + (1 - \alpha)CF(H, \neg E) - CF(H, E_\alpha)} \\ \quad \text{if } CF(H, E) < 0, \, CF(H, E_\alpha) > 0, \, CF(H, \neg E) > 0, \\[4pt] \frac{(1 - \alpha)CF(H, \neg E))}{-\alpha \times CF(H, E) + (1 - \alpha)CF(H, \neg E) + CF(H, E_\alpha)} \\ \quad \text{if } CF(H, E) < 0, \, CF(H, E_\alpha) < 0, \, CF(H, \neg E) > 0. \end{cases} \quad (9)$$

Proof. By (2), Lemmas 2 and 3, it can be verified. □

For a rule $E \to H$, if a human expert offers a value for its ternary strength, both $P(H)$ and $P(E)$ can be found from its ternary strength

$$(CF(H, E), CF(H, E_\alpha), CF(H, \neg E))$$

by using Theorem 3 and Lemma 3. Namely, Theorem 3 converts supplying values for prior probabilities into giving one instance of uncertain reasoning. Clearly, the latter is much easier and more intuitive than the former. On the contrary, in the PROSPECTOR model [9], a human expert is engaged in the very arduous task of supplying a value for the prior probability of its conclusion of each rule in a knowledge base.

Because $P(H) \leq 1$, by Theorem 3, we can get some constraints on the ternary strength of a rule. Let us examine formula (9). There is no problem with the first and third branches of (9), which guarantee $P(H) \leq 1$. However, in order to guarantee $P(H) \leq 1$,

- for the second branch, namely in the case $CF(H, E) > 0$, $CF(H, E_\alpha) < 0$ and $CF(H, \neg E) < 0$, the following constraint should be satisfied:

$$(\alpha - 1)CF(H, \neg E) + CF(H, E_\alpha) \geq 0;$$

- for the fourth branch, namely in the case $CF(H, E) < 0$, $CF(H, E_\alpha) < 0$ and $CF(H, \neg E) > 0$, the following constraint should be satisfied:

$$-\alpha CF(H, E) + CF(H, E_\alpha) \geq 0.$$

In the following table we give some examples of finding prior probabilities by Theorem 3, and further transform $CF(H, S) = 0.8$ into corresponding probabilities by (2), where $\alpha = 0.7$.

$(CF(H, E), CF(H, E_\alpha), CF(H, \neg E))$	$P(H)$	$P(H|S)$
(0.7,0.4,-0.3)	0.5	0.9
(0.7,-0.04,-0.3)	0.907	0.981
(-0.7,0.4,0.3)	0.388	0.878
(-0.7,-0.4,0.3)	0.5	0.9

3 From Instances of the EMYCIN Parallel Propagation

In this section, we will discuss the finding of the values of prior probabilities from instances of the EMYCIN parallel propagation.

3.1   Parallel Propagation Based on Probability Theory

So-called parallel propagation is used to find the value of $P(H|S_1 \wedge S_2)$ when we have found the values of $P(H|S_1)$ and $P(H|S_2)$ from both rules $E_1 \to H$ and $E_2 \to H$, respectively.

Duda et al. [9] showed:

Theorem 4. *If S_1 and S_2 are conditionally independent, given H and $\neg H$, that is,*

$$P(S_1 \wedge S_2|H) = P(S_1|H)P(S_2|H), \tag{10}$$

$$P(S_1 \wedge S_2|\neg H) = P(S_1|\neg H)P(S_2|\neg H), \tag{11}$$

then

$$O(H|S_1 \wedge S_2) = \frac{O(H|S_1)O(H|S_2)}{O(H)}, \tag{12}$$

where O represents the odds. The relationship between odds and probability is

$$O(x) = \frac{P(x)}{1 - P(x)}. \tag{13}$$

By (13), we can transform (12) into the following (14).

Theorem 5. *If S_1 and S_2 are conditionally independent, given H and $\neg H$, that is, (10) and (11), then*

$$P(H|S_1 \wedge S_2) = \frac{P(H|S_1)P(H|S_2)P(\neg H)}{P(\neg H|S_1)P(\neg H|S_2)P(H) + P(H|S_1)P(H|S_2)P(\neg H)}. \tag{14}$$

3.2   Find Prior Probability

In the EMYCIN model, the formula for parallel propagation is as follows:

$$CF(H, S_1 \wedge S_2) = \begin{cases} CF(H, S_1) + CF(H, S_2) - CF(H, S_1)CF(H, S_2) \\ \qquad \text{if } CF(H, S_1) > 0, \ CF(H, S_2) > 0, \\ CF(H, S_1) + CF(H, S_2) + CF(H, S_1)CF(H, S_2) \\ \qquad \text{if } CF(H, S_1) \leq 0, \ CF(H, S_2) \leq 0, \\ \frac{CF(H,S_1)+CF(H,S_2)}{1-\min\{|CF(H,S_1)|,|CF(H,S_2)|\}} \\ \qquad \text{if } CF(H, S_1) \times CF(H, S_2) < 0. \end{cases} \tag{15}$$

Adams [1] and Schocken [23] proved partial consistency between the parallel propagation formula (15) and probability theory. In fact, they proved consistency between (14) and the first and second branches of (15). In other words, the first and second branches of (15) can be derived from (14) and the definition of certainty factors, but the third one cannot.

Notice that $P(H)$ does not appear in the first and second branches of (15). Therefore, we cannot expect that the value of $P(H)$ can be found from an instance of parallel propagation in the situations where both $CF(H, S_1)$ and $CF(H, S_2)$ are greater or less than 0. In other words, only in the situation where one of $CF(H, S_1)$ and $CF(H, S_2)$ is greater than 0 and another one is less than 0, is it possible for us to find the value of $P(H)$ from an instance of parallel propagation.

Theorem 6. *If* $CF(H, S_1) > 0$ *and* $CF(H, S_2) < 0$, *then*

$$
P(H) = \begin{cases}
\frac{CF(H,S_1 \wedge S_2) - CF(H,S_1)(CF(H,S_2)(1-CF(H,S_1 \wedge S_2))+1)}{CF(H,S_2)(1+CF(H,S_1)(CF(H,S_1 \wedge S_2)-2))+CF(H,S_1 \wedge S_2)-CF(H,S_1)} \\
\qquad \text{if } CF(H, S_1 \wedge S_2) > 0, \\[2ex]
\frac{CF(H,S_1)(CF(H,S_2)+1)}{CF(H,S_1 \wedge S_2)(1+CF(H,S_1)CH(H,S_2))-CF(H,S_2)+(2CF(H,S_2)+1)CF(H,S_1)} \\
\qquad \text{if } CF(H, S_1 \wedge S_2) < 0.
\end{cases}
$$

$$(16)$$

Proof. From (2) and (14), we can derive the above formula. $\qquad\square$

In the following table, we give some examples of finding prior probabilities by Theorem 6, and we further transform the certainty factors into the corresponding probabilities by (2).

$(CF(H, S_1), CF(H, S_2), CF(H, S_1 \wedge S_2))$	$P(H)$	$P(H \mid S_1 \wedge S_2)$
$(0.8, -0.3, 0.5)$	0.75	0.875
$(0.8, -0.3, 0.7)$	0.318	0.795
$(0.8, -0.3, 0.3)$	0.847	0.893
$(-0.8, 0.3, -0.5)$	0.531	0.265
$(-0.8, 0.3, -0.7)$	0.492	0.148
$(-0.8, 0.3, -0.3)$	0.575	0.403

4 From Instances of Reasoning in Bayesian Networks

In this section, we will discuss to the values of prior probabilities from instances of reasoning in Bayesian Networks.

Let us consider a single link $X \to Y$ in a Bayesian network [22]. From Bayes' Rule, the belief distribution of X is given by

$$
Bel(x) = P(x|e) = \frac{P(x)\lambda(x)}{P(e)} \tag{17}
$$

where

1) if evidence $\mathbf{e} = \{Y = y\}$ is observed directly,

$$
\lambda(x) = P(e|x) = P(Y = y|x); \tag{18}
$$

2) if evidence $\mathbf{e} = \{Y = y\}$ is not observed directly,

$$
\lambda(x) = P(e|x) = \sum_y P(e|y)P(y|x). \tag{19}
$$

Notice that in a Bayesian network, $P(e)$ and $P(Y = y|x)$ are known.

When evidence $e = \{Y = y\}$ is observed directly, if we ask a domain expert to provide a reasoning instance of the link $X \to Y$, i.e.

$$Bel(x) = P(x|e), \tag{20}$$

it is clear that we can easily find the value of $P(x)$ from this instance. In fact, we have

Theorem 7. *If $P(Y = y|x) \neq 0$, then*

$$P(x) = \frac{P(x|e)P(e)}{P(Y = y|x)}. \tag{21}$$

Proof. From (17) and (18), we can easily derive the above formula. $\square$

Notice according to probability theory,

$$\begin{cases} \sum_x P(x|e) = 1, \\ \sum_x P(x) = \sum_x \frac{P(x|e)P(e)}{P(Y=y|x)} = 1, \\ 0 \leq P(x|e) \leq 1. \end{cases} \tag{22}$$

This is the constraint which the reasoning instance (20) must fulfill.

Example 1. Suppose we have random variables E and Y, which take values on $\{e_1, e_2, e_3\}$ and $\{y_1, y_2, y_3\}$. For the link $Y \to E$, suppose the conditional probability matrix is

$$\begin{pmatrix} P(e_1|y_1) & P(e_1|y_2) & P(e_1|y_3) \\ P(e_2|y_1) & P(e_2|y_2) & P(e_2|y_3) \\ P(e_3|y_1) & P(e_3|y_2) & P(e_3|y_3) \end{pmatrix} = \begin{pmatrix} 0.6 & 0.1 & 0.3 \\ 0.3 & 0.7 & 0.2 \\ 0.1 & 0.2 & 0.5 \end{pmatrix}$$

Again we suppose that we have evidence $e = \{E = e_1\}$ and $P(e) = P(e_1) = 0.3$, and a domain expert gives a reasoning instance of $Y \to E$ as below:

$$(P(y_1|e_1), P(y_2|e_1), P(y_3|e_1)) = (0.2, 0.05, 0.75).$$

Then by (21) we can find the prior probability distribution of the random variable Y as follows:

$$\begin{aligned} (P(y_1), P(y_2), P(y_3)) &= \left(\frac{P(y_1|e_1)P(e_1)}{P(e_1|y_1)}, \frac{P(y_2|e_1)P(e_1)}{P(e_1|y_2)}, \frac{P(y_3|e_1)P(e_1)}{P(e_1|y_3)} \right) \\ &= \left(\frac{0.2 \times 0.3}{0.6}, \frac{0.05 \times 0.3}{0.3}, \frac{0.75 \times 0.3}{0.1} \right) \\ &= (0.1, 0.15, 0.75). \end{aligned}$$

Further, by (1) we can transform $P(y|e)$ into $CF(y, e)$ as follows:

$$(CF(y_1, e_1), CF(y_2, e_1), CF(y_3, e_1))$$
$$= \left(\frac{P(y_1|e_1) - P(y_1)}{1 - P(y_1)}, \frac{P(y_2|e_1) - P(y_2)}{P(y_2)}, 0 \right)$$
$$= \left(\frac{0.2 - 0.1)}{1 - 0.1}, \frac{0.05 - 0.15)}{0.15}, 0 \right)$$
$$= \left(\frac{1}{9}, \frac{2}{3}, 0 \right).$$

When evidence $e = \{Y = y\}$ is not observed directly, if we ask a domain expert to provide a reasoning instance of the link $X \to Y$, i.e.

$$(Bel(x), Bel(y)) = (P(x|e), P(y|e)),$$

we can find the value of $P(x)$ from this instance. In fact, we have

Theorem 8. *If* $\sum_y \frac{P(y|e)P(y|x)}{P(y)} \neq 0$, *then*

$$P(x) = \frac{P(x|e)}{\sum_y \frac{P(y|e)P(y|x)}{P(y)}}. \qquad (23)$$

Proof. By substitute (17) into (19), we get

$$P(x|e) = \frac{P(x) \sum_y P(e|y)P(y|x)}{P(e)}.$$

By Bayes' Rule, we have

$$P(e|y) = \frac{P(y|e)P(e)}{P(y)}.$$

From the above two formulas, we can easily derive the formula (21). $\qquad \square$

Notice that in the above formula, the prior probability $P(y)$ appears. The value of $P(y)$ can be obtained from the value of prior probability of its successor by the above formula. If its successor is not observed directly, this procedure is performed until the corresponding successor can be observed directly. At this moment, we use formula (20) to find the value of $P(x)$.

Again notice according to probability theory,

$$\begin{cases} \sum_x P(x|e) = 1, \\ \sum_y P(y|e) = 1, \\ \sum_x P(x) = \sum_x \frac{P(x|e)}{\sum_y \frac{P(y|e)P(y|x)}{P(y)}} = 1, \\ \forall x, \sum_y \frac{P(y|e)P(y|x)}{P(y)} \neq 0, \\ \forall x, 0 \leq P(x|e) \leq 1, \\ \forall y, 0 \leq P(y|e) \leq 1. \end{cases} \qquad (24)$$

This is the constraint which the reasoning instance (23) must fulfill.

Example 2. In Example 1, we illustrate how to find the prior probability distribution of the random variable Y from a reasoning instance of the link $Y \to E$ as follows:

$$(P(y_1), P(y_2), P(y_3)) = (0.1, 0.15, 0.75).$$

In this example, we continue to discuss how to find the prior probability distribution of the random variable X from a reasoning instance of the link $X \to Y$, where Y is a random variable taking values on $\{x_1, x_2, x_3\}$. For the link $X \to Y$, suppose that the conditional probability matrix is,

$$\begin{pmatrix} P(y_1|x_1) & P(y_1|x_2) & P(y_1|x_3) \\ P(y_2|x_1) & P(y_2|x_2) & P(y_2|x_3) \\ P(y_3|x_1) & P(y_3|x_2) & P(y_3|x_3) \end{pmatrix} = \begin{pmatrix} 0.8 & 0.1 & 0.1 \\ 0.1 & 0.8 & 0.1 \\ 0.1 & 0.1 & 0.8 \end{pmatrix}$$

and suppose that a domain expert provides the following reasoning instance of the link $X \to Y$,

$$(P(y_1|e_1), P(y_2|e_1), P(y_3|e_1)) = (0.2, 0.05, 0.75),$$
$$(P(x_1|e_1), P(x_2|e_1), P(x_3|e_1)) = (0.644, 0.356, 0).$$

Then by (24) we can get the prior probabilities of the random variable x:

$$(P(x_1), P(x_2), P(x_3))$$

$$= \left(\frac{P(x_1|e_1)}{\frac{P(y_1|e_1)P(y_1|x_1)}{P(y_1)} + \frac{P(y_2|e_1)P(y_2|x_1)}{P(y_2)} + \frac{P(y_3|e_1)P(y_3|x_1)}{P(y_3)}}, \right.$$

$$\frac{P(x_2|e_1)}{\frac{P(y_1|e_1)P(y_1|x_2)}{P(y_1)} + \frac{P(y_2|e_1)P(y_2|x_2)}{P(y_2)} + \frac{P(y_3|e_1)P(y_3|x_2)}{P(y_3)}},$$

$$\left. \frac{P(x_3|e_1)}{\frac{P(y_1|e_1)P(y_1|x_3)}{P(y_1)} + \frac{P(y_2|e_1)P(y_2|x_3)}{P(y_2)} + \frac{P(y_3|e_1)P(y_3|x_3)}{P(y_3)}} \right)$$

$$= \left(\frac{0.644}{\frac{0.2 \times 0.8}{0.1} + \frac{0.05 \times 0.1}{0.15} + \frac{0.75 \times 0.1}{0.75}}, \frac{0.356}{\frac{0.2 \times 0.1}{0.1} + \frac{0.05 \times 0.8}{0.15} + \frac{0.75 \times 0.1}{0.75}}, \right.$$

$$\left. \frac{0}{\frac{0.2 \times 0.1}{0.1} + \frac{0.05 \times 0.1}{0.15} + \frac{0.75 \times 0.8}{0.75}} \right)$$

$$= (0.371, 0.629, 0).$$

Finally, by (1) we can transform $P(x|e)$ into $CF(x, e)$ as follows:

$$(CF(x_1, e_1), CF(x_2, e_1), CF(x_3, e_1))$$

$$= \left(\frac{P(x_1|e_1) - P(x_1)}{1 - P(x_1)}, \frac{P(x_2|e_1) - P(x_2)}{P(x_2)}, 0 \right)$$

$$= \left(\frac{0.644 - 0.371}{1 - 0.371}, \frac{0.356 - 0.629}{0.629}, 0 \right)$$
$$= (0.434, -0.434, 0).$$

5 Summary

If the different expert systems in a distributed expert system employ different uncertain models, in order to cooperate to solve problems, transformations of uncertainties among these models are required. This paper discusses the problem of transformations of uncertainties between the EMYCIN model and a Bayesian network. So far, to our knowledge, no paper associated with this problem has been presented.

In a Bayesian network, uncertainties are measured by probability. In the EMYCIN model, uncertainties are measured by certainty factor. But if the values of prior probabilities are known, it is easy to implement transformations of uncertainties between the EMYCIN model and a Bayesian network. Accordingly, the key issue is how to obtain the values of prior probabilities. In this paper, we present three ways of finding the values of prior probabilities. The first way is to find prior probabilities from instances of sequential propagation in the EMYCIN model. The second is to find prior probabilities from instances of parallel propagation in the EMYCIN model. The third is to find prior probabilities from instances of inference in a Bayesian network.

There are plenty of methods for obtaining prior probabilities, yet these methods require a lot of time and money, especially for a large knowledge base. Besides, often statistical data are not sufficient to obtain reliable probabilities. These factors concern builders of systems. Rather, it is easy for domain experts to offer some instances of reasoning. Since domain experts can provide the knowledge with uncertainties, this implies that they have experience of using the knowledge to perform reasoning. In other words, they should have some instances of reasoning. Naturally, it is not difficult to ask them to supply these instances.

In the past, expert systems exploited mainly the EMYCIN model to deal with uncertainties. Currently, expert systems mainly use Bayesian networks for modeling uncertainties. In other words, a lot of stand-alone expert systems which use these two models are available. As a consequence, if we can use the Internet to couple them together, the integrated systems will be able to exchange helpful information with each other, and so improve each other's performance through cooperation. The work in this paper makes an important progress towards this end.

Acknowledgement

The authors would like to thank the referees for their comments. Besides, the authors are very much obliged to Mrs Meg Vivers for her proof-reading. In addition, the Maple system is used to derive all formulae in this paper.

References

1. J. B. Adams, "Probabilistic Reasoning and Certainty Factor", *Rule-Based Expert Systems*, B. G. Buchanan and E. H. Shortliffe (eds), pp. 263–271, Addison-Wesley, 1984.

2. D.I. Blockley, B.W. Pilsworth and J.F. Baldwin, "Measures of Uncertainty", *Civil Engineering Systems*, 1, 1988, pp.3–9.

3. R. Buxton, "Modeling Uncertainty in Expert Systems", *Int. J. Man-Machine Studies*, Vol. 31, No. 4, pp. 415–476, 1989.

4. E. Charniak, "Bayesian Network without Tears", *The AI Magazine*, Vol. 12, No. 4, pp. 50–63, 1991.

5. A.Y. Darwiche, "Objection-Based Causal Networks", *Proc. of the Eighth Conference on Uncertainty in Artificial Intelligence*, Dubois, D. et al.(eds), Morgan Kaufmann Publishers, Inc., San Mateo, California, pp. 67-73, 1992.

6. M.J. Druzdzel et al., "Elicitation of Probabilities for Belief Networks: Combination Qualitative and Quantitative Information", *Proc. of the Eleventh Conference on Uncertainty in Artificial Intelligence*, P. Besnard et al. (eds), Morgan Kaufmann Publishers, Inc., pp. 141–148, 1995.

7. D. Dubois and H. Prade, "Handling Uncertainty in Expert Systems: Pitfalls, Difficulties, Remedies", *The reliability of Expert Systems*, E. Hollnagel (ed), Ellis Horwood Limited, pp. 64–118, 1989.

8. D. Dubois and H. Prade, "A Discussion of Uncertainty Handling in Support Logic Programming", *Int. J. of Intelligent Systems*, Vol. 5, No. 5, pp. 15–42, 1990.

9. R.O. Duda, P.E. Hart and N.J. Nillson, "Subjective Bayesian Methods for Rule-Based Inference Systems", *AFIPS Conference Proceedings*, Vol. 45, AFIPS Press, pp. 1075–1082, 1976.

10. Gaines, B.R., "Fuzzy and Probability Logics", *Information Control*, Vol. 83, pp. 154–169, 1978.

11. J. Guan and C. Zhang, "Analysis of the Unit Element in Inexact Reasoning in Expert Systems", *Proceedings of the Second International Conference on Computers and Applications*, Beijing, pp. 391–393, 1987.

12. O. Heckman, "Probabilistic Interpretations of MYCIN's Certainty Factors", *Uncertainty in Artificial Intelligence*, L. N. Kanal and J. F. Lemmer (eds), North Holland, pp. 167–196, 1986.

13. P. Hájek, "Combining Functions for Certainty Degrees in Consulting Systems", *Int. J. Man-Machines Studies*, Vol. 22, pp.59–76, 1985.

14. J. Ihara, "Extension of Conditional Probability and Measures of Belief and Disbelief in a Hypothesis Based on Uncertain Evidence", *IEEE Trans. PAMI.* Vol. 9, No. 41, pp. 561–568, 1987.

15. X. Luo, "A Study of Probability-Based Uncertain Reasoning Model in Rule-Based Expert Systems: Prospector-Type Scheme", *Automated Reasoning*, Z. Shi (ed), North-Holland, pp. 123–135, 1992.

16. X. Luo and C. Zhang, "A Unified Algebraic Structure for Uncertain Reasonings", *PRICAI'96: Topics in Artificial Intelligence*, N. Foo and R. Goebel (eds), Lecture Notes in Artificial Intelligence 1114, Springer, pp. 459–470, 1996.

17. X. Luo and C. Zhang, "Transformations of Two Dimensional Uncertainty in Distributed Expert Systems: A Case Study", *Proceedings of International Conference on Computational Intelligence and Multimedia Applications*, B. Verma and X. Yao (eds), pp. 366–372, 1997.

18. X. Luo and C. Zhang, "The Favoring-Opposing Cause Model for Uncertain Reasoning", *Proceedings of International Conference on Computational Intelligence and Multimedia Applications*, B. Verma and X. Yao (eds), pp. 373–379, 1997.

19. Luo X. and Zhang C., "A Solution to the Problem of Prior Probabilities in the PROSPECTOR Uncertain Reasoning Model", *Proceedings of the 1997 Joint Pacific Asian Conference on Expert Systems/Singapore International Conference on Intelligent Systems*, D. Patterson, C. Leedham, K. Warendorf and T. A. Hwee (eds), pp. 306–313, 1997.

20. J. McDermott, "Making Expert Systems Explicit", *Proceedings of the IFIP-86*, North Holland Publishing Company, Amsterdam, Dublin, pp. 539–544, 1986.

21. W.V. Melle, "A Domain-Independent System that Aids in Constructing Knowledge-Based Consultation Programs", *Ph.D. Dissertation Report STAN-CS-80-820*, Computer Science Department, Stanford University, CA, 1980.

22. J. Pearl, *Probabilistic Reasoning in Intelligent Systems: Networks of Plausible Inference,* Morgan Kaufmann Publishers, Inc., San Mateo, California, 1988.

23. S. Schocken, "On the Rational Scope of Probabilistic Rule-Based Inference Systems", *Uncertainty in Artificial Intelligence*, J.F. Lemmer and L.N. Kanal (eds), Vol.2, pp. 175–189, Elsevier Science Publisher B.V. (North-Holland), 1988.

24. G. Shafer, *A Mathematical Theory of Evidence.* Princeton, NJ: Princeton University Press, 1976.

25. E.H. Shotliffe and B.G. Buchanan, "A Model of Inexact Reasoning in Medicine", *Mathematical Bioscience,* Vol. 23, pp. 351–379, 1975.

26. C. Zhang, "HECODES: A Framework for Heterogeneous Cooperative Distributed Expert Systems", Ph.D thesis, University of Queensland, 1990.

27. C. Zhang, "Cooperation under Uncertainty in Distributed Expert Systems", *Artificial Intelligence*, Vol. 56, pp. 21–69, 1992.

28. C. Zhang, "Heterogeneous Transformation of Uncertainties of Propositions among Inexact Reasoning Models", *IEEE Transactions on Knowledge and Data Engineering*, Vol. 6, No. 3, pp. 353–360, 1994.

29. C. Zhang and D.A. Bell, "HECODES: A Framework for Heterogeneous Cooperative Distributed Expert Systems", *International Journal on Data & Knowledge Engineering*, Vol. 6, pp. 251–273, 1991.

30. C. Zhang and X. Luo, "Heterogeneous Transformation of Uncertainties of Propositions among the EMYCIN and PROSPECTOR Uncertain Models", *Proceeding Second International Conference on Multi-agent Systems*, AAAI Press, p. 465, 1996.

31. Chengqi Zhang and Xudong Luo, "An Issue on Transformation of Interval-Based Uncertainty in Distributed Expert Systems", Post Proceedings of the Tenth Australian Joint Conference on Artificial Intelligence, Perth, Western Australia, 2–4 December 1997.

32. C. Zhang and M. Orlowska, "On Algebraic Structures of Inexact Reasoning Models", *Advances in Information Systems Research*, G. E. Lasker, et al. (eds), pp. 58–77, 1991.

Using Multi-agent Approach for the Design of an Intelligent Learning Environment

Dong Mei Zhang*
Leila Alem*
Kalina Yacef**

(*) CSIRO Mathematical and Information Sciences
Locked bag 17, North Ryde 2113 NSW, Australia
(**) Thomson Radar Australia Corporation and
Laboratoire d'Intelligence Artificielle de Paris 5
dong.zhang@cmis.csiro.au
leila.alem@cmis.csiro.au
Tel: 61 2 93253100
Fax: 61 2 93253200

Abstract

This paper presents FILIP, a multi-agent framework for the design of Intelligent Simulation-based Learning Environment (ISLE). Such a learning environment assesses the learner and provides adaptive instruction when the learner is developing his/her operational skill in dynamic and highly risky domains. The FILIP framework offers a great hope as a means of helping learners develop the skill necessary for effective performance. It is geared towards skill development and acquisition in order to develop and support operators performance. FILIP is designed as a multi agent architecture, which includes the seven agents: a simulator; a user interface; a domain expert agent; a learner agent; an instructor agent, a curriculum agent and a skill development agent. FILIP framework is distinguished from other traditional ISLE by its skill development agent and the curriculum agent. The skill development agent is to advise the instructor on issues related to the skill development of the learner so that it can be taken into account in the planning of the instruction. The curriculum agent is made of a Curriculum Formalism for Operational Skill Training (CFOST). It provides information for skill development agent to assess skill development and for the instructor agent to provide adaptive instruction.

As an application of FILIP in the context of Air Traffic Control (ATC) training, ATEEG is described. It adopts a blackboard architecture based on a multi-agent approach, in which major tasks of the training are distributed into agents. The architecture of ATEEG is composed of an air traffic control simulator; a domain expert called here the *ideal ATC* which represents an ATC expert and provides expert's problem solving strategies and solutions to given traffic situations presented to the learner; a *learner* which gathers the learner's actions during the execution of a training exercise and derives a bi-dimension learner model; an *instructor* which adapts instruction to the individual learner's needs at two levels: tailoring training exercises and adapting instructional methods; an *ATC curriculum*, which provides a hierarchical network of ATC training topics, training situations and instructional methods; and an ATC *exercise base* that represents existing ATC training exercises in terms of underlying training topics presented, complexity of training situations. An object sever facilities the data flow and communication among ATEEG agents.

Keywords
multi-agent training system, agent modelling, intelligent tutoring system, simulation-based learning

1   Introduction

We are concerned here with the design of an Intelligent Simulation-based Learning Environment (ISLE) using a multi-agent approach. Such a learning environment assesses the learner and provides adaptive instruction when the learner is developing his/her operational skill in dynamic and highly risky domains such as Air Traffic Control, nuclear plant operations, etc.

The use of intelligent simulation-based learning environment for training offers a great hope as a means of helping operators develop the knowledge and skills necessary for effective performance. They provide learners with the opportunity to apply their knowledge and to practice procedures in realistic problem solving situations. Allowing personnel to develop and hone their skills on an ISLE has shown to have numerous benefits including the increase of training effectiveness and the reduce of training periods and cost. In this paper we present FILIP, a multi-agent framework for designing intelligent simulation-based learning environment. Such a framework is dedicated to skill development and training in order to develop and support operators performance. It allows learners to develop their skills and assists/supports the instructional planning process based on the nature of the learning target. The framework provides the learner with extensive practice which is essential for learning complex problem solving skills.

This paper first presents the multi-agent architecture of FILIP framework. Its major agents are described: learner agent, skill development agent, domain expert agent, curriculum agent and instructor agent. As an application of FILIP, ATEEG ([1], [2]) is then presented, which is designed as a training system for Air Traffic Controller (ATC). Relevant design issues of ATEEG are addressed.

2   A Multi-agent View of FILIP Architecture

FILIP's architecture is based on a multi-agent approach. Two main characteristics have led us to adopt the approach: First an ISLE is a complex system, in which the complexity of each task needs to be distributed to increase the system performance. Second, the independence feature gives each task the autonomy needed to perform insetting across the learning session. FILIP's multi agent architecture is shown in Fig1.

It includes the five traditional ISLE agents: (1) a simulator (ie the learning environment); (2) a user interface; (3) a domain expert agent; (4) a learner agent and (5) an instructor agent. FILIP also involves two extra agents (6) the curriculum agent and (7) the skill development agent.

The type of simulations we are interested in here is an interactive high-fidelity representation of some world, where the learner manipulates the elements of the situations (the control is actually shared between the learner and the system), and these situations reflect an accurate representation of the real world. Such type of simulations is often used for acquiring process knowledge ie. "how to do it" knowledge. We exclude uses of simulations as a demonstrating tool or any other use where the learner does not interact with the model. The user interface provides a platform for learners to interact with the intelligent learning system through a simulator. The rest of section describes the learner agent, the skill development agent, the domain expert agent, the curriculum agent and the instructor agent of FILIP framework.

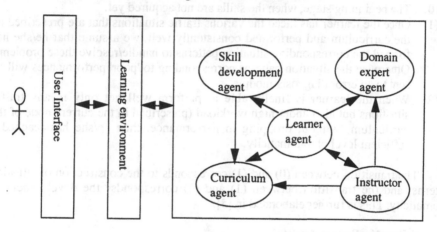

Fig1. FILIP multi-agent Architecture

2.1   Learner Agent

The learner agent is a core of FILIP, which severs functions of (1) gathering the learner's actions and performances; (2) referring to domain expert's actions and solutions; and (3) deriving a learner model. The learner model provides inputs to skill development agent and instructor agent.

The learner agent is composed of a set of task performance measures, (ie., accuracy, speed and quality of strategy in the context of ATC) which are provided with a related set of training situation characteristics. The training situation characteristics describe the problem faced by the learner and its level of complexity. The learner model produced in the learner agent is a bi-dimensional overlay learner model which captures performance measures and the situation characteristics in which such performances have taken place [5].

2.2   Skill Development Agent

The role of this agent is to advise the instructor on issues related to the skill development of the learner so that it can be taken into account in the planning of the instruction. The input of the skill development agent is the learner model from the learner agent which states performance measures with relevant training situation characteristics. As a result, the skill development agent advises the instructor agent for the promotion/demotion of skill training progress.

Assessing the level of the skill acquisition process requires the definition of key stages in the process. We consider the following stages:

(0)   The beginning stage, when the skills are not acquired yet.

(1)   Once the learner has faced the various traffic situations that are prescribed by the curriculum and performed consistently well, we assume that he/she has formed the corresponding situation patterns to handle/resolve these problems. Otherwise the situation patterns corresponding to 'poor' performances will be sent to an error diagnosis module.

(2)   When the learner is finally able to perform well not only in any traffic situations but also under high workload (prescribed in the current node of the curriculum) without dropping in performance, then he/she has reached a sufficient level of automaticity.

The transition between (0) and (1) corresponds to the construction of situation patterns; and the transition between (1) and (2) corresponds the development of automaticity. This is further elaborated in [5].

2.3   Domain Expert Agent

Domain expert agent represents an domain expert's problem solving strategies and solutions to given training situations presented to the learner. Such information is used for the learner agent to measure the learner's performance. The domain expert can be represented as a black box, glass box or process models. Black box models produce the correct solution to the problem but cannot produce instructionally useful explanations of their behaviour when glass box and simulation models can. When considering the class of model available one has to weigh the cost of development against the cost of sacrificing power. For example glass box and simulation models require more extensive knowledge engineering effort than black box models, and as a result are more capable but more expensive to built.

A "translucent *box*" expert model has been proposed in ATEEG, that combines features of "glass box" and "black box" models: it models the general frame of the activity in which the learner is being instructed, with some parts being transparent and some others being opaque. A generic model of the activity is used to describe activities in the domain and the problem-solving activity. Associated with each task is the relevant knowledge to guide its performance. With this mode, it is possible to judge the correctness of the learner's actions as well as provide some diagnosis of his knowledge.

2.4   Curriculum Agent

The curriculum agent is made of a Curriculum Formalism for Operational Skill Training (CFOST) [6]. It provides information for skill development agent to assess skill development and for the instructor agent to provide adaptive instruction. Fig 2 gives an illustration of CFOST framework. Each node represents a training topic. Training topics are characterised by concepts, procedures, elementary skills, (complex) aggregated skills. The prerequisite relationships among training topics are represented by the links among nodes, which help determine promotion/demotion of the learner's training progress. When the learner has mastered some elementary skills (eg., elementary skills (1) and (2)) at certain levels, his or her training can be promoted to the topic for an aggregated skill (eg., aggregated skill (1)). If he or she fails to master an elementary skill (eg., elementary skill (1)) after several exercises on this topic, the training progress may be demoted to acquire relevant concepts/procedures (eg., concept (2), procedure (1)) before this topic becomes an active objective.

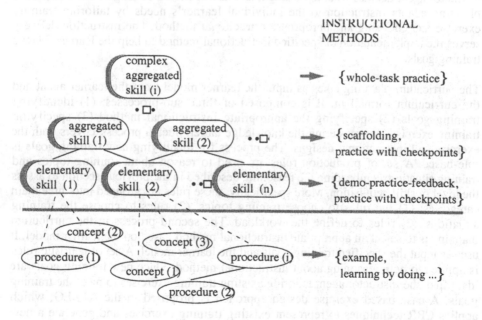

Fig2. A Curriculum Formalism for Operational Skill Training (CFOST)

CFOST integrates training topics, training situation characteristics and instructional methods into one formalism which is then used by the curriculum planner agent for specifying the next training goals. Associated with each skill node topic are (1) a number of applicable instructional methods that can help achieve the training goals, and (2) a set of various training situation that are recommended for practicing the topic, and (3) the workload threshold that the learner must reach successfully.

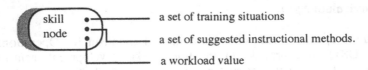

2.5 Instructor Agent

The instructor agent severs the function of adapting instruction to the learner's skill development level. Both the learner model of the learner agent and CFOST of the curriculum agent form the basis for planning the instruction.

The adaptation of the instruction can be done at various levels: adaptation of tutoring strategies, tailoring of exercises, activation of remedial instruction and so on. This agent is composed of curriculum planning and instruction delivery. In other words, the instructor agent decides what to be taught and how it should be taught. The curriculum planning adapts instruction to the individual learner's needs by tailoring training exercise and choosing an appropriate instructional method. The instruction delivery serves the implementation of specified instructional method to help the learner achieve training goals.

The curriculum planning takes as input the learner model from the learner agent and the curriculum formalism. It is composed of three sub-processes: (1) identifying training goals (2) specifying the appropriate instructional method (3) specifying training exercises for mastering the knowledge target. Such a process covers both the exercise and instructional designs. The process for identifying new training goals is rule-based. A set of production rules are used to reason about training topics and training situations, embedding the reasoning described in the previous section to assess the level of skill acquisition. More specifically, these rules are grouped into three main categories: (1) the rules to choose training topics, (2) rules to choose the training situations, (3) rules to define the workload. The second process in the curriculum planning is to select an appropriate instructional method based on the learner model. It uses as input the specified training goals and the learner model. A set of heuristic rules is applied to help reasoning about instructional method. Once new training goals are identified, the instructor agent tailoring existing training exercises to meet the training goals. A case-based exercise design approach is proposed in the ATEEG, which applies CBR techniques to represent existing training exercises and generate a new exercise by adapting existing exercise. The generation process includes two elementary steps: (1) retrieving and selecting relevant exercises from the case base by using the training topic and situation characteristics in new training goals; (2) adapting relevant training exercises to produce a new exercise to meet identified training goals.

In the instructor agent, the instruction delivery is to implement the specified instructional method in order to help the learner achieve the training goals by providing adaptive support and intervention while the learner executes the training exercise. Based on the tutoring strategies implied in the specified instructional method, the instruction delivery performs corresponding actions.

3   ATEEG: A Training System for ATC

The framework FILIP has been used for the development of a simulation-based training system for air traffic controllers (ATC) called the ATEEG system ([1], [2]). The architecture of ATEEG is composed of an air traffic control simulator; a domain expert called here the *ideal ATC* which represents an ATC expert and provides expert's problem solving strategies and solutions to given traffic situations presented to the learner; a *learner* which gathers the learner's actions during the execution of a training exercise and derives the learner's knowledge level and performance; an *instructor* which adapts instruction to the individual learner's needs at two levels: tailoring training exercises and adapting instructional methods; an *ATC curriculum*, which provides a hierarchical network of ATC training topics, training situations and instructional methods; and an ATC *exercise base* that represents existing ATC training exercises in terms of underlying training topics presented, complexity of training situations.

ATEEG adopts a blackboard architecture based on a multi-agent approach, in which major tasks of the training are distributed into agents. An object server is used to store objects shared by several agents as shown in Fig2.

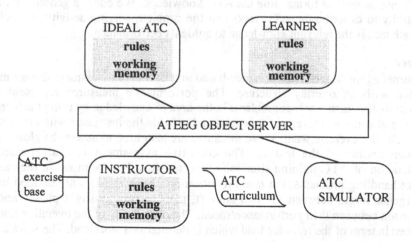

Fig2. Architecture of ATEEG

ATEEG Object Server

The object server facilitates the interaction among multi-agent in ATEEG. It provides a platform for the communication among agents. More specifically, agents communicate each other by accessing the objects stored in the ATEEG object server. For example, the object "conflict" is shared by multiple agents: the learner agent and the ideal ATC agent. The two agents provide relevant information about the conflict status, eg. when the conflict is detected by the learner and/or the ideal ATC. If the learner recognises the conflict, the object "conflict" is then activated and updated. The learner agent can use the object "conflict" to measure the learner's performance based on the time difference between the learner's and ideal ATC's actions concerning conflict detection. As another example, the learner agent and instructor agent shares the object "learner model". The learner agent records information related to performance measures with situation characteristics in the object "learner model". The instructor agent then accesses this object to obtain the learner's current skill level for providing adaptive instruction.

ATC simulator

The simulator gives a physical display of air traffic situation that will be updated according to the learner's actions in the execution of the exercise. Information shown on the simulator contains the lateral and vertical limits of the airspace, positions of aircraft, route structure, navigation aids and weather pattern, etc..

Ideal ATC

The ideal ATC model is a translucent type and uses a generic model of the ATC activity and its associated expert knowledge. ATC activity consists of a set of underlying operative tasks (INSPECT, CONTROL and SEPARATE) each of which is performed according to certain principles based on relevant ATC knowledge. Modelling the expert requires understanding these underlying tasks and their associations as well as formalising the ATC knowledge. We adopt a generic model of the activity to describe the ATC tasks and the problem solving activity. Associated with each task is the relevant knowledge to guide its performance.

Learner

The learner agent adopts a performance-based and cognitive assessment learner model enriched with an overlay structure. The performance measures represent how successfully the learner solves problems in the area of knowledge by using the learner's answers and some measurement functions and provide the instructor with elements of "how well" the exercise went. These measures are also used to assess the global level of understanding of the learner. The cognitive assessment is characterised by consideration of ATC training situation characteristics. For example, in the case of conflict handling problems, the *training situation characteristics* are defined by the convergence angle between the two aircraft, their respective flight phases and the comparison between their performance/speed. The complexity of the overall *training* is described in term of the resource load which is defined as a workload. The *workload* is a function of the number of aircraft flying at the same time in the sector during the interval and the average complexity of the aircraft. The learner model is a bi-dimensional overlay and composed of a list of performance measures for each task, with the specific situation characteristics in which they were done. The overlay model represents the learner's knowledge as a sub-set of the expert's knowledge, ie. procedures, rules and skills. These structures contain *contextual* information regarding training situation characteristics.

Instructor

The instructor agent serves the following functions of a human instructor: (1) it identifies new training goals (defined as training topics, training situations and expected workload value) based on the learner model and ATC curriculum; (2) it determines an instructional method to help the learner achieve the training goals; (3) it generates a training exercise by adapting existing exercises based on new training goals; (4) it also implements the specified instructional method while the learner executes the given training exercise providing adaptive support, context-sensitive help and interventions.

ATC exercise base

The ATC exercise base contains a number of existing training exercises. Each case represents a variety of information relevant to an ATC exercise, including three types of information: (1) description of physical information related to training situations. (2) underlying training topics that are reflected in training situations. (3) complexity of training situations.

ATC curriculum

The ATC curriculum represent an ATC training model using CFOST (Curriculum Formalism for Operational Skill Training) [5]. It integrates ATC training topics (concepts, procedures, elementary skills, aggregated skills), instructional methods and training situations characteristics to help the instructor specifying new training goals and instructional methods. The prerequisite relations among training topics help the instructor determine promotion/demotion of the learner's training progress.

ATEEG is developed on an UNIX basis using ILOG Rules and ILOG Server. Each of the ideal ATC, the learner, the instructor agents contains a set of reasoning rules and a working memory. The reasoning rules supports the operational functions of an agent, for example, generating a solution to the given traffic situation in the ideal ATC agent; identifying new training needs based on the learner model in the instructor agent. The working memory provides a set of objects applicable to the agent in the current moment.

4 Conclusion

In this paper we have presented FILIP, a multi agent framework for designing an intelligent simulation based learning environment (ISLE), targeted towards skill acquisition. The basic design of this framework is based on our experience with ATEEG, an ISLE for operational skill training of ATC. Multi-agent architecture has been used in the design of other intelligent tutoring/training systems [3] [4]. MATHEMA [3] is an intelligent learning environment based on a multi-agent architecture. Its main idea is to integrate a human learning in a micro-society of artificial tutoring agents with the objective of promoting his learning. Frasson et al. [4] designed an intelligent tutoring system that uses multiple learning strategies based on a multi-agent architecture. In this system each learning strategy is supported by several agents. Our FILIP framework offers a great hope as a means of helping learners develop the skill necessary for effective performance. It is geared towards skill development and acquisition in order to develop and support operators performance. Its key innovative aspect is the skill development agent which knows about the nature of skills development process and can assist the planning of the instruction by specifying

ATEEG adopts a blackboard architecture based on a multi-agent approach, in which major tasks of the training are distributed into agents. An object sever facilities the data flow and communication among ATEEG agents. The main features of such an architecture include: (1) extensibility. ATEEG can be readily extended, eg., adding more agents, reasoning rules; (2) modularity. ATEEG is implemented using an object-oriented design approach the learning situation that will influence positively the development of skill. Examples have been given in the ATC skill training, our view is that such a framework could also be used as a basis for the design of an ISLE for hight-performance task that requires extended training to develop proficiency, such as electronic troubleshooting, piloting etc.

Acknowledgment

We acknowledge the CRC-IDS for their coordination and funding on the ATEEG project. We are very grateful to Air Services Australia and Royal Australian Air Force for the time and effort their staff have spent us on the project. We also thank all the ATEEG team members: Ian Mathieson from CSIRO CMIS Melbourne, Bernard Lucat from Thomson Radar Australia Corporation, David Kemp from University of Melbourne, Gil Tidhar and Jamie Curmi from the Australian Artificial Intelligence Institute.

5   References

[1] L. Alem & R. Keeling (1996). Intelligent simulation environments: an application to Air Traffic Control training. *Proceedings of SimTecT'96* , pp 323-328.

[2] L. Alem, B.P. Woolf, A. Munro & W. van Joolingen (1996). *Proceedings of Simulation-based learning technology workshop*, held in conjunction with the

Third International Conference in Intelligent Tutoring Systems (ITS'96), Montreal, Canada.

[3]   E. Costa, A. Perkusich (1996). Modelling the cooperative interactions in a teaching/learning situation. In *Intelligent Tutoring Systems*, Ed. C. Frasson, G. Gauthier & A. Lesgold.

[4]   C. Frasson, T. Mengelle, E. Aimeur, G. Gouarderes (1996]. An actor-based architecture for intelligent tutoring systems. In *Intelligent Tutoring Systems*, Ed. C. Frasson, G. Gauthier & A. Lesgold.

[5]   K. Yacef & L. Alem (1997). Towards an assessment of skill acquisition is student modelling. *Proceedings of AI-ED'97*, Kobe, Japan

[6]   D. Zhang & L. Alem (1997). From task sequencing to curriculum planning. *Proceedings of AI-ED'97*, Kobe, Japan.

A Case-Based Strategy for Solution Synthesis Among Cooperative Expert Systems

Minjie Zhang

School of Computer, Information, and Mathematical Sciences
Edith Cowan University, W.A. 6027, Australia
m.zhang@cowan.edu.au

Abstract. Most synthesis strategies for solution synthesis in distributed expert systems (DESs) are developed based on analytic methods or inductive methods. A synthesis strategy presented in this paper is developed by case-based reasoning based on an analogical method. In this paper, the basic frame work of the strategy is introduced and preliminary results are demonstrated. Furthermore, this strategy is compared with related work.

1 Introduction

Synthesis of solutions has been become one of critical issues among cooperative expert systems for more than ten years [8]. Some synthesis strategies have been developed in distributed expert systems (DESs) such as [2, 7, 9]. These strategies were mainly based on the mathematical analysis of the characteristics of the *inputs* (multiple solutions from ESs). In recent years, we have developed some synthesis strategies [10] using neural networks. These strategies were based on a number of samples with both *inputs* and corresponding *outputs* (final solutions after synthesizing corresponding *input*). Such samples are called *patterns*.

In current literature, there are two methodologies used for designing synthesis strategies to solve synthesis problems. They are analytic methods, and inductive methods [11]. An analytic method is a methodology which can be used to define a synthesis strategy from *inputs* to *outputs* by analyzing the characteristics of *input*. These characteristics may include relationships among original evidence sets from ESs which derive the *inputs*, the factors which affect the final solution, and the weights for all factors. An inductive method is a methodology which can be used to find the general relationship between *input* and *output* based on sufficient patterns.

Different kinds of strategies are good in different kinds of problems. Analytic methods can work well for some simple problems if the relationship between *inputs* and *outputs* can be summarized by an analytic method. In particular, this method is perfect for use with cases where the *outputs* can be derived from some formulas based on *inputs*. Inductive methods can solve some complicated synthesis problems when the enough patterns exist and an inductive function can be found.

There are two major limitations in the above methodologies: (1) if the synthesis problem can not be summarized by a mathematical model, it is very hard to solve the problem by an analytic method; and (2) if an inductive function does not exist for the problem solving, or there are no enough learning patterns available, it is impossible to use inductive methods such as neural network strategies.

In this paper, we introduce a new synthesis strategy, case-based reasoning, which is an alternative way for overcoming the above limitations, by using an analogical method. Analogical methods are different from analytic methods and inductive methods. Analytic methods are based on only analysis without taking real examples into consideration. Inductive methods need too many real examples which are not available in most application fields. Case-based reasoning is an instance of analogical methods which is a popular method used in the learning science even in human society [5]. Case-based reasoning is an approach for problem-solving based on retrieving and applying stored solutions. In case-based reasoning, only some real examples are needed.

This paper is organized as follows: In Section 2, general procedure of solution synthesis in DESs are described. In Section 3, the system architecture of a synthesis strategy by case-based reasoning is proposed and described in detail. In Section 4, case matching rules and several examples are introduced. In Section 5, this strategy is compared with related work. Finally, in Section 6, this paper is concluded and the future direction of this research is outlined.

2   Description of solution synthesis

Let's see an example first. Suppose there are three ESs (e.g. ES_1, ES_2, ES_3) to decide the identity of the organism for a specific patient. ES_1 says that it is pseudomonas with uncertainty 0.06 and proteus with uncertainty -0.9, ES_2 says that it is pseudomonas with uncertainty 0.5 and serratia with uncertainty 0.4, and ES_3 says that it is serratia with uncertainty 0.1 and proteus with uncertainty 0.80. Because ES_1 doesn't mention serratia, we believe that ES_1 has no idea about it. We can represent this unknown by using uncertainty 0. Then the above solutions are represented in Table 1.

	Pseudomonas	Serratia	Proteus	Authority
ES_1	0.06	0	-0.9	0.6
ES_2	0.5	0.4	0	0.8
ES_3	0	0.1	0.80	0.9

Table 1. The uncertainties for each attribute value obtained by the ESs.

The purpose of the solution synthesis here is to decide the final uncertainty distribution among pseudomonas, serratia, and proteus according to Table 1.

We now formally describe the problems. Suppose there are n ESs in a DES to evaluate the values of an attribute of an object (e.g. in a medical DES, the identity of an organism infecting a specific patient). The solution for an ES_i can be represented as

$$(< object >< attribute > (V_1 \; CF_{i1} \; A_i) \; (V_2 \; CF_{i2} \; A_i) \; ... \; (V_m \; CF_{im} \; A_i))$$

$$2.1$$

where V_j $(1 \le j \le m)$ represents jth possible value, CF_{ij} $(1 \le i \le n, 1 \le j \le m)$ represents the uncertainty for jth value from ES_i, A_i represents the authority of ES_i, and m indicates that there are m possible values for this attribute of the object. The authority A_i $(1 \le i \le n)$ is the confidence level for the solution from ES_i. It can be assigned for each ES by human experts or generated based on the historical performance of ESs.

From the synthesis point of view, all ESs are concerned with the same attribute of an object. So we will only keep the attribute values, uncertainties, and authorities in the representation. Here is the representation of m possible values with uncertainties from n ESs:

$$\begin{bmatrix} CF_{11} \; CF_{12}... \; CF_{1m} \; A_1 \\ CF_{21} \; CF_{22}... \; CF_{2m} \; A_2 \\ \cdots\cdots\cdots\cdots\cdots\cdots\cdots\cdots\cdots \\ CF_{n1} \; CF_{n2}... \; CF_{nm} \; A_n \end{bmatrix} \qquad 2.2$$

The synthesis strategy is responsible for obtaining final uncertainties (CF_{*1} CF_{*2} ... CF_{*m}) based on Matrix 2.2 where * indicates the synthesis result from corresponding values with the subscriptions of $1, 2, ..., n$ in the same place.

3 A basic framework of a case-based strategy

3.1 Definitions

Throughout this paper, we make the following definitions:

Definition 1: *An input* of a synthesis strategy is the matrix representation of multiple solutions from different ESs (recall Matrix 2.2).

Definition 2: *An output* of a synthesis strategy is the final uncertainties of the vector (CF_{*1} CF_{*2} ... CF_{*m}) after synthesis of the input matrix.

Definition 3: *An input case* is a set of multiple solutions from different ESs for the same problem. It can be represented by an input matrix.

Definition 4: *An existing case* consists of an input matrix and an output vector.

A general case representation is demonstrated in Figure 1.

Examples of both an input case and an existing case in the PROBABILITY model are shown in Table 2 and Table 3.

	ES_s	$Value_1$	$Value_2$	$Value_3$
multiple	ES_1	0.04	0.14	0.40
solutions	ES_2	0.3	0.01	0.50
	ES_3	0.11	0.83	0.05

Table 2. A example of an input case in the PROBABILITY model

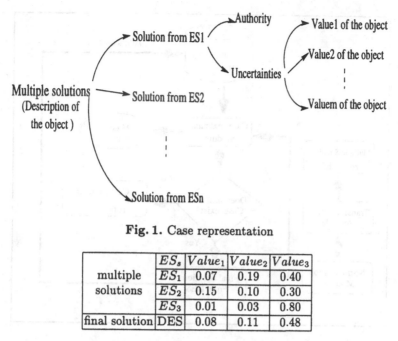

Fig. 1. Case representation

	ES_s	$Value_1$	$Value_2$	$Value_3$
multiple	ES_1	0.07	0.19	0.40
solutions	ES_2	0.15	0.10	0.30
	ES_3	0.01	0.03	0.80
final solution	DES	0.08	0.11	0.48

Table 3. A example of an existing case in the PROBABILITY model

3.2 System architecture

The basic idea of the case-based strategy is to solve a new problem (an input case) by reusing solutions that were used to solve old problems (existing cases) [5]. In this preliminary research, we explore how to solve synthesis problems by a case-based approach. It involves (1) how should an input case be generated from multiple solutions from ESs if these ESs use different inexact reasoning models; and (2) how is the relevant case selected? In current stage, we do not use adaptation and we directly apply whatever solution is retrieved from past solutions to the new situation. The reason for without doing adaptation comes from special features of synthesis of solutions in DESs. Results of solutions themselves are very simple, but reasonings leading to solutions are very complex and involve many factors such as the sizes of knowledge bases in ESs, methods used for a synthesis, and the weights used to measure each factor. If a suitable matching case does not exist, the system will offer some roughly matching cases to users. In this situation, a user can make his choices or choose other strategies.

The basic principle of this strategy are: (a) For an input case, the system will search the case base to find the best matching case. If a matching case exists, the final solution part in the matching case is used as the solution for the input case. Both the current case and the final solution might be added into the case base. (b) If there is no similar case available in the case base, the matching procedure is not successful.

Figure 2 is the architecture of the synthesis strategy by using a case-based reasoning.

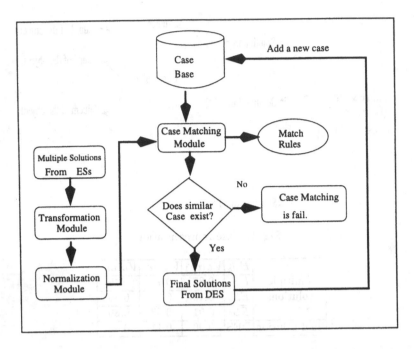

Fig. 2. The principle of the case based approach

This strategy consists of a transformation module, a normalization module, a case matching module, a case base, and a matching rule set. The strategy works in the PROBABILITY [1] inexact reasoning model. The area of uncertainties should be in the range [0, 1]. The following is a brief introduction to each module and a case base.

(a) **Transformation module** — If the range of uncertainties of a proposition is not in the range [0,1], the uncertainties of the proposition are transformed from that range to the range of [0, 1] by using the heterogeneous transformation functions [7] in the transformation module. For example, if an ES uses the EMYCIN [6] model, the range of [-1, 1] should be transformed into the range of [0, 1] in the PROBABILITY model [1].

(b) **Normalization module** — After transformation, the sum of uncertainties may not satisfy the requirements in the PROBABILITY model [1]. If such a case happens, the normalization function is used to normalize uncertainties in the PROBABILITY model.

(c) **Case matching module** — Multiple solutions from ESs are as an input case to the case matching module. In this module, the system examines the case base and searches for the best matching case. Once a suitable case is found, its corresponding solution might be used as a refereed solution for the input case. The refereed solution will be considered as a new case which may be added to the case base.

(d) **Case base** — The case base is a main resource used in this strategy. Currently, there are 180 cases stored in the case base.

(e) **Matching rule sets** — There are six match functions in this set which are implemented case matching rules in different levels. These functions will be introduced in detail in the next section.

4 Case searching procedure and examples

Definition 5: The mean error $\overline{error}$ for a case matching is defined as

$$\overline{error} = \frac{\sum_{j=1}^{n} \sum_{i=1}^{m} |CF_{ij} - CF'_{ij}|}{m * n}$$

where CF_{ij} represents the uncertainty for jth value from ES_i for the input case, CF'_{ij} indicates the uncertainty for jth value from ES_i for an existing case, m indicates that there are m possible values for this attribute of the object, and n is the number of ESs in a DES (recall Matrix 2.2).

Definition 6: The maximum error $error_{max}$ for a case matching is defined as

$$error_{max} = max\{|CF_{ij} - CF'_{ij}|\}$$

where $i = 1, 2, ..., m; j = 1, 2, ..., n$.

If for a case matching, $error_{max} = 0$, we call this matching a perfect matching.

Normally, it is not easy to get a perfect matching for most of our problems. After searching the case base, the system advises the nearest matching case which most nearly solves the problem.

The classification of case matching is shown in Figure 3.

In order to increase the system efficiency, the searching space is classified into 6 levels according to ranks of $\overline{error}$. We use the nearest neighborhood approach to reduce the searching area. If a user doesn't choose a starting level, searching normally starts from level 1 (L_1 in Table 4). If a matching case is not found in level 1, the searching area will be extended to level 2 (L_2), and so on until a similar case is found or whole searching space has been examined. Table 4 describes the performance for each level.

4.1 Examples

In this subsection. we demonstrate some examples by using this synthesis strategy.

Suppose that there are 3 expert systems using the PROBABILITY model to evaluate the values of an attribute of an object. Table 5 is an input case which shows the uncertainties of values obtained by ESs. The synthesis strategy is to find a similar case which can reasonably match the input case from the case base, then solve the synthesis problem by choosing the matching case.

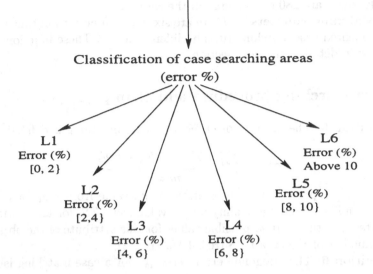

Fig. 3. Classification of case matching

$\overline{error}$	Function name	Performance	Matching result
2%	L_1	Choose the solution from the matching case	*Good*
2%–4%	L_2	Choose the solution from the matching case	*Good$^-$*
4%–6%	L_3	Choose the solution from the matching case	*Acceptable$^+$*
6%–8%	L_4	Choose the solution from the matching case	*Acceptable*
8%–10%	L_5	Choose the reference solution from the matching case	*Acceptable$^-$*
> 10%	L_6	These is no solution for the current case from the case base	*Fail*

Table 4. Case matching rules

	ESs	$Value_1$	$Value_2$	$Value_3$
Input case	ES_1	0.02	0.14	0.60
	ES_2	0.1	0.01	0.50
	ES_3	0.11	0.03	0.80

Table 5. Example 1: Input case

After searching the case base in the area of L_1, there is no case which matches the input case in this searching area. The system then extends the searching area to L_2. In L_2, three cases are considered as suitable cases to match the input case. The detailed information for the matching results is shown in Table 6.

Matching cases	ESs	$Value_1$	$Value_2$	$Value_3$	$error$	Matching results
	ES_1	0.13	0.15	0.66		
$Case_1$	ES_2	0.15	0.01	0.55	2.3%	$Good^-$
	ES_3	0.11	0.15	0.66		
	$Solution_1$	0.13	0.10	0.61		
	ES_1	0.10	0.15	0.7		
$Case_2$	ES_2	0.15	0.01	0.57	2.8%	$Good^-$
	ES_3	0.16	0.20	0.66		
	$Solution_2$	0.17	0.15	0.64		
	ES_1	0.05	0.05	0.35		
$Case_3$	ES_2	0.1	0.11	0.70	3.9%	$Good^-$
	ES_3	0.01	0.03	0.80		
	$Solution_3$	0.05	0.07	0.6		

Table 6. Example 1: Matching cases from the case base

From the above table we find that solutions of $Case_1$ and $Case_2$ are very similar. The matching results fall in the area of L_2 (recall Table 4). The user can choose one of solutions from the above two cases based on their preferences.
Now let us look at another example.

	ESs	$Value_1$	$Value_2$	$Value_3$
Input case	ES_1	0.20	0.40	0.20
	ES_2	0.00	0.10	0.05
	ES_3	0.05	0.05	0.90

Table 7. Example 2: Input case

Matching cases	ESs	$Value_1$	$Value_2$	$Value_3$	$error$	Matching results
	ES_1	0.13	0.15	0.66		
$Case_1$	ES_2	0.15	0.01	0.55	8.3%	$Acceptable^-$
	ES_3	0.11	0.15	0.66		
	$Solution_1$	0.13	0.11	0.62		

Table 8. Example 2: Matching cases from the case base

In example 2, only one case in the case base can roughly match the current case. The matching result falls in L_5. In this situation, if there is no an alternative strategy available, the solution can still be used as a reference.

5 Comparison with related work

We have introduced the basic principle of a case-based strategy and its preliminary results. Case-based reasoning is an instance of analogical methods. Now we compare analogical methods with related work in this research area from a methodological point of view and analyze features of different methods.

- *An analysis method* is the methodology which can be used to evaluate *output* from *input* (as defined in Subsection 3.1) by analyzing the characteristics of *input* using mathematical theories. This method is useful for areas in which the individual solution from each expert can be described by uncertainties, or numbers, and the relationships between *inputs* and *outputs* are not so complicated [2, 7, 9].
- *An inductive method* is the methodology which can be used to find the general relationship between *inputs* and *outputs* based on sufficient patterns [10]. It is obvious that the first condition of using this method for a strategy is that enough patterns must be known (this requirement differs from the analytic methods above). The second condition is that the patterns are distributed fairly randomly. The third condition is that an inductive function can be found (such as 'converges' in neural network terms).
- *An analogical method* is the methodology which can be used to find an *output* by comparing an *input case* to similar known cases. This method is useful for application in areas with limited patterns (or cases). The advantages of analogical methods are: (1) The principle of problem solving is only based on the similarity without knowing the mathematical relationship between *inputs* and *outputs*. This advantage overcomes a limitation of analytic methods which cannot work well if the relationship between *input* and *output* cannot be summarized by mathematical models. and (2) The major limitation of inductive methods is that they need too many real examples which are not available in most application domains. Analogical methods can overcome the limitation of inductive methods since analogical methods only need some real examples. Disadvantages of analogical methods are that (1) the final solution after synthesizing multiple solutions is not very precise; and (2) the adaptation of a new solution by a used solution is a hard problem and has not been solved so far.

After comparison, our conclusion is that they compensate each other. Based on different kinds of synthesis problems and available information, different methods should be used to design synthesis strategies.

6 Conclusion

In this paper, a basic principle of new synthesis strategy has been proposed for solving synthesis problems in DESs and results of using this synthesis strategy have been demonstrated. This strategy is developed based on an analogical method by case-based reasoning. This preliminary research has proved that analogical methods can overcome some limitations of analytic and inductive methods. Case-based reasoning is considered as a good tool to implement an analogical method [4]. The original contribution of the strategy presented is to offer an alternative way for solution synthesis in DESs.

Further work aims at researching the problem of case adaptations and investigating how to combine analogical methods with analytic and inductive methods.

Acknowledgments

The author wishes to thank DR Chengqi Zhang and MR Jirapun Daengdej for their support during this work at the University of New England.

References

1. R. Duda, P. Hart and N. Nilsson (1976). Subjective Bayesian Method for Rule-based Inference System, *AFIPS*, **Vol. 45**, pp. 1075-1082.
2. N. A. Khan & R. Jain (1985). Uncertainty Management in a Distributed Knowledge Based System, *Proceedings of 5th International Joint Conference on Artificial Intelligence*, Los Angeles, pp. 318-320, 1985.
3. V. Lesser and D. Corkill (1983). The Distributed Vehicle Monitoring Testbed, *AI Magazine*, **Vol. 4**, pp. 63-109.
4. K. Sycara (1987). Planning for Negotiation: A Case-Based Approach, *Proceedings of Darpa Knowledge-Based Planning Workshop*, pp. 11.1-11.10.
5. C. K. Riesbeck and R. C. Schank (1989). Inside Cased-based Reasoning, Lawrence Erlbaum Associates Publishers, New Jersey.
6. W. Van Melle (1980). A Domain-Independent System That Aids in Constructing Knowledge-Based Consultation Programs, *Ph.D. Dissertation, Report STAN-CS-80-820*, Computer Science Department, Stanford University, CA.
7. C. Zhang (1992). Cooperation Under Uncertainty in Distributed Expert Systems. *Artificial Intelligence*, **Vol. 56**, pp. 21-69.
8. M. Zhang, Synthesis of Solutions in Distributed Expert Systems, *PhD Thesis*, The University of New England, Australia, 1995.
9. M. Zhang and C. Zhang (1994a). A Comprehensive Strategy for Conflict Resolution in Distributed Expert Systems, *Australian Journal of Intelligent Information Processing Systems*, **Vol. 1**, No. 2, pp. 21-28.
10. M. Zhang and C. Zhang (1996). Neural Network Strategies for Solving Synthesis Problems in Non-conflict Cases in Distributed Expert Systems, *Distributed Artificial Intelligence: Architecture and Modeling*, LNAI **Vol 1087**, Lecture Notes in Artificial Intelligence, Springer Verlag Publishers, pp. 174-188.
11. M. Zhang and C. Zhang (1996). Analysis and Methodologies of Synthesis of Solutions in Distributed Expert Systems, *Proceedings of the Second International Conference on Multi-Agent Systems*, Kyoto, Japan, pp. 417-424.

Author Index

Lecture Notes in Artificial Intelligence (LNAI)

Lecture Notes in Computer Science